FEET

This survey was made singlehanded, with no satisfactory previous map available. Corners of the property were found and included in the triangulation net. A traverse with stadia rod was run along the main trail towards the cabin site. Trigonometric method of leveling was used by taking for the starting point the 500' contour of the U.S.G.S. map, which necessarily gives but approximate elevations above the sea level, the scale of the Government map being too small. Filling in topographic details between triangulation and stadia points was done by pacing.

Life on Two Levels

Camille Showalter

The best of truths is of no use unless it has
become one's most personal inner experience.

It is the duty of everyone who takes a solitary
path to share with society what he finds on
his journey of discovery.

−Carl Jung

Life on Two Levels

AN AUTOBIOGRAPHY

JOSEPHINE WHITNEY DUVENECK

INTRODUCTION BY WALLACE STEGNER

WILLIAM KAUFMANN, INC.
ONE FIRST STREET, LOS ALTOS, CALIFORNIA 94022

Library of Congress Cataloging in Publication Data
Duveneck, Josephine Whitney, 1891-
    Life on Two levels.

    Includes index.
    1. Duveneck, Josephine Whitney, 1891-
2. Friends, Society of—United States—Biography.
I. Title.
BX7795.D83A34   289.6'092'4   [B]   78-17903
ISBN O-913232-56-4

            WILLIAM KAUFMANN, INC.
            One First Street
            Los Altos, CA 94022.

Acknowledgements

I wish to express gratitude to the following persons who encouraged me to write this book: Edna King, who first said "Print it!"; Michaele Grudin, who read and revised the initial attempts; John Short, who volunteered to edit and organize the manuscript into orderly and presentable form; Audrey Johnson, who cheerfully typed and retyped innumerable pages of chaotic longhand copy; and Virginia and William Kaufmann, who eased me into publication.

Contents

viii

Introduction

The story of a full, eventful, disciplined, generous, useful life is at least as much a moral as a literary pleasure. Shallow lives need dressing up; good lives don't. The life itself matters far more than any literary flourishes in its telling. The prose, the devices, the evocations of people and places, the ambient history of a period—these are only the instruments of revelation. Like a windowpane, they are most successful when they seem not to be there at all.

Josephine Duveneck's autobiography is gracefully and charmingly written, but many readers will not notice that fact. Nothing intervenes or interrupts. Whether in the autobiographical narrative itself, or in the poems which show her in attitudes of self-searching and self-knowing, or in the excerpts from her girlhood diaries with their earnest setting of goals, we see Mrs. Duveneck always in historical and social context, always against a dense and varied background, but as plainly and without distortion as if we had just run into her in the lane at Hidden Villa, and stopped for a minute of talk. Those who have known her in life will find her interestedly and energetically and reassuringly *there*. Those who meet her for the first time on these pages will know at once that they have met someone special. This is an un-retouched portrait. She couldn't have touched it up if she had wanted to, and it would never have occurred to her to want to.

As for the moral effect, that is achieved without preachment. Simply by summing up what she has learned through a long life of service to others, simply by her effort to understand herself and the world she has made better by living in it, she clears away our dissatisfactions and demoralizations as ephedrine clears a stuffed head. By being what she has been, she makes us think better of ourselves and of the damned human race.

Her life could have gone many other ways than the way it has gone. She was born a Whitney, and like so many of the well-born she might have become simply another conspicuous consumer of the world's goods and services, the sort of woman her mother seems to have been. But Josephine did not follow her mother's lifestyle; she thought her mother worldly and ambitious for the wrong things, and though she did not actively resist the social life into which her mother thrust her as a 19-year-old debutante, she got only a fleeting satisfaction from it. Educated mainly by governesses and tutors, she had had the experience of living with people her own age only during brief school years in Paris and Berlin, so that coming out in Boston had its thrills. They did not last. Before the end, she felt herself a misfit in Boston society, dissatisfied with its activities and at odds with its aims.

From that life Frank Duveneck rescued her by marriage. He was himself a sort of international waif, son of a famous painter and that fabled Lizzie Boott with whom Henry James was rumored to have been intrigued, and whom he incorporated into *The Portrait of a Lady*. After his mother's early death, Frank had been brought up in Boston by her Brahmin relatives. It was all but inevitable that two such young people, after a year of world traveling, should settle down somewhere outside Boston. The fact that they ended up in California was California's good fortune.

Life on Two Levels, Josephine Duveneck calls her book. Readers may find in it more levels than two. Not only has she spent her life, ever since adolescence, in the attempt to reconcile private and public drives and satisfy antagonistic urges toward quietism on the one hand and public service on the other. She also, and long before it became a cliche, discovered that she had more energy than could be consumed by the needs of even a close, affectionate, and growing family. Inevitably she was led outward into a career—for it must be called a career even though she probably never earned a dollar from it, and undertook it without reference to what it might do for herself. She inherited a New England conscience as well as wealth and privilege. She could not help wanting to be somebody and do something. She could not help wanting to *matter*.

She was very unlike—perhaps deliberately unlike—her mother. Being so well off, so happily married, so secure in the home that she had bought in Palo Alto while Frank was in service during World War I, she felt guilty. Since she *was* her mother's rebellious daughter, in determined flight from Boston, the East, privilege, and conservatism, she could not help interesting herself in the problems of the new, growing community she found herself in. It was probably inevitable that her sympathies and her public stance were invariably progressive, and aimed toward the satisfaction of some public need.

The first tentative step was the employment service she set up in the Palo Alto Community Center to bring together young mothers and the part-time help they so often could not find by themselves. By the rule which says that volunteers will be asked to volunteer, and that doers will be given something to do, she was led from that modest beginning to a seat on the Community Center Board, and later to its chairmanship. Through her work at the Community Center she was put in touch with a dozen programs in health, recreation, education, and the arts, in which she acted as an enthusiastic organizer and expediter. Now and then she ran into opposition, as when she found herself having to defend free speech against the American Legion, or when she was rebuked by the Daughters of the American Revolution for nailing the flag up backwards. About the Legion, she could do nothing except resist it. About the Daughters of the American Revolution, she might have done more, and was tempted, she admits, to cite her qualifications, join, and bore from within. But instead, she let the flurry pass. Shortly she was a member of the Palo Alto City Council.

Four years on the Council constituted her entire political experience. Asked to run for a second term, she declined because she found the routine details of city housekeeping tedious. Later, when she was asked to run for the state legislature, she remembered her first and only political experience as a kind of imprisonment of the spirit, and declined again.

She had other and more rewarding things to do, for even before she left the Palo Alto City Council she and Frank had involved themselves in the two places to which they would devote the rest of their lives. One was the Hidden Villa Ranch, in Los Altos Hills, whose thousand acres of ranch and wild mountainside they bought in 1924. The other was the Peninsula School, which Josephine organized in 1925 and which occupied her in a dozen capacities for sixteen years, until all her own children had passed through it and gone on. Hidden Villa, at first only a weekend retreat, became in 1929 the Duveneck's home; and because they could not own a home without sharing it, it became the center of the whole extraordinary complex of social, educational, environmental, and humanitarian activities which have made and kept them the number one couple of the San Francisco Peninsula.

It is characteristic of the Duvenecks that they do not merely sponsor things, they work at them, share them, lead them, and on occasion even back away from them to let them develop strongly on their own. The Peninsula School grew out of Josephine's interest in progressive education, her reading of John Dewey and the Montessori experiment, and her visits to progressive schools in the East. She enlisted other women, most of them Stanford faculty wives, who wanted for their children something more personal and imaginative than the public schools provided. What began as a primary day school attached to the Harker School in Palo Alto developed quickly (but not without strenuous effort) into an independent institution housed in an old estate, at first rented and later acquired, in Menlo Park.

Having been a somewhat isolated child, Josephine wanted the benefits of companionship for her children. Having been the daughter of a socially-preoccupied mother, she wanted parents closely involved. And having been always of an independent turn of mind, she wanted her children encouraged to grow from within, not coerced from without. More than any other two people, she and Frank shaped the Peninsula School. He taught mathematics and mechanics, she served as organizer, director and teacher, fund-raiser, master of ceremonies, bookkeeper, and sometimes even scrubwoman. What they built has affected the lives of thousands of Peninsulans, and will continue to.

Hidden Villa is an even more remarkable monument to one couple's imagination, energy, humanity, and good will. It has been a Youth Hostel, the first on the West Coast. It has been a sanctuary for every sort of displaced person, from war refugees to relocated Japanese-Americans. It has been a center—*the* center, the only true center—of social betterment groups, racial minorities, conservation organizations. Its picnic grounds and horse rings have been the site of church, ethnic, and conservation group picnics and of benefit horse shows and gymkhanas. In summer it has been a youth camp, with special emphasis on minorities, ghetto children, and the generally disadvantaged, and in the last decade it has developed into a great outdoor classroom to which are brought from all over the area busloads of children, many of whom have never seen a cow or a pig, or ridden a horse. For a day they inhabit the ranch, pat animals, offer fingers to suckling calves, walk in the woods and are taught to observe the little wild things that live there.

These activities too have affected lives deeply, and all the more so because Josephine and Frank Duveneck are so infallibly present, interested, and active in what goes on, and so perceptive of the needs of those who find a refuge with them. The summer camp has now been in operation for so long that the third generation of some families are attending it. I have a young relative, a polio victim, who remembers as the most wonderful hours of her life the times when Josephine had a group of campers snuggle down on sofas and floor in her big living room, and read aloud to them while they blinked and dozed through their after-lunch nap.

A woman with an infinite capacity for loving kindness, an incorrigble impulse to serve others rather than herself. Judged by her humanitarian activities, her life seems as singleminded and purposeful as it could possibly have been. Yet there was always a religious mystic lurking in Mrs. Duveneck. The introspective girl who wrote poems in secret, and confided to her diary aspirations of a nun-like spirituality, has always been there. So has the woman who recognized in herself an authoritarian imperiousness, and had constantly to restrain herself from imposing her will on others. This life has been on two levels at least. Josephine has not only had to choose between faith and works, mystical withdrawal and social activism; she has also, in her public life, had to learn to become the kind of leader who shares, not the kind who commands.

She was tempted by a number of mystical religious leaders, including Baha Ullah, Sri Vivekenanda, and Ramakrishna, before she found her true place among the Society of Friends. What made her resist the attractions of pure mysticism was its withdrawal, its focus upon the self even to the self's annihilation. She herself could never have been content unless she was devoting herself to others, and in the summary of her life, the humanitarian takes precedence over the mystic. Yet there is a little retreat back up on the mountainside above Hidden Villa which Frank built for her, and to which Josephine retires when the world gets too thick around her.

What has happened, it seems, is that she did not ultimately choose the level at which her life would be lived. Her vitality was so great that she simply overflowed, like the Mississippi in the June rise, and flooded *all* the levels, reconciled them, made them one.

Love has marked every stage of her life—love given and love received. There is an incident reported in her book by which I, at least, will always want to remember her—a morning when she came out of the ranch house at Hidden Villa and found the grass, the shrubs, the trees, the fences and gardens, quivering and moving with thousands of monarch butterflies, mysteriously arrived from somewhere and settling gently down for an hour as if in thanks.

—Wallace Stegner

A portrait of Grandmother Whitney (courtesy of Laura Dodge Brown);
Grandmother and Grandfather Green;
Henry M. Whitney, my father; Margaret Green, my mother.

I

Forebears

English and American ancestors;
Whitney Fortune,
family and parents.

Most people become interested in their ancestors only when they arrive at the stage of turning into ancestors themselves. We become conscious of a certain continuity of disposition that appears to be carried on from one generation to another. As we gradually come to understand ourselves better we begin to wonder how we got to be the way we are. We realize that there was a great deal there to start with, not just a vacuum. Indeed the whole evolution of mankind is siphoned through each of us at birth by the medium of one unique genetic lineage that reaches back to the beginning of time and that will pass on through us to as yet unborn incarnations. Sometimes this primordial residue bubbles up into our subconscious; (concrete data usually can only be gleaned from one's own lifetime—a relatively short span of years).

My grandparents died before I was old enough to appreciate them. One of my grandfathers—my mother's father, for whom I was named—was Admiral Joseph Green. He served in the Charleston Fleet under Farragut during the Civil War. My only remembrance of him is of an old gentleman whose sideburns tickled my cheek when he kissed me. He wore a tan vest from a pocket of which he sometimes drew a large gold watch and held it to my ear so I could listen to its chimes. I inherited his sea chest where I now store extra blankets. That is the only surviving memento of him except for a portfolio of naval appointments signed by six different presidents including Lincoln in 1863. This portfolio was donated to the Library of the Boston Athenaeum by one of my sisters some years ago.

The memory of my Whitney grandmother consists of an austere, impassive face crowned by a starched white cap. She always dressed in black with a cameo brooch at her throat. She was the mother of six children. Her husband, my grandfather, died before I was born, but I have been able to learn of his career and have traced other family records as far back as the Doomsday Book, in which an ancient English chronicler commented, "The River Wye winds away to the town of Whitney, which gave name to a famous family."

A Sir Randolph de Whitney served under Richard Coeur de Lion in his crusade to the Holy Land (1190). The story has it that one day, carrying a message to the French commander, he encountered two Saracen guards who engaged him in combat. He was hard pressed to deal with them when a black bull, attracted by the scarlet tunics of the Saracens, charged across the field and put the assailants to flight. The Whitney Coat of Arms bears witness to this episode. A black bull's head stands over the knight's crest and the crusader's cross. The motto is "Fortis sed non ferox." In 1306 Sir Eustace de Whitney was knighted and sat in Parliament. A direct descendant, Robert, disapproved of Henry VIII's 1533 marriage to Anne Boleyn, but managed somehow to remain in favor at court.

More than a hundred years later, in 1635, John Whitney (who apparently did not carry on the title) embarked from the port of London for the New World with his wife, Elinor, and five sons. They settled in Watertown just outside Boston. In 1637 John became one of the Selectmen of the Community. Their fourth son, Thomas, was chosen "to take care that no dogs come into the Meeting House on sabbath days, and to have for his pain 30 shillings per year." Joshua, John's sixth son, was the first Whitney to be born in America.

John Whitney's will, probated at East Cambridge, contains the following excerpts:

I, John Whitney, Senior, of Watertown in ye County of Middlesex, being perfect and sound in memory and understanding, blessed be God for it, do declare this to be my last will and testament as followeth:

First—I commit my spirit into ye hand of God who gave it, and my body unto ye earth whence it was taken.

Secondly—I give unto my son John Whitney my meadow called Beaverbrook Meadow with ye upland yt doth apertaine thereto: and a yoke of oxen: and 9 lbs. 10 shillings: and 10 acres of my land called devedend land and a trunke and a paire of sheets and 1 paire of pillow beers and 2 pewter dishes—a great one and a small one: and the bed whereon I lie with all ye furnitures thereunto belonging.

Thirdly—I give unto my son Richard Whitney 10 acres of my land called devedend and 2 cows and a great sea chest.

Fourthly—I give unto my son Thomas Whitney 10 acres of my land called devedend and two cows and a sad colored sute namely a paire of breeches and a close coate and powder dish.

Fifthly—I give unto my son Jonathan Whitney one iron kettle and a great brass skillit.

Sixthly—I give unto my son Joshua Whitney twenty acres of my land called devedend and a cubard and a little table and a cheste and a great kettle and a warming pan and skillit.

Seventhly—I give unto my son Benjamin ye old gray mare if she live."

Poor Benjamin. Not even a coat of many colors!

We next hear of a Whitney in 1776 when General Josiah Whitney commanded a battalion to defend Boston Harbor. This gentleman had 25 children—sixteen by his first marriage, nine by his second. Thirteen by the first wife died young, but apparently the survivors were prolific enough to scatter the seed and the name to a large number of descendants.

My grandfather, James Scollay Whitney, was born in Deerfield, Massachusetts in 1811. He inherited his father's store, but being more interested in public affairs than in store keeping, he sold out his interest to his partner and served several terms in the State Legislature. He reorganized the State militia and became Superintendent of the Springfield Armory. He was a Jacksonian Democrat and in 1860 President Buchanan appointed him to the office of Collector of the Port of·Boston, a position he forfeited when the administration changed with Lincoln's election. Shortly before his death he established the Metropolitan Steamship Line operating between New York and Boston, a popular means of travel between the two cities. This company, inherited by his two sons (one of them my father), provided the starting point for the extension of their financial careers. Born in a small town in western Massachusetts, as adults they became influential in business enterprises in Boston and New York.

Those were the days when private enterprise enjoyed a free rein in the development of natural resources like coal and gas. Trade and travel facilities such as railroads, steamship lines and urban services of all kinds, from street cars to garbage collection, were waiting for the vitalizing drive of a promoter. There were no restrictions on corporations, there were no personal income taxes and labor laws were extremely lenient. This was the period of the "robber barons" when the fabulous American fortunes were built. Almost anyone with imagination, organizing genius and sufficient capital could develop a business empire subject only to the limits of his own dictatorial capacities.

My uncle William C. Whitney built up the Whitney fortune partly by means of an astute business acumen, but also by means of the enormous financial resources which were at his disposal through his marriage to Flora Payne, a daughter of Senator Payne of Ohio and sister of Colonel Oliver Payne. The Paynes, a family of great wealth, bought a house in New York City on the corner of 5th Avenue and 57th Street and gave it to the couple as a wedding present. It is recorded that the reception hall in this mansion was large enough for a two horse team pulling a wagon load of hay to turn around without backing. On the birth of her first child, Flora received a check from her father for a million dollars!

Uncle Will became prominent in politics as well as in business. He was urged to be a candidate for the presidency of the United States, but withdrew in favor of Grover Cleveland, in whose cabinet he served as Secretary of the Navy. His son, Harry Payne Whitney, became well known as a polo player and as the owner of stables that produced many champion race horses. In recent times, younger members of the family established the Whitney Museum of Modern Art, the John Hay Whitney Founation, and even provided an American Ambassador to England: John Hay Whitney, from 1957 to 1961. The October Mountain Preserve in the Berkshire Mountains in Massachusetts was donated by the family, and in the next generation some 60,000 acres in the Adirondack Mountains is destined to be donated to the State of New York for a recreation and park area. Dorothy Whitney, the only daughter of Will and Flora, married Willard Straight. Together they founded and financed the *New Republic,* a weekly which has continued to present the liberal point of view during the changing political eras of the last fifty years. Willard Straight died in Paris during the flu epidemic of 1918. Dorothy married Leonard Elmhirst, an Englishman who assisted Rabindranath Tagore in building the rural school Santiniketan in Bengal, India. The Elmhirsts developed Dartington Hall in England, a rural community famous for its 'progressive education,' its school of dance, and interesting experiments in agricultural and cottage industries.

My father, Henry M. Whitney lived with his parents in Brookline, a suburb of Boston. Like his brother Will in New York, he utilized the profits from his share of the Metropolitan Steamship line to develop more ambitious projects. He became obsessed with the idea of electric street cars to supersede the horse-drawn vehicles then in use. Against great skepticism and timidity on the part of the public, he succeeded in establishing the first electric transportation system in the United States. It is interesting to note that in the terms of the charter, granted in 1888, provision was made for possible underground operations—a long time before the subway under the Boston Common was planned. The West End Land Company, of which he was president, bought up large tracts of vacant land on Beacon Street through Brookline to Chestnut Hill. When the electric car line was installed, the value of the lots increased prodigiously.

My father's activities also reached into eastern Canada, from which coal for New England could be shipped more cheaply than from Pennsylvania. The Dominion Iron & Steel Company was a great asset to Nova Scotia and to all of Canada, as well as to Massachusetts. My father became an ardent advocate of reciprocity with Canada, joining with Sir Wilfred Laurier, premier of Canada, in trying to achieve this entente. These contacts undoubtedly led to his involvement with a little known product, asbestos, and his purchase of a large mine in the province of Quebec. The development of the many uses of this new substance fascinated him, of which I shall say more in Chapter II.

Father was not so much interested in making money; he delighted in the challenge of promoting a scheme or product. Once a new thing or a new idea was established, he lost interest in it. The routines of management involved in continuing production bored him and he started looking for some other creative venture. I remember a succession of experiments—some on how to preserve orange juice and how to manufacture dry ice, and others on the development of a new kind of roller bearing, or submarine signals, or on nests for hens that would record egg-laying performance. His interest and enthusiasm were contagious. His larger projects included a proposed central railway station near the Back Bay in Boston,   electrifying the steam railway at some point in the suburbs, thus eliminating smoke and dust in the city. He suggested the Cape Cod Canal long before August Belmont thought of it. He ran for Governor of Massachusetts on the Democratic ticket in 1906 but was defeated. He became president of the Boston Chamber of Commerce. As a result of a run-in with President Theodore Roosevelt, he was a charter member of the Ananias Club (the group designated as *liars* by Roosevelt).

Unfortunately Father's enthusiasm for undeveloped potentials finally led him to invest heavily in a coal mine in Rhode Island. He was then in his 80th year, and he would not listen to competent scientists who told him the product was unuseable. (Some said of it that on the Day of Judgment Rhode Island Coal would be the last thing to burn.) Stubbornly he continued to pour money into the coal mine—a fiasco that ended in his bankruptcy. He who had controlled millions ended as a pensioner. But in spite of this failure I think my father had a lot of fun living. He enjoyed the excitement and risk of each new venture. He made several fortunes which he used for some new and original schemes. Although he made a mess of things late in life, he could look back on a previous long life of accomplishments that benefitted mankind. He had a lot of conquests to remember and chuckle about. I was in my late teens when he went through bankruptcy.

Thinking back to the relationship between my parents that created the background of my childhood, I find a complex diversity of human attributes. They were married in 1878. Both of their parents' families lived on Pleasant Street in Brookline. By the time they were married, my father was 41, had already attained a prominent position as a businessman, and possessed virtually unlimited income. My mother was only 20. She had always lived in Brookline and was used to the modest household of a retired Admiral and small town living. She was a beautiful girl, without much formal education, but possessed a brilliant mind and a driving ambition. The offer of marriage from an older man flattered her vanity and also held the assurance of an affluence she had never had. It was an opportunity she could not reject.

Soon after they were married they moved into a large and charming

Home in Brookline, Massachusetts.

ivy-covered mansion not far from where their two families lived in Brookline. It was quite a change for my mother. The furnishings and interior decoration were selected by her under the guidance of experts who were not limited by expense. Even the library was supplied with leather bound sets of all the classics, encyclopedias and reference books. There was a Steinway Grand piano and there were oriental rugs. The walls along the staircase held large plaster replicas of the Parthenon frieze. There were even some Whistler etchings and two water colors by Winslow Homer. Later, over the mantel piece were hung three life-size portraits of my sisters by Dewing, a society portrait painter in vogue in 1880-1890. The house gave the impression of containing a large number of heirlooms like any bonafide old New England home.

It appears to me now, as I consider the circumstances of her marriage, that my mother did a remarkable job of self-education. She must have read and studied and sought out intellectual opportunities and associated herself with sophisticated people until she became at ease in her surroundings and could win for her daughters an entree into the exclusive social milieu of Boston society. She had to do this pretty much on her own because my father remained a simple person. Apart from providing the finances, I don't think he cared very much about high society. He suffered through the dinner parties, but I suspect he hated them. My mother, on the other hand, really attained her ambition of becoming a cultivated personality. She had an instinct for excellence, and the world of letters, art, philosophy, music and education filled her later days. To her I owe my varied intellectual interests, but my father taught me to feel love and compassion, to be interested in new things, to laugh and to enjoy animals and country living.

Josephine Whitney, age 2

II

Early Childhood

Friends, governesses, father, schools and early memories.

After my parents' marriage in 1878, three daughters, Ruth, Elinor and Laura, were born in quick succession. My brother Jim was born in 1886 and I followed five years later in 1891. I have always had the idea that I was an accident. At all events, my late arrival resulted in my growing up much like an only child.

Memories of my very early childhood are few. The only concrete memory is of a baby carriage on runners like a miniature snowmobile (minus the engine). I was buttoned up into a red woolen bag with a hood and pushed around in the snow by one of my big sisters. The wind kept blowing light powdery snow off the branches of the trees onto my bag and into my eyes. I remember opening my mouth to catch the tiny flakes and wondering what happened when I tried to chew them. Another early memory is connected with the open grate in the Franklin stove that warmed my nursery. After I was put to bed and the lights were extinguished, a little smoldering fire sometimes remained. As the flames flickered up through the coals they were reflected on the ceiling in rosy shifting patterns. I lay in bed watching this play of fire fairies. They entered my dreams after my eyelids closed. In the morning when the first daylight sifted through the shadows, I listened for the daily procession of garbage carts that went by on Boylston Street. The stable was in Chestnut Hill, a few miles up the road. There must have been fifteen or twenty carts painted bright blue, drawn by sturdy work horses. They started off from a central depot at the same hour and branched off to distant routes along the main artery of Boylston

Street—*klop! klop! klop!*—the horses' hooves sounded on the cobble-stones, first faint in the distance, gradually louder and louder as they passed our driveway in their steady syncopated rhythm. *Klop! klop! klop!*—growing fainter and fainter as they dispersed and left the quiet of dawn behind them.

One traumatic experience rises out of the memories of early childhood. It still sends a shiver down my spine. The facade of our brick house was completely covered with English ivy like some of the college buildings in Oxford or Cambridge. The English sparrow, which had become a formidable pest in Massachusetts, nested in these vines by the hundreds. They were prolific breeders. In early spring mornings their chattering was deafening. The litter on the terrace near the wall was unsightly and offensive. Relief from this nuisance was offered by a certain company that made a business of destroying undesirable birds. They brought in huge nets rolled up on tall bamboo poles. These were lifted up and suddenly placed against the wall of ivy. The birds, startled by the sudden pressure of the net, were frightened and flew off their nests to be caught in the meshes. The nets were then lowered back onto the lawn with their screeching burden of captured birds. The workers went over the nets with clubs, exterminating the creatures and ending the uproar. No one in our household had told me that this massacre was contemplated, so when I woke up at midnight and heard the frantic chirping, looked out the window and saw ghoulish forms rushing about, I thought I must be dreaming. When the net was laid down and the slaughter began, I was terrified. I was glued to the window, afraid to move until someone, thinking I might have been awakened by the rumpus, came and told me what it was all about and carried me back to bed trembling with horror and unable to sleep. The next day the men climbed ladders and destroyed the nests. I heard my mother say that over a hundred and fifty birds had been disposed of.

My nursery was entered from the hall by a small vestibule where wardrobes and drawers provided ample storage space. The room, situated on the corner of the second story, had windows on two sides. A smaller room connected with the nursery was the bedroom of my nurse. I had a bed and a dresser, a couch under two gas jets, a three-storied doll house and a stove. In front of each window was a comfortable seat with padded cushions where I could sit and read or look out the window into a big copper beech tree that grew on the south lawn. The gently sloping bank under this tree was especially warm and sheltered. Here I used to find the first snow drop of the spring season and a week or two later the first yellow crocus. These were news items of great importance to me. I tried to tell everyone who would listen. I remember the egg man with whom I shared my excitement exclaiming enthusiastically, "You don't say so my dear! Ain't that something!"

My sisters and brother lived up on the third floor. My father and mother had separate rooms, and the servants' quarters were in a wing added onto the back of the house. The ground floor contained a dining room and storeroom. Originally there was only one bathroom in a dark, dingy hall. The tub was tin or steel and raised up on legs. A second bathroom had been improvised in a bedroom next to my father's room. That held a white enamel tub with claw legs. I remember kneeling beside it with a towel pressed against my eyes while Stella Babcock, the Negro hairdresser who came once a month to go the rounds of all the heads, rinsed my head with a metal pitcher of water. An agonizing experience. A third, somewhat more modern plumbing arrangement, was installed in one corner of the trunk room on the third story. My sisters considered it a great luxury not to have to go downstairs. I think there was a fourth lavatory and bath behind the servants' dining room. That was also a dark and spooky place with a peculiar odor. Of course every room had a wash stand with bowl, large pitcher, small pitcher, soap dish and tooth brush holder. In a little compartment underneath was the chamber pot and a slop jar. I still have two large pitchers and a bowl that date back to that Victorian era. The house was equipped with a coal furnace, numerous stoves and open fireplaces for heat, fishtail gas jets, kerosene lamps and candles for light.

Today there is much discussion about the 'disadvantaged child.' The term usually refers to the youthful inhabitants of an urban slum or to those growing up in dire rural poverty, but it can also be used to describe the child who grows up in a palace over-supplied with every material need, yet is starved for affection and deprived of meaningful human contacts. I know, because I belonged in this category—a little alien in an adult world, isolated from family life and cared for by people paid to do so.

My sisters were ten, eleven and twelve years older than I. They were becoming 'young ladies' and the closest contact I had with them was watching them dress for dinner. Their silk or satin dresses were so elegant, I liked to run my hands over the fabric. They needed help in hooking their dresses up in the back. Sometimes, if the maid was busy, I could do this for them. My brother, five years my senior, was away at Groton, a fashionable boarding school for boys. I saw very little of my mother, who spent much time entertaining and going out in the evening to dinner, receptions, concerts and lectures. She was determined to launch her daughters into a social whirl. I think for one not 'to the manner born,' it took a great deal of tact, intellect and judgment to overcome the social barriers of Boston society. By sheer determination, backed up with almost unlimited financial resources, she was able to realize her ambition and to edge her way into the outer fringe of Boston Brahminism. And of course her daughters sailed in her wake like so many ducklings following their mother across a pond. There was not much time for the ugly duckling in the nursery. Until I was 12 or 13 I did not have my meals downstairs, except for breakfast with my father. My mother had her breakfast in bed. And on Christmas Day, New

Year's Day and my birthday, I was included at the family table. Twice a year my mother took me to buy clothes at Hollander's, an expensive store in Boston; twice a year we went to the shoemaker, white-haired Mr. McCowan, who measured my feet and made boots to order. (I especially remember the ones that had about a dozen buttons to fasten with a button hook.) I was taken to the Unitarian Church, but I did not attend Sunday School.

I never went to my mother's room unless she sent for me. "Your Mama wants to see you" was a command that chilled my blood. It usually meant that some misbehavior had been reported to the high tribunal and sometimes I lingered a long time before knocking on the door and facing her terrifying presence. I remember one occasion when I had done something evil and she ordered me to sit in a certain low ladder-backed chair in my nursery till I was ready to say "I'm sorry," which I refused to do. I sat there all day with firmly closed lips. Towards evening I was exhausted. So was my nurse. In despair she dragged me back to my mother who was angry at being disturbed again, and although I am not sure I think I remember that she slapped me. I finally snarled "I'm sorry," but as I went out the door I called back "But I'm not." My mother chose to ignore that recantation.

However, during those early years I was not wholly alone. My father could not get very much satisfaction from his older children who were involved in the network of educational and social engagements, so he sought me out. He always knew that he could find me in my nursery, and he was always sure of an enthusiastic welcome. Between the time he reached home after his business day and his dinner hour (which never came before seven or eight o'clock) he used to visit me. He would sit and read to me. I remember the Uncle Remus stories especially. He would chuckle over Brer Rabbit's exploits as heartily as I did. He called me "Josie," a name I have always disliked but which sounded different on his lips. I have never let anyone else use it. One of my nurses told me, "You act so nice with your Papa. You are so naughty the rest of the time." If I was in the middle of one of my tantrums (which were frequent and violent) and I heard him coming through the vestibule outside the nursery, I would end my dramatics instantly and present an angelic and smiling face to my father. Often he stayed so long with me that the butler would have to come and tell him "Dinner is served, Sir", and he would leave reluctantly to face the burden of hosting formal guests at an elegant five course dinner. I think he, too, was somewhat of an alien in his own home. He had a flair for making money, but he was essentially a western Massachusetts country boy and not really comfortable in the social milieu that my mother was promoting. As I grew older our relationship became more meaningful for both of us.

The other people in my life at this period consisted of the household help and the nurses who came in rapid succession to look after me. I remember them only vaguely. They were strong, wholesome peasant girls fresh from Germany. I recall their names: Amalia, Karolina and Appolonia. They taught me German. For a period I talked a jargon described by one of my sisters who heard me say to my mother, "Geben Sie mir some Handschuh. I freeze," while holding up two mittened hands with holes in every finger. Somewhere in the picture came Nellie, an American girl born in New Hampshire who discouraged the German jargon and tried to teach her little heathen charge the rudiments of religion. She took me to the Catholic Church and when she suddenly made her genuflexion in the aisle, wearing the then fashionable ankle length skirt, I, who was immediately behind her, walked right up it, much to her discomfort and my chagrin. She bought me a book about Jesus which had a picture of the Good Shepherd on the cover. My mother saw it one day when she came into my nursery. She removed it and I think Nellie was dismissed for her attempts to convert me.

I am not quite sure when I graduated from nurses to governesses. It may have been a division of labor during a transition period. Be that as it may, Carol A. Dugan was the most important individual as teacher, companion and friend during my formative years between eight and fifteen. She was the daughter of a Cape Cod sea captain. She trained to be a kindergarten teacher in the early days of the educational system originated by Froebel. I do not know why she did not continue teaching in this field, but she came to our family as a home teacher for my sister Laura who was in delicate health. With the exception of two summer months each year when she returned to her beloved home on the Cape, she worked for my family for 25 years. Sometimes she lived in our house, but at other times she rented an outside room and came by the day. She was a truly cultured person—a great reader and a composer of songs and poetry. She wrote a series of plays in which my sisters and brother and one or two friends acted. These plays were given at Christmas time for the dinner guests. They were afterwards published in a book, *The King's Jester*, which was the title of one of the plays. I was not old enough to be in these productions except for the last one—a Japanese play about the Sun Goddess. I was to be the maid and on being given an order to fetch a cup of tea, I was to say, "I fly!" According to legend I uttered this line and then stood transfixed, gazing at the audience with a beaming smile till a hand reached out and pulled me off the stage. Miss Dugan had a dumpy figure. She was plain, but she had all the best qualities of a New England gentlewoman, with no self-righteousness or snobbery and no intolerance of those with less integrity than herself. She managed to maintain her dignity with my mother who came to trust her completely. She ignored the jealousy and back-biting of the servants and met guests pleasantly, but unobtrusively. She provided for us children all the little criticisms and encouragements and consolations that growing spirits need. When my sisters were off to Europe or caught up in society, I was the only one left. For about seven years she was responsible for my welfare and loved me without sentimentality. I resented often that I had to be chaperoned wherever I went and let her know it. She understood and sympathized with me but nevertheless it was her job and she carried it out. I did not, of course, realize it at the time, but she must have had a very frustrating life. She called me "Childie." I was her child, but not her child. And after twenty-five years of devoted service and the close ties were broken, it must have been a devastating termination. Luckily she owned her old family mansion on Cape Cod, a beautiful colonial house which provided not only a home but a pond, a pine grove and a strip of beach. She had paying guests to augment her income, took beautiful photographs and helped organize the "Brewster Ladies Library." Years later, during the depression, my husband made it possible for her to retain the property.

The only friends near my own age in Brookline were three little girls in the Lee family who lived in a big yellow colonial house which shared the driveway with us. They never came into my house and I was forbidden to go into theirs, but we played outdoors together. Bessie, Florence and Margery played hide-and-seek with me, we coasted together in winter and picked daisies and buttercups in the spring. I became *persona non grata* for several weeks one winter. It happened this way. We had a neighbor, living on the other side of the Lee house. Mr. Beal disliked children and would become infuriated if one of us crossed the edge of his land. He had a vicious dog who barked and snarled at us. We were equally afraid of the dog and of his master. I made up a story about how at night we children went through a mysterious opening into the walls of Mr. Beal's house. Here were passage ways and hidden treasure, skeletons, ogres and magic creatures. We were in constant danger of pursuit by Mr. Beal and our narrow escapes were terrific. The girls would ask me, "Did we really do that last night?" I would assure them, "Yes, you really did. You just don't remember because you went back to sleep afterwards." So realistic were the episodes I told that the Lee children began to have nightmares and wake up screaming around midnight. Their mother tried to find out what was troubling them; their talk about the walls of Mr. Beal's house was unintelligible to her. Finally she learned that Josephine had been telling them stories. "It's really true, Mother," they told her. "It really did happen. Josephine told us so." Mrs. Lee came to my mother and complained. The Beal series came to an end and our companionship was suspended for awhile.

About this time I added to my natural wickedness by stealing. I believe I received an allowance of 25 cents a week. When I had saved enough, Miss Dugan took me in to Boston where there was a fascinating Japanese store that imported all kinds of small bits of pottery, little china animals, baskets and vases. When we went shopping there, it took me hours to pick out the few objects my savings would allow. One day I paid for what I had chosen and surreptitiously pocketed a few additional items. When we got home I got out the spoils and set them up along with the legitimate purchases. Miss Dugan's eagle eye spotted the difference. "Where did you get these?" she asked, pointing to the stolen articles. "Oh, Bessie Lee gave them to me," I answered glibly.

A few days later Miss Dugan asked if she could borrow my Japanese things. She wanted to show them to a little girl she knew. I gladly consented. When she had a chance she showed them to Bessie and asked, "Have you ever seen anything like these little dishes?" "Oh, no," said Bessie. "Aren't they cunning? Where did you get them?" Miss Dugan did not tell her why she asked, but she confronted me with the fact that Bessie had never seen them before. And I of course then confessed to the theft. A few days later she took me back to the store with the little dishes and insisted that I tell the Japanese owner how wicked I had been and that I was sorry. She told me later that he wanted to let me keep them, but she was standing behind me and shook her head. He caught on and accepted the loot graciously and I was saved from a life of depravity.

She was a wise woman. She taught me how to sew and mend, how to knit and crochet. I made all my Christmas presents: needle cases, pincushions, washcloths, and greeting cards. I also made picture books for the Children's Hospital. The pictures I cut out of magazines were pasted onto colored cambric cloth and sewed together with yarn, the edges finished with blanket stitching. Once or twice a year Miss Dugan would take me to the hospital bringing these albums and a big bunch of daisies and buttercups. In those days a child could visit the wards freely. I went from bed to bed offering little bunches of flowers and occasionally a book to the occupants. I remember one day there was a little black face on the white pillow. I had never seen a Negro before. When I got to his bed I hesitated and looked at Miss Dugan. She nodded her head and I gave the little boy his bunch of flowers. I always remember the white teeth that showed suddenly in a smile as he accepted them. This was my first experience with racial difference and Miss Dugan started me in the right direction.

I had lessons at home most of the time, but at some point I went to school. It was a little red schoolhouse run by two maiden ladies, Miss Emily and Miss Sadie Cushman. All I remember about them was that they were amazingly ugly. I visualize Miss Emily to this day as a grotesque African mask. The children teased me at recess. Using little sticks, they whipped my legs to make me dance. My only other memory of that school is an astonishing episode (not to be proud of). A golden haired boy, Jimmy Minot, dressed in a dark blue sailor suit sat in the seat fastened to the row in front of my desk. When we had "clay" everybody was given a lump about as big as your fist and a black-headed hat pin with which to make a design. I was incapable of making anything except a sort of bird's nest or bowl and I kept looking at the sailor suit in front of me and wondering what would happen if I stuck my hat pin into it. I wondered and wondered and finally curiosity overcame me and I jabbed the hat pin into the unsuspecting back of Jimmy Minot. He shrieked and chaos broke out in the classroom. "Why did you do it?" they asked me. My reply was, "I wanted to see what would happen." Well, I found out and spent the rest of the school day in the dark cloak room which smelled of stale lunches and damp rubbers. That part of my education was not a success.

So far I have described the winters of my childhood. When school was over for my sisters, the family moved to our summer place in Cohasset. Moving day was always an excitement for me. It took four or five carriages to transport all of us, plus the maids. For the journey we always had delicious cold chicken, hard boiled eggs, ham sandwiches, oranges and cider. It took all day to go the twenty-five miles. Years later I could not believe it when we made the trip by automobile in half an hour. I loved going to Cohasset because of the greater freedom I enjoyed there. Most summers I was alone with my father and a governess substitute for Miss Dugan who always spent her vacation at the Cape. These governess ladies never made very much of an impression on me. I remember vaguely a Miss Stutz from Switzerland who tried to teach me French and a Miss Jacoby, a large bosomed lady with dark hair and a big nose. I don't remember that the latter taught me anything. I think she made the most of her peculiar position in the household by attempting to charm my father and to dominate the domestics. She played the piano ostentatiously and sang in a high rasping voice. I have the impression that she had led a hard life so that the two months spent supervising me provided her with a rare interlude of leisure and luxury. The role of governess so well described in *Jane Eyre* was an anomalous one, neither master nor servant, poised uneasily between class distinctions and as an adjunct to an already complete household.

My father must have spent a good deal of time at home in the summer months. I rode and drove with him frequently. We went to the farm almost every day. There we visited the big red barn which provided a double row of box stalls for the horses. Papa was interested in trotting races. He built a circular half-mile track and employed a man named Arthur to train the colts. I enjoyed seeing the young animals harnessed to a sulky or breaking cart, being coaxed to go ahead in a straight line. Papa had a stop watch and used to keep records of their time around the track. I remember a bay filly, Miss Flora Whitney, who held the national record for a two-year-old trotter.

My first pony was a strawberry roan called "Merry Legs." He was succeeded by "Lady Grey," a spirited mare who sometimes ran away with me. That did not matter too much because Papa always rode at top speed and his horse, "Chika," was so fast that Lady Grey could never pass him. There were many miles of woodland trails, shady and cool for horse and rider. One of our favorite objectives was Turkey Hill from where we could look over the towns of Hingham and Nantasket. Like all

The summer house in Cohasset, Massachusetts

Josephine Whitney and "Lady Grey", ca. 1903

New England female riders of that era, I rode side saddle. I mounted my horse as follows: while the groom held my left foot in his hand, I said "one, two, three" and jumped. He boosted me up to where I landed on the saddle and then I curled my right leg round the pommel and inserted my left foot in the stirrup. To me now it seems humiliating to think of needing a man to help me, but in those days I didn't know any better. With the coming of the automobile, we had trouble with some of our horses who were terrified by the noise and smell and strange aspect of a carriage running without a horse. Some horses never became accustomed to the new invention. I remember riding a big bay who climbed a bank or jumped the fence if he chanced to meet one. He was sent, like a number of others similarly afflicted, to Mt. Desert, Maine, where no automobiles were allowed. There he pulled a Victoria for a New York society lady and never had to worry about encountering the dreaded monsters for the rest of his life.

My father, who was hard of hearing due to effects of scarlet fever in his youth, delighted to read aloud and my evenings were often spent listening to passages from Shakespeare, Mark Twain, Longfellow, *The Virginian* (by Owen Wister) or Thackeray. If the story were humorous he would laugh so hard he almost choked and the tears would run down his cheeks and he had to stop reading to get his handkerchief out and mop his eyes. I did not always quite understand the humor, but I liked to laugh with him. His enjoyment was contagious.

As I mentioned in Chapter I, he was always promoting some new scheme or product. I remember the samples he brought home for us to taste when he was trying to develop bottled orange juice. They were uniformly horrible! Although most of these new efforts did not materialize, I remember one that paid off. A greenish fibrous rock that he brought home could be pounded down into a sort of fluff that looked like cotton wool. Only unlike cotton wool, it was not flammable. We put bits of it in the open fire, but it did not burn. We held twists of the fibre over the lamp chimney, but it would not ignite. Later he brought pressed slabs of the stuff. They could remain in the kitchen stove all day and still be unscathed. He used to try these experiments and say, "I think this has a great future." And indeed it had. He bought most of the mines in Canada that produced asbestos—open pit quarries where it was easy to extricate the brittle rock. At one time he controlled the asbestos market of both Canada and the United States. He took me with him once to the little town of Thetford in Canada, close to the mine. The populace turned out to give him a big reception. However, the only thing I can remember about it now was seeing a much dressed up dowager unwittingly sit down on a plate of ice cream that someone had left in a chair. I waited, fascinated for her delayed reaction and was not disappointed. I am not sure why Papa sold all rights in the business to the Johns Manville Company. He probably wanted money to develop some new product.

In addition to morning lessons from my summer governess, I was given the morning chore of "fixing the flowers." About eight o'clock Richard Mulcahy, the gardener, brought up a whole tray of cut flowers. It was my job to bring the vases of withered flowes to the side porch and use the fresh ones in new arrangements. It usually took me about an hour. There were three rooms to decorate. At first I found it irksome, but as my skill increased, I enjoyed working with the lovely blossoms still wet with dew that filled the air with the fragrance of opening buds. I read a great deal and I wandered "lonely as a cloud" around the gardens and the barns. I was not supposed to milk the cows or curry the horses or go into the kitchen. What a sterile life for a child surrounded by so many opportunities! I am shocked when I think about it now, but it never occurred to me at the time that it could be otherwise. My rebellion took another form, which I shall tell about in the chapters that follow.

III

Dream World

Childhood's world of imagination.

It was in the summer that my inner life really began. Not having any associates of my own age, I invented companions who were invisible to the eye but vividly alive in my imagination. The Cohasset estate was isolated from town and bordered on untrammeled New England landscape, with its characteristic wild pasture land interspersed with outcroppings of grey granite rock and second growth woodland. The house itself was surrounded by well watered lawns and planted shrubbery, but the wild areas were readily accessible. This was my domain. It was there that my introspective self emerged, nurtured by the kindly Earth, the mother of all creatures who dwell on our planet. I could wander at will, learning the trees by the shapes of their leaves and the textures of their bark. Birds, rabbits, wood rats and squirrels amused me by their antics. The ground cover yielded surprises of lichen, fern and miniature flowers. Lying on my back on a sunny rock, I found excitement in the ever-changing procession of clouds that loitered across the sky, dissolving and reforming in dramatic and suggestive shapes. I have never felt lonely out of doors, doubtless due to the early communion with nature that was my refuge in early childhood.

I also entertained visitors in my sanctuary. People out of books I had read joined me for brief periods. Jack the Giant-killer, Siegfried, Robin Hood, Ivanhoe, Joan of Arc, Evangeline, and the Pied Piper of Hamelin were a few with whom I remember carrying on interesting conversations. But more often, my companions were born out of my own fantasy. They were fairies, gnomes, elves and leprechauns, all creatures of the

wild wood. I discovered a little dell, carpeted with soft green moss and edged about with ferns. This I designated as the fairy dance hall. I removed all stones and fallen twigs. On conveniently situated toad stools I arranged acorn cups of dew and wild huckleberries for their refreshment. I never saw the "Little People" but I knew they had been there because in the morning the berries were gone and the acorn cups were scattered. Once they left me a beautiful swallowtail butterfly in the middle of the dance floor. I thought he was asleep, for the color of his wings was still irridescent and the golden fuzz on his body was still unblemished. By the next day he did not waken so I considered that he was a gift from the fairy queen and I took him carefully to my bureau and placed him in a little white jewelry box in my drawer of treasures. A song I used to sing to myself was William Allingham's:

> Up the airy mountain,
> Down the rushy glen,
> We daren't go a'hunting
> For fear of little men,
> Wee folk, good folk
> Trooping all together
> Green jacket, red cap
> And white owl's feather.

As I grew older I became less interested in the "Wee folk." Instead I conjured up a galaxy of nature personifications who were influenced, it would seem, by Norse sagas and Greek mythology. I developed a cult for myself reminiscent of the theology of the American Indian or of any other primitive tribe.

I had, of course, frequently heard the name God. I do not think it held very much meaning for me at that time. My meagre religious instruction consisted of:

> Now I lay me down to sleep
> I pray the Lord my soul to keep
> And if I die before I wake
> I pray the Lord my soul to take.

"God bless Papa, Mama, my Sisters and Jim and all the dogs. Amen." This recitation was part of the going-to-bed ritual, like brushing my teeth, putting on a nightgown and winding the clock.

However, whether I used the word God or not, I reverenced some form of Supreme Being. I think the sun symbolized the Creator and the Preserver and that other elements, such as wind, rain, moon, stars, rocks, trees and grass, also claimed my homage. I set up a big stone as my altar, successor to the toad stool. Here I left pretty pebbles, bird feathers, flowers, even bits of cake or candy as offerings. They also disappeared. Sometimes I executed dances, or what I considered dances, before my altar. There was no one there to see my twirling and leaping and the happy stretching of my arms toward the heavens. Once at night when there was a thunder storm I tiptoed out to the lawn, took off my nightgown and lay down to let the torrents of rain beat down on my naked body. The zig-zag, startling streaks of lightning in the sky and the bloodcurdling explosions of thunder struck terror to my heart. But at the same time I felt myself somehow caught up in the universal cosmic whole. I became a part of all that tremendous disturbance in earth and sky. I was very frightened but very exalted. That was the first esoteric revelation I can remember. Other great moments were to come later to my inner consciousness. But that was the first.

I never spoke of these experiences to any of the people with whom I lived. Indeed, I do not think I have ever shared them with anyone. Writing of them now and stirring up these early memories, I am surprised at what I discover. It is almost like reading a book of fiction about someone I have never known and at the same time I discern my own self emerging out of the shadowy past. Was I really like that? What an odd little girl!

As a protection to my secret preoccupations I maintained two retreats safe from intrusion by adults. One of them was close to the house. A flat outcropping of granite outside the western porch disappeared at the further end underneath the branches of a large white pine which grew up from the base of the rock. The branches spread out over the ledge. I discovered that just below them was a convenient shelf about seven feet wide which I could reach by sliding under the pine boughs. I could be standing on the side steps and in a twinkling of an eye I could disappear as if into thin air. It was a cool, fragrant place in which to read or to dream. And, as I could jump off a drop of four or five feet to the ground below, I could return to civilization by an entirely different route. Often I huddled there when my governess was calling only a few feet away. If a response seemed diplomatic I could jump off the shelf and come up from quite a different direction.

"Where were you, Josephine?"
"Down by the tennis court."
"What were you doing?"
"Oh, just looking 'round."

My other hideout was a little further away. It was also a granite rock reached by an unfrequented path. It also dropped off sheer, twenty feet into a meadow of golden rod and asters belonging to a neighbor. I used to pretend it was a fortress. Somewhere I heard the song, "Rock of Ages, cleft for me,/ Let me hide myself in thee." I used to sing that on my upward journey. I still bear a scar on my right knee where I fell while scrambling upon my "Rock of Ages."

I had been told repeatedly not to go too far on the wood roads because "you might meet a tramp." I wasn't quite sure what a tramp was, but it sounded interesting. About four miles from our house, still on our property, was a place called Turkey Hill to which I used to be driven by my father, or go there with him on horseback. It was only a little hill, but I thought it was a great mountain. I became obsessed by the idea of adventuring there by myself to see the sunrise. I didn't think I would dare risk it and yet I hated myself for being scared. I plotted about going and gave it up repeatedly. Finally I decided that I *had* to go. I could no longer resist the pressure of my inner compulsion. I laid my plans carefully. Early one morning in midsummer I got out of bed just as the stars were beginning to fade and the darkness was giving way to light. It must have been about 3:00 a.m. I tiptoed downstairs in the sleeping house and out the front door. The world I was accustomed to appeared eerie in the half light and I almost turned back. But I forced myself to continue. Our Irish setter was startled by my sudden and unexpected appearance, and when she poked her muzzle into my hand and I realized that she meant to accompany me, I felt reassured.

It was dark in the woods where the tree tops met overhead, but there were no tramps. In fact, I met no one, not even a cow. At the farm house and barn no one was about, and at the railroad crossing I had to pass, the gate house was empty. The dog and I climbed Turkey Hill as the sky was turning pink in the east. I had not long to wait before the color deepened. Soon the curved edge of the sun poked up from the rim of the horizon. Slowly it swelled up into a golden semi-circle and at length there it was, a complete flaming disc that I could not even look at for dazzlement. All around, the fields and fences and trees were aglow with light. I noticed that the shadows, including my own, fell at a different angle. Almost immediately the birds began to sing. My eyes and ears were filled with beauty and my heart with wonder. How fortunate for a child thus to learn the miracle of dawn!

But then I remembered that I had a long way to retrace my steps. I ran all the way down the hill. The crossing was still deserted and no one saw me at the farm, although the roosters were crowing and the yearling colts hung their heads over the pasture fence to wish me good morning. The woods were no longer somber, but flecks of sunshine penetrated their branches and made patterns on the road. Here, too, the birds were singing, and I saw a red fox disappear into a thicket. The house looked familiar and welcoming. Not even the cook was up. The dog lapped up water from her dish and collapsed panting on the veranda. I patted her head and whispered my thanks for accompanying me on our momentous journey. Then I pulled off my shoes and crept stealthily upstairs, where I slipped off my clothes and got into bed. I pulled the blanket up to my chin, snuggled into the pillow and hugged myself for happiness. I had a wonderful feeling of relief and achievement, and—perhaps for the first time—a sense of self-confidence in my own strength, courage and judgment. It was a good adventure.

Thus, the inner level of my life developed quite apart from my apparent existence. The secrecy with which I guarded my inner preoccupations established a pattern that prevailed through later years. Seldom, if ever, have I been able to share the spiritual drama that unfolded for me over the years. Perhaps no one can. Perhaps the isolation of the deeper consciousness exists in every human being. I only know that this was my way. In telling of it now and trying to analyze its evolution, I am hoping to find a key to the meaning of life, this strange, individual manifestation in a strange planet in a strange and incomprehensible universe.

IV

Adolescence

School in Boston; sisters' marriages and parents' separation.

There is no definite boundary line separating my childhood and adolescence. If one were to try and construct a graph it would be characterized by widely divergent lines, hitting both high and low extremes with nebulous spaces in between. Academically, I was doubtless well advanced. Emotionally, I was immature, still living in the world of fantasy and socially hampered by scanty experience in human relationships. I was fiercely independent and protected myself both from criticism and approval by an almost fanatical secrecy.

I recall one step in passing out of childhood which I think is characteristic of my psychology. When I finish with something I am through with it for keeps. I do not go back on my decisions. One day I told Miss Dugan that I was through with dolls. She expressed incredulity. I got a large sized dress box and some tissue paper, packed the dolls carefully away and relegated them to the top shelf of my storage closet. Miss Dugan tried to arouse my sympathies by dramatizing the loneliness of the abandoned dolls. She prevailed on me to remove "Frankie," my favorite rag doll. I set him up in a baby chair but I never played with him again. The same thing happened with my stable and the little skin horses that all had names and private stalls and pasture on a green carpet in my nursery. They, too, were packed away never to be resurrected. I don't know what happened to them, but "Frankie" was somehow preserved. Fourteen years later, he was resurrected for my first daughter, Elizabeth. His features had been rubbed out, but De Neal Morgan, an artist in Carmel, California, painted a new face on the old cloth and he again became a member of the family.

From my tenth to my fourteenth year I no longer had a nurse, but according to modern—and even Victorian—standards, my freedom was strictly limited. When I went shopping or traveled by streetcar, I had to have a chaperone. This was a great trial to me, and I am sure it must have been an onerous duty for Miss Dugan, who sympathized with my desire for independence. I was safeguarded from contacts "below my station." I was not, for instance, allowed in the kitchen where I might have come in contact with unseemly words and manners. I wasn't allowed in the stable where interesting conversation took place while horses were curried and harnesses oiled. I was not even permitted to watch the cows being milked. The one time I defied that prohibition, I had the misfortune—in trying to get a good view of the pulling process—of kneeling in a "cowpie" and soiling my stockings and cotton drawers. I washed them out in the watering trough and was returning with them under my arm when I ran into my summer governess and the scandalous confession could not be avoided.

I think Miss Dugan tried to introduce me to the "other side of life" as much as she could. She took me to see a blind girl called Melissa, who liked to have me read to her. Another time, in the spring when the fields were laden with daisies and buttercups, she took me to the Children's Hospital, an old red brick building located on Huntington Avenue. Before making the visit, I picked big bunches of flowers to distribute to the little patients in the not-too-sick ward. Our coachman's wife had a baby, and she was nursing it when I went to call. I felt horrified that the child was chewing its mother. Miss Dugan tried to explain, but I still thought it was an indecent performance.

When I was about twelve years old I started going to Miss Haskell's School on Marlboro Street in Boston. There I met some very nice girls I thought were just as clever as I was, and I found some real friends among them. Eleanor Cabot came from Brookline and lived not far from me, so I could see her on afternoons and weekends. Barbara Bolles lived in Cohasset, and I met her a few times every summer. Eleanor and I became "best friends", and it was a godsend to me to associate with someone my own age with whom I could share my joys and sorrows, who liked to do the things I liked to do and whom I could trust. Our friendship lasted for many years. She went to France with the Red Cross during the first World War. Later, she made an unhappy marriage and we seldom met. Distance and the differences of our living patterns rendered communication difficult to maintain. But she was my first real love. I used to go to visit her in Dublin, New Hampshire, where she spent her summers. In her home I saw for the first time a normal relationship between a mother and children. Mrs. Cabot's warmth and devotion to her family contrasted painfully with my arid environment. She must have sensed my hunger for affection, because she included me in the bedtime ritual of good night kisses. I hated to go home after these visits.

Once when visiting her in Dublin I was invited to the home of Samuel Clemens, alias Mark Twain. It was his custom to invite all the children of the community to help him celebrate his birthday. We played games and explored his house and grounds. When it came time for ice cream and birthday cake, an impressive looking gentleman with bushy white hair and mustache, dressed in a white suit and smoking a big cigar, came sauntering in. He did not speak for a while, but looked us all over. I think we were more interested in the pink ice cream than we were in him. Presently he began to tell us a story in a quiet, modulated way. I don't remember what the story was about, but I am sure it had some funny things in it because I remember hesitating to laugh because he looked so solemn, never cracking a smile; when the older people began to chuckle we knew it was all right to do likewise. One thing I noticed were his light blue eyes that had a mischievous glint in them. When we started to go home, some officious parent insisted that we must all shake hands with Mr. Clemens. "Someday," she said, "you will want to say you shook hands once with Mark Twain." So the poor man had to shake the hand of every little youngster who had shared his birthday cake. He muttered pleasantries as they filed by him. I am sorry I was not smart enough to listen and record the historic moment more carefully. But I did shake hands with Mark Twain.

While in Dublin I saw a good deal of the artists Abbott Thayer and George DeForest Brush. Thayer had three children, Mary, Gladys and Gerald. His wife and two of the girls had great beauty. They were the models for most of his pictures. Gerald became a pioneer in the study of protective coloration in nature and wrote an authoritative and beautifully illustrated book on the subject. George Brush had a large family of children which he, too, used as models. Their manner of living was most informal. Once, a visitor called by appointment to find no one at the house. Mrs. Brush called from her perch in a tree, "Come up if you want." But they were not dressed for tree climbing so they remembered a previous engagement and departed. Another time, when the Brushes had invited friends to supper, the guests arrived to find a note on the kitchen table, "We changed our minds and have gone up Mt. Monadnock. Help yourselves. There is plenty of food in the ice box." Sometimes I have been tempted to follow their example.

I enjoyed Miss Haskell's School. The classes were small, the teachers well trained and the standards high. I became scholastically ambitious and had to work hard to keep myself at the head of the class. I also had fun and engaged in quite a few pranks. Mrs. Lucinda Prince was the first teacher Eleanor and I had. We were her favorites. She was in the habit of inviting one or the other of us to sit beside her in front of the class while she taught. Whichever one of us sat next to her would make faces at the rest of the girls facing us at their desks. Since we were close beside her, Mrs. Prince could not see our grimaces and never could understand why the class erupted into giggles at some crucial moment of

her instruction. Twice a week a French woman came in to teach us. We used Miss Haskell's dining room for this class, and we sat on folding chairs. Sometimes these really did fold up and suddenly the sitter would shoot under the table. Mademoiselle would cry out, "Oh, la la!" and the other girls exploded into delighted giggles as the victim crawled out from under the table and set the chair up again. It took many minutes before order was restored, in spite of poor Mademoiselle's reiterated pleas of "S'il vous plait, Mesdemoiselles." I think that each day before we went downstairs to this class it was pre-arranged which of us would collapse. Miss Haskell eventually caught wind of the matter and scolded us. Because we all liked her very much, the "accidents" became less frequent and we learned a little more French.

In my last year in that school I learned a great deal. Having struggled through Julius Caesar's conquests in beginning Latin the year before, I progressed to Ovid and the fascinating Graeco-Roman myths. In history I had an inspiring teacher who carried me through the Middle Ages and the Renaissance with a mixture of enthusiasm and that scholarly curiosity that made history a living experience. I did all the supplementary reading she suggested and much more. We acted (or thought we acted) Shakespearean plays. Because I was so tall, I always got men's parts. In *Twelfth Night* I impersonated Sir Toby Belch; but my greatest triumph was in the *Taming of the Shrew*, in which I starred as Petruchio. This part gave me a great opportunity to express my aggressive frustrations. I remember that I had a hat with a long black ostrich feather and a sword. I cannot recall the shrew, but I must have given her a horrid time in rehearsals.

One day, the walls of the reception and dining rooms of the school were covered with a collection of extraordinary drawings. They were pencil sketches of nude figures in strange symbolic attitudes executed with great skill and delicacy. I did not understand them very well, but they aroused a deep emotional response in me and I kept returning to look at them whenever I had time between classes. Years later I was amazed to see those drawings again as illustrations in Kahlil Gibran's *The Prophet*. I never knew how the drawings happened to be hung on the school walls, but it seems that Mary Haskell came to know Gibran soon after he first came to the United States from Lebanon. Her letters to Gibran were published in 1972. Miss Haskell was a dynamic, warm, glowing personality. She must have been far ahead of her time in teaching methods, and she was certainly able to attract a superior staff to carry out her ideas. Her interests and contacts must have reached far beyond the school. I only knew her as someone who aroused my intellectual aspirations and who helped me believe in my own ability to achieve. She gave me a good start.

To get to school in Boston I had to drive in from Brookline. It took about forty minutes. Thomas Ayers, the second stable man, drove me in and came to take me home early in the afternoon. He was a ruddy-cheeked Irishman. His light blue eyes always seemed to be twinkling at some secret joke and he had just enough brogue left to make his conversations spicy. He had many yarns to tell of the "old country" and of the horses he had taken care of over there and in Massachusetts. We drove in all kinds of weather, rarely missing a trip because of a storm. In winter we traveled in a sleigh, with a string of bells on the horse making a lovely sound as we sped along. Often it was bitterly cold, and although Thomas tried to bundle me up in the buffalo robe, I sometimes arrived at school with a frost bitten ear or nose and fingers too numb to untie my bonnet. Usually he let me drive, although he had strict orders not to do so. My father owned an extremely nervous and spirited gelding called "Attair." Thomas liked to drive him and so did I. One day, on the way home when we crossed Massachusetts Avenue, two noisy streetcars were converging from different directions. The trolley had been knocked off one car and sparks were showering over the street. Attair took one look at the fireworks and proceeded to rear up and prance round on his hind legs, adding to the excitement of the spectators on the sidewalk. I was handling the situation with presence of mind and skill when, on the other side of the street, at the very moment of Attair's gymnastics, my mother appeared in her victoria, which was drawn by a well-mannered sorrel pair and driven by John Gaffey, the head stable man. Unlike Thomas's face, John's never lost its stolid dignity, and he sat up on the box in his trim, green uniform looking straight ahead, apparently oblivious to the vulgar throng on the other side of the street. Thomas and I caught sight of Mother's equipage at the same time. When I had quieted the horse and passed beyond the danger point, Thomas said, "Faith, I'll be catching it now, Miss, and like as not you will too." His prophecy was correct and for a few days I could not wheedle Thomas into giving up the reins. However, after a bit he relaxed, and I promised to keep a sharp look out ahead for approaching victorias and to hand over the reins pronto if I saw danger approaching. I did once and the transfer was perfectly timed.

Elinor was the first of my older sisters to marry. She was married to Pennington Gardiner in 1904. My mother was not pleased with this match and for many years refused to have anything to do with Elinor or her family. Ruth, the oldest, was the next to go. She married Herbert Lyman in 1906. Mama was delighted, for not only was Herbert a fine person, but he also came from one of the old aristocratic families of Boston.

After Ruth's marriage, my sister Laura and I were the only ones left at home. My brother, who had spent four years at Groton, was now at Harvard and came home seldom because of the critical atmosphere he encountered. My sister Laura was lovely to look at, very slender, with curly brown hair shot through with golden glints. She played the violin well and I used to enjoy listening to her practice. She had a delightful sense of humor and could be enchantingly silly even in the sombre atmosphere of our household. For about a year I enjoyed getting to know her. For me she was "the blessed damozel," the embodiment of everything sacred and beautiful. When she told me she was planning to be married, I pretended to rejoice in her happiness, but at night I wept bitter tears at the thought of losing my beloved companion. Especially since she was marrying Phil Dodge, a native of Omaha, Nebraska, and would be living far away. Mama did not oppose this marriage, even though Phil's midwestern accent and political views were a little hard for her to take. Once, in the midst of a discussion of public affairs at a dinner party, he became exasperated, pounded on the table and said, "Oh, you God damn *Easterners!*"

After Laura's marriage, the relationship between my parents had become so untenable that they agreed to live out the rest of their lives separately. The Brookline house was altogether too large for just my mother and me. Furthermore, she wanted to travel in Europe. So the house was closed, and my father went to live with Aunt Mary on Pleasant Street in Brookline. I was destined to accompany Mama and continue my education abroad. This was a momentous change for me. It necessitated my bidding goodbye to Miss Dugan and my friends from Miss Haskell's school and entering into continuous association with someone whom I hardly knew and whom I had always regarded with apprehension bordering on fear. It was a difficult upheaval in my life. However, it was somewhat alleviated by the prospect of seeing new lands and strange people and finding out what the world outside of eastern Massachusetts looked like. I was frightened at the prospect of being alone with my mother but excited about traveling.

Before I left, my sister Elinor asked me to come see her one afternoon and to my surprise told me she thought I ought to know some things about life. She asked, "Do you know where babies come from?" I was very much embarrassed and answered, "I guess they come from God."

"Yes," said Elinor, "but how do they come?"

"I thought they were just there."

"Just as I was afraid," she continued, "you don't know a thing about it. And I think you ought to know."

She then entered into a detailed and specific discourse on the realities of sex, the male and female functions and the procreation of offspring. It is difficult for me to understand how I could have reached the age of fourteen or fifteen and not had the slightest inkling of this aspect of life. I was curious about so many things and read such sophisticated novels that I find it hard to imagine now how I could have been so unaware of fundamental facts. Although I had plenty to eat, and a luxurious home, I was a deprived child in that my experience with life itself was curtailed at almost every point. The common knowledge of street and playground, the homely realities of animals and soil and the comforting sense of belonging somewhere were all denied to me. Luckily, Miss Dugan, my father, Eleanor Cabot and my sister, Laura, provided channels for my affections. They undoubtedly saved me from bitterness. I was often unhappy and often lonely, but I could not despair when I had such good friends whom I loved and who loved me in return.

My sister's revelation was a profound shock. Apparently no one had even approached me with the "birds and the bees." I had terrifying dreams and waking nightmares. Elinor certainly did me a kindness by telling me, but I wonder if she herself had not been almost as innocent as I before her marriage. She dwelt only on the physical aspects of union and did not mention the deeper spiritual significance. It seems to me she left me with a distorted view and a false emphasis, but that may have been my fault. At all events, for some time after our conversation I regarded all men with disgust. As one approached I wondered what he looked like without his clothes on and I shrank from having him come closer. I imagined that he had evil intentions and I didn't care to have anything to do with the monster.

Two years later, when I started going to dances, I continued to feel shy and apprehensive and I kept my friendships on a strictly platonic basis. I never let any boy kiss me or even hold hands until I was engaged. If I had not married an unusually sensitive and patient man I might have proven to be a very unsatisfactory wife. In bringing up my children I saw to it that they were knowledgeable, but I think I was still somewhat puritanical in regard to their social activities. They did a good deal to educate me. My grandchildren have done more; they have given me a post-graduate course, and I do not know how much more I can learn from my great grandchildren!

Attitudes have certainly changed since I grew up. Much of today's sex attitudes and practices seem to me to be crude and self-indulgent, but I am glad there is no longer a veil of secrecy concealing the true nature of love and parenthood. I still believe that the family is the most important unit in society and the best training center for the young. The creation of a lasting marriage is a long process of adaptation and acceptance. It seems a pity to jump into it without realizing the self-discipline involved, and the deep faith and purpose that are needed to bring the relationship to mutual satisfaction. Promiscuity disturbs me. The bloom is off the rose and love becomes a tarnished commodity in the secondhand market. The superficial gratifications are easy to come by, but they are short-lived. The most precious things in life demand a price. Today too many young people (and older ones also) are in too much of a hurry or too selfish to pay. And so they never experience the deeper fulfillments of life.

V

European School Days

School in Paris and Berlin;
Bayreuth and the opera;
travels in Germany.

On my first trip abroad, my mother and I landed at Liverpool. Our first stopping place was the picturesque village of Clovelly, where the little white cottages seemed to cling precariously to the steep hillside, and where the cobblestone streets were barely wide enough for two carts to squeeze by. It was a charming introduction to England. When I arrived in London my previous years' study of history had provided me with the clue to many of the sights: the Tower of London, Warwick Castle, Kew Gardens, the Thames and its bridges, Fleet Street, the slums, Newgate Prison and Trafalgar Square. I spent many hours in the London museums. Of all the great picture collections in Europe, the British National Art Gallery seems to hold the least number of second rate paintings and contains the finest masterpieces. To my adolescent taste, however, the Tate Gallery offered the greatest stimulus. The Pre-Raphaelite School, and especially the paintings by Watts (Hope, Despair, Sorrow, Death, etc.), appealed to my sentimental searchings. I sat and looked at these mystical paintings till the tears came. I collected as many reproductions as I could find. What had struck me in the drawings of Gibran on the walls of Haskell School was reemphasized here.

We traveled in many parts of England, visiting universities and cathedrals and picturesque towns. Automobiles were rare and the hawthorne-lined lanes were quite adequate for the dogcart and the dray. Three weeks in the Lake Country gave me a wholly new appreciation of Wordsworth's poetry. I had never cared very much for his mellow, restrained style of writing. But living in the landscape, and skirting the edges of Windermere and Grassmere Lakes, I came to realize the special quality of the environment, and of Wordsworth's low-keyed descriptions of the hills and dales he knew so well. His devout moralizing was quite a contrast to the melancholy Rossetti and the fiery Byron, the ecstatic Shelley and the enraptured Keats, all of whom I had been reading. For a few weeks I abandoned my old loves and immersed myself in Wordsworth, cultivating the "inward eye," which is "the bliss of solitude." The fluency and homeliness of his sonnets made me try that writing medium, but I soon found that the ease was apparently Wordsworth's and not mine.

When summer ended, the question of my further education arose. My mother decided to spend the winter in Paris, and rented an apartment on the Avenue d'Iena near the Etoile. She took me to visit several schools that had been recommended to her and allowed me to choose whichever one I liked best. She favored a small select family who took in three or four girls, but I did not fancy the cramped quarters nor the ultra sophisticated atmosphere. I preferred a larger institution outside the city in the suburb of Neuilly. This place was known as the Villa Leona, or "L'Ecole de Madame Yeatman pour Les Jeunes Filles." Some fifty girls from divers countries were "finished" under the guidance of the headmistress and several other teachers. There was a big, white, three-story building, set in a spacious garden which was surrounded by a high metal fence. Most of the girls came from England, but there were representatives from most European countries, even from Australia and South Africa. There were only six Americans. The school was ungraded but there were three divisions, beginners, medium and advanced. There were eight in the advanced group, who sat in the front row, and I was one of these. Sitting next to me was Enid Bagnold from Woolwich, England. She later became famous as the author of *National Velvet* and several other books and plays. She was a brilliant and stimulating person and we enjoyed companionship and rivalry. Enid carried a little black notebook in her pocket in which she jotted down any *argot* (French slang) which she could pick up. Whenever a workman came to the school to make repairs or to deliver merchandise, she would listen in on his conversation, and when we went on sightseeing trips she paid more attention to the street boys and the trades people than she did to the monuments. At school she used the phrases she had collected with gratifying reactions from the teachers, *"Tiens, Enid, ou avez vous entendu ces mots?!"*

Towards the end of the term, there was a competition for the best translations from English into French, and from French into English. The texts were chosen from the classics in both languages. The prize was a volume of Victor Hugo's poems bound in red leather. Enid and I were evenly matched, and we were both equally ambitious. We worked very hard over the passages. When the name of the winner was announced

FONDATRICE: MADAME YEATMAN.   VILLA LÉONA·   DIRECTRICES { MISS EASTON
                                                               { MADEMOISELLE CHARPIOT·

and I received the ribbon-tied package, I was surprised and elated. It was the first time I had come up against any real intellectual challenge, and I could not believe that I had won over Enid. The congratulations of the teachers and the applause of the other pupils were music in my ears. I was a little embarrassed about Enid, but my triumph was so important to my ego that it did not allow much consideration for my rival, even though she was my friend.

The schedule of the school included lectures on French history and literature given by Sorbonne professors. Madame Girard, a retired actress from the Comedie Francaise, gave us lessons in diction. She used to wring her hands in despair over my New England reticence and Enid's sense of the ridiculous. Mme. Girard's efforts to induce us to express passionate laments or soulful ecstasies usually ended in disrespectful paroxysms of laughter on our part and grieved incomprehension on hers. We were hopelessly Anglo-Saxon. Once a week, a lady journalist reported current events to the school assemblage. She was an anaemic, somewhat faded lady dressed in pink who wafted an aroma of heavy perfume through the schoolroom as she mounted to the podium. Almost every paragraph in her discourse was prefaced with the commentary, "Figurez vous, mesmoiselles" (Imagine, young ladies!) Our name for her became "Figurez Vous." One morning M. Porret, the history professor, had the misfortune to begin a sentence with these words, whereupon everyone exploded into a shout of merriment. He stopped in his description of the court of Louis XVI and blushed to the roots of his blonde hair. In his confusion, not knowing what he had said amiss, he appealed to Mme. Yeatman. All she could do was to rap sharply on her desk with her pencil and cast severe looks on the giggling girls.

The best moment of each day occurred at midmorning when the bakery boy brought a big basket full of hot croissants. We were allowed all the milk we wanted but there were always just exactly enough croissants to permit one apiece. They were hot and flaky from the oven. Nothing ever tasted so delicious.

On Thursday we had only half a day of school. In the afternoon we went sightseeing in Paris. Several different excursions were posted, and we could sign up for the one we wanted. The designated chaperone for each group often determined our choice. Before returning to school in the late afternoon, we were allowed to go to a patisserie where we could purchase no more than two cakes apiece. I can still recall the agonizing moments of decision, poring over the case of pastries trying to eliminate all but two of the delectable concoctions. I think this must have been a trying period for our duenna.

Every morning, after we had all rattled off the Lord's Prayer in French, we had roll call and each of us reported how many English words we had spoken the previous day. Often we could not remember and the answer would be "Beaucoup" or "Je ne sais pas," but as the weeks went by some of us could honestly say that we had not reverted to English at all. We really did learn to speak French, although I suspect the accent was not much better than what one hears today from British tourists on the continent. We gained a superficial knowledge of French literature and history, although I never could get all the King Louis's between ten and twenty sorted out in my mind. Lamartine was my favorite poet and Pierre Loti my favorite novelist. I read plays by Racine and Moliere and was fortunate enough to see Coquelin in his famous role of Cyrano de Bergerac. I believe I heard the Mozart operas and La Boheme for the first time that winter. But in addition to this abundant menu of culture, the most significant aspect of the school was the chance it gave me to become acquainted with girls from widely varied backgrounds. Muriel and Madeline Ashwell, American girls from New York, and Marie Vedder from Holland were my special pals. But the most significant experience for me was my *affaire du coeur* with one of the teachers. Her name was Gabrielle Boissier. She was not a very good teacher and she was not at all pretty, but she was a warm and sympathetic young woman who, like me, craved affection and who felt lonely in the monotonous and impersonal role in which she found herself. Mme. Yeatman and her assistant, Miss Strong, discouraged unhealthy attachments between the girls and the mistresses, so our intimacy had to be somewhat clandestine. On excursion days, I usually managed to be included in her group. For that afternoon, the other girls would go on ahead and we could stay close together behind and look at the museum or the church or whatever the sight might be, sharing our thoughts and our sympathies as we passed along. Sometimes she visited me in my room after lights were out, as she was in charge of the second floor of the dormitory. Visitation after hours was strictly prohibited, so she ran a considerable risk of being caught by the head mistress who often snooped around the corridors at night. But Gabrielle succeeded sometimes in eluding surveillance, and she would slip in stealthily and sit on my bed and we would talk in whispers far into the night. She called me "Ma Grande" because I was much taller than she. She taught me a lot about the Catholic religion and the meaning of many of the symbols and the characteristics of her favorite saints. After I left the school, I used to receive fat weekly letters bearing French postage stamps which aroused my mother's curiosity and evident disapproval. As the months passed, the letters became less bulky and arrived at wider intervals. Gabrielle left the school and eventually married, while my interests turned to other directions, and our communication gradually ceased. I am sure, however, that the intense infatuation that we held for one another satisfied a pressing need for a brief period. Although it was short-lived, I know it deepened my capacity for affection and loyalty. How does love increase save through the practice of it?

I remember very little of the weekends that I spent with Mama in her apartment in Paris. I was allowed to go there once a month. She had a delightful French maid who took care of the apartment and cooked for her. She always wanted me to tell her what I especially liked to eat on my monthly visits. She made a delicious dessert called "Mont Blanc." It was a chestnut puree, a mound of it surmounted by whipped cream to suggest snow. She always made it for me. Once, after I was married, I decided to try and make it for my husband. I felt guilty in retrospect, when I found out what a tremendous amount of work that chestnut puree involved. It took me at least four hours to cook, peel and mash Mont Blanc and shape it up before adding the creamy peak.

When school was out, we went to Trafoi, a small town in the Austrian Tyrol half way up the Stelvio Pass. There was a big hotel that faced a towering barrier of snowy peaks almost frightening in their austere, icy stillness. The moonlight on that stupendous backdrop was so crystalline that I spent several nights rolled up in a blanket by the window, enthralled by the ethereal light. When the sun set the whiteness turned to deep pink and lavender just for a few moments, a fleeting glorious illumination to bid farewell to one more lovely day. At dawn every morning, the goats from the little village of Trafoi were rounded up by the goatherds and driven to the high Alpine meadows to feast on the flowers and gambol on the rocks. Every goat had a bell, and as they joined the procession on the hillside trail, there was quite a din. When they returned at evening one heard the bells far off in the distance, sounding louder and louder as they reached the village. Each goat would go into her own shed and bleat for her owner to come out with his bucket to take the sweet milk from her bag overflowing with the juice of the pasture grasses. I climbed up to some of these flower-sprinkled meadows. There I saw gentians and Alpenroschen. I even found an Edelweiss at the edge of a snowdrift. If I met any man on the trail, he wore Lederhosen and like as not a feather in his round green hat. He always greeted me with *"Grüss Gott, Fraulein."* This place was a pleasing interlude between the months of formal schooling. Who can say through what media a child learns? Mountain goats and sunsets are not bad teachers.

The second part of my European education took place in Berlin. I am not sure why Mama chose Berlin rather than one of the other less austere and ugly German cities. But there we were installed in an apartment on Friedrich Wilhelm-Strasse not far from the Siegesallee, that blatant avenue lined on both sides with atrocious statues of German heroes past and present. A few blocks from our temporary home I was enrolled in Fraulein Wittig's Mädchen Schule. Here I was the only foreigner so it did not take me long to acquire fluent German. I had learned German grammar and vocabulary while still in school in Boston. That basic foundation was important. I have a natural facility in languages, due in part to a sensitiveness to the cadence of speech, so that I could hear the verbs holding their breath till the end of the sentence. My knowledge of grammar gave me the clue for the correct endings. It was a small school of about twenty-five girls. All the teaching was done by Fraulein Maria and Fraulein Margarethe, the two homeliest women I ever met. When the girls arrived in the morning they made a *knix* and kissed the hands of each of the ladies. I could manage a *knix*, but I balked at the kiss. The girls could not understand why. I explained that in America we didn't kiss people's hands. I thought it was an unsanitary custom. They were all very docile and well-behaved. I found them rather uninteresting except for one tall blonde, Hilda von Zedlitz, whom I liked. She invited me to her home one evening where I made the mistake of sitting down on the livingroom sofa, considered the seat of honor for grandmothers and persons of high rank. I did not realize this protocol at the time; I only knew I had committed some sort of *faux pas* as I saw Hilda and her mother exchange shocked glances. Her brother was a typical *Junker Officier* resplendent in blue uniform and gold braid who treated me as if I were some sort of inferior animal. I did not enjoy my visit very much and I was never invited back. Hilda and I corresponded a couple of times a year, but with the advent of the First World War our communication ceased.

The winter of 1908 saw an effort at rapprochment between Germany and England. George V visited his cousin Kaiser Wilhelm in Berlin. I joined the spectators who watched the parade down Unter den Linden when the King and the Kaiser, both wearing hats with ostrich feather plumes, rode side by side in an open victoria to the rhythm of marching feet and the Royal Band. Flags were flying from all the houses, and the populace cheered lustily. The veneration for the royal family was hard for me to understand. One afternoon, the Wittigs took their pupils to see an exhibition of paintings at one of the galleries. While we were there, the word went round that the Kaiserin was coming to the gallery. Such excitement on the part of the girls and the mistresses! We were herded into a corner of one of the exhibition rooms so as not to interfere with the royal progress. As the Kaiserin came in with her entourage, the girls all curtsied and bowed low and so did the Wittig ladies. I stood stolidly, like a misplaced fence post, in the middle of all this commotion. The Kaiserin, a tall, heavy-set blonde, tightly corseted in yellow, stopped to look at us through her lorgnette. The girls said, "She noticed us! Did you see? She noticed us! And why did you just stand there, Josephine, without bowing at all? I don't understand you." Of all the Hohenzollern family I think the Kronprinzessin Cecilie was the most attractive. The Crown Prince was a conceited, ineffectual type. The next son, Eitel Fritz, a big hearty blonde like his mother, was more popular.

A feature of German international relations before 1914 was the exchange of university professors with the United States. Dr. William Davis, a geologist from Harvard, and Dr. Felix Adler, founder of the Ethical Culture Society in New York, were the two incumbents whom Mama knew. Because we knew them, we were invited to some occasions involving high society where we met the ubiquitous officers, Herr Professors, Doktors, Hoch Wohlgeborene Geheimrats, etc., etc.

Very formal and sedate. Sometimes there was very nice music which broke through the tedium. Mr. and Mrs. Davis did not have any family with them. But the Adlers had four children. Two of the older ones lived in the apartment directly over ours. Margaret, who had been an honor student at Smith College, had suffered an attack of polio the year before which prevented her return to school and handicapped her movements. Lawrence was studying piano with Rudolph Ganz in Berlin. It was arranged, therefore, for Margaret who needed care and Lawrence who needed to practice, that the two should live apart from their parents whose social life was very demanding. A pleasant German girl took care of the brother and sister, and I was delighted to have some young Americans close overhead. Margaret and I always insisted that Lawrence should play Liszt's *Liebestraum* for our delectation. Their little Dienstmädchen made excellent coffee cake and we enjoyed many pleasant evenings together. This friendship lasted all our later years.

I found Southern Germany more to my liking than Prussia. We attended the summer Wagner Festivals at Munich and Bayreuth. I became familiar with the Nordic myths and the librettos of the operas. The *Ring Cycle* aroused my romantic notions and during the week of the festival I was completely absorbed by the drama that unfolded through all its tragic sequences. I wept when Wotan put Brunhilde to sleep on the rock, when Lohengrin departed in the Swan boat, when Isolde sang her lament for Tristan. And I gloried in the Valkyrie battle cry (what a ghastly thing to sing!), and the coming of spring in the woods when Siegfried found he could understand the birds. The performances began at 2 p.m. There was a forty minute break about 4:30 and the audience wandered through the corridors drinking beer and munching *belegtes Brödchen* (sandwiches). We returned to our seats for another act. A second intermission allowed time for a complete dinner before the final curtain went up. It was a leisurely manner of absorbing an opera. You were not exhausted at the conclusion because of the relaxing intervals which gave time to refuel the engines and allow the emotions to cool off.

All the time I was in school I studied German literature. Both Berlin and Munich had excellent theatres. Plays by Hauptmann and Ibsen were frequently given. I remember also the Marionetten Theater in Munich which gave the ancient version of Doktor Faustus so beautifully that you entirely forgot the smallness of the stage and the hugeness of the audience. I loved the poems of Heine, but I found most of Goethe rather hard going. I enjoyed books by Peter Rosegger and the German fairy tales. I felt at ease using the language and even after all these years I find I can speak it passably on the spur of the moment. I loved Germany very much better than France but I never wanted to go back after World War II. Too many tragedies that could not be forgotten. Not the same Germany ever again.

In the fall and winter of 1909-1910 I was destined to "come out"—in other words, to be introduced to society. We were known as "buds",

Margaret Green Whitney, my mother

and the opening of the rose consisted of qualifying for the Junior
Assemblies, getting your name on the list of eligible young ladies in the
Social Register and becoming a member of that year's Sewing Circle.
(Perhaps in the Pilgrim days the sewing was in evidence, but that must
have been very long ago. A monthly luncheon took the place of
needlework.) For this traditional social splash an extensive wardrobe was
a prerequisite. My mother figured that it would be much less expensive
and also more chic to purchase the clothes in Europe, and she chose
Vienna as the desirable market. We had rooms there for two or three
weeks. The dressmakers came to the hotel and brought their models

from which we selected the most desirable. They took measurements and returned some days later for fittings and then again for alterations. It was a gruesome process selecting what Mama liked and standing up while the dressmakers pinned and cut and adjusted the different raiments. I don't remember all of them, but there was a white satin with a train, a blue silk, a pink afternoon dress with flounces, a flowered dinner gown and an old rose suit with a lace waist and a long coat which I detested. When the wardrobes were finally completed and packed they filled a trunk. Mama also ordered a very handsome purple outfit for herself.

The only other thing I remember about Vienna was a procession which took place on Corpus Christi day, when the Host was carried through the streets by the Archbishop, accompanied by dignitaries of church and state and military contingents. The old Kaiser Friedrich Wilhelm walked bareheaded behind the priests. He was followed by his special regiment of Hungarian Huzzars. Without doubt they were the most magnificent band of horsemen I have ever seen. They were dressed in red coats and yellow breeches with high black patent leather boots. Over their shoulders hung a leopard skin and on their heads they wore black astrakhan hats in which a white egret feather stood high up above the fur. They were mounted on magnificent white Arabian horses who seemed to dance along in perfect unison. This parade must have been one of the last public appearances of the old Emperor who had ruled for fifty years and whose polyglot empire with all its pomp and glory was to crumble and disintegrate within a very few years. I wonder what happened to those young men who so proudly rode their horses that day in 1908. I was fortunate to have been in Europe at the end of an era. When I open the atlas to the map of Europe, I try to find the old boundaries, but the lines are all different and the old names no longer exist.

The Victorian age was a pleasant time to live if you were economically well off. Life was relatively safe and sane for the affluent. The arts flourished, taxes were low, the clutter of motor vehicles had not begun, the aristocracy was respected and open space was not threatened. I started life in this comfortable and predictable milieu which was so soon to disintegrate. Before I became an adult, the foundations of the world's social structure started to crumble and the whole fabric of our life gradually became frayed and torn apart. Those of us born around the turn of the century have had to change not only our physical ways of life but also our ideological and spiritual ideals and concepts in the face of continuingly fluctuating patterns of social, political and ethical change. I am afraid none of us will live to see the new renaissance established, but perhaps the era of experimentation and search will prove to be the most rewarding. Perhaps it is true that to travel is more exciting than to arrive.

VI

Awakening

*Growth of religious feeling;
quest for faith.*

Sometime about my twelfth year I discovered the Bible. I don't remember seeing one in our own library, but I had noticed one in the guest room in a house that I visited. I knew very little about the Bible, but I had heard it spoken of often and alluded to in other books I read. My own first copy came from a secondhand bookstore—the King James version, in a worn, black leather binding, printed on thin paper. This book became my secret treasure. I kept it hidden under the nightgowns in my bureau drawer. While I was reading, if anyone chanced to knock on my door, I slid it under the bed before saying, "Come in." The marvelous drama that unrolled from the pages of the Old Testament held me spellbound. I had always thought of Adam and Eve and Noah as somewhat comic figures, but as the antecedents of the Great Prophets they assumed a new dignity and fell into line behind Moses and Joshua, David and Solomon and the great Hasidic succession. The concept of Jehovah—a great King above all other gods—filled my mind with new and magnificent images. The resonance and rhythm of the texts, especially the Psalms, reverberated under the surface of my daily activites and at night as I fell asleep under the shadow of His wings I murmured, "in His hands are all the corners of the earth and the strength of the hills is His also."

The struggle for righteousness that dominated the lives of the Hebrew leaders, and the high moral demands laid on them by God, influenced my aspirations. The idea of sin became poignant. I already had a sense of inferiority due to my family environment. As I became conscious of the transcendence of the Almighty, the unworthiness of me, the creature, deepened. After concluding the Old Testament, I came to the story of Jesus in the four gospels. I have always been thankful that this was my own discovery. My mind had never been cluttered with artificial dogmas or pious reiteration. I came to the story of Jesus with a fresh and open mind. In all their simplicity I read the scriptures so that the lineaments of the Great Teacher and His message of love and brotherhood came through to me as a new and overpowering revelation. I could not stop reading. I remember long after I was supposed to be in bed, standing under the gas light with my hand on the valve, ready to switch off the gas if I heard the carriage coming up the driveway or someone moving in the hall who might see the light under my door.

From the Bible, I turned to the lives of the saints and other devotional books. I undertook penances, such as lying on the floor instead of on a soft bed, going without certain foods I enjoyed, mortifying my flesh by tying an itchy string round my waist. I even went so far as flagellation. As I consider this phase of the "deeper level", I realize the romanticism that inspired these extremes. But at the time they seemed very real. Doubtless they served a purpose and satisfied a need for discipline.

Meanwhile, my actual church life was irrelevant and perfunctory. I never went to Sunday School. On Sunday mornings my sisters and I were dressed up like fashion plates, and we were driven with Mama to the Unitarian Church near the reservoir in Brookline. Our pew was halfway down the church. We were usually late, and I can remember heads turning to look as we sailed down the aisle, with my mother in the lead, followed by her girls, including little me. Dr. Lyon was the minister. I don't remember anything about the services or the sermons. I think there may have been a quartet that sang an anthem and led the hymn singing. My only vivid memory is of a family who sat in the pew in front of ours. When the mother passed away, the several sons who lived elsewhere returned home for the funeral. They attended church the following day. They were all dressed in black. One of them, a tall handsome man, was overcome with grief. He sat bent over, head in his hands, and sobbed openly. That a grown man could cry was a startling revelation to me. That he should care that much about his mother and be unable to restrain his emotion was a completely new idea which shocked me and at the same time moved me to admiration. I dreamed about him for several weeks.

The human spirit is never satisfied. It resembles a sea creature moving its tentacles hither and thither, sifting and filtering the tidal flow for bits of nourishment to appease its insatiable hunger. After my acceptance of the Christ image and the mystical interpretations of the Gospels, what chance did I have to associate this revelation with any other aspect of my life? Traveling in Europe as a tourist might not seem to offer much opportunity to deepen one's consciousness, but fortunately my mother's sightseeing programs introduced me to some of the magnificent Christian churches in England and the continent. While she studied architectural details, I found emotional excitement in the altars, the candles, the statues, the shadowy chapels and the upsweep of the arches to the high vaulted ceiling. They seemed to take me along with them towards heaven. I think Lincoln Cathedral was my first experience of such a building. We came in there when a service was in progress, and the ethereal boys' voices rose up from the choir and seemed to mingle with the streaks of sunlight that struck across the nave. It was a breathtaking moment. Beauty personified to the eye, the ear and the inner yearning.

As I look back to those months in Europe, the churches stand out most vividly in my memory. What I remember most about the English cathedrals is how they dominated the narrow streets and the low houses clustered around them. Durham, which was started before the Norman Conquest, had a marvelous crypt with massive original pillars of solid rock. At York, the glass windows were particularly memorable. It seemed as if the walls were formed of radiant translucent screens set in a network of stone. All the cathedrals had the immense height of Gothic arches sweeping one's gaze up to the vaulted roof. In all of them, the pipe organs thundered forth majestic anthems that echoed from every aisle and chapel and whispered back from clerestory and dome. In France, Notre Dame, the Sainte Chapelle, St. Denis and Chartres offered me equivalent ecstasy.

When I settled down at school, I was allowed to spend one weekend a month with my mother in Paris. Just around the corner from her apartment there was a small High Anglican chapel presided over by a priest from England. My mother attended service there every Sunday morning. The notice board at the entrance displayed a list of services offered in addition to the one we attended. I noticed that the first one came at 5:00 every morning, so I made it my practice to creep out about 4:45 without disturbing Mama. Perhaps half a dozen worshippers attended matins at that hour. No one paid any attention to the tall teenager who knelt in one of the back benches. I looked forward to these solitary vigils even more than to the delicious dessert that Mama's French maid produced in my honor for Sunday dinner.

This habit of attending early services reached its climax in Cologne. The hotel was located just across the square from the Dom (the cathedral). There masses began at 5:00 a.m. I arrived about 4:00 a.m. and stayed in the beautiful building until after 6:00 a.m. Out of the valley of shadows my soul seemed surrounded with a great company of celestial beings. I seemed to be drenched in light. On returning reluctantly to the hotel, I received a quizzical look from the night clerk as I passed through the lobby on my way upstairs. I can imagine what he was thinking. I doubt if he ever had had an American guest who spent two early morning hours in the cathedral.

Of course by frequenting so many churches I became very much drawn to the Catholic faith. I could follow the ritual in the small missal which I purchased, and I familiarized myself with the church calendar and holy day observances. I used to watch the people going to confession in the little wooden booths behind the screen in which the priest lay in waiting. I wondered what would happen if I went and recited the "Mea Culpa" and told him I was a Protestant. I never had the courage to try. Although rejoicing in the forms, I could not quite bring myself to accept the philosophy. The discipline of the church appealed to me strongly, as did the beauty of the architecture and the stately music of anthems and the rhythms of praise and prayer chanted in Latin or in the King James version of the Gospels. My desire "to belong" was obstructed by some of the doctrines that as a postulant I would have to accept. The Virgin birth, for instance, the resurrection of the *body* and the menace of hell. Also, the sacrament of communion, in which the bread and wine was supposed to be transformed into the actual blood and body of Christ, seemed repugnant to me. As a symbol of sharing in the divine fellowship of the disciples it had meaning, but as a literal act it seemed to me sacrilegious. I also felt that I should be responsible for my own sins, which were many. I suppose it was my New England heritage which made me unable to welcome the idea of a saviour who would assume responsibility for my transgressions. However, doctrinal obstacles did not prevent my joining freely with others present in the adoration of the Godhead. I have always felt perfectly comfortable in worshipping with any sincere group, even though the form and manner of expression might be incompatible. The seeking spirit is the essence of all religious sects and no barriers exist within that profound quest.

I tried very hard to follow the teachings of Jesus in my daily life, and it was not always easy. Living alone with Mama in a big city I could not escape her moods of criticism and disapproval. Sometimes she would not speak to me for two or three days. One evening, after she had been particularly hard to please, I retired to bed with a book. About 11 o'clock she pounded on my door and said it was time for me to put out the light and go to sleep. I did turn off the light, but I did not sleep. I lay in bed seething with resentment. I said to myself, "I hate her! I hate her! I hate her!" Suddenly it came to my mind that Jesus had taught that we should love our enemies and cherish those "who despitefully use us." It became evident to me that Mama was my enemy whether she was my mother or not, and it was my business to learn to love her. The next day at supper time she objected to the way I put the little spoon back in a salt dish. All of a sudden it struck me as so ridiculous to be finicky about a salt spoon and I burst out laughing and to her amazement kept on laughing. I guess it was a bit hysterical. "I don't see anything funny in that," she said, glaring at me, which made me laugh all the more, thinking how she was really only a petulant little girl under a tyrannical mask. And suddenly I felt a great pity and began to understand the frustrations which made her act as she did. From that time on I was much more tolerant. Her criticisms no longer bothered me very much, and I accentuated in my mind the great qualities she possessed, and I thought how she, too, was probably as lonely and unfulfilled as I. By admitting the hatred to myself I suddenly became aware of a new sense of freedom. While I could not immediately control my inner reactions, by invoking the power of love I found that the old resentments no longer irked me. Gradually I came to appreciate and relish the brilliant and complicated personality behind the forbidding exterior. I have often thought how fortunate I was to have been honest enough with myself to admit that I wanted to kill my mother. It might have cost me many hours and thousands of dollars in later life if I had had to discover it under the guidance of a psychoanalyst.

Later, as a debutante in Boston, I seem to have satisfied the duality of my religious groping by going to Kings' Chapel, the Unitarian Church in Boston, which continued to use the Anglican liturgy, but where Howard N. Brown preached eloquent sermons based on profound scholarship and high ethical principles. I went to hear him on Sunday mornings, but often on week days I visited a church in a very poor district somewhere behind the State House. The Cowley Fathers operated this humble little chapel. What a contrast to the austere white interior of Kings' Chapel! There the congregation occupied private pews which were entered from the aisle by a separate gate and were "owned" by enormously respectable and prosperous leaders of New England aristocracy. The other sanctuary seemed dark when you entered by the small flickering votive lights which made bright circles in front of the altar and in the side chapels. At any time of day suppliants knelt or meditated on the wooden benches. Most of them were shabbily clad men and women who were heavy laden and in need of solace. The atmosphere was sweet with incense and prayer. Here, on Good Fridays, I joined the believers in the Stations of the Cross.

As an outlet for my emotions and a means of clarifying my thoughts I started making occasional notes relating to my perplexities. Looking through these pages now, they seem to me to have been written by someone else. At the same time I recognize the struggle as my own. I quote from one page:

"I am restless and groping for some high satisfying religion but I can't find it. One thing suffices my intellect but it gives no comfort or cheer. The soft symbolic religion that appeals to my emotions does not convince me as truth so that the practice of it is insincere. It would be enough if I could be just a plain Christian but I am not even that and I have no idea what means is best to make me one. I am not sure I want to be one. I am not sure that is the goal. The only name I can give myself is Truth *Seeker*. How poor for an object that is as compared to Truth *Finder*—one who reaches the faith which answers to every call that the individual personality can make. And yet the *Highest* is surely higher than human understanding so that perhaps it's better to love the Unknown and strive ever toward the Ideal, the Perfection, than to be content with lesser creeds although they stifle the hunger of the soul. (Do they really, I wonder.)"

During my sojourn in Oxford two years later, my mind was so fully absorbed by my studies that at the deeper level I felt less driven in the pursuit of godliness. My great solace during this period I found in the exquisite chapels ensconced within the enclosures of each separate college. When I completed my reading at the Bodleian Library in late afternoon I would go out and find my way into one or another of the college chapels just as the bells were tolling for evensong. Only a very few people attended. Usually there was only one priest whose chanting echoed and reechoed in the empty spaces. Sometimes boys' voices sang the responses. Evensong in the English Book of Common Prayer is a particularly touching service. "Lighten our darkness we beseech Thee, O Lord, and by Thy great mercy defend us from all perils and dangers of this night," and "Lord, now lettest Thou Thy servant depart in peace, according to Thy word." And the final benediction, "The grace of our Lord Jesus Christ, the love of God and the fellowship of the Holy Spirit be with us all for evermore"—these texts seemed to me a comforting conclusion to my day's work. I can remember singing them to myself as I walked home through the foggy English twilight, passing the lamplighter on his rounds to light the gas lights along the sidewalks. The collects and the psalms and some of the ancient Anglo-Saxon hymns to the Virgin and to the "tiny blessed chylde" blended together sweetly in my peaceful mood.

I do not know the exact date, but I accompanied my mother on two occasions when she was invited to some philosophical meetings in private homes in London. The first of these was a discourse by Mrs. Annie Besant, a co-worker with Mme. H. P. Blavatsky who organized the Theosophical Society. When Mme. Blavatsky passed away in 1907, Mrs. Besant became head of the movement which claimed to have an international membership of 100,000 converts. The doctrine was based on Hindu interpretations of the nature of God and the powers latent in man, and laid particular stress on reincarnation. Mrs. Besant was a large, heavy-set woman with a powerful voice and an impressive manner, acquired no doubt through her previous campaigning for the Indian Home Rule League. She believed that every so often a Mahatma or divine teacher appears on earth to reveal the Truth. She had discovered a child in India who corresponded to the specifications required for such a leader and she was promoting the spiritual ascendancy of Krishnamurti. (He later repudiated her claims and her domination.) But at the lecture I attended she was interpreting the idea of Karma in a forceful manner. It is strange that my mother and I never discussed religion, so I do not know what she thought. I was impressed.

The other meeting was held in a garden studio on the outskirts of London. Its purpose was to listen to Abdul-Baha, son of Baha Ullah, the founder of the Bahai religion in Persia. Out of the misty maze of London streets we entered a drawing room where some twenty persons were seated in a semi-circle. Before them in an ample armchair sat an elderly bearded man. He was dressed in a full brown robe and wore a white turban. One look at him convinced me that I was in the presence of a prophet. His eyes were piercing, but tender, and gave the impression of being deep and far-seeing. They radiated light. Half a dozen young followers sat behind him in the posture of meditation. As we came into the room, an excessively blond lady rose from her chair, deposited a long bunch of American Beauty roses into his lap while she sank to the floor and draped herself at his feet. I can see him now, tossing the flowers onto the table and bidding her to get up and go back to her seat. I was impressed by his kindly repudiation of her sentimental dramatics and his refusal to assume the role of seer. He spoke in Arabic about universal brotherhood and non-violence. One of his disciples translated his words into English. It was the second time I had encountered a religion of the East. The truth of his words and the nobility of his personality made a deep impression on me. In later years the remembrance of that awe-inspiring teacher and his consecrated band of young devotees made me receptive to the Vedas and to the teachings of the Buddha. It seems to me that Abdul Baha and Baha Ullah are the last great spiritual leaders to appear on the earth. Perhaps the time is ripe for another manifestation in our time. An incarnation of the divine Spirit might indeed point the way out of the mechanistic era in which we find ourselves living in the twentieth century.

VII

Misfit in Society

*Return to Boston; coming-out balls,
social life, study.*

After the "grand tour" of Europe in 1909, we did not return to
the Brookline house, as my parents had agreed to no longer live together.
My father stayed with my Aunt Mary in Brookline, and Mama rented a
house in Boston from which I could be properly "launched" into society.
The house was at 54 Beacon Street, about two blocks from the State
House, and the front windows looked out on the elm tree mall of the
Boston Common. This setting was calculated to insure status because of
its location. Somehow the proper wires were pulled to have me included
in the debutante list. I was enrolled in the 1910 Sewing Circle and in
the Junior Assemblies, and also subscribed to the Brattle Hall Dances in
Cambridge, and other affairs, and had my picture in the paper. Every
debutante was expected to have some sort of invitational affair, a tea or a
dinner or a dance, which constituted her formal introduction to the
social whirl. Other maidens of the group were invited "to pour" at teas.
Sometimes well-established matrons combined as hostesses for a dance.
Many dinners preceded the balls which were held at the Somerset
Hotel and lasted until 3:00 o'clock or 4:00 o'clock in the morning,
sometimes even until 5:00 o'clock.

If there was a cotillion, called "the German," the couples lined up in a
colorful procession and paraded round the room. "Pomp and
Circumstance" was one of the favorite marches. On these formal
occasions the ladies had trains on their dresses. It was really a pretty
sight to see their dignified sweeping approach and the deep curtseys and
low bows of their escorts when they presented themselves to the

receiving line of hosts and hostesses. Great mounds of favors were brought in to be selected and bestowed on the partner of one's choice—trophies to be taken home and shown as a sign of one's popularity. Some of these favors were very elaborate. I remember Dorothy Draper's dance (her father was Governor at that time), when large paper roses on a four foot staff had electric lights in the calyx. When they turned off the chandeliers, the dancers were like fire flies flitting in the twilight. Another time someone had canaries in paper cages. They were released and flew round the ballroom twittering and hurling themselves against the lights. Many of them died. It was a cruel exhibition of ostentation which spoiled the festivities for some of us.

I felt very apprehensive about the whole prospect of "coming out." Having lived in Europe for the previous two years, I had very few girl friends, and I knew almost no boys. I had not been to dancing school for the last two years where I might have met young people of my age and learned how to dance and become accustomed to ballroom etiquette. It apparently never occurred to me in those days to refuse to follow the established pattern. It was made to appear to me as an inescapable step in the process of growing up. During the later years of my life, I have learned about the initiation rites of puberty among primitive tribes and in early civilizations. In days of chivalry the candidate for knighthood spent an all night prayer vigil, and the confirmation service in the Christian church afforded a similar initiation. Nowadays, it appears to me that obtaining a driver's license to operate a motor vehicle on the road represents about the only tangible evidence that our young people receive to prove their coming of age. I was docile enough at that time to accept the inevitable. I decided that, however disagreeable, it was a process that I had to go through, and it was up to me to play the game and see if I couldn't find something in it that was interesting and perhaps even enjoyable. A letter I wrote to my sister Laura dated October 17, 1909, had this to say:

> This is a real autumn day. It has been snappy, clear and windy. The kind of atmosphere that makes your heart thump against your ribs and sets your feet dancing before you know it. I am sure a day of such exhilaration is worth a host of teas, dinners and balls. But here I am going back on my pledge to put the thing through. We shall not move in town till November 1st, and I am glad. Really I think the New England autumn is one of the wonders of the world. There's nothing like it abroad. The dreary falling of grey leaves in Germany and France, the plunge into bleakness of winter in Switzerland, the constant semi-tropicalness of Italy give no inkling of this glowing, brilliant moody New England autumn. The twilights are melancholy but the moon's so athrill with life and vigor one could race along with the wind forever and never be weary.
>
> My tea is to be on November 11th. Just think how soon! The first one was last Saturday.

There follows a list of ten teas scheduled in November, and six dances.

Doesn't that sound very gay? The Sewing Circle lunches begin in December. I was thinking the other day—five months at the outside will cover all of this business. I'm glad it isn't six.

I started keeping a diary in 1910. One of the first entries states:

Nothing is ever as good as you hope, and nothing is ever as bad as you dread. But I cannot escape this feeling of aloofness. At the luncheons with the girls I feel ever so far off as if something pushed me away from their real selves. Hideous idea, this gap between you and other human souls. The palaver of coming out has made me more reserved than ever before.

At most of the balls, the girls were taken in to the hall by ushers and deposited in seats lined up along the wall. Here you waited with a smiling face and a frantic uncertainty till some condescending male decided to pick you up from purgatory. At a few parties the hostess presented the invited guests with dance cards which had small pencils attached by a silken cord. The dances were numbered and the young men chose their partners ahead of time, writing their names in the empty spaces on the girl's card and her name on theirs. This was a pleasant arrangement because you knew what to expect. Ordinarily it was the custom that your partner stayed with you until he was relieved by someone else. If you were what was known as a "pill," you might get "stuck" with a boy, and if he could not get rid of you to someone else he might become an unwilling captive. This was an embarrassing situation for his partner—the only solution being for her to feign fatigue and leave for home, or discover a tear in her dress and use the pretext of having it sewn up in the dressing room. If someone really wanted to dance with you, he could "cut in" on the dance floor and take you away from your partner. This happened to me very rarely, whereas some girls could not dance half way round the room without interruption. I used to wonder how they managed to be so desirable. I wanted to be flirtatious too, but I couldn't seem to get the hang of how to do it. As the winter progressed, however, I began to have some boy friends who would ask me to dance more than once in an evening. This was enormously gratifying and gave me a little more confidence. In another letter written to Laura shortly after Christmas that year, I made these further comments:

Well, now, really it's awfully easy to scoff at coming out, but in spite of the trying-ness there's real sand under the salt water. It's a very new thing to me to get to know men. It's upsetting at times but sometimes wonderful. I must admit it's pleasant when somebody comes and speaks to you at a party or at the theatre or on the street. It's very nice to realize you have a friend whom you can count on to rescue you when you're "stuck." I like matching wits and learning about another person's attitude, his blue fits, etc. Everybody else knows all about this but it's just opening up to me.

I cannot now remember many Harvard students I came to know that winter. The ones I recall most vividly were a little out of the ordinary. There was a musician and a poet, a boy who worked one summer as a stoker on a railroad train and the next year as a horse wrangler on a Montana ranch. There was the socialist, Roger, whose father was a high official in Massachusetts. He preferred to live with an Italian laboring family in South Boston rather than with his family on Commonwealth Avenue. (The Italian family's baby was named for him—Roger Garibaldi Lugano). Mama did not approve of Roger and would not invite him to the house, but I saw him elsewhere. After graduating from college he worked in the law office of Justice Brandeis. And there was Frank Duveneck, whom I met occasionally, but he never came to call. I thought little about him until the following summer.

When the social season dwindled to a close in early April, I became restless and began to wonder about the future. Just to sit around waiting to be courted did not appeal to me. It would have been logical, and in my case highly desirable, for my mother to have planned for me to go to college. She told someone that she sent my oldest sister Ruth to Bryn Mawr College, because she needed to become more self-reliant; she did not send Elinor, because she didn't have the brains; nor Laura, because she was not physically strong enough. "—And Josephine was too independent, anyway." The fact of the matter was, although I did not realize it at the time, that she wanted my companionship and she realized that if I went to college she would never get me back. I did not have enough worldly knowledge to initiate such a break for myself, and no one pointed out the possibility. Today it is almost a foregone conclusion that a girl of "good family" will go on to college. But of my fellow debutantes in 1909, I do not remember any who were then planning to go. Some came to it a year or two later if they had not married by then.

The turbulence of my mind at that juncture was expressed in another letter to my sister:

You see, I don't want to go the way most of the Boston society girls do— not a bit. I want to know such a lot of things. I want to learn about flowers and birds and nature, and all about *all* literature and history, and I want to keep up my music and I want most of all, but mixed up with all the rest, to become a habitual writer. I don't mean that I think I could ever be anything great, but I ought to be able to do more than I am doing now. What on earth are we given inclinations for if not to follow them and make the best possible out of them? I don't mean that I'd like to live entirely secluded from the world (I would in a way) but sometimes I should like to see people in a good sort of way—not dance-and-tea assort-ment, but something more vital and intimate. This of course is probably an impossible and crazy idea but wouldn't it be nice? Also I should have to do something with children. I do adore kids and I do like to tell people about things I know and am interested in. At Haskell School, once in awhile Mrs. Prince used to give me some of her little classes and I never enjoyed anything more in my life. She used to tell me to be a teacher. I should like to. . . . The more I go on, the more I realize how superficial the life of many people is. I don't believe I think it's right for people to smother their real selves. It's dangerous and false. Why do it anyway? I don't care about conventionality and if I'm not so inside, what is the sense of being so outside? I feel a certain power in me growing stronger and stronger, and I have more and more things and ideas waiting to be expressed or created. I don't understand the feeling in me that I *must* work and study and live the life I want because it's undoubtedly selfish and perhaps misguided. But I want freedom, that's the thing!—and I could soon find out about myself. I don't think I care so much about being great—yes, I *do*, of course, though not for fame but I sort of want to find my own place more and establish *myself*.

Among the important results of my social year were the friendships I developed with girls my own age. With the exception of Eleanor Cabot, who went to Haskell School and lived near me in Brookline, I really had no intimate girl friends in Boston. But during that winter at teas and luncheons and Sewing Circle, I came in contact with a lot of extremely attractive and intelligent young ladies, some of whom proved to be most congenial. Edith Storer, Ruth Eliot, Katharine Thaxter, Ann Stedman, Erica Thorpe, Barbara Bolles. I visited their homes and spent the nights talking well into daylight hours, sharing deep secrets and noble thoughts, embellished with gossip and silliness. That such nice people seemed to like me broke through my sense of inferiority, enabling me to overcome my self-consciousness. If I had gone to college as a regular four year student, such associations would have been part of the whole learning experience. I would probably have become involved in student organizational activities, which would have helped me to avoid some of the mistakes I made in my early direction of Peninsula School ten years later. It was fortunate for me that I encountered the girls I mentioned above and that deep intimacies developed with several of them which lasted well into adult life. The sharing of emotional motivation loosened up my protective shell and helped me become more open with other people, as well as more interested in them.

The letter to my sister quoted above expresses the quandaries I was caught in now that the business of "coming out" was disposed of. I apparently arrived at a temporary solution by discovering that I could attend courses of my choice at Radcliffe College on a non-resident basis by passing enough entrance examinations to accumulate 16 points of credit. These credits allowed me to be classified as a "Special Student." I had not had any college preparatory training in any schools I had attended in Europe, but I decided to try my luck and signed up for the June examinations. Social engagements in April and May had pretty well petered out, so I concluded that if I studied for two months I could make it on my own. I knew I could pass Advanced French and German and I felt confident I could manage English A (Freshman English, necessary for admission to more advanced courses). I knew I never could succeed with any mathematics, but I liked Latin and I was fairly familiar with English history. I went back to Caesar and the elementary

Latin grammar and obtained a syllabus for English history to fill in the gaps in my memory. From April till the middle of June I crammed on these two subjects. It was a great relief to have a purpose in life besides looking for a husband—whom I was not very eager to find then anyhow.

I passed the exams in June and spent half the summer in Cohasset with my father and half of it with my mother in Northeast Harbor where she arranged some house parties for me, which I thoroughly loathed. My memory has retained no record of who came or what we did, but the days with Papa are still vivid. I wrote to my sister Laura, describing my feelings about being with him:

> Sometimes when I think how perfectly happy Papa and I could be together and how altogether contented I should be to be able to make the latter part of his life a sunny one and how much I could work in such a life, then the impossibility seems cruel. I can never forget the summers when Papa and I were alone together at Cohasset. I was only a little girl then, but nobody knows but he and I the gladness and joy we had. One thing when I was a kid, I never used to talk just to talk, and I remember often how we'd go along in the woods or on long drives hardly speaking and yet both of us perfectly happy. It's funny, but silence is the greatest test of communion between two people. Do you find it so?

In the fall I enrolled in two courses at Radcliffe College. It was an exciting day for me when I took the subway for Harvard Square, clutching my pen and pencil case and a loose leaf notebook. Walking into the registration room and becoming one of the noisy, pushing throng of students was terrifying, and I had some difficulty finding my way to the desired lecture hall. Though no one had time to give comprehensive directions, I eventually arrived, panting but eager. The technique of getting into the chair with the bookrest attached to it puzzled me considerably, but with some friendly advice from another girl I managed to install myself. A student at last!

The courses I chose were English Literature with Professor Nielsen (who afterwards became President of Smith College) and English Composition with Charles Copeland, or "Copey" as he was always called. He taught for years at Harvard College and only occasionally gave a course at Radcliffe. I think he thought the feminine intellect much inferior to the male. "Copey" was the inspiration and mentor of a whole generation of young men who became distinguished writers, poets and journalists in the early twentieth century. He remained a bachelor, and his rooms were always open to students. Rumors of the informal seminars, debates and hilarious fellowship spread far afield. He was too unconventional ever to be recognized as a full professor, but his influence on young men of talent was greater than any in the English Department of the University. He was impatient with mediocrity and pretentiousness, and his wit could be devastating. But his critical sense was infallible. When he found someone with real talent and serious intentions, there was no limit to his help and guidance, nor even, I suspect to his generosity when someone's funds were low. He read aloud with consummate dramatic skill. No one ever went to sleep in his classes. His lectures were somewhat rambling, but always full of wit and intellectual challenge. Incidental occurrences were similarly provocative. Copey hated loud noise. In one class I attended, a door was about to slam shut. I noticed what was about to happen so I jumped out of my seat to intercept it. "Copey" paused, took in the situation and said, "Thank you, Miss Whitney. You showed great presence of mind and considerable agility." Another time, a student came in late and climbed over two rows of seats to a place nearer the front so as not to make anyone get up to let her pass. "Copey" stopped in the middle of a sentence saying, "Observe the antics of the mountain goat." The class observed and roared with laughter. He did not tolerate late arrivals. No one committed that error more than once.

I did well in both classes and had several literary efforts printed in the Radcliffe Magazine. I should have liked to continue, but Mama was getting restless and wanted to return to Europe. She artfully introduced the idea of my spending a term in England at Oxford University, where I could study Old English and Chaucer, for whom I had conceived a liking. An English friend of hers then living in Oxford was just embarking on a round-the-world tour, and she offered us her house, complete with furniture and fixings, including two maids and a weekly chore boy. It was too advantageous an offer to overlook, so in the summer of 1910 we traveled again across the Atlantic Ocean in search of that illusive quality known as culture.

VIII

Quest (One)

*Journal; the inner life;
philosophical thoughts.*

When I was a child I thought as a child. I find it difficult to recall
the true nature and the pattern of the years and the experiences in my
inner life between the ages of 17-20. To carry one's thought back
seventy yeas to the "Sturm and Drang" period in one's own life is not an
easy feat. Memory fails to re-establish the aspirations, the yearnings, the
absurdities and naiveties of that long past period. It is easier to see the
inconsistencies of the youth around us today than to recapture our own
revolts and frustrations in adjusting to society at the turn of the century.
The world of 1910 has retreated into mythology.

I kept a diary at times during my late teens. Several times over the
years I have had the impulse to burn them up. But I desisted each time,
because I thought I might like to look at them again sometime, the way
one resurrects old snapshots. When I dug them out of the 'archives' and
reread them, finally, I realized that they contained live material which I
couldn't possibly describe today from memory. In fact, I was amazed at
the contents. Did I really do those things? Did I think and struggle and
philosophize thusly? Its authenticity is unquestionable. I have to admit
that this *was me* during the turbulent years between adolescence and
coming of age. I started to say maturity, but I am sure maturity came
much later.

In going over the little brown notebooks, begun in 1910 and carrying
through the spring of 1912, I note that various passages from these
jottings seem to fall under three or four main topics: the search for God;
the desire for independence; the urge to write; and the need to love and

to be loved. The entries were not a daily record of events. Sometimes weeks went by without notations, and at other times I wrote every day. It seems that those notebooks provided an escape from the pressures of a restrictive life and a means of trying to clarify the emotional and intellectual drives which swept over me. For what they express of that period of my life I quote them here:

January 8, 1910—Read *Jeanne d'Arc* by Percy Macaye and later *Quintessence of Ibsenism*. I wonder if he's not right, cowardice and the accepted standard of "goodness" are often identical.

January 9—*Ich bin mude. Ich arbeite und mein leben geht um nicts hin. Ich habe mit einem armen Man gesprochen. Er sagt "Ya, Ich muss immer arbeiten um Essen und Trink, Kleidung und Haus zu verdienen - Traume - keine mehr."* How sad!

January 16—In Cohasset. What a night! A child moon but oh, so brilliant. Hosts of stars dimpling the whole face of heaven. Snow up to my knees, feathery soft and sparkling in the moonlight. I lay on my back on the pool rock and looked up. What a thing it is to lose oneself in the universe, to have no more knowledge than a stone, to let the wind blow in your hair as in the boughs of a tree, to become almost an inanimate object, one unobtruding atom of the great snow white earth. Nothing and yet part of the inconceivable vastness of astral legions.

January 20—Since the world began children have been different from their parents. What is wrong to the mind of an old man may be right in the mind of a lad. It is hard for parents to realize that children *grow up* and as men and women must decide and act for themselves. Freedom and independence alone develop character. Youth ought not to be suppressed.

January 30—New York. On a visit to Aunt Sue in New York. After lunch the girls talked gowns, engagement rings, orchids and foreign princes. I held my tongue and played with the dog. I thank the dear Lord in heaven that I was not born into a coterie like that. Such driveling nonsense, such jets of rarified laughter! Wouldn't I just like to hear Papa tell one of his stories and nearly burst with uproarious guffaws. I should revel with Silenus and let Juno and her peacock and handmaidens show their well bred resentment. Je m'en fiche!

February 16—I am so selfish and impure. I have not been true to my vision. Sometimes the yearning for perfection tears one in two. "We see through a glass darkly." So very dark. Tomorrow is Ash Wednesday. I do believe. I have to believe. Sin is like quick sand, the more you struggle the deeper you sink in. What power can free you? Christ? I cannot find the faith. Yet He did live. Of all men the most perfect and beautiful. Therefore it cannot be wrong to wish to keep His fast day even if I do not call Him "Domine."

March 4—Went to King's Chapel. Mr. Brown talked about the water and bread of life. He said the reason people are restless is that they don't *dare* face in thought the facts of life and intellectual beliefs. I wonder if I'm like that. I am restless and evermore groping for some high satisfying religion but I cannot find it. One thing suffices my intellect but I get no comfort or cheer. The soft symbolic religion that appeals to my emotions does not convince me of truth so the practices are insincere. It would be enough if I were a plain Christian but I'm not even that. I have no idea what means is best to make me one. I am not sure I want to be one. I am not sure that is really the goal. The only name I can give myself is *Truth Seeker*. Will I ever change it to *Truth Finder*?

March 15—Today I escaped with my little packet of two sandwiches tightly grasped together with my purse and notebook. Off to Vagabondia in the spring! I took a street car as far as it would take me and walked out over a field and later on a road, making a wide detour to avoid a drunken fellow mortal.

The view from the hill was very striking today. Blue was the general tone—a "grey day" of course. The hills seemed to have lent bits of themselves to mix with the clouds. The sun came out for a brief survey and the instantaneous glow of warmth was surprising and pleasant. If my voice had not been sunk deep under a choky cold I should have sung and the baby leaves would have heard a new lullaby. As it was I only peeked at the tips of their noses protruding from their brown winter blankets. I wondered if they would be pretty when they grew up.

I had the good fortune to come upon a typical New England barnyard. I never before enjoyed the conversation of hens but I discovered wonders in it today. I sat on the fence with my eyes partially closed enjoying the soft air that floated gently by. The subdued clucking, the low scratching and the occasional flap of wings seemed to me to express the two things that I at that moment felt most keenly—spring and contentment. It was not the bursting movement of the season, nor the exuberance of joy, but as the Germans say, the "Stimmung" was all there.

The turkey amused me mightily as he stood surrounded by the group of hens. He felt himself a great lion, vastly superior to the cackling flock. "Pride goeth before a fall." These creatures are so like us. How many a one struts and swells with his own importance oblivious to oncoming fate, whether it be in the form of axe or fortune.

The woods were full of things. There was a bit of woodland carpeted with brown leaves and in the fitful sunlight it was a golden lacework of sun and shadows. A brook flowed beyond under a grey bridge. I leaned over as every pedestrian does to look into the water. A wheelbarrow had met a sad fate and was upturned in midstream against a large stone. I mused idly on its position and why it was there and what happened to it. I never saw a wheelbarrow just like it. It was an old fashioned shape, painted a Chinese red mellowed by the stream. I thought of rescuing it but the moveable stone and green slime looked damp. And my cold!

I came home. Of course we all come home like the cows. I suppose one would feel worse off than beasts if there were no place to return to at night. That is one of the primal instincts common to all life. The butterfly's home is death. And at the last ours is too, be we banker or beggar.

June 16—I like sometimes after a long day to think what I have seen and done. It's like watching a cinematograph for the pictures pass along before the mind's eye in a shifting procession of details. There was the locomotive and the tiny sparrow with a cherry stone in his beak (think of the history of that cherry stone), the quick eager face and the sordid miserable one. There were big stores and horses asleep, flowers, papers, puddles and extraordinary millinery. The town gives amusement to the wayfarer.

I suppose good people turn to the image in their temple and lose all their pain in worship and adoration. I wish I could. The Thought is to me one lone burning agony—the Unattainable—like an open wound. People are not real to me, but dreams, and dreams are not weird to me, but real. I seem to walk like a shadow midst a world of dreams. Death seems the only hope.

> *Uber allen Gipfeln ist Ruh,*
> *In allen Wipfeln spurest du*
> *Kaum einen Rauch*
> *Die Vogel schweigen in Walde*
> *Warte nur, balde*
> *Ruhest du, auch.*   —Goethe

And yet one waits and waits. One becomes like an old withered parchment book filled with the close fine penmanship of pain. I tell myself there is lots more that I do not know but must experience. I wonder does parchment ever shrivel up and take no more impressions however much the instrument is applied thereto?

Why should suddenly from the gallery of memory a picture stand forth vividly? It is as if I stood in Keswick out in the field between the village and the river and gazed round at the mountains. I see them, wonderful purples and reds and over the ranges of peaks are moulded great waves of luscious creamy clouds, thick against the azure of the sky. Why it comes to me so clearly all without any previous allusion I wonder? And it means? Perhaps this:

> The white peace of the roaming cloud
> The great strength of the rugged hills
> The still reach of the pale sky
> Be on you to heal your ills.
>
> The sweet smile of the field grass
> The pure youth of the bird on the wing
> The rare spell of the open plain
> Be on you and teach you to sing.

July 13—I have just read a book such as I never before read. It is the *Story of an African Farm* by Olive Shreiner. I never heard of her before though the book is quite old. It made me sit up and say, "But this is I. How can she know so much about me?" It does one good to know that others have striven and toiled and yearned. It makes you feel less lonely, less lost in a world of people.

August 6—Books I've read this summer:

> *Diary of a Man of 50*, by Henry James
> *Bundle of Letters*
> *Poems in Prose*, by Turgenev
> *Dreams*, by Olive Schreiner
> *Threnodies*, by Mitchell Kennerly
> *Les Aveugles*, Maeterlink
> Re-read the *Iliad*
> *Vanity Fair*, by Thackeray
> *English Humorists*

Thackeray says of Swift, "We have other great names to mention, none I think so great nor so gloomy . . ." I like the way Thackeray seizes the worthy characteristics of authors and admires them whole heartedly, as in turn he swoops on their failings and depreciates them suitably.

August 15—Bar Harbor. About 8 this morning as I was looking out of my window I saw two battleships come steaming in to anchor. They are great grey grim things not at all in sympathy with the sun draped hills and dancing water. Yet there was a certain impressiveness such as a discord often brings into music. The band played the Star Spangled Banner ending just as last rumble of falling anchor chains died away. It is extraordinary how people live everywhere and everyway. Think of the summer hotels they infest, little houses, big houses, huts, palaces, camps, steamers, yachts, battleships, stables. Everywhere people. I like the thought of these myriad waves of life beating against mine and thousands more swarming for which I have no comprehension.

August 16—Out on the rocks where the waves dash high against the shore and beyond a vast all surrounding calm of blue—out to the horizon with possibilities undreamed of great human love is like that—with all the dash and spray and exultation in the outward visible relationship—all the wild music and thrill of meeting and parting and living, then beyond the unmeasurable reach of quiet consecration whose strength, power and depth man himself can hardly conceive.

October 3—My objectives for the coming year:
1. Love and universal charity.
2. Firmness towards myself. Greater self-restraint.
3. A faithful search for the Truth.
4. The spirit of a poet.
5. Unselfishness.
6. Fulfillment of my dreams.

Though you have no faith in my soul, I shall yet achieve.

October 4—

> When I sleep I dream
> When I wake I'm eerie
> Sleep I canna get
> For thinkin' o' my dearie.
> — Robert Burns

December 31, 1910—New resolves:
1. Never make a promise of any kind without keeping it.
2. Make more time for meditation.
3. Set aside certain days for seeing people and other days for going into the country.
4. Become more orderly and methodical.
5. Get up earlier. No so much time in sleep.

Most important:
I. Seek Truth faithfully. Never tire from the Quest. Believe without faith.
II. Really to *see* the world and converse with beauty.
III. Subdue my pride.

This year sees in me a great change and some gain chiefly in self-confidence, in intellectual and social power, independence and the capacity for getting joy out of life—of living every moment. Perhaps I am a little kinder and can love a little better but still much too little. Spiritually I'm not progressing. Last of all I have become more humble. I'm like a pigmy who thinks he's the biggest thing in sight because he doesn't realize that what he stands on and the fours walls about him are really living beings too big for him to appreciate.

(Date?)—That goodness and genius are equivalent is a fallacy. Virtue and great art are independent of each other. . . . Burns was not a particularly exemplary character, nor Byron, Shelley, Swift, nor Pope. Milton himself was a hopeless egoist and rendered unhappy the lives of his hearth companions. Yet you can't imagine them in hell-fire. They were singers and they served the world. They must have their reward. But the rest of us whose work is but chaff? We will be left in nakedness having neither accomplished our dream nor labored for our souls.

"Her eyes were filled with perishing dreams and the wrecks of forgotten delirium." What a marvelous sentence of De Quincey! The r's and the s's and m's are so beautiful.

January 11, 1911—The Ayer dance Friday night. I had a joyous time. J. for supper and M. for the cotillion. I felt quite womanly and confident. I saw in men's glances that I was good to look upon. I was gay and glad and the night was one long dance-whirl. Yesterday was not a happy day. No, I don't love him. I care for him more than for most round here but I could never go to him with arms outstretched. He makes my heart throb but I'm afraid it's my reverence for love that I feel coming from him. But not because he is the One Man. I *must* have something big, overpowering, ecstatic in my life—or nothing. I can wait.

January 12—Emerson wrote an essay on "Imperfect Sympathies." I don't remember the point but the title is suggestive. That's what society is. To be so near a human soul and see into it only fitfully if at all, leaves one much regret. I felt as I came in here and threw off my coat that now I could express myself quickly and beautifully but I am so tired that only philosophical drivel is all that comes. I feel I must create, but what and how?

(Date ?)—Reading St. Augustine: *Confessions* and *City of God*. Went to midday service at St. Paul's. Fasted. Walked through East Cambridge to look at poverty. Went to the Advent at 4, organ recital, prayer and Even Song. Felt the Holy Spirit. Read Thomas à Kempis. I felt specially admonished by these words: "The more thou knowest and the better thou understandeth, so much the more grievously shalt thou therefore be judged unless thy life be also more holy."

March 2—"Whether ye live or whether ye die, ye are the Lord's." I sinned three times today, gluttony, pride, irreverence. But that "peace which passeth understanding" has come to me for the first time in months, through no work of mine. God is not angry with us forever.

I don't like the litany very well. The supplications "Spare us Good Lord" are not to my taste. I don't want to avert justice nor beg for things that will be anyway if it is right that they should be. To pray for the kindly fruits of the earth is not only superfluous but presuming. The idea of an avenging and implacable deity shocks me.

> Es bildet ein Talent sich in der Stille
> Sich ein Character in dem Strom der Welt.
> —Goethe

(Date ?)—I am tired. A grand chaos of half conscious thoughts pour in on me. There must be some correlation between all the different daily events. There must be one thread on which to hang all.

(Date ?)—One thing I have just discovered, dummy that I am. It's only by God's mercy that we ever feel Him and it is in the times of exile and doubt that we must be faithful. It's nothing to love and keep Him ever in our thoughts when grace is upon us. We can't help it. But when the awful darkness comes and we labor without comfort then our spiritual strength is called upon. It's clear to me that God withdraws His arm and says, "Struggle a little alone." And then it is necessary to perform one's devotions more faithfully than ever. *Believe* in the midst of despair and doubt.

March 8, 1911—I read Schopenhauer and thought much. The wind rose in the night. Its fury was exhilarating. The curtains waved wildly and one of the doors banged. I was freezing cold but it was a wonderful wild experience. Snowdrifts on my floor and the vase of pussy willows upset.

March 10—There was a rehearsal of the *Greek Tragedy* at 4 in the opera house. It's fun being on that huge stage. Read *Peter Ibbetson* all evening. I tried going to sleep in the "sacramental pose" but it was so uncomfortable that I always rolled over and finally went to sleep in an ordinary manner. I thought about A.M. who told me to read this book. He must be a good deal like Gogo. Physically he is. It's not as poetic as the Brushwood Bay but it's clever, original and well developed.

March 22—Heard Dr. Grenfell at Park Street Church. An open-hearted man. Translated some of Walter Pater into French. I must do something after I'm 20. I can't putter anymore. I must take life seriously. I keep thinking of New York.

I finished the story that has been hanging round in a disgusting state for days. Personally I don't think much of it but I shall send it on its fate to the "Youth's Companion." Read the Divine Fire.

"It is better to be populace in Rome than Caesar in the provinces." I wonder if that's true.

April 11—New York. Uncle Dim's funeral. Sad but beautiful. Hymns "Lead Kindly Light" and "Nearer My God to Thee." He was a sweet person. Talked to Felix Adler about Ethical Culture interpretation of immortality.

June 2—London. A new journey with my mother. We landed yesterday. It seems like weeks so quickly does life at home become an illusion and the old life lived before I came out returns as characteristically as ever. I am upset and bewildered by the suddenness of transformation. Two weeks ago I was free, now again I am bound, but having been free it irks more than ever. The constant fret and worry, the censoriousness and worst of all the absolute detailed domination is most killing. I can stand a lot but to feel one's personality squeezed and pinched and nozzled and stamped is a weakness on one's part. It would be easy to become a mere dummy, a bundle of nerves without will as I was before. I suppose if my character's any good it's going to stick it out and be itself. I'd give anything to hear some music or go to church alone. But I am never let off the leash. Perhaps tomorrow.

June 15—Tonight it took me an hour to write three sentences. I think they are good ones. Now I feel absurd and sleepy. Matthew Arnold would not discover in me that "high seriousness" which he holds up to aspiring literary novices. He says it is not found in Burns or Chaucer! Arnold didn't have much humor. Humor is really a saving grace—an excellent demi-god.

And what about the whole God?

July 14—Scotland. A month of a reflective vegetating existence at Braemar, Scotland is a mood. The moors became my friends and the hills. I climbed Morrone, Crag Coynach, Cairn-na-Drocheide and the unknown one from the Dee Bridge. The Duke's deer against the sky, in the swamp and on top of the braes. The falls of Carriemulzie. Elsie Harper's wee house, the rivers Clive and Dee, the Sunday afternoon walk over the ridge, the Queen's Drive, Coronation Day festivities and the old woman sitting on the hill leaning her chin on her oaken staff.

September 20—Vespers at Christ Church. Ethereal boy's voices—"O hear ye this, all ye people ponder it with your ears, all ye that dwell in the world. High and low, rich and poor, one with another." Who says socialism is modern? The *Psalms* are inexhaustible. There is always a "packende" passage that seems completely new and modern.

September 29—Whatever you do, do it wholeheartedly. No matter what it is, you will gain more by concentrating your efforts. It would be better to wallow in vice than to make desultory excursions into the back alleys of morality. At least you might acquire a thorough knowledge of wickedness which could enable you later to resist temptation. Skimming through life is the most discouraging trait of character. It prevents inheritance from the past and looks forward to nothing in the future.

October 1—In momentary glimpses one foresees the future. Now and then it is given us in a fleeting abstract way to comprehend the whole trend of one's individuality. How and why are still dark. Perhaps the ultimate issue of spiritual consciousness is acceptance. The knowledge lasts only a second. I have had this flash only once or twice. It was when my mind was particularly keyed up and *impersonal*. If one could get away from introspection and cultivate another habit of mind, treating yourself as an indifferent unit of human nature, would this realization of the consummate ideal develop into a steady revelation? Or is step by step the only rule for spiritual progress, as it is for learning grammar? Or still another alternative. Does there come a time after learning the syntax when you begin to comprehend the complete structure? You divine it (the German *"ahnen"*) though you can't express it in words. If you can get an *ever increasing* sense of validity you could get rid of fractional presentiments and concentrate only on the ultimate. Is there really a short cut to culmination? I don't know if my mysterious vision is possible for daily use. If one was aware of subconscious certainty, instead of conscious surmise, how blessed that would be!

October 22—Heard Canon Scott-Holland preach this morning. Lots of dogma. He said that Christianity only began with the resurrection. He said to take it as a symbol was not enough. You must believe in the body. There was a storm outside, the doors of the church rattled. I thought it could be the Spirit of Truth protesting. A bit of thistle down came sailing from behind the altar. The unresisting wayward passage of this common bit of white fluff was so casual and exquisite. None of the Canon's learned protestations could ever equal the performance of the falling thistledown.

Eternal beauty versus blustering dogma. Christ's victory didn't depend on any glorification. Maybe the disciples needed a resurrection to interpret the meaning of poverty and suffering for themselves, but the real revelation is in His life and His teaching and His acceptance of death.

November 26, 1911—Surely half the battle of life is to determine the relation of one part to another. Intellectual thought must be correlated with the unseen and the unknown. Unity is the principle not only of the centuries but of each man within himself.

February 5, 1912—There always seems to be a *behind* for every action and for every aim. There may be a Great Principle underlying God of which the world has as yet not even begun to dream.

March 12—We dined tonight at the B—'s and conversation turned on the unrest in the world. Mrs. B sadly lamented the good old times when there was peace and wholesome leisure. Mama pointed at me saying, "She doesn't want peace." "Peace." What a beautiful word! But there can be no rest for us because a new age must be baptized with the bitter waters of restlessness and striving. Even if we shut ourselves away from the world so that no rumors reach us in our seclusion, yet in our own breasts the struggle would go on. Each of us individually would have to solve the problems of the hour. Indeed the Spirit allows us no peace.

April 11, 1912 (My birthday next day)—This is the last day of my childhood. If I could I would go and dream it out in some cool grassy slope with a little brook babbling somewhere near. But the hour glass will not cease even for one last golden hour of youth and the little sands run out impassively just like a glacier melting in the sun.

IX

Year of Decision

Return to Europe; Scotland and Oxford.

Returning to Europe sometime in June or July 1911, we stayed for a short time in England, completing arrangements for our winter in Oxford, and then went to Scotland. Mama had some friends who recommended an inn at Braemar. They urged her to join them there for three or four weeks. Braemar is close to Balmoral Castle where the royal family used to spend several days each year. A large portion of the countryside represented an old feudal estate belonging to the Duke of Fife who owned an elaborate mansion with lavish gardens and stables. He also had his own herd of deer (shades of Robin Hood). Almost every afternoon while the adults were napping or drinking tea, I roamed across the moors and went "a-hunting." I carried neither gun nor camera, but when I came stealthily out of the mist and spied the deer, I would see how close I could get to them, walking soft-footed on the heather. The bucks were usually the first to detect my approach. The wise old leader would lift up his head with its many-pronged antlers and gaze fixedly in my direction. Then the younger bucks stopped grazing and followed his gesture. Unless I moved they could not see me clearly but the wind carried my scent and the old buck, wishing to play it safe, but not wanting to alarm his charges unnecessarily, would turn with great dignity and start walking off very slowly away from me toward the shoulder of the hill. The does and fawns did likewise. However, if I came on them suddenly, the leader would blow through his nostrils, "Beware! Run!" and the whole herd would move away like a brown wave and be swallowed up in the ocean of fog. Then, like a bonafide hunter, I would trail them to the next feeding place. Once or twice I got lost and became a little frightened by the white shroud of mist that obliterated familiar landmarks. I have always had a good sense of direction which served me well when I groped my way back to the village through the chiffon wilderness where the sun did not shine and there were no stars visible.

In the evenings sitting by the open fire at the inn I read Walter Scott and Robert Burns:

> My heart's in the Highlands,
> My heart is not here
> My heart's in the Highlands
> A-chasing the deer
> A-chasing the wild deer
> And following the roe
> My heart's in the Highlands
> Wherever I go.
> —Burns

If you have been out on the windy moors yourself, those words can make you catch your breath or feel the tears start in poignant remembrance.

I met some of the village people and was fascinated by their manner of speech, akin to old Anglo-Saxon unpolluted by Norman influences. The postmistress, Mrs. McDonald, talked about the "braw bricht moonlit nicht," and Mrs. Morrison, our landlady, wore a bonnie plaid shawl that had once belonged to her "Mither." One day as I passed by the parish church I saw a sign that said "Tomorrow's Sermon—The Real Meaning of Samson's Restored Hair." Unfortunately it was Monday morning when it came to my notice so I never found out that secret.

I remember very little about the rest of Scotland except for watching the Royal Regiment of Scotch pipers parading in the courtyard in front of Edinburgh Castle. Back and forth they marched in perfect unison, with leggings flashing, sporans swinging, and the skirling of the pipes resounding from the hilltop where the Castle is located. The unearthly raucous music of the bagpipes has always excited me and recreated in my mind the eerie loneliness of the highlands and "the Scots wha once wi Wallace bled."

In England an incident occurred which was most disconcerting for my poor Mother but was amusing in retrospect. We always traveled with an outrageous number of trunks. On this trip I think we had nine or ten. They were divided into three divisions: one containing winter clothes for Oxford, one with old clothes, stout walking shoes and faded sweaters, for Scotland and Switzerland, and one with our grandest wardrobe to be worn while visiting at an English country estate. Somehow, I don't know how, Mama had met Sir William and Lady Mather in Boston and they had invited her (and me) to spend a week at Something-or-other Downs

Mrs. Whitney and her daughters go coaching in England.

in Devonshire. In London, we stored some of our superfluous baggage, but planned to take the two trunks with our fancy raiment to the Mather's. At Mama's request I gave the directions to the local porter about which to send and which to retain. Either he or I got the pieces mixed. We took the train at Paddington and were met in Devonshire with a trap. Our baggage was to come later. When we got to the Mather's lovely house the family was in the garden. We joined them for tea, crumpets and strawberry jam and thin slices of bread and butter. Mama gave her keys to the maid to unpack our belongings. After tea we wandered through the gardens and eventually retired to the guest rooms to array ourselves for dinner at eight. Imagine Mama's dismay when she opened the closet door and beheld our mountain climbing apparel instead of the evening gowns and smart afternoon tea dresses we expected to find! The worst of it was the underwear, some of it a bit ragged, neatly folded by the maid in the bureau drawers. The storm burst over my head and extended to profuse apologies to our hosts and dispatching of telegrams to the concierge in London, for the substitution of the other set of trunks. The proper baggage arrived after two days, restoring our prestige with the servants (I hope) and Sir William and his Lady. I do not remember another thing about that visit.

In my diary I noted a stay with a certain Canon Cary, who apparently took us to the Archbishop's Palace in York:

> We passed under a turreted gateway, through a Gothic portal supported by slender columns into this wonderful restored house of the fourteenth or fifteenth century. Dining hall looking way off over the fields, the Archbishop's study—books!—red and blue glorious carpets, chapel with excellent restoration, royal apartments upstairs. After service in the Cathedral, dinner at the Canon's. Good food. Interesting lady who had lived seven years in South Africa. She told about the Zulus and the compounds and the almost rebellion averted by the tip-off by a little boy devoted to his master. A narrow escape. She and her husband traveled by night in oxcarts.
>
> The next day Canon Cary took us to the Treasurer's house. All sorts of luxurious old things—clocks, tables, chairs, vases, pictures, etc. Great canopied beds and rich stuffs. Great hall with staircases leading out of it. Tapestries. It has taken fifteen years to get it all together.
>
> In the glazier's shop we saw the bell window of the Cathedral. We could pick up pieces and feel them. Imagine!

On my first visit to Europe I had visited a great many art galleries, and during one of my Boston sojourns I took a course in History of Art at the Boston Museum. I enjoyed studying the different types of architecture as we traveled through European cities, and in museums I could easily recognize the characteristic style of famous painters without recourse to catalog or label. When I looked at the Pre-Raphaelite School, I was surprised at my former enthusiasm for Rossetti and Watts. My taste had become much more discriminating. I collected a large number of photographs and monographs to take home. The familiarity I acquired with the different schools of European paintings enabled me to feel at ease when in later years, through my marriage, I came in close contact with an American painter who had spent his early years in Germany and Italy.

While in London I attended a Congress of Races. I quote from my diary:

> Much unnecessary dullness due to poor management. Two interesting little Japanese with charming smiles, one of them said that differences between races were all due to misunderstanding which in turn was due to (1) Suspicion, (2) Misrepresentation, (3) Differences of custom. Since the white Caucasians have insisted on entering China and Japan, how can we justly bar them from entering our lands?
>
> Mrs. Annie Besant (The Theosophist) was the only orator. Powerful person, great command of language and a magnificent voice. At that time she was the outstanding critic of British imperialism. The four grievances she voiced as being particularly resented by the Indians were:
>   1. Restrictions of their right to travel at will in all parts of the world.
>   2. Denial of administrative posts to Indians. Opportunities limited.
>   3. Personal inviolability. Civil liberties violated.
>   4. Restriction on commerce. Home industries should be protected.
>
> These suggestions raised a storm which ended the meeting. An extra session was proposed which I was unable to attend.

A brief junket to Norway and Denmark and a short return visit to Berlin completed our traveling that season. In late September we arrived in Oxford and settled in the house we had temporarily fallen heir to. Two maids that came with the house were called by their last names—Ryder, the cook, and Rimmel, the second maid. I think my mother was a little afraid of them, they were so eminently proper. And they were not averse, I am sure, to indulging in sly British snickers at the manners and speech of their American employers.

In the days before World War I, English colleges were almost exclusively male. This situation changed because during the war women were so important in the defense of their country. They proved themselves indispensible for all kinds of labor and so gallant under air raid attacks that the men were forced to admit their equality. After winning the right to vote, women overcame many of the restrictions governing higher education. They were also able to assume responsible positions in the professional and business world—positions open to them, in part, because of the numbers of young men killed in action during World War I.

But when I arrived in Oxford, women were not yet eligible for degrees. They were allowed, however, to attend lectures and were known as "Home Students." They were expected to be as unobtrusive as possible and not to engage in any familiarities with the men students or professors. Indeed, a Rhodes scholar whom I had known in Cambridge (USA) could not speak to me in a class we shared, nor did he dare greet me on the staircase enroute to the lecture hall. Students had been expelled for less. I took Anglo-Saxon and Old English (with a professor named Sir Walter Raleigh!), Social Philosophy with a Socialist Churchman and Greek Drama with Sir Gilbert Murray, translator of the Odyssey and the Greek tragedies. It sounds like a scatterbrained schedule but since the time was short and the opportunity unique, I felt justified in skimming off the cream. For Anglo-Saxon I had a tutor, in accordance with the English system, and he corrected my papers and would have prepared me for the final exam if I had stayed longer. There were no marks during the course and no attendance records at the end of the term. You either passed or failed.

Probably the greatest experience I had at Oxford was being able to use the Bodleian Library. My card gave me access to the stacks and allowed me to peruse old manuscripts dating back to the Anglo-Saxon period and to Chaucer. Students were allowed to take their resource material to one of the small alcoves consisting of a chair, a sloping desk beside a casement window affording complete privacy. The smell of old leather bindings, the hushed footsteps of other scholars and the feeling of the precious old parchment in the volumes I studied gave me the illusion of living in a mediaeval world.

This feast of intellectual and esthetic enjoyment more than made up for my lack of social life. I remember one or two evening parties at the home of Sir William Osler, and one frantic cross country beagle hound chase at the invitation of Malcolm, the son of Reverend Arthur Jones. The son was far from reverent. We tore across fields and woodlands, over stone walls, through shallow brooks and broken fences trying to keep up with the yelping dogs. I suppose there must have been a rabbit, but we never saw it. When I returned home with torn clothes, disheveled hair and muddy boots, my Mother exclaimed, "Where on earth have you been?"

"Beagling!" was all I could gasp out as I sank into an armchair.

Oxford has changed since the second World War. I have not been there, but I am told that it has become industrialized and that there are factories and tall buildings, freeways and busy metropolitan streets. My memory clings to the images of a few horse drawn vehicles in narrow streets bordering a river, some small shops, and a series of ivy mantled college buildings, representing many different periods of English architecture. The colleges were self-contained within a quadrangle. Usually there was a tower and a chapel and each one had an atmosphere quite different from all the others. My favorite was Christ Church because of a particularly beautiful chapel and the Christ Church Meadows where sheep grazed on rich green turf. At sunset time, the bells in all the towers rang for vespers, and I got so I could recognize the different tones.

During this period my relationship with my Mother became less exasperating. She enjoyed her manner of life, made some interesting friends and attended lectures on architecture and English history. I was away from home most of the day, and she approved of my pursuit of learning. Although she had never given me any maternal love, I think I really owe a great deal to her. Beginning with her employment of Miss Dugan as my governess and her choice of Haskell School, the associations she arranged for me were of high quality. Traveling with her was certainly a hard discipline, owing to her autocratic and overbearing personality, but she introduced me to a wide variety of cultural experiences which enriched my whole subsequent life. She had a brilliant and analytical mind. At a different period and in a different setting, she could have maintained a salon and been a *femme celebre*. Indeed, my brother-in-law, Herbert Lyman, always referred to her as "The Duchess." She read a great deal and had the money with which to buy beautiful volumes. Her library, which I inherited, contained not only leather bound sets of the classics—which I think she must have acquired *en masse* when she moved into the Brookline house shortly after her marriage—but also many current books on biography, history, architecture, painting, literature and philosophy. By the time we were in Oxford, I was mature enough to share her interests in literature and we could talk about books, providing of course that I agreed with her judgments.

In trying to recall the later years of my adolescence, I am surprised to realize what a lot of education (not in a narrow scholastic sense only) was jammed into a very few years. I must have been insatiably curious and extremely impressionable because I developed enthusiasm for so many things—music, art, poetry, archaeology, and literature. I acquired fluency in three languages and became familiar with the *"feel"* of different cultures. I did not realize it at the time, but I think Mama must have derived some pleasure out of my response to the marvelous things to which she exposed me. Of her five children I believe I was the only one who shared her intellectual interests. I was fortunate to be exposed to such a broad international influence.

Strange as it may seem, my mother was a militant *Anti*-suffragist. She attended many meetings and was an officer—perhaps president—of the Massachusetts Association. She and her active protagonist, Mrs. William Palmer Lucas, the wife of a doctor who later became a well-known pediatrician in San Francisco, decided to catch the girls young before they were contaminated by radical ideas. They wished to start a junior anti-suffrage league. Before I went to Oxford, I had been suggested as the president of this project, and Mama was all set to launch me in it the following autumn of 1912. While I was in Cohasset I decided to try to win a prize of $100.00 offered by *Outlook* magazine for the best article on either side of the controversy. I started out knowing all the reasons why women should not vote and tried to write them for the contest. The strange thing was that every argument with which I started out led me to the exactly opposite conclusion than I intended. Working things out logically on paper revealed the fact that I was convinced that women *should*, of course, share the responsibilities of citizenship enjoyed by men. In the confusion of my discovery, I abandoned the idea of writing any article. Somehow, the process of arriving at this conviction represented an important turning point in my thinking. I don't believe I ever again accepted arguments without trying first to analyze the real significance of their origin and purpose. Also, it indicated that when I wanted to really understand a problem I should write it down. (Even now, so many years later, I find many revelations of meaning by writing these reminiscences.) When I told my Mother that I could not go along with the "anti" point of view any more, I thought she would be furious. But she said very little, only requesting that I refrain from walking in Suffragette parades or carrying banners. This was easy for me to agree to because I was nowhere near ready for that sort of commitment.

The summer after my return from Europe I spent with my father in Cohasset. It was a sad period for him because his last promotional enterprise failed to meet his expectations. He was doggedly trying to sell stock for the coal mine in Rhode Island that he had purchased, but it turned out that the product was non-combustible, despite the enormous amount of money he poured into the black hole. Eventually he lost all that he had invested and was only saved from the consequences of bankruptcy by his nephew in New York, who continued to subsidize him for the rest of his life.

My allowance, which I had always accepted as a matter of course, faded away in the general debacle and I woke up to the fact that I had better get busy and earn something on my own. Imagine a girl of today, twenty years old, just arriving at that conclusion! As a beginning, I found a job tutoring a little twelve-year-old girl who, for one reason or another, did not attend school. I had some difficulty with arithmetic, but I enjoyed teaching all the other subjects and I got along famously with my pupil. I have a distinct recollection of the first purchase I made with my own earnings. It was a grey felt hat with a green bird's wing plastered on one side. Another use for my income was the rental of an attic room (three stories up) in Louisburg Square where I could do my writing free from the oppressive atmosphere of my mother's house. I did not tell her that I had arranged such a retreat for daytime hours, but she found out accidentally and some fireworks ensued. But that time I did not accede to her criticisms, and since it was paid for by my own money, there was not much she could do about it. I wrote several short stories which I sent to magazines. They were promptly returned. I had one or two poems accepted, but I soon realized that I was not going to be able to support myself by writing, without a great deal more skill than I possessed.

My success in tutoring inclined me to look for a teaching position. In those days a college degree was not obligatory for teaching in schools, and I thought I could handle History, English and Languages without

Josephine Whitney, age 21, with her first purchase made
from her own earnings—a new hat.

much difficulty. I determined to consult my old teacher, Sara Dean, whom I had liked at Haskell School. She had become principal of the Brearley School in New York City. At that time it was a day school where daughters of well-to-do families received high grade education with special emphasis on the humanities. I thought that New York would be a stimulating place to live, and at least I could get away from Boston. I wonder now why no one told me that I should go to college and get some training. I don't see why I didn't realize the need myself, unless it was that I was still so incredibly naive and so sure of my own ability. Perhaps it was too bad that I never really followed through with my plans for self-sufficiency. College and a job would have given me a more realistic approach to fundamental problems and might have kept me from making some mistakes that were hard to correct later. On the other hand, my very inexperience enabled me to undertake idealistic ventures without being handicapped by practical considerations. Sometimes these ventures worked, thanks to the cooperation of other more efficient people.

Be that as it may be, I made a decision at this point which radically altered the course that I was to follow.

X

Mating

Frank Duveneck; courtship.

After I returned to the United States from Oxford, I renewed contacts with my girl friends and also with a few young men who seemed to be interested in me.

One of these men lived in Hingham, an adjoining town about six or seven miles from Cohasset. He used to ask me to go sailing in his boat. Papa had given me a stylish little dog cart with bright red wheels and a spirited bay horse who could be ridden or driven at my pleasure. On one occasion, I drove over to Hingham, tied up the horse and cart to a tree in his family's front yard and off we went in his boat. We had a very pleasant sail but before we returned, the wind vanished and we were left at the entrance to the harbor in a dead calm. Just about that time a motor boat puffed by us and someone called out, "Did that young lady you've got there have a horse and rig?"

"Yes," he shouted back. "Is anything wrong?"

"Sure is," came the ominous words. "The horse got loose and went through the hedge and smashed the cart all to bits."

What a predicament! To be stuck out in the bay, with not a breath of wind to propel the boat, frantically worried about the horse and my precious high wheeled cart. When we finally got back to the pier and rushed up to the house, I found that indeed the pony had crashed through the hedge taking the cart with him. The harness broke and let him loose to mess up the neighbor's flower beds and front lawn. He was not hurt but my beautiful turn-out was completely smashed.

The young man who took me sailing was someone I enjoyed being with, but on my side, at least, it was nothing more than a comfortable friendship. I had a funny variety of other swains. There was Enrico, who was half Spanish and sang delightful love songs accompanied by guitar. I remember the tune of one to which the words were something like this: "Every little gesture has a meaning all its own, . . . And every feeling will be revealing . . ." He took me for a buggy ride one evening when I was visiting in Chicorua, a town near Dublin. He held the reins in one hand and the other sought mine, but I sat on my hands, much to his indignation. Then there was Rufus, a tall, long-necked individual who was interested in art and took me to visit galleries. Henry was a divine dancer, but seemed to be without a brain in his handsome head. Thomas, a promising poet majoring in English at Harvard, was the most intelligent and the most sensitive of the lot. I might have fallen for him except that I sensed a lack of stamina in character and body. We read Whitman together and exchanged poems and socialist tracts, but I was glad when he moved out West, and his voluminous letters made enjoyable bedside reading for a while.

I disposed of one suitor by playing a mean trick on him. It happened one autumn when a lot of us were invited by my friend Erica Thorpe to the annual Halloween party in the basement of the Longfellow House in Cambridge. (Erica was a granddaughter of Longfellow, and her mother was "laughing Allegra" in the poem, *The Children's Hour*). Their basement was a huge maze of mysterious passages and cubby holes. When the lights were turned out we wandered about bumping into each other and trying to identify the obstruction. My friend Catherine was being courted by David, an ungainly brilliant young physicist, while Allen, a playwright was pursuing me. Catherine and I decided to try to catch each other's suitors and then to impersonate each other. She did not find my man, but I was eminently successful in catching hers. When the lights were turned on and my victim found out that he had been whispering endearing sentiments into my ears instead of Catherine's, his facial expression of amazement, embarrassment and disgust was a hilarious study. Allen, who was also David's friend, found out what Catherine and I had plotted and told us both off in no uncertain terms. But I did not regret his disenchantment; the fact of the matter was that I found all these nice genteel young men very boring, and I didn't want to get married then anyhow. I valued my emerging independence too much.

However, fate has a way of messing up the best intentions. Youthful plans do not always materialize. One's line of personal procedure is unexpectedly crossed by a line of someone else's personal determination, and the planned course is deflected, rather like a balloon that gets hung up on a telephone wire. The intrusion in my case took the form of an unexpected male animal.

I was surprised one day to receive a letter from Frank Duveneck, whom I had not seen for months and whom I had known only as an occasional dance partner. He asked me for the name of a piece of music by MacDowell that I had once played for him, and suggested that I might invite him down to Cohasset to visit. I sent him the name of the piece and told him to come along. Later he told me that he knew the name perfectly well; the request was just an ice breaker.

He arrived by train at the North Cohasset railroad station, where I met him with horse and buggy and brought him home for lunch. After lunch we went for a walk in the woods and I began to find out a little about him. I could tell that he was a nature lover because every so often he would stop to identify a flower or a tree. He liked animals, and my dog took to him at once. As we walked up Forest Lane, when he was in the right hand side if I chanced to cross over, he would slip behind and move to the other track. I experimented with this maneuver several times, and it always produced the same result. Apparently he did not wish to get too close to me. *Funny!* I thought. Most men had a tendency to snuggle up. He was avoiding proximity.

Since I had seen Frank last, he had received a master's degree in engineering from Harvard University. His first employment was in Pittsburgh, where he served as apprentice at the Westinghouse Company, earning $60.00 a month for a ten-hour day plus Saturday morning. He took pride in living within this budget. At the same time, he had a Steinway Grand piano in his boarding house bedroom. That was an odd combination! He had been brought up under the shadow of the golden-domed State House on Beacon Hill, but he knew all about Europe, especially the picture galleries and folk festivals. He appeared to be related to a lot of influential people in Boston even though his name was Duveneck, not Lyman, Cabot nor Lowell.

When I moved from Cohasset in the fall to live with my mother in the city, he was working as an engineering consultant in Lowell, a mill town fifty miles outside Boston. He used to come up on carefully spaced weekends to call on me. Then I discovered that his mother was a niece of Mr. Arthur Lyman and had been brought up by her father, Francis Boott, in Europe, where she had married Frank Duveneck Senior, an American artist with whom she studied painting. When her baby son was not quite two years old, Lizzie Boott Duveneck died in Paris. It was then that her aunt and uncle adopted "Frankie," and brought him up as a member of their own family. In those days, the sons of well-to-do citizens usually went into the professions of law, medicine, teaching or business. Engineering was for the more plebeian. Here again, Frank seemed to be an interesting combination of opposites, and when he came to see me directly after a day's work in the mill he neither looked nor smelled like a gentleman. Yet he always addressed me meticulously as "Miss Whitney."

As time went on I discovered that, whereas I had forgotten all about him, ever since he first laid eyes on me at a coming-out party, he had decided he was going to marry me. He kept on thinking about it for two years during his Pittsburgh labors and his travels in Europe with his father. He chose a job in Lowell to be near enough to do his courting. I think he ran a big risk by failing to remind me of his existence during those two years—I might easily have run off with someone else. As it was, I was really astonished when he came to the point of asking me to be his wife. Until then, he had always appeared to be so reserved and diffident that our relationship seemed to represent only a pleasant platonic friendship. And all of a sudden it was not platonic at all but a deep and powerful urgency.

I was in the midst of making plans to strike out on my own career in New York, and I resented this unexpected interference. So I refused his offer. But I agreed to consider it further before making a final decision. Here again Frank was different. He did not importune me nor bewail my indecision, as he might have; after all he had been planning this for nearly three years, even though I had only been aware of his intentions for a few weeks. Instead, he agreed to allow me time to consider all aspects of the proposition, the way one puts a halter on a colt so the colt will get used to the feel of a bridle. It was good psychology and it revealed genuine sensitivity—and it gave me a little time to catch my breath.

I explored the implications of the decision facing me. Having witnessed the marital disharmony of my parents, I wanted to make sure that the same thing would not happen to me. I tried not to let my impulses run away with my reason, yet neither did I want my reason to dampen legitimate responses. I resisted all the way, making sure I did not allow myself to *fall* in love. By testing every step, it might be said that I *sauntered* into love. But the inevitable happened; there was no other way. My career as author or teacher went a-glimmering, and I relinquished my independence before ever I achieved it. I had to admit to myself that I was terribly excited by this strange and unusual man, whom I had reluctantly come to regard as the most remarkable person in all creation. I knew I couldn't afford to lose him.

The word *love* in English has so many meanings. There is love of self, love for a friend, love of pleasure, love of work, love of mankind, love of God, love of charity and love between a man and woman. It seems as if special words ought to have been invented a long time ago to express these many different forms of attachment, all the way from "I love mashed potatoes" to the "love of God which passeth understanding." Fritz Kunkel insisted that while sexual desire may be included, it is only a small part of love. The decision to live with an equal partner and to subordinate oneself to the formation of a new subject, a "we" presents the strongest positive experience imaginable. He who exchanges part of his egocentricity for a superpersonal purpose becomes part of a "Great Clarification." After I was married and as time went on, our companionship developed into an integral unity of direction, and events shaped themselves around the fusion of our two personalities. But the discovery and onset of love needs special celebration. I wrote a series of poems for Frank—too many to include here—but I include a few because they were important at the time they were written and expressed what I felt.

DEDICATION 1

One could not show a meadow by one blade
Nor paint an ocean in a drop of dew
I could not speak in words my love of you
Tho all the rosaries of love were said

And yet from out my mind I boldly drew
These most imperfect pearls and humbly laid
Them all before your eyes nor stayed
To count their number were it much or few

Oh my Beloved, take these little songs
They are not worthy of the harp I hear
And yet you will not scorn their good intent
But understand how much my spirit longs
To voice the wonder of the joy we share
And to reveal love's blessed sacrament.

DEDICATION 2

These wanton moods and fantasies of mine
Are yours, Beloved, since they came from you
You are their audience and their author too
I but the instrument, to you consign
What e'er of melody your fingers drew
From all my heart strings. Can you disentwine
My thought from yours and yours again from mine
Or recognize when first the wonder grew?

And yet what I have written as my creed
Is little worth—an echo or a sigh
Of mighty winds about a little reed
While overhead a whirlwind rushes by
All that I have I do on you bestow
And all I cannot say is yours to know.

AN INCIDENT

You walked behind me on the stair
The carpet dulled your tread, I *felt* you there
And by the mirror in the hall where hung
Wood bay-berries—I praised them with my tongue—
I halted, secretly to watch you pass
Behind me, imaged in the looking glass.
And you,

With dream-filled eyes which then I little knew
Gazed too
And caught my look in yours as in a net
One quivering instant only. Yet
Within that brief captivity of soul
You contemplated all my fear, my whole
Encloistered passion and the tears of fire
The hunger and the corporal desire
All this revealed.
And by your glance the scars of patience healed
Oh stranger, you who have such power
In moments shall I trust you for an hour?
And if an hour then why not for a day?
And if a day why should I say you nay
Though months that draw to years are very long
And may be drenched with wrong?
Shall I not trust you who have had the grace
To claim the soul behind the mirrored face?

TEACHERS

Sorrow teaches many things
Patience more
Every day a shadow flings
On life's shore.
But a teacher wiser far
Then the stars above
Shows where light and glory are
That is love.

ABSENCE

You are not here
And yet you are more near
Than mine own dress.
Oh blessedness
O heart-communion fathomless!
I cannot miss you when you are away
Because all thro the night and all the day
You walk with me
Clad with invisibility
And who could miss a friend
When he was close at hand?

ABSENCE

Beloved I am weary and sad and much depressed
And fain against your shoulder I'd lay my head to rest

But you are far away
And I must wait all day
Till night comes creeping darkly from out the sunlit west.

Beloved since I love you and you indeed love me
Why should we tarry longer and not espouse'd be?

The little birds don't wait
A springtime ere they mate.
They look—and love each other—and settle in a tree.

Distance where is it?
Despair who shall visit?
Delight who could miss it
    Since Frankie is home?
The hills call the rover,
The bees on the clover,
Foul winter is over,
    Since Frankie is come.

XI

Marriage and a Wander Year

Marriage in Boston; honeymoon in Europe, Japan, Korea and China.

Frank Duveneck and I were married at Kings Chapel in Boston on June 7, 1913. It is very difficult to really know a person until you actually live with him. The partnership, originating in sexual attraction, depends for continuing satisfaction on a great many other factors. One marries not only a person with ethical values, with discriminations of taste and behavior, with interests, curiosities, problems, preferences, but one also marries a background. Frank brought such a rich inheritance for me to share that my later life was greatly influenced by it. My story would not be complete without the correlated narrative of his genesis.

Frank grew up in the home of his great-uncle, Arthur T. Lyman, whose summer estate was in Waltham and whose winter residence was 39 Beacon Street, Boston, just half a block from the State House. This house represented the opulent period of New England architecture, with steep staircases, spacious parlors and dining room opening into an exquisite blue and silver ballroom. There were stables in the rear, close to the basement kitchen. On the fourth floor were servant's quarters, consisting of small chilly rooms typical of the period when help was abundantly available and easily satisfied. Persons passing along the street noticed the lavender panes of glass in the curved windows of the ground floor reception room. The house has since been converted, with the addition of the twin edifice next door, into the Boston Women's City Club. In summer, the family moved to Waltham to another expansive mansion set in lovely gardens, enhanced by a small river, a pool, green houses and hundred-year-old trees. The copper beech, the white pine, chestnuts, elms, flowering fruit trees and evergreen lawns constituted a veritable garden of Eden. It was known as "The Vale."

How did it happen that this son of Frank Duveneck the painter, who was a descendant of pioneer immigrants born of German peasant stock come to be brought up in the rarified atmosphere of "Boston Brahmins"?

It happened this way.

A group of immigrants from North Germany joined a colony which had settled on both sides of the Ohio River at Cincinnati, Ohio, and Covington, Kentucky around 1832-35. Part of this group left their colony and homesteaded near Piqua in the "badlands of Northern Ohio." My Frank's grandmother, Katarina, was one of the pioneer children. After the death of her parents she returned to Covington where she married Bernard Decker, a recent arrival from Germany. Before their baby was born, most of the Decker family, including Bernard, died of cholera. But Katarina soon remarried, and although Joseph Duveneck was her second husband, her son never knew until he was a grown-up that he was only a half-brother to the large family of brothers and sisters that lived on Greenup Street in Covington, Kentucky, across the river from Cincinnati.

As a boy, Frank manifested marked talent for drawing and was apprenticed to a German artist who constructed altars and painted sacred pictures for the new Catholic churches which were springing up in the middle West. One of the priests persuaded Frank's parents to let him go to Europe to study art. He arrived in Munich in 1870 and very quickly won recognition as the foremost American student. A few years later, he established his own classes and taught both American and German students. One of these students was Lizzie Boott, the only daughter of Francis Boott who had married Elizabeth Otis Lyman, a sister of Arthur T. Lyman of Boston. Elizabeth died while Lizzie was very young. Francis Boott, who was something of a misfit in Boston society, gathered up his small daughter and her nurse and departed for Europe. After living in a number of different cities, he decided to rent a villa at Bellosguardo just outside of Florence at the munificent cost of $50.00 a year. There, he devoted himself to the education of Lizzie. She learned several languages, played the violin, took riding and swimming lessons and developed considerable facility in drawing and painting. The Villa Castellani where they lived became a gathering place for many of the English and American expatriates and travellers. Lizzie's sketch books (all carefully preserved by her father) show portraits of Robert Browning, Henry Savage Landor, Henry Higginson, Anthony Trollope and other distinguished literary figures. Henry James frequented the Villa whenever he was in Italy. He and Lizzie Boott corresponded for many years, and he used the Villa as a setting in one of his novels. Francis Boott composed music—songs and marches and some choral church music. The atmosphere of the Villa was conducive to creative work, and Lizzie became a proficient watercolor artist. Her father had never allowed her to return to New England until she was over eighteen. When she reached that age, they visited Boston and renewed acquaintance with relatives they had not seen for years. Lizzie attended an art class taught by William Morris Hunt, whose reputation as a painter and teacher was, at that time, the latest cultural excitement in Boston. The Hunt Class for Women brought Lizzie in contact with other young American women of her own age. The friendships formed then lasted a lifetime. On returning to Europe, the Bootts spent a number of months in Paris, where Lizzie studied painting with Couture. She was not entirely satisfied with his manner of painting, and having seen several portraits by a painter named Duveneck, she and her father looked him up in his Munich studio and asked if he would be willing to teach an individual female student. He agreed, and the lessons began. Lizzie wrote her former associates in the Hunt Class describing Duveneck's method of starting a canvas and her amazement at his rapid and infallible brush work. She was disturbed by the ugliness of many of his models and wrote, "the very genius of ugliness seems to possess him. . . . The models are all so ugly."

Later, when she contemplated returning to Florence, she suggested that he should try painting in Italy.

"What shall I do with my boys?" he asked, alluding to his class of students.

"Bring them along," urged Lizzie.

And so it happened that a bevy of oddly dressed young artists descended like a flock of pigeons on Florence, and later on Venice. They rushed through the galleries, crowded into *trattorias* and demanded studios and models, using incomprehensible Italian words interspersed with interpretive gestures. (In my book, *Frank Duveneck, Painter, Teacher*, I describe this exodus at greater length.) William Dean Howells portrayed their advent in his book, *Indian Summer*. He calls them the "Engelhart Boys." The impact of Italy brightened Duveneck's color values, and Lizzie persuaded him to exchange butcher and carpenter models for charming young Italian girls and sunny landscapes.

A romance developed between teacher Duveneck and pupil Boott which was to continue for about ten years. Francis Boott opposed their marriage and Lizzie, torn by conflicting loyalties, could not bring herself to hurt her father. Finally she consented, in spite of her father's reluctance, and she and Frank were married in Paris in 1886. Much to her surprise and delight (for she was then about 40 years old) she bore a son, named for her father, Francis Boott Duveneck, who when I met him was called Frank, Jr. A few years of conjugal happiness were tragically terminated by Lizzie's death in Paris in 1888. The two devastated men, husband and father, were left with the delicate little child, who was then barely two years old.

In response to this dilemma, Mrs. Arthur Lyman wrote, offering the hospitality of her home to Lizzie's child, her great nephew. The artist father really had no recourse except to leave his child with his wife's people and Francis Boott took up residence in Cambridge to be near his grandson, the only remaining tie to the daughter to whom his life had been dedicated. That is how and why my husband grew up as he did and belonged, in part, to the genteel tradition of Boston Victorian society. The other part of him came from his father, who represented the Bohemian unconventionality of artistic genius and the rugged pioneer background of his ancestors.

Young Frank Duveneck thus came into a complex pattern of relationships, which consisted of his father, with whom he spent a few weeks in the summer and who visited in Boston during school vacations; his grandfather, who was his guardian and who directed his education and his great uncle Arthur Lyman (affectionately known as "Possie") with whom he lived and shared many happy hours in the gardens of Waltham. Other members of the household were two unmarried cousins, who looked after his material needs; and Bessie the nurse, who had gone to Paris from England shortly before Lizzie died and who had accompanied Frank to the United States. Bessie felt that the child was an almost sacred inherited trust. She gave him the warm, detailed devotion that his own mother might have given him but she was careful never to usurp the mother's role. For his father, his grandfather and his nurse, he was the center of concern, and apparently they often had emotionally-charged sessions to consider the best plans for "Frankie's" development. In addition to these three who were especially solicitous for his welfare, there was a whole bevy of cousins, aunts and uncles representing Lymans, Paines, Cabots, Lowells, all of whom were related to his Mother's side of the family, and who constituted a closely related and staunchly loyal family clan into which he was accepted.

I think it remarkable, in retrospect, that Frank was not outrageously spoiled. Perhaps the very fact of the divergence of personalities responsible for him kept the balance even and on the whole beneficial. Interestingly enough, probably the greatest influence really came from his mother. He did not see her, but his father talked of her incessantly, and his grandfather and Bessie added their reminiscences. Julia and Mabel Lyman, the spinster aunts, idealized her so that she became for him a spiritual reality. Her gentle presence permeated his dreams and his ideals. Quite surprisingly, his talents and interests took a turn quite different from the *modus vivendi* of all the above-mentioned people. He had a knack for scientific and mechanical devices and he created miniature machines out of wire and pins and matches. Instead of a studio or a study he asked for a shop, and instead of paints or books for Christmas he wanted tools. Whatever he did along this line was entirely on his own as his entourage did not include any such branch of knowledge. It was fortunate for him that Mr. Winsor, head master of

Middlesex Preparatory School which he attended, steered him into engineering studies at Harvard instead of business, law or the language arts which were the usual careers open to "gentlemen" of the privileged upper classes in Massachusetts at that period.

Frank had just completed his master's degree, combined with a year of assistant teaching in the University, when I first met him. He had been working for several years in the engineering field; he also had been to Europe with his father and had journeyed to Panama to witness the building of the Canal. He was fortunate enough to have inherited a comfortable income from the Boott estate, and when we married, he suggested that we travel around the world before settling down and contracting responsibilities. I had a predilection for travel, especially if it could be done in a less ostentatious way than I had hitherto experienced. Thus it was that our life together began with a trek abroad that lasted a year and included not only Europe, with which we were familiar, but also the Orient, which was totally unknown to us and unknown by either of our families. Indeed a trip to the Orient represented a faraway adventure that very few Bostonians even thought of attempting in 1914.

Following a brief honeymoon trip to the Adirondacks in New York State, we sailed from Canada to England. We stayed in England briefly, then spent a few days in Paris, took a trip down the Rhine, went to Florence for a week and ended in Munich, where we stayed for three months.

It was not easy to find an apartment with a bath room, which we considered a necessity. Finally, we found one in the house of Frau Haunschild on Gisela Strasse near the *Englisher Garten*. It consisted of an iron tub installed at the end of a corridor behind a green baize curtain. Inside the curtain and next to the tub was a gas hot water heater. We thought this would do (the Germans thought it luxurious), but after we moved in, we found it took about 2 1/2 hours to heat the bath water, so only one of us could bathe of an evening. We had to put money into the gas meter for cooking. Sometimes this would stick, but we developed a technique of hammering it with an umbrella and then it would start up again.

In those days, Munich offered the best of German culture; it was rich in concerts, opera and plays. We used to have opera seats in the front row of the balcony—not only seats, but seats with armchairs which cost about $1.00. We heard all the Wagner operas. They began in the middle of the afternoon. The first intermission lasted about an hour; and the second one, between acts two and three, allowed time for dinner. This gave a chance to recuperate from the emotional tension of listening to the magnificent music, and we returned refreshed to the next act before midnight. Frank rented a piano and spent several hours every day practicing.

In addition to the performing arts, the picture galleries, covering modern as well as classical painting, the craft studios and folk art, the book and print shops and the incomparable beer gardens, all afforded unlimited opportunities for enjoyment. Small carved wooden figures, Christmas cards, colored braid, hand woven fabrics, men's felt hats with feather ornaments, edelweiss jewelry and other creations were displayed in countless little shops in the Marienplatz and elsewhere. We took long walks in the *Englisher Garten* and made excursions to the lakes and villages in the Bavarian Tyrol where the eccentric Ludwig II erected his fabulous palaces.

I began to learn to cook in Munich. Until then, I had never done any cooking—and I mean *any*. Frank knew a little from his camping experience and from watching Olive Siderbotham, the cook in the Lyman house, but I hardly knew how to boil water. Meat was sold in small separate stores in Munich, and in the mornings, the *Madchen* who worked for well-to-do families would do the marketing for their employers. They carried little market baskets and approached the counter to ask for a piece of meat to fry, or to boil, or to bake. At first, I watched and listened and I would imitate their requests, and then I at least knew what to do with my *"Stuck Fleisch"* after I got it home. One time I cooked a duck. It was pretty tough, but edible, and I decided to make the carcass into soup for the next day's lunch. But what I produced was so greasy that even my long-suffering husband couldn't eat it, and I was so mad and disgusted that I just shoved the pot to one side on the drainboard. To my amazement, the next morning I found a beautiful white layer of fat covering the top of the soup. I discovered that I could lift it off, and there underneath was a nice, clear broth—duck soup! I made a number of discoveries of this kind during our three months' stay in Munich.

We came back to Boston to spend Christmas there, and then we started out again. This time we headed in a different direction, west instead of east, and our first stop was in Pennsylvania where Frank had worked in the Westinghouse Factory at Pittsburgh. I wrote in my diary my impressions of Pittsburgh and other places we saw enroute to California:

> Pittsburgh is one of the most dramatic places I was ever in. The city coils round between the hills. They divide it from itself and hide miles of chimneys from miles of more chimneys hardly a league apart. The tops of most of the hills are bare while up their sides clamber lopsided little houses—a gigantic slum. Trees have fallen down here and there, and lie rotting for want of someone to carry them away. How different from Europe where every scrap of lumber is eagerly seized upon by the poor people. The soil is not brown, but dirty black. . . .
>
> Today we have been traveling thro' Kansas, passing cornfields and wheat fields, endless stretches of flat country all beautifully cultivated. Pigs, cows, horses are grazing in the close shorn fields. The pigs and cows don't mind the train a bit, but the horses and mules kick up their heels and

rush away, making little dust clouds around their hooves. The scarcity of churches is noticeable to one who has traveled much in Europe.

In the desert we saw some of the Indians with their gay colored clothes and glossy black hair. The colors of the earth are richer than the *Rosengarten* in Tyrol. Imagine riding across such country. Nothing to bar your way over unending stretches of sand and gentle dunes—nothing but the great sky above, and the wind blowing out of nowhere into nowhere.

As I get further into the great open spaces, I realize that Boston is a kind of happy hunting ground for elite souls. But not for us. We must have a hand in moulding the future, be it ever so slight a part. Boston is all made and finished. It can be improved, of course, but it is like Europe—the birthpains are all over. Out here everything is in a state of unfoldment— there are marvelous possibilities.

Trip down Grand Canyon. . . . The descent on the narrow path which was very icy took one's breath away. The burros and horses go just as near the edge as possible, and at the corners there is not much except edge and infinity below. At the lowest depth of the canyon we found the brown river flowing over rapids between towering walls of stone. Looking up from the abyss the sky was such an intense blue that it looked like hard polished metal. . . . I would not have missed the trip down for anything . . . although the view from the top was also breathtaking. Marvellous place. No words can tell. . . .

My sister Laura, who had not been well, was staying with her small son at San Ysidro Ranch, Montecito, just outside of Santa Barbara, California. She had invited us to visit her. From Boston to California took us about five days on the Santa Fe Railroad. I shall never forget coming out of the bleak, snow-driven desert lands into the lush acres of orange groves, wave after wave of them, on the slopes of the San Bernardino hills. We stopped at a small station to take on water for the engine, and the fragrance of orange blossoms pervading the warm, caressing air almost smothered us with sweetness. It was such a contrast to the wintry weeks of December and January in which we had been living. It seemed unreal to us. The ranch where Laura stayed was also in the midst of an orange grove, and every day we could walk out of our guest house along the paths and listen to the hum of countless bees gathering honey, and pick up luscious fully ripe orange culls from the ground. It was then and there that we lost our hearts to California. We never got them back!

Our stay in San Francisco, our next stop, was brief, but it did nothing to diminish our enchantment with the West. We had never before seen a city built on hills and served by cable cars, nor had we ever met more than one Chinese person at a time. And not even in some of the most exclusive restaurants in Europe had we ever had a better dinner than we enjoyed at the (something) d'Or Restaurant located on a corner near Union Square, where for one dollar we had a five course dinner . . . complete with wine! The street corner flower stands, the Fairmont Hotel, Golden Gate Park, Fisherman's Wharf and the ferries made a great impression on us. Two Bostonians at the Golden Gate in 1913 really had their eyes opened.

Our trip across the Pacific to Japan took about 21 days, and the sea trip from Japan over the China Sea lived up to its terrible reputation. As the ship approached land, I told Frank I wasn't going to move from my berth till the ship was serenely tied to the dock. He said, "It's not very rough," and got up vigorously to get dressed and prepare to land. However, that time his pride played him false; he caught a devastating excess of nausea as he was buttoning up his shirt and he, too, had to retire to his couch—to my roars of uncharitable mirth.

As I remember Seoul, it was the dirtiest, most unsanitary place I ever saw. A canal ran along the streets. It was used, most of all, for cooking and drinking water, but also for women to wash clothes in, for children to urinate in, for kitchen slops to be poured in, for dogs and ducks to swim in. There was mud and filth everywhere. At night, we were kept awake by a strange rhythmic pounding coming from all directions. It turned out to be the Korean method of ironing. Everyone was dressed in coarse white clothing made of some fibrous thread. Flat sticks pounding on heavy boards smoothed out the wrinkles and gave the material a shiny surface gloss. Everywhere we went, women seemed to be engaged in this drudgery. The men were resplendent in their starched white garment. On their heads they wore little black brimless hats fastened by cords under their chins. Their wives were often in ragged clothes with unruly, dishevelled hair and toil-worn hands.

On the highest hill in Seoul there was an enormous Catholic cathedral. Many people were constantly going and coming through its porticoes. We noticed that the Christian women were clean and kempt, and no longer bore the downtrodden aspect of slaves.

Peking was an exciting place. We stayed in a hotel in the legation quarter. This area was in the center of the city and surrounded by a high wall with one large gate which had three lanes. I do not think there was more than the one entrance and exit. As you walked along the wall, on one side you saw the elegant chateau of the Belgian Embassy, the green lawn of the British, and other European mansions and parks. In the other direction, you looked into the swarming masses of the Chinese populace, clad all in blue cotton suits, pulling or pushing all manner of vehicles, crowds upon crowds of them moving incessantly like swarms of ants or locusts. The sound of voices and the shuffling of many sandal-clad or bare feet filled the air with a dull, incessant murmur. On the wall we were truly standing between two cultures. It was fascinating but frightening. We were there shortly after the Boxer Rebellion and the dethronement of the Manchu Dynasty. There was much conflict between the war lords, each group hoping to gain control of the government, and one day, we saw a tripod in the street to which was fastened a head hung by a long black pigtail.

Our trip to the Great Wall was a never-to-be-forgotten experience.

The Great Wall of China, 1913

We left Shanghai Kwan early in the morning riding on donkeys and
accompanied by the two donkey boys. We rode through desolate
country, which probably had been forested in former centuries, but
which was stony and barren of any vegetation. Approaching the north
gate, we could see the wall all along the ridges of the hills, leaping from
pinnacle to pinnacle in an unbroken sequence disappearing into the
distance both east and west. A thousand miles of masonry still standing,
testifying to the tremendous initiative of great dynasties on the one
hand, and on the other, to the ephemeral nature of culture. Every so

often along the wall there were outlook towers. We climbed up the one overlooking the gate. As we stood there gazing across the boundless Mongolian plain, we discerned a cloud of dust out of which, as it drew nearer, emerged a caravan. The camels, led by camel drivers on foot, were laden with packs bulging on either side. As we watched their slow approach I felt transported back in time to the days of Marco Polo and the Great Khan. I had a strange feeling of standing on the outpost of civilization and looking into the vast expanse of northern unexplored wilderness, and also of being suspended at some point of human evolution confronting a future as mysterious as the unexplored physical horizon—a sort of punctuation mark in geography and history.

When we returned from the Great Wall, it was late afternoon. Frank's donkey was much faster than mine, and he got further and further ahead of me on the trail, then finally disappeared. I was left alone on my donkey (with a man with whom I could not communicate) in the fast-approaching darkness. I had read of the kidnapping of two white women by Chinese bandits the week before, and I felt considerable uneasiness. I wondered why Frank had left me in such a precarious situation, but of course he also was unable to communicate with his donkey driver, so any chivalrous sentiments he may have had would not have been of any avail. As it turned out, my fears were unfounded, and my donkey and my "boy" brought me back, a little late but otherwise intact.

Our stay in China was cut short by the development of a cholera epidemic in Canton. Foreigners were advised to depart, but we did spend a few days in Soochow and Shanghai before leaving. Soochow is the equivalent of Venice in an Oriental setting. The streets are canals, and at that time many families made their living in boats by operating duck farms. A flock of a hundred or more ducks would surround a sampan and would be fed from it. They followed that particular boat and would not be lured away by any other flocks or other boats. I was not sure if they laid eggs on certain locations on the bank, or if they nested in the boat itself, but it was interesting to see how they recognized their own aquatic clans and seemed to maintain separate but equal domains.

Shanghai epitomized the least attractive aspects of British colonization. The harbor was filled with English war ships and merchant marine vessels, and the recreation areas along the bay were reserved exclusively for Anglos. The native Chinese city was unsanitary, impoverished and unbelievably crowded. The police in the white man's city were recruited from India, all of them Sikhs—huge, bearded men who wore turbans as their heads and cutlasses in their belts and showed imperiousness in their traffic controlling gestures. In most of the hotels and restaurants, Chinese were not allowed.

Those few months that we spent in Japan, Korea and China were an important part of our education. Before marriage we had both had considerable familiarity with European countries, but for both of us

Frank and Josephine Duveneck on their first trip to the Orient.

these lands of the Orient were totally new explorations, which we experienced together. The countries we visited had not yet lost their savor or uniqueness, and we were open to first-hand spontaneous impressions because we had arrived without previous indoctrination.

We were there long enough for us to become enormously interested in the Oriental civilizations and aware of their importance to our world. In New England, enlightened citizens turned their attention almost exclusively to the European scene, and very few bothered to understand what was happening in the other hemisphere. Our sojourn gave us an early perspective on world affairs, and a little understanding of the problems that developed on the international stage in the next three decades. It made us skeptical about the superiority of the West and industrial capitalistic society. Our thinking was greatly enriched by the brief contacts we had with Japan and China.

When we returned from our travels, we stopped in Omaha to visit my sister Laura. There we found Papa, who had had a severe illness and who had also gone through bankruptcy. In spite of these handicaps, he was on his way to British Columbia where he thought there was opportunity to promote a new enterprise and a chance to recoup his financial debacle. He was in no physical condition to warrant such a trip and in no financial shape to even consider it. But he was determined to go.

Frank and I had no success in dissuading him, so we agreed to accompany him, hoping to keep him from a relapse of pneumonia and also from an unwise involvement in a questionable business venture. We went to Victoria, the provincial capital of British Columbia, where he met with a group of *"entrepreneurs"* who were bent on developing a coal mine on Vancouver Island. Somehow or other, we succeeded in playing our cards well and showing up the shady character of their schemes. Papa agreed to cancel his final meeting with them, and we left by an early boat. When the entrepreneurs arrived at the hotel for what they hoped was the settlement, they found that the bird had flown, eluding the snares they had so surreptitiously laid.

On the boat returning the short distance from Vancouver Island and Victoria to the city of Vancouver, Papa was in a jovial mood, perhaps relieved from the tensions of the last few days. He got talking about the fact that a great territory like British Columbia should have its capital in Victoria, way down in the southwestern corner of the province, just across the border from the United States boundary. He started playing with the idea of moving the government seat to a more central place in the province, such as Prince Rupert. He outlined the strategy of arousing public opinion to demand the change and with increasing hilarity he described how the movement could be expedited. "Then we," he said, "would buy up all the land around the newly-chosen site and sell it for ten times its original value," and here he laughed so hard that the tears ran down his cheeks, and he got coughing and laughing and we had to laugh with him. A very proper Canadian matron sitting near us on the deck got up at this point and, with marked disgust, moved to the bow. Papa saw her disapproving looks and laughed still more. "She doesn't like the idea," he gasped, "but we won't let her in on any of the profits when we sell the lots. We'll keep the fortune ourselves."—and he went into more paroxysms of ribald mirth. This was one of my last memories of him, and I have always thought it was an example of his indomitable spirit that he could come through all his reverses and his illness and the disillusionment of his newest dream and could enter so whole-heartedly into the development of such fantastic nonsense with almost childlike exuberance.

On our return to the east coast, we went to Gloucester where Frank's father had rented a house for the summer. Thus I had a chance to become acquainted with my father-in-law, and I developed a deep affection for him. He was painting off and on, usually when one of the younger artists around persuaded him to accompany them on an outing. They often provided the canvas and the paint and brushes so that he could not plead the lack of equipment as an excuse for not painting.

One weekend, in August 1914, we were invited to stay with my sister Ruth and her husband Herbert Lyman at Sandy Cove in Cohasset. Ellery Sedgwick, the editor of the *Atlantic Monthly*, was their dinner guest one evening while we were there. About half way through the meal, he was called to the telephone. When he returned to the table he said, "England has just declared war against Germany." We were surprised and shocked. But it seemed far away and of no immediate concern to our personal lives. We little realized that this was the end of the era of peace in which we had been living, that nothing would ever be the same again, and that all of us, our whole society, would be involved in continuing conflict for the rest of our lives.

XII

Family and World War I

Birth of first child; move from Massachusetts to California; Frank joins the Signal Service; wartime living; peace at last.

For over a year after our marriage we had been footloose and fancy-free, and we were now expected to "settle down." This appeared to be the more urgent because I was pregnant now, and it was considered the proper thing for Frank to find himself a job. So we slipped right back into the pattern of newlyweds in Boston society; we rented a three-story house on Brimmer Street and had two maids. It seems incredible to me now that we could have started out in this aristocratic manner, but we did not really know anything else then. Frank found a teaching position at Middlesex, his old school in Concord, and he commuted every day in an open roadster with no windshield, sometimes through snow and zero temperatures. We got our first Scottie dog that winter. All his life Frank had wanted a dog, but the Lymans did not like dogs, so he had never had one until now. We named our dog Peter.

Our first daughter, Elizabeth Boott Duveneck, was born at home, early one morning in April 1915. She was named for Frank's mother. Frank was busy during the dark hours of the night carrying buckets of boiled water up three flights of stairs from the kitchen. He said that Peter followed him all the way down—flop, flop, flop and up again, jump, jump, jump over every stair, with a stop for breath at each landing. I had a very starched and rigidly professional nurse, Miss Turnbull, whom Frank named secretly "Miss Turnbaby." She would not have appreciated the nickname. We thought our baby was absolutely beautiful. Early photographs reveal that she, like most babies, was really quite ugly, but she grew into a beautiful woman.

The experience of motherhood was the second profound human experience that came to me. I had always loved children, and after I married I planned secretly to have at least six, perhaps even ten. Frank was as excited as I about our first child! Now he had a wife and a daughter and a little dog, too. He did not have to feel lonely any more.

When summer came we gave up the Boston house and adjourned to the Lyman estate in Waltham where we lived in three different houses during our stay of about nine weeks. I remember best being at the Vale and putting Elizabeth to sleep in her baby carriage under the great copper beech tree on the side lawn. This time was memorable for my association with Possie (Arthur Lyman, Frank's Great-Uncle). He had a way of making sly little jokes in an almost inaudible undertone, the subtlety of which required alertness to catch. He gave provocative nicknames to people, such as "Puffball" for a pompous gentleman whose son Theodore was called "Do," but referred to as "Doughball" by Possie.

Possie was a staunch Unitarian, a pillar of King's Chapel in Boston and a little suspicious of Episcopalians. I remember that a well-known preacher of that denomination was a certain Doctor Pusey. Possie referred to his followers as "pussy cats." And described them as somewhat "furry," with a sly twinkle in his eye. You had to guess what he was talking about until you became familiar with his vocabulary. He would sometimes bring me a single rose or a sweet-smelling blossom, saying as he looked down shyly, "You might like this." It was such an eloquent expression of his sensitivity to beauty, and his regard for me—much more eloquent than any florist's bouquet could have been. His private name for Frank was "Sam" (no one knew why). When we left the Vale he said, "Goodbye, Sam." They both knew it was to be a long goodbye.

We had been pursuaded by Frank's father to spend the next winter in Cincinnati, Ohio, hoping that Frank might find a professional opening there as an engineer. After we settled in Cincinnati, a Negro woman was hired to help me part-time. I was surprised to find her quite slovenly and prone to petty theft. Older residents told me, "You have to know how to handle *those people*; you can't trust them," but it made me uncomfortable to scold or threaten Bella Mae. No doubt she took advantage of my ignorance, but she was such a hearty, spontaneous soul, always ready to enjoy a joke. And she loved my baby. I could overlook a few irregularities for the sake of her good-natured friendliness.

We saw a great deal of Frank's father that winter, and the idea came to me that I should try to gather material for an article about him, or even a biography. He seemed so little appreciated at that time, outside of the small group at the Museum and at the Art School where he was known as "the Old Man." In the Cincinnati Library I managed to do quite a little research on the pioneer communities on both sides of the Ohio River and found out what the German immigrants had encountered in making settlements there. At the Mutter Gottes Church

Frank Duveneck, Senior, ca. 1915 (courtesy of Frank and Elizabeth Boott
Duveneck Papers, Archives of American Art, Smithsonian Institution)

in Covington, I found old family records, and I even made a trip to
Piqua, in Northern Ohio, where Frank's grandmother had homesteaded
with her parents in the 1830's. I unearthed names in the church archives
there and also made notes of these matters. Although it was a long time
before I was able to incorporate them into a book, they furnished
invaluable data when that time came.

Nothing in the way of a job for Frank turned up in Cincinnati,
because he was unwilling to engage in the making of war materials and
at that time industry was absorbed in military preparedness. At one
point it appeared that there might be an opening in Philadelphia with

the Baldwin Locomotive Works. We even hunted houses on the main line where we were infatuated with the suburbs of Chestnut Hill, Wallingford and Swarthmore. It was early spring, and the gardens were festive with flowering shrubs and sprouting bulbs. We were certainly not averse to living in such a charming place if the job should materialize. We were very near to committing ourselves to that decision when fate intervened. Frank received an offer from the Merrimac Mills in Lowell, Massachusetts to work for a year on a special engineering problem with the probability of permanent employment at the conclusion of the special assignment. This offer presented an interesting challenge for his technical knowledge and skill, and for his propensity for experimentation. So it came about that Lowell became our next home, in April 1917. Back to New England—hot humid summers, icy frost-bound winters.

Lowell was one of the oldest of the mill towns in Massachusetts. The mill buildings were built of bricks and were located along the banks of the Merrimac River. The Lyman family owned several of these mills. The Boott mill had been established in the late 18th century by Kirk Boott, an uncle of Frank's grandfather. In the old days, the workers lived in houses within a brick quadrangle which included the mill itself, the company church and a school. The whole life of the employees was centered there. They labored 14 hours a day, six days a week. On Sundays they had to go to church and were expected to support the minister out of their meagre salaries. Children worked in the mill also, nine or ten hours at a stretch. Much of the blue cotton cloth worn by coolies in China in the nineteenth century was woven in the Massachusetts mills of Lowell and Lawrence. It was taken in Yankee clipper ships round the Horn to Canton or Shanghai. On the return journey, the ships carried fine bronzes, jade, silken garments, and the celebrated blue and white Canton china featured on the dinner tables of the rich Boston merchants. I still have half a dozen platters dating back to this trading era.

When Frank started work at the mill, the communal living system had, of course, disappeared and child labor was on the way out. Most of the workers were immigrants from Italy and Ireland. Supervision was in the hands of a manager who lived in the town. The owner and the administrative board did not live in Lowell but visited from time to time and were in charge of marketing the products and introducing new processes. I think the Jacquard method of weaving was just coming into use. Frank was asked to devise easier and cheaper ways of cutting velvet. The town had a few handsome old houses set in elm-shaded estates, several churches, a couple of schools, a newspaper, a department store, a movie theatre, a crowded slum area and a district of rather shoddily built houses for the middle-class residents. This was where we rented a ramshackle house with four small bedrooms and a pleasant back yard.

During the month of May we hopefully planted quantities of flower seeds, most of which never came up. The soil was thin and run out, and we didn't know enough to spade it up and use fertilizer. The house was adequate for summer, but when winter came it was a different matter.

I was expecting another baby in September and I found the heat in Lowell exhausting. We had a big open car—a Peerless with a jump seat behind. When he returned home from work, Frank and I often took a picnic supper and drove off into the woods round Exeter or Billerica where it was possible to find an occasional breeze. My brother and his wife (also a Josephine) were expecting a baby in September. We had many jokes about "Labor Day," and on our evening excursions, when my unborn baby carried on somewhat violent gymnastics, we thought if he should arrive suddenly it could be called a "Rural Free Delivery." But that did not happen. Jim Whitney, Jr., won the race, arriving four days before Francis Duveneck, Jr.

Across the street from us lived two old maiden ladies. They were much interested in all that went on at our house, and eagerly awaited the baby's arrival. They sat on their porch and rocked, keeping our house under strict surveillance. But Dr. Worcester arrived after dark the night the baby was born, and he left again about half past six in the morning, so they never saw his car parked in front of the house. Frank went to work at the mill and told the foreman about his newborn son. When Mr. Clark went home for lunch he informed his wife. She in turn telephoned the news to the two old lady watchers. They were most indignant that this important event had taken place without their knowledge and observance!

When winter arrived, we found out about our house. When the wind blew, bringing sleet and snow in its wake, the curtains at the windows would billow out into the room, and the carpets would ripple across the floor like waves. If you took a hot water bottle to bed and happened to kick it out during the night, it was frozen solid by morning. The radiators froze and the roof leaked, and the pipes in the bathroom leaked. To cap these disasters, both children got the measles and the baby had pneumonia. From Thanksgiving to March was one long nightmare.

Our thoughts kept going to the visit we had made to my sister Laura in Santa Barbara two years before. When there was a place like that available, why endure the rigors of New England weather? We were also experiencing considerable pressure from our families about how to bring up our children and organize our social lives, and we felt that distance might provide more independence. Our planning to move was somewhat complicated by the increasing pressure on the United States to enter the war. Woodrow Wilson had won the election by his pledge to keep us out of the conflict, but as events developed in Europe it became evident that we could not remain neutral. Everyone told us we should not leave the security of New England and our family cohesiveness, but we were so fed up with the winters and with conservative advice that we did not allow ourselves to be dissuaded. My sister Ruth expostulated with us that because we were planning to travel on the Southern route it would be very dangerous: the Mexicans were shooting across the border and we might get hit in passage. Her comments exemplified the ignorance of New Englanders about the geography of Western America. The United States declared war on Germany the first week in April, just before we planned to leave.

There was great confusion in the government. After all, with the exception of Indian skirmishes and Mexican sorties and the Spanish war in the Philippines, we had not had any major wars in the United Staes since 1865. We were in no way prepared, nor were our people united in accepting the responsibility of a foreign war. It had taken three years of German submarine destruction of our ships and livid accounts of German atrocities to wake us up to the crisis. Even the German-American citizens in the Middle West and the sheltered residents of the West Coast were forced to accept the moral obligation to save democracy from the threat of world domination by German war lords. Congress voted large sums for war material, ship yards operated day and night, college students and others hastened to enlist. The draft began commandeering all available manpower. Factories converted their output to uniforms, firearms, ammunition and trucks. The Red Cross, better prepared than most agencies, recruited doctors, nurses and medical supplies. In spite of all these preparations, Frank and I went through with our plans to move, packed up in a hurry and moved West. I had the conviction that if we did not depart then we would get caught in the meshes of the war effort and might never escape. I think I was right, and I never regretted the move. We could not avoid involvement in the war, but we succeeded in altering our base of operation and attaining personal independence.

At San Ysidro Ranch, near Santa Barbara, we introduced Elizabeth and Francis to the delights of orange groves and Pacific beaches. Unfortunately, soon after our arrival, a very bad fire started in the hills beyond the Ojai Valley, and the wind carried the smoke, heat and cinders westward. The daily temperature rose to 100°, to 110°, to 115°. It was stifling. The children wilted, and I could hardly bring myself to move away from the electric fan. Even the nights were unbearable. Everyone who could do so was fleeing north, and we decided to follow suit. "Where shall we go?" we asked. "Where it is cool?" Someone said that a place called Carmel was always cool. "That's where we'll go." Packing was an ordeal, but I soaked a sheet in cold water in the bathtub and wrapped it around myself while I emptied dresser drawers and tied up baby paraphenalia. Every five minutes the sheet was dry and sweat was pouring off my back in steamy trickles. We squeezed ourselves into an already crowded night train and arrived at Monterey early in the morning. At the hotel the children and I collapsed on a double bed while Frank caught a bus to investigate the cool place called Carmel. After a couple of hours of sleep, I heard the telephone ring. I answered, and Frank said, "I'm in Carmel."

"What's it like?"

"Well, I don't know. It's sort of a funny place."

"How is it funny?"

"I can't exactly describe it. It's not like anywhere else. But I think it'll do. There's a hotel that has cottages. I rented one for us near the beach."

A cottage near the beach away from forest fires sounded like heaven to me. And that was our introduction to Carmel, a place we and our family have frequented on and off for fifty years. It was a fascinating village. We arrived just before the halcyon days of the artist-writer colony ended. The names of George Sterling, Redfern Mason, Michael Williams and Ina Coolbrith still echoed on the fog that drifted through the pines. Other younger and equally talented artists and writers remained to sustain the tradition: Mary Austin, Robinson Jeffers, Lincoln Steffens, William Ritschel, Edward Weston, the photographer, Dr. MacDougal, head of the desert laboratory, and many others.

The main street, Ocean Avenue, boasted about six stores. There were two groceries a block apart, Devendorf's and Leidig's, a meat market, Slevin's stationery store, Curtis' ice cream parlor, a real estate office and the post office. There was a garage, a library and a milk depot somewhere in the background. The town constable, Gus Englund, rode a horse up and down Ocean Avenue. He was very straight and official looking in his saddle, but I never heard of his arresting anyone. Along Ocean Avenue and some of the adjacent cross streets, the pedestrians could travel on board walks set up to avoid the winter mud and summer dust. Travel over them could be hazardous, as boards were often broken or missing, and it seemed that no one had the responsibility for replacing them. Travel was particularly hazardous if you ventured out at night. You carried a so-called "Carmel lantern" which consisted of a lighted candlestick, its flame encircled by a glass chimney. The light it shed did not always reveal the board walk, and usually the middle of the road was safer.

As a shopping center, Carmel left much to be desired. Typical of its limitations was the butcher shop. A small glass case well visited by flies, contained the day's available supply—usually a few weiners, hamburger, bacon, ham and once in a while a stringy steak. The proprietor sat behind the counter in a rocking chair reading his Bible. A friend of mine ventured in to inquire the price of a steak she saw in the case. The butcher took it out and held it up for her to see, stating the price. "Oh," she said, "I can buy that in Monterey for half that amount."

"It's a damn lie, Madam," he answered. Slapping the meat back in the case and adjusting his spectacles, he returned to his Bible and his rocking chair.

Once a week I used to rent a horse and buggy from the town livery stable and drive to Monterey to purchase my week's supplies. Many of the old ladies of Carmel learned that I made this weekly trip and they used to requisition me to make all manner of purchases in the metropolis. In addition to grocery items, fresh fish and stew meat, it might be a spool of purple thread, a couple of spoons, hair nets, or face cream. It took me almost all day to make the round trip. That was long before the Carmel Hill had been graded, and I can remember my old white horse plodding up from Monterey on the long climb to the top which took at least an hour. What a relief the downgrade to Carmel was for both of us! Like as not, some of the old ladies were waiting at the post office for their commissions. Sometimes there ensued a period of frenzied finance while accounts were straightened out and the proper change collected.

The momentum of war preparedness was accelerating and penetrated even to the back country along the Pacific Coast. I remember a so-called emergency meeting, advertised in the *Pine Cone*, the weekly journal. It was to be held in the movie theatre, the largest hall in town. The subject was the threat of German submarines landing down the Coast near the Big Sur, and what we should do to prevent their taking over California! Someone reported having seen a periscope somewhere near Palo Colorado. Perry Newberry was the chairman, and the meeting started with a sensational description of what was likely to happen. From his impassioned words, you could almost visualize fully equipped Prussian regiments, having marched twenty miles up the coast, swarming into the quiet lanes of Carmel and commandeering the redwood homes and hotels and making slaves of the population. This talk produced great excitement, both pro and con. There were those who pointed out the absurdity of the idea, but they were shouted down by others who were carried away by a patriotic fervor and were prepared to protect their homes and womenkind from the "Ruthless Hun."

The meeting resulted in the organization of volunteer patrols who were to be stationed at strategic points of lookout along the coast road. A number of elderly spinsters, whose time hung heavy on their hands, agreed to devote four hours a day to this arduous duty. Since August is the month of heaviest fog along the coast, there was no chance of seeing anything, much less a small periscope on the fog-enshrouded waters of the Pacific. Nevertheless, they wrapped themselves in shawls and blankets in their exposed lookouts, and staunchly carried out their voluntary assignments until well into the autumn.

However, the call to arms and the urge to enlist had become more insistent as reports of the weakening of French and British forces filled newspapers and magazines. It became more and more apparent that our whole civilization was threatened by the German war machine, and we could no longer remain passive in the face of this catastrophe. The draft

Frank Duveneck in Carmel, California with "Pete", our Scottie, 1917.

was in process of being organized, but many young men were enlisting without waiting to be called. Frank felt the pressure, and when he learned about a special all-California regiment being recruited for the Signal Service, he felt that he could contribute his technical skill without being involved in shooting his fellow men. After enlistment it was about two months before he was called up and assigned to Camp Lewis, just outside of Seattle, for training in the 322nd Field Signal Battalion.

Meanwhile, the Carmel branch of the Red Cross had been organized, and a lot of the women of the town spent many hours preparing military supplies for the medical corps and knitting for the men in the trenches. We made and folded bandages of various kinds, and stitched up night shirts for the hospitals. Mrs. Josselyn, the mother of three boys already in the army, and Mrs. Myrtle Criley from the Carmel Highlands, Nora Ritschel, Yvonne Winslow were the most constant and indefatigable workers. The upstairs apartment over a store was a center for more than medical supplies. It was a place where the latest gossip was brought in red hot, and in the six or seven weeks I worked there, I learned a great deal about the people of the town and their family histories. As you stitched or knitted, you could engage in most enlivening conversations. I think this was the only time in my life when I took part in such a traditional female pastime.

Many people in town preferred to work at home. We supplied the olive drab yarn, and they brought the finished products back to us to ship to the boys overseas. Although directions in regard to measurements and styles were given out with the wool, we received some very strange looking garments. I recall one muffler which seemed to be a beginner's effort. It had numerous gaps and odd lumps and the rows were of uneven width. Another donation consisted of a pair of socks varying in size from nine inches to thirteen. Sometimes the sleeveless sweaters had such small openings that only a pin-head would have been able to pull them on. When such labors of love were too unusable, one of the more proficient workers would unravel the yarn and rewind it for a second try.

Late in the summer, we exchanged the horse and buggy for a Model T Ford. It was important for me to learn to drive before Frank had to leave for training. My instruction took place on the back road which passes the Carmel Valley and goes straight up the hill, merging with the Monterey Road near the present entrance to the 17 Mile Drive. At that time, it had almost no traffic and furnished a series of small ups and downs—good practice for a beginner. The only trouble was that every time I stalled the motor, which was pretty often, poor Frank would have to get out and crank the engine by hand, since this was the era before selfstarters. He must have performed this arduous duty at least fifty times in one afternoon. Eventually his patience won; I learned the feel of the motor and the rhythms of shifting in time to keep it from stalling. My final initiation consisted in driving down the coast to the Big Sur on what is now Highway 1. In those days, even experienced drivers were intimidated by that route. It was very narrow and unpaved, and it wound in and out of the innumerable canyons. On one side there were steep banks above you, and on the other side, there might be a thousand foot drop straight down into the Pacific Ocean. I was pretty scared, but I made it without mishap, and from then on I could tackle any cow paths or mountain passes without hesitation.

Cars often got stuck in the sand at the edge of the roads in and around Carmel. Wheels of the car would spin ineffectually, and the owner would become completely frustrated. Often, if the driver was a lady, she cried; if it was a man, he cursed. The village tow truck was in constant demand. I always carried a roll of small mesh chicken wire in my car. Chicken wire under the wheels packs down the sand and gives traction for the car to pull out. I often helped out people who did not understand the nature of sand. Some of those I assisted were very grateful. One man, who drove a big Cadillac, offered me a ten dollar tip. I refused, but he was insistent. Finally, after the third refusal, to satisfy his gratitude, I said, "O.K. I'll give it to the Red Cross." He then doubled the amount. The ladies of the sewing room were delighted.

In November 1917, our little family was separated for the first time when Frank was called for basic training at Camp Lewis in Washington State. We planned to be reunited as soon as he had the opportunity to find a place for us to stay. For a time he was not permitted to leave camp because he did not have a hat: there was no hat big enough for his head in the outfitting department! Finally, when he received the appropriate headgear, he went into Tacoma and got the addresses of several summer shacks located in the woods near Steilacoom Lake. One place he saw seemed suitable for our needs. As he left the house, a captain and his wife drove up evidently also looking for a place to live. Frank telephoned the real estate office on his way back to camp and stopped in to pay the first month's rent before the captain returned.

When the rest of us arrived in Tacoma from California, Frank met us at the depot and drove us out to the little green cottage in the woods. He was able to spend that night with us but had to leave early the next morning. It was December 19th, and he promised to be back the following day when we would go shopping for the children's Christmas.

The next day he did not appear. Nor did he show up on December 21st, nor the 22nd, nor the 23rd. Nor was there a telephone call. He just seemed to have dropped from existence. I had no money, no transportation, and having just arrived, I knew no one. When I tried to call the camp headquarters, I was emphatically rebuffed, and I thought Frank must have been shipped overseas. Here we were, five miles out in the woods without funds and Christmas just round the corner. On the morning of the 24th he finally called on the telephone saying that he would be with us shortly. He explained that when he got back to camp, after settling us in the cottage, he was put under quarantine. His dormitory was guarded by an M.P. armed with a pick handle (the guns had not yet arrived). No one could leave the barracks, which was quarantined because of a case of spinal meningitis. Unfortunately, the only telephone was across the street in another building, and Frank was stuck, completely incommunicado. What a relief it was when he showed up at last and we could go shopping for food and little treasures to tuck in the stockings for the children and for Eloise, the high school girl who had come with us from California. Frank was able to stay for a couple of days, long enough to make a wonderful snow fort for the children. Elizabeth was only about three at the time, but she remembers these early experiences.

The winter climate in Washington was dreary. During the four months we were there, I only saw Mt. Rainier once. Drying diapers for two babies was a never ending problem; it was no use hanging them outside, so I festooned lines above the kitchen stove. To this day, when I visit the homes of families where clothes are being dried in similar fashion, the smell of the damp linen takes me back in a vivid flash to the steamy little kitchen near Steilacoom Lake. Frank was usually able to spend Saturday afternoon and all day Sunday with us. Our Model T Ford was kept in a shed. To get Frank back to camp on Monday morning in time for 7 a.m. reveille and roll call, we had to get up at 5 o'clock. That was before the days of anti-freeze, and we had to drain the radiator of the car before we went to bed each night. We developed a system to expedite our departure. We left a bucket of water on the stove before retiring so that it would still be luke warm by morning. Before getting dressed, I poked up the wood and coal fire and put the tea kettle on the hottest hole. When we were ready to go, we poured warm water into the radiator and boiling water over the carburetor. And off we went with a bang through the darkness and snow and slush. When we reached the camp the mud was terrific. None of the roads were paved, and the army trucks had worn holes and ruts in which your car got stuck, unless you kept going full steam ahead. One day after I had let Frank off at Company A, I was returning home, when a bus load of belated soldiers hailed me, asking for a ride to camp. I turned around, the thirteen men piled into the Model T car, and I raced back, crashing the shock absorbers and spraying muddy water all over my windshield. We arrived at their quarters just as the battalion was lining up outside for morning inspection. They fell out of my Model T and one boy yelled back, "Lady, you sure can drive!" In a few seconds they were all standing stiffly at attention, saved from a day in the guard house.

Despite the winter weather, the time passed all to quickly, and rumors began to spread about the end of the training period for the 322nd Field Signal Battalion. Meanwhile, Frank had won recognition by constructing a remarkable barber chair which tipped back and enabled the officers to enjoy luxurious treatments from the company barber. They found out that he had considerable manual skill as well as a master's degree in engineering. He passed an examination which earned him the position of Master Sergeant Electrician, the highest non-commissioned officer in the outfit. This gave him more privileges than an ordinary private, and was a more congenial job.

In view of his departure overseas and the fact that I was eight months pregnant, it seemed wise for me to find a more permanent domicile. In April I moved to Palo Alto, California and the Model T Ford followed by freight. The soldiers had been forbidden to tell their families when they were leaving camp, but Frank and I had arranged a code sentence which would indicate when he was about to be on his way. A few days after receiving his letter with this information, my sister Laura telephoned me from Omaha, Nebraska, to tell me that she had been working evening shift for the Red Cross at the depot meeting troop trains, when to her amazement she found herself offering Frank, her brother-in-law, a cup of coffee! After he had arrived at camp in Massachusetts, his father came on to see him. They spent the afternoon and evening together and his father said, "I'll come back and see you again tomorrow, Frankie." Frank knew, but could not tell his father, that he would be gone by dawn. That was their last meeting. Frank Duveneck, Senior, died in January 1919.

On the way across the Atlantic the 322nd was part of a large convoy. There was great danger from submarines. Just as it was getting light all the men were mustered out on deck and told to watch the waves for any sign of a conning tower. Frank said it was spooky, all standing silent—they were not allowed to talk—in the dim dawning light, everyone's eyes apprehensively staring across the expanse of waters for a signal of danger.

Josephine Duveneck with Hope, 1918, and with Francis, Elizabeth and friends.

The day before he sailed Frank had received a telegram at camp from me announcing the birth of our second little girl, whom we had agreed to name "Hope." If he had not received the news then, it would have taken six or eight weeks before he could have received word. Mail service was not very speedy in World War I.

The house I rented for three months was on the corner of Addison and Cowper Streets in Palo Alto. It was very pleasant except that the mud was so deep that I dared not drive to the front door after a rainy night. Hope was born in May, and I moved back to Carmel at the end of June. We reclaimed Peter, our Scottie, much to the children's delight and Peter's satisfaction. I had exchanged the horse and buggy of the former days for the Model T which made housekeeping easier. Of course I resumed the role of professional shopper for the old ladies, but now the Carmel Hill was no longer so formidable.

Except when it was too foggy, I spent the afternoons with Francis and Elizabeth, the two older children and Peter, the dog, on Carmel Beach. We dug tunnels and erected sand castles, and chased sandpipers along the fringes of the ebb tide. If it was windy, we found refuge in the dunes

where we could play hide and seek and get lost in the hills and valleys, or cuddle up on a blanket and read *Mother Goose* and *Peter Rabbit*. One of the most popular books was *Becasine,* a French picture book Frank sent us. I translated it as I read. If it happened that I used a different word from my original version, I was quickly corrected by Elizabeth, who suffered no deviations in her favorite story. The homeward trek pushing the go-cart up the rough road from the beach was somewhat arduous. Francis (called Buddy at that time) was a very solid heavyweight, and Elizabeth often insisted on squashing in beside him. It was easier to push the extra load than to cope with a tantrum in the middle of Ocean Avenue. When we reached home, Walser, the dear companion who lived with us for several years, had supper prepared for us. Baby Hope was ready to be played with, and aside from missing Frank we were very happy.

News came from Father Duveneck which was disturbing. He had intended to spend the summer with his grandchildren, but just after Hope was born he was troubled with a soreness inside his mouth. It was diagnosed as cancer (he had always been an inveterate smoker) and so, instead of coming to California, he had gone to a specialist in Philadelphia for an operation. The outcome was not encouraging. He lived in a hotel with his sister and went to the hospital each day. His brother Charlie asked me to come if I possibly could, because he felt the sitation was becoming impossible. I hated to leave the children, especially the baby, but they would be well taken care of, I knew, by the faithful Walser. About the middle of September, I went to Philadelphia. There I found Father Duveneck very ill, and the hotel arrangements were thoroughly inappropriate. I conferred with his sister and brother, consulted the doctors, and got him moved into a hospital. This required considerable pressure, as the flu had hit the east coast just at that time and all medical facilities were overtaxed. I had found a room in a boarding house and one night there, just after supper I was seized with nausea, a terrible headache and a raging fever. I had not yet heard about the flu epidemic, so I had no idea what had hit me. I didn't know any of the people in the boarding house, nor anyone in Philadelphia except my sick father-in-law and his brother and sister. I kept drifting into a sort of coma due to the high fever. I thought I was going to die. Because I was in a strange city and none of the family knew where I was lodging, I imagined that no one would know who I was nor where I came from. Frank would never guess where I had disappeared to—and my three little children, what would happen to them? I never felt so alone and so powerless in all my life. But I was determined not to leave my loved ones in the lurch. I made a supernatural effort of will—a declaration to myself that I was *going to live* and a sort of declaratory prayer to fate and to the great Unknown, asserting my independence of choice. I believe—and have seen my belief confirmed more than once—that there is a Power in the Universe that can be evoked when the need is great, that if one has faith, healing will take place and the seemingly impossible is vouchsafed. It may sound incredible, but it is a fact that by seven o'clock in the morning the fever had passed. I was completely exhausted and slept all the next day, but the flu was gone. As soon as I could, I made arrangements for Father Duveneck to be moved by ambulance to the train station and taken to a Cincinnati hospital. I made a brief visit to my family in Boston and on my way back to California I stopped in Cincinnati to see Father Duveneck. He was in a Catholic Hospital. The nuns were very kind to him. He was as comfortable as it was possible for him to be. He could not talk, but he wrote me several tender little notes. I reassured him about Frank and told him about his grandchildren. I hated to leave, but there was nothing further I could do for him. I felt I had been gone from my precious kids, who were my first concern, much too long already. As I went down in the hospital elevator, I could not restrain my tears. As I got out, the elevator man patted my shoulder and said, "Don't take it so hard, Miss. We all have to go sometime."

My arrival in San Francisco, after having come across from Oakland by ferry, took on the aspect of the most extravagant phantasmagoria I had ever imagined. I wondered if I were dreaming. Because of the flu epidemic, everyone was wearing white gauze masks over their noses and mouths. In the dim street lighting this made them look positively ghoulish. In addition, whistles were blowing, bells ringing, automobile horns blasting, dogs barking, and everyone was shouting and yelling at the top of his lungs. Market Street was pandemonium. I screamed into the ear of one of the shriekers asking, "What *is* going on?" "Don't you know yet?" he screamed back. "The war is over!" I had been on the train and ferry for the last few hours and had not heard the welcome news. Someone standing on top of a taxicab waving a flag howled through a megaphone, "The war is over! We've beaten the krauts! Hurrah for our boys! Peace! Peace at last!" At that point it didn't seem very peaceful, but I felt like shouting a bit myself. It was on November 11, 1918. I hurried on from San Francisco to Carmel to share the good news with the children and my friends. Great was our rejoicing. The swords could be shaped into ploughshares, and the soldiers would soon be coming home. "The war to end wars" was over. Peace at last. Peace for the whole world. *We believed it—then.*

XIII

Establishing a Home

Purchase of a house in Palo Alto; Frank's return from the war; bringing up our children.

After leaving Father Duveneck in Cincinnati and returning to California, I decided to live in Palo Alto. However, I was unable to find a house to rent. Finally, an agent hoping for a quick sale, offered me a five bedroom house on an acre of land just outside the city limits. I was especially attracted by the garden. The property had formerly been part of an extensive orchard. Twenty-three cherry trees remained. There was a formal rose enclosure with box hedges, a grape arbor, a small lawn and some fine Monterey pines with shrubby underbrush along the road, ensuring privacy. A two car garage and a children's playhouse with electric lights and running water was an added attraction. All this was offered for $7,500.

Since my marriage, I had lived in thirteen different houses. The thought of owning a place from which I would not have to move after a few months seemed desirable. I consulted the bank and Frank's financial trustee in Boston. Both approved, and I wrote Frank telling him of the opportunity and saying that unless he cabled disapproval I would go ahead with the deal. He never received the letter, only a later one that started out with the news, "Well, I bought the house." He did not even know of its location! I was a little startled by my temerity on going ahead on my own to assume what seemed to me then an enormous expenditure.

Since the war was over, I thought that Frank would be returning home soon. His battalion had served from July 15 until November 11th in all the major American engagements—the Aisne-Marne offensive in

July, the Vasle and Toule in August, and the St. Michiel and Meuse-Argonne in September and October up to the time of the Armistice. What I did not know was that about October thirtieth he had been transferred to an officer's training camp at Ste. Aignon. When peace was declared, there was no longer any need for more officers. He expected to return to his battalion, but until the disposition of that unit had been decided by the higher authorities, Frank was marooned in mouldy old French barracks in Ste. Aignon, where the so-called "casuals" were housed. He ate his Thanksgiving dinner of stew from a tin plate resting on a stone wall in the pouring rain. When he finally got routed back to the 322nd Field Signal Battalion, he learned that it had been designated as part of the Army of Occupation which was to remain in Coblenz, Germany, during the whole period required for negotiating peace terms. This involved another six months of service. Although the clean and orderly barracks formerly used for German troops were a welcome contrast to shabby French accommodations, the tedium of waiting and the inactivity made the "Battle of Coblenz" a trying experience. Luckily, someone had the idea of organizing a school for enlisted men. Frank taught mechanical drawing and elementary engineering. The post library and concert programs organized by local German citizens also helped to pass the time.

Meanwhile, I was busy moving into our first real home, getting our furniture and wedding presents out of storage, unpacking china, books and pictures and arranging them in their new locations. It was a wonderful place for the children. They could pedal their wheel toys around the driveway and the paths, play at housekeeping in the playhouse, climb trees and make mud pies. The bit of jungle out front became "Sherwood Forest." Fairies lived in the back garden. We raised rabbits and a baby goat, acquired a Saint Bernard puppy and numerous pussy cats. Our Scottie, Peter, protected us from intruders. That one little acre seemed like a whole dominion to me. It held unlimited possibilities.

Our happiness was temporarily disturbed by the severe illness of our baby, Hope. A heavy cold developed into mastoiditis, an ear infection for which there seemed to be no remedy. She was in great pain and cried incessantly. This condition is easily cured with penicillin today, but at that time an operation was the only recourse. This operation on a ten-month-old baby was delicate and crucial. The doctor arranged for me to stay with her in the hospital, because it was important for her not to cry. It was a terribly anxious period, but Dr. Jerry Thomas was skillful and tender and the baby's life was saved. The hearing in the infected ear was destroyed, but otherwise she convalesced quickly and was home within a week.

The big event of that summer was the return of Frank. He had completed the long and tedious waiting period in the Army of Occupation in August 1919. He was discharged finally at the Presidio in

San Francisco. At last he could meet his new daughter, now nearly a year and a half old, and renew acquaintance with the other two older children. It was a surprising reunion to them. All of a sudden, here was a complete stranger with a mustache, arriving from somewhere and acting as if he belonged in the family. Elizabeth and Buddy had heard about "Daddy," but it didn't mean much more to them than "Little Boy Blue" or "Old King Cole," legendary characters—just someone Mother told you stories about. And all of a sudden here he was, a real somebody dressed in Khaki. Hope especially eyed him with suspicion and it was several days before she would let him pick her up.

He showed us his gas mask, and the children tried it on gleefully. Little did they know of its ghastly implication. We unpacked his civilian clothes out of mothballs and used the same box to put away his uniform and overseas cap. Then his concern was to round up a few tools and become a useful citizen once more. Frenchie, the gardener who had been coming to help me once a week for the last six months, was greatly relieved to meet him. All spring he had been telling me to go find myself another man. He knew all about soldiers. "Soldiers never came back." "A fine young woman like you, what for you wait?" He suggested the president of the local bank, a bachelor. Why didn't I go after him? *"Beaucoup d'argent! Tres chic! Depechez vous!"* He didn't believe Frank would return. But seeing was believing. "You were right after all," he had to admit. *"C'est bien, c'est tres bien."*

We had so many things to talk about. All his experiences overseas and mine at home, his father's illness and Hope's. The new friends I had made in Palo Alto and observations about the children and their unique personalities, talents, interests, quirks and problems. Very soon he was making little automobiles for Buddy, tiny little teacups and spoons for Elizabeth, and whistles for Hopey. And he could mend broken chairs and patch screens and fix the toilet. Yes, it was good to have a Daddy round the house!

Perhaps this period was the happiest one in my life. At least it was the most serene. We were a united family, we had a little piece of land of our own, a comfortable house, good health, no financial worries, an automobile and a garden. The "war to end all wars" was over. The other problems of society seemed far away and irrelevant to our daily lives. To watch the children as they emerged from babyhood into individual personalities was fascinating. They were always busy. I read books and told them stories, and they concocted dramatic plays out of these tales. Hansel and Gretel visited the witch in the grape arbor, Robin Hood and his Merry Men lived in Sherwood Forest. We sang songs: "Here we go looby loo;" "Lazy Mary, will you get up?;" "Monday comes for washing." It soon became apparent that Elizabeth had marked facility for arts and crafts, and Francis was concerned with nuts and bolts and mechanical construction. I collected all sorts of scrap material and fundamental tools like scissors, screwdrivers and hammers. As parents, we relived our own childhoods —I with books and fantasies, Frank with ideas for gadgets and how to construct them out of wood, tin and wire. Our children's little bodies were so beautiful. I loved to bathe and dress them. Getting them ready for bed was often hectic, but tucking them in and good night songs and final hugs were so much fun. Even the inevitable glass of water demanded after final rites was the source of an extra exchange of mutual reassurances. The physical care of their bodies and the nurture of their spirits was a completely absorbing vocation. All the modern propaganda about "women's lib" should not overlook this prerogative of motherhood in the first years, which is too precious to forgo even in the interest of a professional career. To cheat a woman of this experience is to deprive her of her most basic human function. The complete dependence of the baby lasts such a short time and can never be repeated. Psychologists say, too, that love expressed and received physically and mentally during the early months of childhood is most important for subsequent development. I believe this to be true.

Some of my jolliest memories are of overnight camping trips. We loaded sleeping bags, cooking pots and food into the "Tin Lizzie," and all five of us would go bouncing over the hills and stop near a stream or near the ocean. In those days everything was open, there were no private property signs. One could light a little campfire with impunity, and after cooking supper snuggle down in our sleeping bags and watch the stars as they moved leisurely across the sky. One of the children, I don't remember which one, called out one night, "Mother, I thought you said stars were fixed up in the sky. But that one has moved. It was just beyond that oak branch when I first went to bed. Now it's way over near the mountain." Frank and I had both been fairly familiar with the trees and flowers of New England, but in California we encountered completely different species. We spent many evenings identifying specimens we brought back from our trips. Sometimes Frank went fly fishing and the children waded up stream, and I lay in the grass and listened to the running water. Sometimes we camped under the giant redwood trees where there is a great quietness. In adult life all our children and most of our grandchildren have manifested a love for camping and the great out-of-doors. I am sure no other source of recreation is as satisfying, and no other remedy for overburdened minds and frazzled nerves is as effective as getting away from routine into the untrammeled wilderness.

Before committing ourselves irrevocably to remaining on the West Coast, Frank wanted to canvas the employment opportunities, and both of us felt the urge to renew contacts with our families. So, in the summer of 1921 we went East again. We made Cohasset, Massachusetts, our headquarters and visited relatives who lived in Boston or nearby towns.

It was an uneventful summer. The children enjoyed the beach, and I was glad to see some of my family and Eastern friends again. A letter about my visit with the children to Grandmother describes some occurrences:

"On Sunday we went to Boston and Elizabeth and Buddy and I went to King's Chapel with the Lyman's. They sit in the balcony where the seats in the pew are quite high. The music is splendid as the boys sing well. When they got through a particularly stunning Latin hymn Buddy whispered, "Those men were roaring, weren't they?" I had him all dressed up in blue velvet trousers and a frilled waist. The first time he leaped down from those high seats he pulled three buttons off his shirt and left about three inches of gash where they had pulled out. I had one safety pin with me but he wrenched that loose too. Then he rubbed one of the dusty pillars with his fingers and then rubbed his nose. You can imagine the result. The children chortled with glee when the minister crawled up that staircase into the pulpit which Elizabeth called "a funny little box." But on the whole they behaved with acceptable propriety. I did catch Buddy making faces at Mrs. Bradford who must have liked his looks because she never once took her eyes off him during the whole service. I thought the faces served her right. Buddy is funny. Yesterday we met a little short lady and an enormously tall man. "There's Mr. Sky," says Buddy in a loud voice. On returning to Otis Place (where my Mother lived) I sent Buddy out in the Esplanade with Miss H. There are altogether too many things in that china shop. Hope had a nap and emerged smiling and winsome. At lunch, each thing that appeared, Buddy said, "I don't like that." The Duchess was disgusted with him, but says she likes him. I don't know why. When she was eating pudding, he said to her, "You've got a great white gob under your nose," pointing to a bit of whipped cream that had landed there. "And also," he said, "If you left any of that on your plate, I might take it." After lunch we went upstairs to the sitting room. Missing Buddy, I got to the foot of the stairway just in time to see the Winged Victory statue rocking precariously while Buddy crawled in behind her pedestal. I caught Victory with one hand and caught Buddy's leg with the other. I was glad to take the kids to the station to go back to Cohasset on the 2:15 train. Miss H. said she had a circus on the way Hope had everyone in the car looking at her, and Buddy burst the rest of the buttons off his shirt. On the whole, though, I think the visit was fairly successful, but I'm glad we don't have to do it again. It's too hard on me."

I was delighted when Frank decided at the end of our brief return to New England that he really belonged in the West. From the moment when I had first stepped off the Overland Train before the War I felt that this Western land was where I belonged. I never changed my mind. Frank, however, like a good many New Englanders, had to make a return trip before he was quite convinced that the change in habitat was congenial.

On December 29, 1922, my fourth baby was born, a boy whom we named Bernard, in memory of Frank's pioneer grandfather who died of cholera. This was the first time I had been to a hospital for delivery. The three previous children had all been born at home. There was an amusing story connected with this event. Frank took the three older children and their nurse to Carmel to simplify the household for about ten days. We had an old Chinese cook named Wong Chong working for us. When I realized I would have to go to the hospital in a hurry while Frank was gone, I called a taxi and asked Wong to come upstairs and get my suitcase. He said, "Where you go?"

"I have to go to the hospital now. The baby is coming."

"Oh, no. You no go hospital till boss comes home."

I had a hard time to persuade him that there are moments in a woman's life when you do not wait for "the boss."

This old Chinese was a very dear person. When the transcontinental railroad was built a large number of Chinese coolies were imported to California to work on the western end. When West and East met in Utah and the golden spike had been driven in, many of the workers preferred to stay in the United States instead of returning to China. However, they were often subjected to violent treatment by unfriendly gangs in small towns. For protection, they took refuge in San Francisco, where Chinatown was in the process of formation. They opened little shops and tea houses, gambling dens and opium parlors. The government would not allow their women to immigrate so that the community consisted mostly of single men. They frequently sent for their sons to join them and their numbers increased. A great many fortunes were being made in California during this time, and large homes were being built which required domestic helpers. People of wealth often entertained lavishly, and they soon discovered the efficiency of the Chinese cook and general servant, by whom all their culinary and maintenance problems were solved. "The house boy" occupied a unique position. He became like a member of the family, often managing the household, bringing up the children, deciding major issues and serving all the members with indefatigable toil and the deepest, most loyal devotion.

We were fortunate to have "discovered" Wong Chong. First we had Ah Low, but on his day off he got into some kind of trouble with the police and was put in jail. Ah Low insisted on calling me to say where he was and to tell me he would send somebody else. I did not believe he would do anything of the kind, but the following day an old man appeared at my door and said, "I work for you." He went into the kitchen, looked all round, examined the pots and pans, walked into the living room and upstairs, and asked, "Where I sleep?" I showed him and he said, "You pay?" I told him how much. He said, "O.K. Tomorrow I come." And come he did and stayed for several years. He loved the children and brought them gifts from Chinatown, especially at Chinese New Year. He told us all what to do and how to behave, and he knew all our friends and protected us from some of them. He suffered no irregularities in family life, and that is why he objected to my going to the hospital without the sanction of "the boss."

The three older children were delighted with the arrival of a new little brother. As he got older, their delight was somewhat tempered with other feelings, for although his golden curls and his angelic smile were irresistible, yet there were occasions when he did not appear so lovable. He had a way of prying into their possessions which they did not fancy, and his persistence was not easy to overcome. Everyone learned that being part of a family affords valuable disciplines in give and take, appreciation and tolerance.

A balanced family of two girls and two boys seemed a satisfactory family to us. To be sure, I had envisioned a family of ten at one time, but like many early ambitions which come up against the living reality, I found my enthusiasm for a larger family modified. I decided that since I was satisfied with the quality, I could forego quantity. At all events, life seemed very full and challenging with four personalities vitally different from one another, possessing such complicated inheritances and constantly surprising me with their funny, dynamic or tragic ways. Nurturing these young lives entrusted to my care seemed to take all the love and wisdom I had, and a little more. It was a period of dedication and singlemindedness.

XIV

Skirmish in Politics

Problems of peace; Palo Alto Community Center.

Although the cataclysm of the First World War was over and the fighting had stopped, the aftermath was yet to be dealt with. The destruction of land and resources, the loss of youthful lives and the poverty of the vanquished combatants changed the face of Europe. The United States was geographically far removed from battle, and our civilian population had never experienced the realities of warfare. Nevertheless, our isolation had been broken into. Now we found ourselves involved in world politics, forced to deal with secret treaties, balance of power considerations and diplomatic bargaining. But Wilson was no match for Clemenceau and Churchill at Versailles. The fourteen points that he advocated to eliminate war between nations were too naive, and the vision of a League of Nations died with him. He became a prophet without honor in his own country. We are still trying to revive and realize his dream of a peaceful world. I am not a historian, and I am unable to analyze the profound changes that took place beginning in 1914 and which are still going on, but economically the United States profited from the World War. It seems to me that the present frightening complex of military-industrial controls that the United States and other great powers have been establishing all over the world had its origin way back then, when great powers were exhausted by war and large corporations, having been stimulated in the production of armaments, found international markets eagerly awaiting their goods. World War II has, of course, greatly augmented the growth of this new imperialism.

On the one hand, the hope of universal brotherhood and human equality conflicted with the expanding ambitions of capitalism. The privileged class felt threatened, not only by the rise of communism, but also by the increasing strength of labor unions and the growing aspirations of the common man for equality. Symptoms of this unrest were exemplified by the establishment of the weeklies like the *New Republic* and the *Nation*, and by organizations like the Civil Liberties Union, the Fellowship of Reconciliation and Women's International League for Peace and Freedom. It is hard to explain just how the social ferment seeped down into individual lives. But it seems as if some sort of a dividing line took shape about that time in the average citizen's attitude toward change. Perhaps it is always so. In any case, I know that Frank and I became much more concerned about public affairs than we had been ever before. Contrary to our elders and our upbringing, we found ourselves in the advance guard of social and political aspiration.

Soldiers, after participating in any war, find it difficult to resume their peace-time careers. So it was with veterans of World War I. In many cases, their positions were filled by younger men, management had changed, competition was much more intense. In addition to the problems of finding a new job, many of them were still suffering from the psychological effects of battle. Some were burdened by memories they had to live with, and about which they found it difficult to talk. Younger men who had been drafted while still in school and had been drilled into conformity now became civilians again and often were puzzled how to direct their own lives apart from the daily routines of wartime and military orders.

After the relief of getting away from Europe, discarding his uniform and making reacquaintance with his own family, Frank began to confront the choice of occupation. If our living had depended on his salary, there probably would have been no alternative but to return to New England, Pittsburgh or Detroit where engineering jobs were available. The field of mechanical engineering was practically non-existent in California at that time. Yet Northern California was where we wanted to live. He became very much discouraged and depressed and thought perhaps it would be better to go back to Boston and find an opening thereabouts. While we were there, in the summer and fall of 1921, when my sister had rented a house for us in Cohasset, Frank canvassed opportunities but nothing opened up in the East nor the middle West except jobs connected with war materials and armaments, in which he wanted no part. He was too old (32) and too well educated to start at the beginning (so he was told), and the right niche just seemed not to be available. But when he returned to California to try again that October, he made an important decision. That year there had been early rains, and the hills were turning green. It was such a beautiful rejuvenation after the long summer drought that it came over him that, after all, this was his country. Whatever else had to be adjusted, this is where he wanted to live. The four children and I were only too happy to return home and join him in time for Christmas and the approaching springtime.

About this time, I began to feel the need of contributing something to the community. The fact that I was so comfortably off, due to no effort on my part, made me feel guilty. So many people were hungry or sick or the victims of circumstance, and I was healthy and over privileged and idle. I felt obligated to do something for somebody. Also, Frank and I felt that we needed closer associations with the community, more than simply paying taxes and contributing to the Community Chest, the Fireman's Ball and the YMCA. We were living an exclusive life, on an island as it were, with no bridge to the mainland. We fed on each other's resources, unaware of the life around us and the larger world to which we also belonged. We read about what was going on. To be merely an onlooker left me dissatisfied. But where were we to connect? The entering crack soon appeared for us, as it always will if one is determined to find it. Some background is necessary to explain how it came about for us.

The First World War caught the United States almost completely unprepared for military action. A few years earlier, Theodore Roosevelt had intruded on the armchair bureaucracy of the army high command by insisting that they should go out and ride 100 miles in three days. He himself covered the distance in one day. When war was declared by Congress in 1917, the wheels had to be set in motion for the training of hundreds of young civilians in the technique of modern warfare. Camps were set up hastily all over the country as centers for emergency training. One such camp was thrown together in Menlo Park, bordered by El Camino Real, San Francisquito Creek and Santa Cruz Avenue. It was called Camp Fremont (no trace of it remains). To serve the boys in their adjustment to such unforeseen demands, the ladies of Palo Alto, Menlo Park and Atherton organized a branch of the National Defender's Club. The national YWCA erected a Hostess House and furnished it. The Defender's Club ladies provided a volunteer staff to arrange entertainments, provide refreshments, library resources, friendly counseling and hospitality for lonely G.I.'s. About a month before the war ended, they arranged a mammoth Songfest at Stanford in the Football Stadium. Mme. Schumann-Heink, a world famous concert and opera singer, contributed her services, as did local choirs and choruses. The profits from this major effort amounted to some $4000.00. Before they had time to spend this money, the war ended, the army ordered Camp Fremont closed and all barracks and other installations dismantled. The Hostess House was a beautiful and spacious building constructed of wood, and the Defender's Club conceived the idea of transforming it into a community center, provided it could be moved elsewhere. The city of Palo Alto owned the land between the Southern Pacific Railroad and El Camino Real from University Avenue to "El Palo Alto", Palo Alto's Big Tree and the creek. The YWCA was willing to donate the building if the City of Palo Alto would agree to provide the location and would promise to assume responsibility for its maintenance, supervision and program. The City Council accepted the offer and created a Community Center Commission to have charge of the project. The proceeds from the Concert were donated by the Defender's Club to be used for moving the Hostess House onto city property just in back of the depot. It was moved piecemeal and reassembled, complete with plumbing, lighting, telephone and furnishings. The two stone fireplaces were set up at either end of the room, and a reception desk stood by the entrance door. The Painters' Union waxed the floor free of charge one Sunday afternoon. The House was dedicated just one year after Armistice Day, on November 11, 1919. It was estimated that three thousand people marched from the Charter Oak (corner of Waverly and University Avenue) to the site, led by the Stanford Band, the Base Hospital Band, the Stanford ROTC, the D.A.R., the Native Sons and the High School Cadets. Palo Alto's Mayor Swain presided. Mrs. Amy Seward sang and Dr. Harry Reynolds was Orator of the Day. It was a gala occasion.

The Palo Alto Community Center was one of the first municipally operated centers anywhere in the United States. The house was open from 9:00 in the morning until 5 p.m. on week days and on Sunday afternoons. There were programs of lectures, music and dancing, pool games and card parties. Some night classes were organized; a story hour and playground fun attracted the little people.

I had been hearing from some of the young mothers I met in the community that they found it impossible to obtain any part-time help to relieve them for a few hours a week. I also heard of several unmarried women who wished to earn a few extra dollars. It occurred to me that if there were some point of contact for these groups it might be mutually beneficial. My children took naps after lunch, and I felt that I could leave them with my household helper at that time. So I asked the Community Center Board if I could try setting up a part-time employment office between the hours of 12:30-2:30, and I was given the use of a small room. Publicity in the newspaper and in the weekly calendar of events at the Center brought in my first clients. (I may not remember correctly, but I think the going rate was from 50 cents to 75 cents an hour.) I had one file for employers and another for employees, and I had the use of a telephone. As the service became known, I began to receive calls and when I succeeded in making several successful combinations between applicants, I found myself in business. When I think about this venture now, my total lack of previous experience reminds me of the old saying about "fools rushing in." But I seem to have muddled through somehow. I recall several amusing episodes, and one or two disastrous ones. I remember one old Scottish lady who went to take care of a newborn baby and its mother. She weighed about 250 pounds, and she had to carry meals on a tray up to the second floor. One day, she slipped coming down on the stairs, and all the dishes and utensils went clattering down in a great crockery shambles. In telling me about it when she came looking for another place, she said, "Heavens above! Ah fell right on me bottom." One day, I had a request for a man to cut the fronds off a palm tree in a kindly spinster lady's front yard. I did not realize then that this operation called for an experienced gardener equipped with gloves and adequate, sharp tools, and I just happened to have a forlorn little man in my office who had just been released from the county jail. He had no money even for food or lodging, so I sent him out to cut the palm fronds, certain the lady would be sympathetic to his need. The next day I received an irate telephone call from the aforesaid lady: "Why in the world did you send me that awful man? The first thing he did was to fall off the ladder. I washed him up and put mercurochrome on his scratches. The next thing I knew he was at the door again, this time with a spine stuck through his finger. I took that out with difficulty and minutes later he was back. This time he sawed his wrist instead of the palm branch. So then I paid him for two hours and sent him away. Of all the stupid, helpless people he takes the cake! I'll do the work myself," she said, finally, and slammed down the telephone. The hapless victim never returned to me for another assignment.

This modest little part-time employment enterprise turned out to be fairly successful, and it put me in touch with a good many people, including members of the Community Center Board. Mrs. Parker Maddux, the Chairwoman, became a good friend. When she went to live in San Francisco, she recommended me for her place. This absolutely flabbergasted me. It was a most responsible position and I could not imagine why anyone thought I was qualified. As I look back on it now, I imagine that none of the other Board Members could be persuaded to take her place and in desperation they thought of me because I had great enthusiasm and considerable drive and was not involved in any other organization. It was with the greatest trepidation that I agreed to attempt what seemed to me almost impossible. Of course I was pleased that people I admired had confidence in me. The Center offered a tremendous opportunity for imaginative planning and, like my father, I was intrigued by the possibilities of pioneering. With the approval of Frank and some urgent persuasion on the part of Mrs. Maddux and other Members of the Board, I accepted. At my first meeting I was scared to death. I didn't know the first thing about Robert's Rules of Order, and the rest of the people were all much older than I. But they were very kind and I somehow survived the ordeal.

The Palo Alto Community Center continues its work today in a fine building donated by Mrs. Lucy Sterne at the corner of Middlefield and Melville Avenues. It is a model of efficient, well-organized activity. A large part of the operating expense is provided by rental fees for Boy Scout Offices, the use of halls and committee rooms, and by the sale of theatre tickets, and other activities.

In the early days it was operated largely by volunteers, and space was available gratis to any organizations within the town. There were two permanent employees, Dad Moulden, the former athletic coach from Stanford, who had charge of outside games, and the pool room, and Alice Diaz, the resident hostess. Alice was an extraordinary choice for the position. She was the daughter of a strict New England family on her mother's side and of a dashing Spanish interloper who broke into the puritan confines of Plymouth, Massachusetts and carried off his bride. Alice, a mixture of these two divergent traditions, aspired to be a dancer. But she was handicapped by her somewhat squat figure and her angular, unesthetic features which did not go with a *premiere danseuse*. She resorted to giving dancing lessons and occasionally was called on to arrange entertainments for special occasions. She had a warm, outgoing approach to people. At the same time, she maintained a quiet dignity that represented the finest tradition of the New England gentlewoman. Mrs. Maddux had the perspicacity to select her as resident hostess, and it was a happy choice. The location of the Center just at the entrance to the town invited strangers to seek its hospitality. The big fireplaces and comfortable arm chairs attracted poor and lonely people. The athletic programs drew in the teenagers and young adults, and the older volunteers who were responsible for programs were constantly coming and going. Alice made all these people welcome irrespective of status. Although Alice had never done anything like this before, and neither had I, we worked together very harmoniously. It was a most fortunate time to be involved in such a unique experiment, because the town of Palo Alto was on the edge of great expansion. The Center could respond to expressed needs and, not being bound by any past tradition, could instigate new activities on a purely experimental basis. It was very exciting. All kinds of people with all kinds of problems came for help. Our response was unprofessional but genuinely democratic and human. I think I learned first hand from working with these humble people more than I could have absorbed from a year's course in sociology.

Many movements and ideas originated at the Center which later became separate programs and composed the network of agencies and organizations associated with any American town. I have described the beginning of the employment bureau. When I became Chairwoman of the Board, a part-time worker was hired to run that office. Miss Helen Vincent ran it for a number of years until it was absorbed by the State Employment Service. The night classes increased by leaps and bounds. We offered instruction in sewing, embroidery, millinery, home nursing, Spanish, French and mechanical drawing. This last class was taught by Frank. The class fees were very moderate. This was the first night school in Palo Alto, and we persuaded the High School to take over this part of our program because it was becoming too large for us to handle. The Girl Scouts of Palo Alto held their initial meetings at the House, so did their Board. I served for several years and came to know Mrs. Lou Henry Hoover in that connection. That was before she went to

Washington and before the Girl Scouts had their own building. A score of clubs used our side rooms for their meetings—among them the Garden Club, the Bridge Club, the Health Club (organic foods), Church Women, and the Business and Professional Women's Club, which we organized at the instigation of Miss Manaton, the City Clerk, and a librarian from the High School. Once a week there was folk dancing, a Sunday afternoon concert, a Saturday morning baby clinic, various lectures and entertainments, and weekly meetings of the Veterans Associations. The Little Theater group played monthly, using a portable stage and large screens over which scenery could be hung or tacked. This was the original Palo Alto Community Theatre. For a short period one spring we operated a weekly Forum for the discussion of current issues. I remember considerable commotion in regard to a meeting for peace at which Anita Whitney, a labor organizer, was the main speaker. She was a controversial figure, and the American Legion tried to prevent the meeting. But by that time I had become a crusader for free speech, and the meeting was held. It was a stormy session. In order to placate the patriots, we had nailed an American flag on the wall behind the speaker. It was not displayed in the proper position. Stars were in the upper right instead of the upper left, or something like that, and we had the Daughters of the American Revolution on our necks for that breach of etiquette. Since I was eligible I thought of joining their ranks (to work from within), but their meetings seemed terribly boring to me, so I never did present my credentials.

During the years that I was connected with the House Community Center in the late twenties, there was considerable unemployment. Men with packs on their backs were often seen walking the roads to and from San Francisco. The House offered temporary asylum for these wayfarers who would sit by one of the big fireplaces and relax, or ask to see the day's paper, or go to sleep in one of the big armchairs. I think Alice slipped many a sandwich and cup of coffee to these visitors. They were called "bundle stiffs" by some. We also had a score of individuals, both men and women who lived in cheerless rented rooms downtown, and who liked to spend their evenings at the House where they met friendly people and a warm environment. One such was Quinto Pancera, an Italian barber. He came almost every night. Gradually a warm friendship grew up between him and Alice. He told her much about Italy, and she was convinced that he was a nobleman in disguise. She was in her forties, he in his fifties. It was probably her first love affair. The New England side of her family was horrified (there seemed not to be any Spanish relatives). Eventually Alice and Quinto were married in the grape arbor on our Hamilton Avenue place, the first of numerous marriages we have sponsored. They lived very simply but happily for many years.

Through my work at the Community House I found that I had a flair for organization. I was really very much surprised by this, because I had always felt very shy in groups and I never had had any training in sociology or welfare work. When I was asked to run for the Palo Alto City Council to fill out the unfinished term of the first woman member, I was quite overwhelmed at the idea and reluctant to comply. A lot of pressure was applied and finally I said, "O.K., but I won't do any campaigning for votes." The group that had asked me to run said they would do all the electioneering. I don't even remember who my opponent was, but they did such an efficient job that I was elected for a four year term with a large majority. So here I was, in another new situation, sitting round a big table every Monday night helping to decide issues for the fast-growing municipality. Apart from attending meetings regularly I don't think I contributed anything noteworthy except in two instances. One was the acceptance of the estate of five acres belonging to Mrs. Dixon to be used for a park site. Mrs. Dixon was an elderly lady who had one daughter. This daughter passed away in her early twenties. Mrs. Dixon wanted the house to remain just as her daughter had left it—all the china animals and glass vases and candlesticks to stay in place on the shelves and the gardens maintained in the same profusion. It was to be called Elinor Park. The men on the city council thought it was much too far out of town (on Channing Street near Newell Road) and some of them hesitated at the thought of all the keepsakes. I insisted that the town would soon grow beyond Mrs. Dixon's property and it would be a great asset for the future. I persuaded Mrs. Dixon not to insist on making a condition of the gift contingent on the *status quo* of the house and the bric-a-brac. After hours of discussion the proposition passed. Elinor Park lies now in the center of Palo Alto near the Main Library.

The other situation in which I had some influence was in connection with the Police Department. There was clear evidence of irregularity in the use of funds, the responsibility for which led directly to the Chief's office. The investigation made by the Council's Committee on Safety and reported to the Council confirmed the evidence. But rather than raise a scandal they advised hushing it up and continuing the guilty personnel in office. The Council was divided on this issue; a few members, of which I was one, believed that the Chief should be removed. The others for political reasons did not wish to override the Committee on Safety. The Chairman of the City Council asked for a voice vote and the result appeared to be against dismissal. Any member of the Council had the right to ask for a roll call on any vote in question. I asked that the individual votes be taken and it turned out that the majority agreed that the Chief should be removed from his office and members of the Board of Safety also should be dismissed. This prerogative of a call vote was rarely taken and one of the councilmen who had voted with me said, "You were very courageous." I couldn't see what courage had to do with it, but of course I was not involved in business and could act without fear of reprisal. All members of the police department were dismissed with the exception of one officer recently sworn in. He was a man with considerable education and unquestioned integrity. One innovation that I was interested to see added to the force was a *police woman*. It seemed important to me that in dealing with juveniles as well as female offenders, there should be a qualified woman available. Miss Wyckoff applied for the position in spite of the skepticism of her friends and the ribaldry of her fellow police officers. She was not dismayed by these negative reactions; indeed, she expected them. She took up her duties resolutely and with a dry humor that soon won over her male associates. Parents and teachers found a valuable ally in dealing with young people who were in trouble, and the judges came to rely on her case reports when forming judgments in court hearings. Miss Wyckoff was one of the first women police officers on the West Coast. I used to help her sometimes to meet the needs of an individual boy or girl who did not fit into the general pattern and whose problems extended far beyond the restraints of the law. She was gentle and patient with first offenders, but she could also be very tough when the occasion required it. No nonsense with Miss Wyckoff, but no cruelty, either.

After I had served four years on the Council, I was asked to run again for a second term. But I had found much of the business somewhat tedious. I could not get up much enthusiasm about set-back lines, street widening and traffic regulations. An inordinate amount of time was spent developing and reiterating arguments with the Southern Pacific Railroad in regard to the University Avenue crossing. It was a source of great danger but the railroad was reluctant to install the necessary underpass, because it would involve considerable expense. A bad accident finally brought results when the gates came down a little too late on a prominent citizen, causing his death. At the Community Center I had enjoyed contact with a great variety of people from all walks of life. As a member of the City Council, I found that most of the problems I had to deal with involved finances and technical decisions which did not arouse my interest. Also I had become involved in an educational project which took a great deal of time and thought. I had to make a choice at this point, and the field of politics failed to appeal to me. Some years later I was asked to run for the State Assembly from my district but I had no difficulty in refusing. Aside from doing propaganda for certain bills and for desirable candidates and making a brief foray, speaking from a box on street corners in the Santa Clara Valley towns during Robert LaFollette's campaign for President in 1924, I left political activity to my husband, who became prominent in Democratic State and County organizations. He did considerable precinct work. I put on Christmas parties for the Americans for Democratic Action and fundraising picnics for local candidates. I signed my name to countless petitions and newspaper advertisements, and I wrote letters to several Presidents and a great many congressmen. Not that these things are

particularly effective, but I believe that every citizen should vote
faithfully and support the ideals of democracy that he believes in. My
causes have usually been unpopular ones, and I have seldom been on
the winning side, but once in a while, after several attempts, the right
has prevailed. Votes for women, child labor laws, civil liberties, fair
employment practices, conservation of open space and socialized
medicine are examples of battles partly won. The democratic processes
often seem exasperatingly slow, but as William Blake wrote:

> I shall not cease from mental fight
> Nor shall the sword rest in my hand
> Till we have built Jerusalem
> In England's green and pleasant land.

America is no less green and pleasant, and the need to continue mental
fight is equally imperative for building Jerusalem in these United States
of America as it was in England two hundred years ago.

XV

Pioneer Adventures and the Discovery of Hidden Villa

Exploring the countryside; hikes and expeditions; purchase of Hidden Villa Ranch; building our home.

After World War I, when we were again a united family, we spent a great deal of time exploring the out-of-doors. Almost every weekend we would pile the kids into our Model T Ford and chug over the Santa Cruz Mountains to the Big Basin Redwood Park, to the Santa Cruz County beaches, or to creeks then unpolluted, unposted and free to vagrants like us. A frying pan, water bucket, tin plates and cups, blackened coffee pot and sleeping bags, ax and shovel were assembled in the camping closet ready for sorties on the spur of the moment. We were familiar with all the back roads on the San Francisco peninsula. Longer trips were in order also. On these excursions we made little fires to cook our evening meal and warm us in the darkness. It was so lovely to sleep under the stars, to wake in the virgin whiteness of the new day and watch the sunshine gradually illuminate the tops of the trees. Bacon and pancakes never tasted so good. When we left to go home, we took care to leave our camp so clean and neat that no one could tell that anyone had ever camped on that piece of ground.

Our first really primitive adventure was undertaken by just Frank and me. At that time the coast road south of Carmel only extended a short way beyond Big Sur. We drove as far as Post's, a ranch where we left our car and rented a burro. Mr. Post packed our gear on the pack saddle and we started off on foot, leading the animal. It was easy to unload the first evening, but in the morning when it came time to pack up, we found that we didn't know much about the techniques of packing. We did what we thought was a pretty good job and tied it all down securely with ropes. That afternoon, as we were making our way out of Big Canyon, we noticed that the pack was slipping over the hind quarters of the donkey. The trail at this point was a sheer foot path at the extreme edge of a cliff, only about a foot and a half wide. On one side of the trail, the bank went up abruptly above us, and on the other side we looked down into the seething white foam of the ocean breaking on the rocks a hundred feet below. What to do? I went ahead to lead the burro and pull on the front of the pack saddle while Frank at the rear tried to push the load up on the animal's hindquarters. It was touch and go with the pack veering over to the right and threatening to pull the poor beast off the precipice and us with him. When we finally reached the top we were breathless and exhausted, but what a relief it was! Later, when we were going downhill, the pack threatened to spill over the donkey's ears, but we could cope more easily with that. Before that trip ended we had become excellent packers; only the final professional secret of the "diamond hitch" still eluded us.

It was a beautiful experience to follow the trails back into the dark canyons and out again through wild, sunny pastures, or along the foggy shoreline. After two days of tramping, we arrived hot and dusty at Slade's Hot Spring's, later to become the Esalen retreat. A wicket gate led into a pasture. A notice on the fence told would-be bathers there to leave the gate open while bathing and to close it when they left. A path led across the field to the edge of the bank overlooking the ocean. Halfway down the bank, we came to a platform on which, side by side, stood two white enamel bath tubs half filled with cold water. We discovered that the technique was to unplug the pipe of boiling hot sulphur spring water and fill the tubs to the desired temperature. So we took off our sweaty garments and each of us enjoyed our tub of steamy water. It was simply wonderful to feel our tired muscles relax while we gazed over the wide expanse of the Pacific Ocean with gentle breezes ruffling our hair and sea birds flying overhead. Frank looked so funny to me, sitting there stark naked in the middle of the endless panorama of land and sea, and I am sure I looked equally comical.

On the hundred miles or so we traveled, we only met one other person. We explored a number of deserted homesteads, and in one camp ground I found an Indian mortar and pestle. Today, whenever I traverse Highway 1 between San Luis Obispo and Carmel, I try to visualize that expedition. Sometimes it took us all day to trudge from the rim of a canyon down to the crossing point of a stream shrouded by dark redwoods and climb up and out again on the other side into the sunlight where now, a bridge close to the shore takes you across in two or three minutes. I am glad that I can remember some of the secrets of that remote back country which a present-day tourist can only imagine.

Our second big trip included the children, Edith Storer, Frank's cousin from Waltham, and Pansy Redfield, our household helper. The summer before Bernard was born (I was in my sixth month of pregnancy) we visited Sequoia National Park in Southern California, driving two cars and pulling a baggage trailer. Palo Alto friends had lent us their campsite in the park where they had a tent all set up on a wooden platform with a fireplace and grill, and a regulation table and benches. Running water, a privy and trash container were nearby, so we had the comforts of home under those marvellous towering Sequoias. All kinds of birds and little animals shared our seclusion, as did occasional larger animals like deer or bear.

One night, we were awakened by a great clatter inside the tent. Examination by flashlight revealed a black bear who had upset the cooking utensils and broken into the oatmeal carton and the sugar sack and was sitting on the egg box enjoying a free meal. We routed him out that night, but we were sure he would return, and the next morning, when we were buying fresh supplies at Park Headquarters, we purchased a long rope and a sturdy box which we could hoist over a branch of a tree and leave suspended several feet about bear height. The bear's next visit was unproductive, and after that he left us alone.

Jennie, a small grey donkey, joined us on hikes. The adults would walk and the children took turns riding double. Jennie had only one bad habit. Whenever she came to a stream or even a trickle of water, she insisted on jumping over it—much to the discomfiture of her riders. We took some fairly long hikes with Jennie's help. I distinctly remember one bad night I went through after we had been on an all day climb. I was tired and I went to bed early. Around midnight I woke up with strong pains inside, and I was sure I was about to have a miscarriage. The ground seemed awfully hard and my sleeping bag very cramped. Since medical help was nonexistent, I worried all through three hundred minutes of five dark hours, squirming and twisting in my hard and narrow cocoon. Dawn showed in the paling of the sky before I finally went to sleep. When I awoke, the children had already prepared breakfast and there apparently had been nothing wrong with me that rest couldn't cure.

The road into the National Forest at that time was an old logging road, rough, circuitous, narrow and incredibly steep. It was a long pull up for the Model T Ford, which I was driving, and several stops were necessary to allow the engine to cool off. We renewed its water supply from the canvas bag we always carried hung on the back of the car. The return trip was all downhill, and although we had no engine trouble, the brakes presented a hazard. About quarter of the way down, the footbrake became completely useless. Then, as was customary, I had recourse to the reverse pedal. That held for a few more miles before it also succumbed, leaving only the low speed pedal and the hand brake. The last twenty miles was a nightmare, as we coasted speedily downhill, intermittently pulling the hand brake gently on and occasionally, when we got going too fast, running into the left bank to slow up our speed. My passengers, Edith Storer and our daughter, Elizabeth, luckily did not know anything about driving a car, so they were serenely enjoying the scenery and were quite unaware of my anxiety. What a relief it was to emerge on the valley floor and find the first garage where the brake bands could be relined.

Frank also had his adventures on that trip. He was driving our other children in a hefty old Stanley Steamer with a trailer attached. As he was going round a sharp turn, the trailer tipped over. Sleeping bags, blankets, towels, coats, shoes, pans, tin cups, everything else we had so neatly packed, tumbled out in confusion, even our little pink potty which rolled across the road. What a task to retrieve and pack all those accoutrements again!

Several years later, we made another trip to Sequoia National Forest. This time, Frank, Elizabeth and I were accompanied by Mrs. Eliot Mears and her daughter, Helen. Both girls were thirteen years old. We engaged two guides, seven horses, and five pack mules and headed for the wilderness by way of King's Canyon. Sometime in the middle of the first night I woke. It was bright moonlight. I heard a sound of breathing and raising my head I saw a bear sniffing at the bottom of Mrs. Mears' sleeping bag. It was her first night in the wilds. I hoped she would not waken, and I kept very still. Soon, not finding any provender, the bear ambled off, his dark form submerged in the shadow of the redwood trees.

We made this trip before the King's Canyon road was built. I had never been so far from civilization for so many days, nor had I ever been at the altitude of the mountains we traversed. Deadman's Canyon, Mirror Lake, and Alta Peak are some place names I remember. Best of all were the meadows, lush with alpine flowers, where we made camp, drank the crystalline water of mountain streams and looked up at the encircling granite peaks draped with snow. Just to breathe that high-altitude, tingling air brought exhilaration.

Every morning before we could start on the trail, we went through the ritual of catching the horses and mules. In spite of the hobbles put on their hind legs at night, they could travel quite a distance in search of forage. There was a bell on one of the horses, too, but it was sometimes difficult to locate where the sound of the bell came from. One morning, we could not get started on the trail until nearly noon. We had searched a long time for Romeo, the most independent of the mules. We finally found him, but after he was retrieved and fitted with his pack saddle and burden, he pulled loose from the packer—and away he went across the meadow, bucking like crazy while our possessions went flying through the air. We found sweaters and shoes, dishes and cups in the sagebrush. I discovered my hair brush obstructing the entrance to an ant's nest. After we collected all the items, they had to be repacked in the saddlebags on the reluctant Romeo. Fortunately, he was a model burden bearer the rest of the day.

It is amazing how, in the high country, the petty concerns of urban living drop away. The majesty of the mountains and the vast silences produce a different perspective. Subtly and imperceptibly the traveler is absorbed into this great immensity, no alien observer but an essential part of the whole. And one knows, for the first time perhaps, the strong, deep peace and the abiding miracle of creation of which one is a part.

While we were making our excursions into the open spaces, we always had in the back of our minds the hope of finding a location which we could purchase for a permanent home. We had picked out several places which we called "our ranches." We imagined ourselves living in any one of these spots: one was in Marin County, another on the road between Carmel Valley and Salinas, and a third near the Big Sur. On our excursions to Black Mountain and the skyline drive west of Palo Alto, we used to go past an open place on Page Mill Road from where we could look down into a seductive little green valley. We often wondered how we might get into it without attempting a descent through heavily matted, almost impassable chaparral, but we never found out until one afternoon, when we were returning home to Palo Alto by way of Los Altos. We drove by a green iron gate which was slung between tall redwood posts and surmounted by white metal flags. The flags were labeled 'Hidden Villa,' and a sign on the gate announced the sale of 1000 acres for clearance of the mortgage. Although we had no idea of ever purchasing any such sizeable acreage, we decided to investigate. We opened the gate, passed by a closely planted olive grove and continued up the lane past open pastures in which a few cows were grazing. As we rounded a corner under overhanging bay branches, it suddenly struck us both that this was the secret valley that had been enticing us for so long. And as we continued on our way, we discovered there was an old ranch house, a splendid wooden barn and a number of outbuildings. Most exciting of all, a running stream came meandering down out of the hills and through the fields to the road. What a beautiful place! What a playground for children! What opportunities for gardening, for raising animals, for country living!

We left with growing excitement, noting the address listed on the sale notice on the gate. As soon as possible, we contacted the agent and investigated cost and terms, and after checking county records for title, and doing other legal necessities, closed the sale.

FOR SALE
ONE THOUSAND ACRES
J.C. WOOD

And in a reckless mood
We push the iron gate,
It opens wide.
We find ourselves inside,
Where olive trees their silver-facing leaves,
Matted together like autumnal sheaves
Make a tight canopy above our heads.

The old ranch house and barn, Hidden Villa Ranch.

> The little lane led on across a bridge
> And up a rise and then along the edge
> Of meadow on the one hand, oak and bay
>   upon the other.
> Far up the canyon where the creek swirls brown
> An old white house with porches tumbling down
> Stands guarded by magnolia trees so tall
> That each is like a forest in itself.
>
> All of a sudden we become aware
> This is the place we looked at from above
> This the secluded valley deep ensconced
> Among beneficent and gentle hills.
>   "For sale
>   One thousand acres
>   J.C. Wood"
>
> What strange and willful fate
> Has led us through that gate?
> What secret potent pull
> Makes consciousness so full
> And every ounce of feeling
> Conclusively revealing
> That here is home?

Because the property was so much larger than we had envisioned acquiring, we first thought we could easily sell off portions and reimburse ourselves for part of the outlay. However, as we explored the property, it seemed to us so complete a land configuration that it would be almost sacrilegious to chop out pieces. Castilleja School in Palo Alto made a bid for the canyon where the hostel now stands. They wanted a weekend retreat near enough Palo Alto to bring their pupils. Discussing it one day Frank said, "Wouldn't it be a pity to have a lot of screaming girls up there?" I agreed, and we turned down the offer. Since that time many individuals and many groups have interceded with us to release a few acres, but we have resisted all inducements. Except for the exchange of some of the borderline acres to gain watershed control of the stream up to the original springs, the property has remained pretty much intact, as it was when we bought it in 1924. Much of it was valued then at $25.00 an acre. Today, people wanting to build in Los Altos Hills must pay $15,000 to $20,000 for a minimum one-acre site. In 1924, of course, we did not have any preconception of this development.Indeed, we have not been pleased with the invasion of the "urban sprawl." We purchased the land because we fell in love with it, and it has been our policy ever since to preserve and cherish its pristine beauty for other lovers of nature now and in future generations.

I have always had a sort of esoteric reaction to environments. Sometimes I feel that a certain location has absorbed an atmosphere of good will and charity, while in other places there are evil vibrations that frighten me. When I first walked up the road in Hidden Villa, I was overwhelmed by a sense of past lives lived in serenity and harmonious fulfillment in this place. Indians perhaps, Mexicans, who knows? I find it hard to describe what I felt, but I am convinced that it was a positive and valid spiritual residue. I have continued to have an abiding sense of the sacredness of this environment, especially after all of our years here, because of a sense of the accumulation of enjoyment and appreciation left behind by children and adults who constantly visit us. I often hesitate to say we own this land. How can a person own what he has not created? "The earth is the Lord's and the fulness thereof." We are only its custodians.

The acquisition of Hidden Villa Ranch was probably the most important event in our lives. It had the most momentous consequences for Frank and me, for our children and grandchildren, for our Eastern relatives and for many, many people of the wider community who have shared our hospitable environment.

From 1924 to 1929 we continued to live in Palo Alto, but our summer months and weekends were spent at the ranch. Friday afternoon was a joyous scramble to exchange school clothes for jeans and sweaters and be off to Hidden Villa. Sunday afternoon came all too soon, and it was not easy to call the family members in from their favorite pursuits and gather them together to return to Palo Alto for hot baths, clean clothes and homework. Those were busy, exciting years, as our ranch activities grew. One day, I saw an advertisement in the *Palo Alto Times*: "Horse for Sale $10.00." I went to Marsh Road in Menlo Park to see the horse, and after trying him out, bought him. His name was Tempe which was short for Temporary—as his owners had named him, expecting to buy a more fiery creature soon. We led Tempe back to the ranch with the Model T Ford. Francis sat in the back seat of the sedan and held the rope which went through the rear window. Even at low low speed, Tempe would stop occasionally, plant both feet straight out and pull back. The Ford would stall, and Tempe could catch his breath before starting again at a slow trot. Arriving at the ranch, we encountered the horse who came with the ranch. He was an old racer that someone wanted to dispose of and had left inside the gate. He lived out a comfortable old age with plenty of grass and a water supply all his own. We considered him to be permanent, so he was nicknamed 'Perm' to keep company with Tempe.

Our next four-footed resident was Snowball, who started out in Palo Alto as a pet kid, Hope's special charge (Francis had Gwendolen, a brown baby pig). Unfortunately, animals do not remain soft and cuddly for long, and Snowball soon grew to be a very large white goat with formidable horns. We took her to the ranch in the faithful Model T and told her what a lovely time she was to have there freely roaming the green wilderness. But Snowball did not appreciate the wide open spaces. She stuck close to me when I prepared to leave. I gave her the slip after leading her behind the barn, where she found some alfalfa to nibble, and then I ran to the car, jumped in and went down the road. But when I looked back, I saw Snowball galloping down the road after me, making great leaps. I thought my speed would soon discourage her and kept going. At supper that evening we had a visitor, who inquired in an Italian accent, "Does that young lady who was at Hidden Villa today own a goat?" "Well—yes," was my puzzled reply.

"She's here under my chicken house and the chickens are all upset," he said. "I can't get her to come out. Will you please come and get her?" And of course we did.

So many memories like this crowd into the drama of the children's early years. Helping reshingle the big barn, making dams in the creek, cutting trails, trapping animals, identifying flowers and birds and trees, camping out, building tree houses, installing a bag swing, learning to ride. Before long, there was a special game played out of my sight in the lower field where the kids filled pockets with green olives and rode after each other on horses. If you received a direct hit from an enemy olive you were expected to drop off your horse no matter how fast he was going.

As time passed and our house in Palo Alto was gradually surrounded by subdivision planning, the call of the ranch became more insistent. We decided to build a new home, so that we would not have to leave every Sunday afternoon, and we spent the winter in the old ranch house in order to watch the new house being built. That winter was a good discipline for all of us—almost a pioneering experience. We had no electricity and had to depend on coal oil lamps and candles. The kitchen stove was fueled by wood, and coal heated the dining room. The living room had an open fireplace, but the bedrooms were unheated. The bathroom was a makeshift addition on the back porch. Although it did have running water and a flush toilet, there was only a smelly coal oil heater to alleviate the outside chill. It was rugged living, but we found we could get along quite well without modern conveniences; in fact, necessity opened the way for new ideas and often led to ingenious contrivances. An example was our cooler—a tall rough box with shelves covered with burlap sacks and kept moist by a dripping faucet overhead. Fresh milk stayed sweet there for several days.

The planning and building of our new house was a family affair. Everybody's ideas were incorporated: a big living room for folk dancing, music and parties was imperative, several bathrooms (remembered exigencies of only one), plenty of closet space and a separate room for each child, plus a guest room. I insisted on tile on the dining room floor, and Frank wanted green tiles on the roof. We all collected stones from the creek for the fireplace. After we selected the location, I wrote what I felt about excavating the ground.

EXCAVATION

Turn, turn, good red earth,
Never pierced,
Never broken,
Inviolate hillside
Forgive us that we intrude
On your virginity—
Open your heart to us we pray
Make room for our lives
Close to your bosom.
Red earth,
Washed by the winter rains,
Baked in the summer sun
Harried by autumn winds
Fragrant from masses of bloom
That cover your slopes in the spring.
Red earth
Forgive us that we intrude
On your virginity.

The lumber for the living room ceiling came from a redwood grove near Pescadero on the coast just over the mountains west of us. The beams were rough-hewn and the ridgepole, which was forty feet long, was brought over from the coast by truck, supported by a dolly. Here is what this great rafter symbolized for me.

RIDGEPOLE

Not far from Pescadero on the coast
Along the canyon called the Butano
Where fog drifts in like hoary autumn frost
And ferns are deep, the ageless redwoods grow.
Of all earth's steady works the most steadfast,
Their roots go tapping secret springs below,
Emerge in columns that delay the last
High-showered ruddiness of sunset glow
And chant great paens as the winds sweep past;
Or sometimes catch a wreath of lace-like snow
To trim the nests of all the little host
Of birds and spiders, flies and bats who boast
A redwood tree is all the world they know.
Sun wind and rain, and moonlight drifting through
Leaf mould and fragrance of the early dew
Oh, ridge pole as you hold the roof secure
Make these immortal memories to endure
Safe in the bronzed and timeless heart of you.

After we brought in the stones we had gathered from the creek, an elderly mason who was a craftsman of the old school put them together in a massive fireplace. The hearth fire has always represented the center of family or tribal life, and our fireplace inspired these thoughts in me:

THE FIREPLACE

Fire and water,
Water and fire,
These two
Since the beginning—
Dim lost beginnings—
Man's eyes have watched.
Stream in its flowing
Whence never knowing
Life-rebestowing.
Fire and water,
Water and fire,
These two
Warming the night,
Enthralling the sight,
Of deep gazing eyes in the dark—
Hearth fire sacred,
Temple lamp holy,
Funeral pyre—
Always the fire
Sacrament, symbol.
Fire and water,
Water and fire
These two

We have taken the stones
From the heart of the creek.
They have listened long to the voice of its singing,
They have lain embraced by its cool caresses
They are worn with the ardor of endless rushing.
Here we set them to hold the fire
The life of the house—
The communal altar
Sacrament, symbol.

Fire and water,
Water and fire
Since the beginning
Always these two.

The architect with whom we worked wanted to put four small windows with leaded panes on the view side of the living room. This was before the era of "picture windows," but that was what I wanted:

CONVERSATION ABOUT THE BIG WINDOW
IN THE LIVING ROOM

"A window pane as large as what you want
Is unattractive for a nice abode.
It makes an ugly surface, blank and stiff.
Small panes are really much more a la mode."

"I'm sorry, sir, it really has to be
To chop the mountain up would be a sin!
A window should be looked at inside out
And never outside in."

(We got the big window.)

When the house was almost completed, we arranged with the Pacific Gas and Electric Company to bring electricity in from Moody Road. When their line was finished and the inside wiring was all installed, we went over in the evening and turned on the main switch. Then, one by one, we tried out the fixtures. It was exciting!

LIGHT

The house was like a shell—
Smooth, polished, crisp, with new paint,
Dormant, unresponsive, empty.
But tonight
Suddenly
A miracle happened.
It came alive.
For out of the darkness,
Through hidden arteries
By one miraculous touch,
Came Light!
Came Light!
And behold, the soul of the house entered into it
And its shell
Was no longer a shell
But an organism
Open to life
Warm, vivid and luminous
Welcoming our entry.

A portion of Hidden Villa Ranch with its new house (far right).

Now all we had to do was to move in. We did so a few days before Thanksgiving 1930. One evening not too long after the move, I was alone sitting on the stone seat on the hearth by the open fire. As I looked around the room which was lighted by the flickering light of the burning logs, it seemed to me that our dream had materialized. The room was indeed a lovely setting. Yet something was missing; it was still only a backdrop with no inherent quality—no soul. I realized that human relationships provide the only real dynamic in an environment. The subtle essence that we call atmosphere was still to be created by those living within the four walls and by the friends or strangers who would pass through. What happened here would make the difference between just a house and a home. This thought laid on me a deep responsiblity for the development of the quality that I desired. As I sat there in the semi-darkness I invoked the inspiration of the Great Spirit to sanctify my purpose. The drama was yet to be played.

XVI

Peninsula School
is Born

Making a start; moving in; the staff, the syllabus and the childrens' progress.

When our children reached school age, they were ready to go further afield. I thought they needed more contacts with children from other families, too. I visited the public kindergarten in our district, but was dismayed to find it overcrowded and lacking in constructive activity. Most of the "busy work" I saw there had already been done by my children at home. The songs were insipid, and there was very little freedom of movement in the classroom. I had been reading books by John Dewey, the American philosopher, and Pestalozzi, the Swiss educator, and I recalled the ideas of Mme. Montessori whom I had heard speak in Boston about modern education before my marriage. I learned about the Progressive School movement and the "new schools" springing up in the Eastern United States, whose basic philosophy seemed to fit in with my own ideas, and I hoped that our children could participate in the creative aspects of the new approach.

Not far from where we lived there was a girls' boarding school run by the Harker sisters. In addition to the main dormitory and classroom building there were tennis courts and spacious lawns and gardens. I went to talk to Miss Sara Harker and suggested that she might set up a primary day school on part of her property. I told her I would recruit the children if she would provide a place and a teacher. The idea seemed to appeal to her, and she took steps to design and build a new building adjacent to the already existing institution. While it was in process of construction, Miss Sara rented the downstairs rooms in Dr. Alderton's house on Channing Avenue, and at my instigation, she wrote to John Dewey asking him to recommend a teacher who had worked under his direction. He submitted a name, and the young lady was hired by correspondence without our having seen her.

Our hopes were high when the school opened for morning sessions with twelve or fifteen boys and girls in attendance whose parents I had persuaded to join in the experiment. We warmly welcomed the new teacher and left our children with her, not staying to infringe on her authority. At the end of the second week, however, we began to wonder about things because the children seemed to be so keyed up and nervous when they came home. By the third week they began to protest against going to school. I thought it was time to visit, even though I did not know exactly what I should be looking for in a "new school." I found that the class was permissive all right—wildly, devastatingly permissive, with no apparent program, no direction, just unmitigated freedom and disorder, resulting in boredom and quarreling. I wondered what to do and consulted Miss Sara.

"What do *you* think about it?" she asked.

"It's incredibly awful!" I said. "That can't be what progressive education really means. The teacher seems helpless." Miss Harker agreed.

"I'll get rid of her," she said, "tomorrow. She appears to me to be psychopathic." I volunteered to run the class with the help of one of the other mothers until another teacher could be found.

A few days later, Miss Sara called me to say that this unfortunate person, who had been so highly recommended by John Dewey, had just been released from a mental institution before coming west and was in no condition to accept any kind of employment, let alone assume responsibility for the supervision of young children. Miss Sara soon found another teacher who was far from inspiring, but at least she could maintain an orderly classroom and a planned routine. The children calmed down, and the parents sighed with relief. This was my first experience with a "child-centered school."

Although the children continued at the Harker School in the new building which had been completed and which was pleasantly commodious, I still did not feel satisfied. I encountered other parents who were disenchanted with both public and private elementary education and who also had been trying to influence teachers to broaden the curriculum to include more types of learning and to provide more individual initiative to students. We held meetings to discuss the ideas of Jean-Jacques Rousseau, John Dewey, Kirkpatrick, Horace Mann and the implications of the psychological discoveries of Sigmund Freud, C. G. Jung and Karl Adler. Frances Wickes' book, *The Inner World of Childhood*, passed from household to household and increased our awareness of basic human needs. But none of us had had the opportunity to visit any schools which were putting the new ideas into practice. We had only read about them in the magazine published by the Progressive Education Association. First-hand observation seemed imperative; accordingly, I planned a trip combining a stay with my mother in Boston with visits to some of the schools in question.

In New York, I visited the Lincoln School, and the Horace Mann, City and Country Schools, Walden, Ethical Culture and the Little Red School House. They filled me with excitement. Subsequent contacts with Francis Parker School at the University of Chicago, and various Country Day Schools organized by parents in New England and the middle West added to my sense of commitment. Some of the Country Day Schools were housed in make-shift quarters, such as an abandoned barn near St. Louis, and a greenhouse near Detroit. The Hocking family's kitchen in Cambridge, Massachusetts, was the original home of Shady Hill School. Nowadays, in educational circles the term "progressive education" has evil implications, and it is hard to recapture the fervor that inspired teachers and parents who revolted against the formal, academic, restrictive classrooms of that time and who dedicated themselves to evolving wider conceptions of learning and individual growth. The apostles of the new order could hardly talk of anything else, especially parents who, because of the brief span of childhood, were consumed with urgency to provide the desirable environment for their children before it would be too late.

When I returned home from my trip and reported to our group how others had overcome obstacles of time, place and financing, the reaction was, "Let's go!" The leaders of the group were Mrs. Anna Webster, wife of the head of Stanford's Physics Department, Mrs. Marjorie Tatlock, whose husband was in the English Department, the Cloughs and the Blackwelders, who were also connected with Stanford. We felt we needed a wider range of local interest, so we arranged for a series of lectures to be given by Marietta Johnson, whose school at Fairhope, Alabama had received nationwide publicity. She was one of the first of the progressive innovators to put in practice the new philosophy of education. Miss Lockey, principal of Castilleja School, a private school in Palo Alto, permitted the use of her auditorium. This lent us considerable prestige and insured that our publicity would be effective. Between one and two hundred people attended the series, and from them we derived several new adherents. Miss Lockey volunteered to establish an experimental class on the Castilleja campus, but mindful of our experience with the Harker School, we decided to be independent. We formed ourselves into a board to govern a non-profit corporation to be called the Peninsula School of Creative Education. We had no money, and our hunt for a suitable place took us into barns, and rundown houses, once even into an abandoned dog kennel. We were becoming pretty discouraged by the alternatives, when someone mentioned a "haunted house" in Menlo Park and suggested we take a look at it. It turned out to be a huge Victorian mansion, built by a Mr. Coleman for his bride, but never lived in because she was drowned

Photo by Morley Baer.

Peninsula School, a former "haunted house".

before its completion. The Archdiocese of San Francisco had used the building for students while the Los Altos Seminary was being built, but they had recently moved out, and the big building was again empty, except when some Stanford students used it for Hallowe'en revels. When we inquired about the property, which included ten acres of open land, we discovered that we could rent it for a hundred dollars a month! The inside of the building was still in good condition, and new plumbing had been installed. Thirteen high-ceilinged, spacious rooms offered us unlimited freedom of movement, and the fields outside were beyond our wildest dreams of space. We were able to raise enough money to insure a year's lease and about $1500 more to purchase chairs and tables, blackboards, paper, pencils and other basic supplies. Additional furniture including a piano, library books, athletic equipment and cooking utensils were donated by interested families. Our paid staff included Philip Rulon, at that time a graduate student at Stanford and later a member of the Mathematics Department at Harvard; Julia Wyckoff and Charlotte Rideout, recent graduates of San Jose State Teacher's College; Mr. Alliger, a worker in wood; and Helen Moore, a musician. The volunteers were Mrs. Webster, who took on the arts and crafts program; Mrs. Mears, who conducted the orchestra; and myself. I agreed to be office girl, secretary, receptionist, bookkeeper and janitor. A variety of other (transporation, library maintenance and public relations) duties were carried out by willing parents. Most of the new schools had started modestly with kindergarten or first grade and had built up by degrees. But, because the families interested in our project had children of all ages, we were forced to start off from the beginning with all eight elementary grades.

I shall never forget the day before we opened our doors. We all spent the day cleaning and scrubbing tables and floors, washing windows and arranging our meagre equipment. Late in the afternoon, I was down on my hands and knees working on the floor of the large entrance hall when a much bedizened lady wrapped in an expensive fur coat walked in. I looked up from my lowly position and asked, "What can I do for you?"

"Oh, nothing," she said in a haughty voice, "I just wanted to see Mrs. Duveneck. When can I find her?"

I knew if I told her who I was in my bedraggled condition, she would never come back. So I told her, "She'll be here all day tomorrow, but she will be very busy in the morning." When she returned the next afternoon, I was suitably dressed, and I don't think she recognized the cleaning woman of the day before.

On the momentous day when school actually opened, we welcomed 45 children between the ages of five and thirteen, whom we divided into five age groupings. The parents hung round the school most of the day. Everybody was jubilant and excited and anxious. During the next few weeks a few more children showed up, and before the end of the year their number was up to nearly seventy.

For all of us who were involved in the beginning—parents, teachers, children—the experience was profoundly meaningful. We felt we were pioneers inaugurating a new society and for the first time in our lives were free to translate our ideals into reality. The children, released from the restrictions of the traditional school, reveled in the opportunity to explore the many facets of learning which appealed to them. When weekends came, they were impatient for school to open again on Monday. The parents were happy because of the children's response, and teachers found themselves free to carry out long-dreamed-of experiments. They were learning along with the children, and they rejoiced to find themselves able to function as guides rather than as dictators. The cooperation of all these different elements determined to make the school succeed was almost like a religious conversion.

Weekly staff meetings, where the curriculum was developed, were enormously stimulating and the frequent parents' symposiums received almost 100% attendance.

My function at the school was somewhat ambiguous, and I was alternately receptionist, telephone girl, accountant, trouble shooter, hot lunch cook, supply clerk, first aid dispenser, transportation organizer and general handy man. I couldn't resist taking part in teaching also, and somehow wangled myself into a literature class for 12-year-old boys. I introduced them to Howard Pyle's version of King Arthur, and we established a Round Table (which was really square) in the Library. The idea of putting on a play enacting some of the legends came when each member of the group chose to impersonate his favorite knight. There were plenty of knights to go round. But an obstacle arose when our King Arthur insisted that he must have a queen. But this was a strictly masculine group; no girls were allowed! What to do about Guinevere? Then John, one of the most all-boy and non-nonsense members of the group, amazed us all by volunteering for the part. He had a clear peaches-and-cream complexion and dark eyelashes curving over his china-blue eyes. I had an old blue silk Renaissance costume which had come from Father Duveneck's studio. It fitted John to perfection, and arrayed in this silk finery, he was transformed into a ravishing beauty. He carried off his disguise with all the airs and graces of an experienced flirt. The play was a success.

Miss Crumby's class centered on an imaginary, six months' tour of Europe. They actually visited a ship in San Francisco Harbor, just before it was starting south and east via the Panama Canal. Afterwards, they imagined themselves on the boat, keeping diaries about all the stops enroute. This introduced them to geography, mathematics (for distances and costs), science (for weather) and a variety of cultural possibilities in the countries visited. These two projects stand out in my mind as salient starting points of our educational adventure.

I am not sure just how it came about, but in the second year, I found myself director of the school as well as group teacher for 7th and 8th grades—the oldest children in the school. I had never had any professional "teacher training," and considering this today, when there is so much emphasis on method and technique, I am amazed that the group was willing to accept me just on face value. I am sure I had no idea then what I was undertaking, and it was only my ignorance and my great enthusiasm for the cause that carried me through. I had had an inconsistent and hit-and-miss education, never even graduating formally from any high school, let alone college. The wide reading I had done in my childhood, the European travel and bits of schooling in my adolescence, the courses at Oxford and Radcliffe stood me in good stead. The Oriental journey after I was married also added another dimension to my concept of world culture. This varied background, although superficial, enabled me to plan a rich social science curriculum calculated to arouse curiosity and interest in the children which I could explore with them enthusiastically. Compared to the meagre content offered in most schools of that period, the Peninsula School's literary and historical program was revolutionary. Music, arts and crafts also held an important part in the over-all concept. I was not on familiar ground when it came to science and mathematics, but I had sense enough to recognize my inadequacies and refer to others who were knowledgeable in these fields. Among our parents, we had some top scientists from Stanford University who contributed valuable suggestions. Frank was a most helpful adviser and taught some classes. His feeling for work with the hands inspired the shop program where tools and wood and metal encouraged the youthful artisans to construct marvellous creations from their own original ideas. Dr. Percy Davidson, professor of education at Stanford, who had been preaching the "new school" doctrines for years, became our most devoted partner. He attended staff meetings, shared our ambitions and kept us on an even keel. He loved the school because it represented a demonstration of his educational philosophy. His wise counsel was invaluable to us amateurs.

Without the executive board of the school we would not have survived the first ten or twelve years, for when our receipts fell below our income, a number of our wealthier families with several children in school were willing to finance the deficits that continued to worry us. Initially, our fees were too low, our collection techniques too mild and our bookkeeping inefficient. I was outrageously impractical, and it was not until we added Mabel Weed to our staff as business manager that I was relieved of this responsibility and the school succeeded in operating within its budget. The teachers should also be especially remembered during these years, for they gave their services for a pittance, way below what they could have earned in a public school.

A few pages back, I described our first performance of King Arthur's Round Table. This initial project was followed by a succession of other dramas which became one of the main features of the school. I especially recall our plays about Odysseus, Aladdin, Moses and Pharoah, King

Richard and the Crusades, the History of Science (in twelve scenes), Sir Francis Drake and Siegfried. During this period, Frank was sales agent for the Stanley Steamer automobile in Northern California. He used one of these cars to enhance several of our plays. Secreting the automobile in the bushes, he built up pressure in the boiler, and when the genie of the lamp appeared to Aladdin, a jet of steam concealed his magic entrance. The dragon that Siegfried slew belched smoke through his nostrils, and when Wotan placed Brunnhilde on the rock to sleep till Siegfried came to awaken her, a pipe around the built-up platform emitted a circle of smoke lighted by red spotlights. It was stupendous.

The staff, inspired by the children, had their try at dramatics. We dramatized *Alice in Wonderland, Winnie the Pooh* and the *Wizard of Oz*. The art room and the shop were beehives of activity when stage properties, swords, helmets, costumes, crowns—not to mention dragons and ghosts—were needed.

Anna Webster, who presided over arts and crafts, was a vigorous, dynamic and infinitely resourceful person who loved kids and whose room was always aglow with color and enthusiasm. She had been greatly impressed by an exhibition of the work of Cizek's pupils. He was a Czechoslovakian teacher in Vienna who was one of the first to put brushes and paint into the hands of children and encourage them to do whatever they wanted with the material. He was well known in Europe, and his exhibition in this country caused a great excitement among art teachers and psychologists wherever it was shown. Anna followed his ideas of giving large pieces of paper and free rein to the young artists. The high white walls of our building offered marvellous backgrounds to carry out large-scale imagery. Equipped with big brushes and jars of poster paint, the youthful artists painted sweeping landscapes and brightly arrayed figures directly on the walls. As visitors walked through the hall, they were often startled by coming across a boy or a girl perched on a ladder and splashing away at a fresco twice his size with no apparent adult supervision. I shall never forget those paintings on the walls—such delicate scenes of the Santa Clara Valley when the orchards in bloom still existed, like pink mists on the hills—nor the playground areas with brightly colored children in action, nor the massive sweep of the mountains that overlooked our valley. These pictures were allowed to remain only for a year, and then they were all washed away to allow for fresh inspiration to fill the space. Only one picture in the Assembly Room was allowed to remain for many years. It was by our gifted Chinese pupil, Wah Chang. He painted a life-size portrait of a great buckskin mare with flowing black mane and tail, standing with her newborn colt in front of an old wooden barn, which everyone recognized as the Hidden Villa barn. The mare was our "Sweetheart." When this masterpiece had to be washed away, some of us had tears in our eyes.

The main staircase of the school was broad and impressive. There was

Peninsula School Days: a Greek Festival; the front cover of a booklet about the school; some "Duveneck discipline."

a long straight flight of stairs to the first landing. Mrs. Webster encouraged my son Bernard, then about ten or eleven years old, to utilize the wall along the staircase to depict an engine and a train of cars chugging up a hill. Using a big brush and black paint, he started at the bottom with the caboose and then put in the engine at the top, filling in the cars between under a great trail of black smoke. The staff was somewhat taken aback by such a bold and startling representation in such a prominent place. Some accused Anna of playing favorite to a child of the director, a youngster who was something of an *enfant terrible*, anyway, and not particularly talented in art. What was her delight when the Mexican artist, Diego Rivera, visited the school and, after viewing the hall paintings with polite interest, stopped at the stairway and threw out his arms saying, "Ah! Ah! Bueno! That is good." Anna was vindicated. One of our most talented students, Emmy-Lou Packard, studied with Rivera in Mexico after leaving our school. She is one of the best "home grown" artists in Northern California today. Like Rivera, she embodies revolutionary movements in society in her murals and decorative panels. Her color prints are especially delightful.

Rivera's visit to the school reminds me of another visitor who became outstanding in the field of music. This was Henry Cowell, who lived in Menlo Park during his childhood and adolescence. With the help of friends he built a small house where he could live and work with the piano and other instruments. He needed a bathtub and shower, but plumbing was expensive even in those days. In the school, there were a number of bathtubs that had been set up by the Catholics when they were running a boarding department. Bathtubs were of no use to a day school, so we exchanged one of these fine white enamel tubs for a concert by Henry Cowell. He was just beginning his composing, and that very early performance was given for our parents and children. He was considered an eccentric by many people in the community, who laughed at his musical innovations. But the children responded with immediate comprehension. He fascinated them by opening the lid of the grand piano and playing "The Banshee" on the strings. Indeed, he himself was like a little Irish leprechaun—slight of figure, quick-moving, and whimsical. He had translucent blue eyes and a mysterious smile, and there seemed to be something primitive but ages old in wisdom, about him. When he played *The Tides of Connemara* (an Irish rhapsody), you could hear the surf pounding as he rolled great chords up the piano till the instrument trembled with the sound he drew from it. One of our teachers who was there at that time, Sidney Robertson, later married Henry Cowell and assisted him in collecting folk music and instruments from all over the world, and this collection is now in the Library of Congress.

As the initial excitement of our first two years at Peninsula School sobered down, a number of changes were made in the physical accommodations. The Board of Trustees raised enough funds to purchase the land, and then by selling off two or three acres, acquired money enough to put up a kindergarten building, a shop and ceramics work room. In Menlo Park, the old Schwabacher estate contained a large barn no longer in use. The barn was donated to the school, and its removal which was accomplished during one summer vacation by the joint efforts of the Merrills and other family groups and staff personnel, under the leadership of Amy Burt, the indefatigable nursery school teacher, who was determined to get her charges into a spacious, detached environment away from the noise of older classes. It was wonderful to see workers of all ages putting up barn sections and shingling the roof on hot summer days. The building became known as "Amy's Temple." A fenced area outside called for improvised play equipment, most of it constructed by the older children and parents on weekends. A kiln was purchased for the clay shop by Mrs. Francis Crosby (Kitty Crosby), who offered $5.00 for every child who would swear off eating candy for two months. She was a fruit-vegetable-raw-food zealot, who arrived at school driven in a Packard by Lee, her Negro chauffeur. Impeccably dressed, she would descend into the basement to prepare wholesome lunches for the students. The children grumbled sometimes about raw spinach and some of the health foods, but it did them no harm. The example of Kitty, with her cheeriness, good humor and dedication to her beliefs, impressed them, even though they made fun of some of her idiosyncracies. I believe that unusual, odd personalities are valuable for children (or adults) to encounter. They enlarge understanding and appreciation of behavior patterns different from those inherited from one's immediate environment. Kitty Crosby also represented a striking feature of Peninsula School that encouraged fulfillment of parental aspirations while at the same time contributing to the richness and diversity of the program; and in her care, a good example of providing a means of expression to someone hampered by her wealth but anxious to serve in some humble way.

The constructive use of parent potentiality was exemplified by the development of our health program by Dorothy Lee, wife of Dr. Russell Lee, whose five children attended Peninsula. She developed our medical questionnaire for incoming students and recommended more sanitary practices in class rooms, at lunch tables, and in washrooms. She brought about better communication between the school and the family doctor when it was advisable. Another parent trained in child psychology volunteered to give tests to individual children when problems developed. In fact, the testing program throughout the school was conducted almost entirely by interested and well-qualified parents.

At an annual meeting of the parent body in April, 1934, I made a general report on the progress of the school. One of our parents connected with the Schwabacher Frey Company had it printed as a small pamphlet entitled "After Nine Years" and distributed it widely in the community. I quote from parts of this report which, as I read it now, seem to me typical of the evolution of most independent or 'free' schools, *which survive* even today, when the 'winds of freedom' blow so vociferously over the fields of youth.

CHANGES IN THE READING PROGRAM—As to changes in the curriculum itself, I seem to apprehend two distinct and marked changes. The first has to do with our attitude towards the tools of learning and the second with our choice of content.

In the beginning it was our chief desire to do differently because we felt that what most schools did was not good; therefore, if we did just the opposite, at least we'd be better, and perhaps a lot better. We were very sure that the child's spirit should be nurtured, so we gave him a chance to create beautiful pictures and to sing lovely songs and to act noble dramas and to fulfill himself in many ways. And that was all right for the children who were ten and eleven. Incidentally, our first group of children was an unusually gifted, dynamic lot; they undoubtedly did more than any of us adults to establish certain enduring standards. However, the rub came when children who started with us at six or seven were not sufficiently possessed of the mechanics of reading and writing to enable them to do the research work we believed in. So the whole plan for creative individual work fell down right there and it was necessary to try to make good the lack for those children and also to see that such a condition did not re-occur. Then ensued a long and heated and occasionally bitter fight among the members of the faculty and one or two valiant parents, to determine the age when reading should begin and how it should begin and whither it should tend. The echo of that controversy has not entirely died away. But, we do now start reading at six, in a very mild form, and we do expect that by ten or eleven they begin to do so-called individual research work in texts applicable to their age. The dispute about phonics—whether they come before or after, whether too much or too little—is still, I believe, unsolved; but the same altercations go on in state schools and in teachers' colleges, and I have an idea we shall solve the question for ourselves at least within a year or two. Because of individual attention during the beginning period, the attitude towards reading in the younger groups at the present time is uniformly excellent; there are no serious problems; with the exception of one or two children in the upper groups, all are good readers. A year or two ago the children who lacked the proper first foundations had great fear, often amounting to emotional complexes. So, as Eeyore said to Pooh, "That was not a good idea, Pooh Bear." It brought about just the opposite effect from that desired.

TEACHING MATHEMATICS*—With mathematics much the same procedure took place, but with slightly different results. It was the fathers who were always after us about arithmetic. We haven't heard so much about it lately, not since Mrs. Chapman took to asking the parents "in meeting"' some of the mental arithmetic problems she gives her groups. The answer to the queries about the teaching of this skill is the same as about reading—individual attention and complete accuracy in the beginning processes—with this important exception however; that you should not begin too young to handle numbers detached from concrete material; that each year you should review everything already learned or forgotten; that most of the material in the eighth grade arithmetic books is a waste of time. An introduction to algebra or geometry is a much better preparation for High School. Speed in combinations and tables, real understanding of fractions and decimals, and to be able to reason out problems mathematically are our objectives for arithmetic. It is interesting that the San Mateo Special Committee, Teachers' College, Columbia, and English authorities advocate these reforms also. We discovered it for ourselves, but it is cheering to find others have reached the same conclusion. I have always had the idea that mathematics might be for some children a fascinating study not only as a tool or skill, but for itself. The real understanding of the world and the universe at the present time seems to be based almost entirely on mathematics. I hope our children will possess this key which would unlock so many mysteries of earth and air and the waters that are under the earth.

CHANGES IN CONTENT—So much for the so-called fundamentals. Now as to the matter of content: when I come to think of it at first one of our great slogans was co-relation. We couldn't dare do anything unless it fitted in neatly with something else. We thought we were getting unity, but sterility was the only result. I remember in the early days when we were trying so hard to tie the program all up together, and with much effort I had finally found a literature book which fitted in with the Social Science work. I produced it with pride and one of the girls remarked, "Oh, do we have to go on and do that same old Greek stuff all day long? I'm so tired of Greek things, I want to do something else and come back to it tomorrow fresh." However, with the bunch of individualists that we were, teachers and children alike, that couldn't last long and we soon freed ourselves. But then each teacher of Social Science raced off in any old direction her children pulled her and maybe they would spend two or three months studying ducks—ducks' feathers, ducks' bills, ducks' eyes, where ducks are found, where they aren't found and why, how to cook duck and how to make duck soup, etc., etc. And another group would live like Hottentots and eat and sleep and dance Hottentot, and jabber Hottentot and spell Hottentot for weeks on end. And that was all right because the children suggested it. It was Dr. Davidson, who came so patiently to our faculty meetings week after week and questioned our practices so trenchantly, that made us realize that there is a difference in value between this subject matter and that, and since knowledge is vast and school years are numbered, the choice must always be made not only because the children will enjoy the subject matter, but because in itself it is a contribution to their understanding of the world they live in. A good teacher can pick up on any thread she pleases and have it lead, like the golden thread in the Palace of the Minotaur, straight to the heart of a central idea. It is her business to set the stage. That does not mean that one can never follow the children's lead—they constantly give us leads; but we can select unproductive ones or pick up the significant openings. Surely this is in what the art of teaching consists.

THE PLAN FOR SOCIAL SCIENCE—We have in our school developed a certain loose system for our Social Science teaching. Social Science, under Miss Crumby's deft and masterly handling, was from the beginning the pivotal point in the group life. It still remains so, and should. Social Science comprises the subjects of history, geography, litera-ture, civics, science—almost all phases of human activity. We try to teach it in a social manner by means of reports, discussion, debates, dramatics, etc., so that it may also provide a laboratory for living and working in a group. Parallels between man's life in the past and his problems in the here and now are continually drawn, and from these comparisons and analyses certain social attitudes are developed. The opportunity for ac-tivities involving student initiative, leadership, responsibility and follow-ing, within the group, provide the social experience without which "Social Science" is only an empty, meaningless term.

The first two groups concern themselves with the world immediately around them; the third group, still exploring their own environment, learns about the sun and stars and the earth's surface. At that point a certain transition is made to the historical approach quite easily—from learning about how the earth was formed to the study of man's first life upon the earth. Because of our early cultural roots in the Mediterranean civilizations and because of our later relationship to England and its place in the world today, both those cultures are studied in the fourth group. The great explorers and the opening of the new world fit in logically before or after a study of England. This we have found is a good place to acquire a knowledge of maps, locations of seas, countries, mountains, etc. Games are used to increase facility in this respect. Flexibility in the Social Science program is most important, however. Pertinent events may point the way, or a teacher who has first-hand knowledge of a country. Thus Miss Gorman gave her group an invaluable interpretation of Russia; Mrs. Shaw has carried out studies of Mexico and Central America, based on her experience.

With the older group I used to feel that a history of the world, a study of empires, a survey of the Middle Ages, etc., had great value. But in these days it seems imperative at least to suggest that society is under-going a change. I don't think it is enough to dwell in the romance of the past, nor to build up a sense of historical continuity. It seems to me in-cumbent on us teachers to give something of the immediate background of the present transition and to cultivate an open mind towards change. I feel very deeply the fact that a new attitude must be born if we are to emerge from racial and class strife. People should cultivate the spirit of sacrifice; but they also need knowledge as to the causes of all this upheaval. They require clues to find their way out to the light. And our hope for a new world rests in the new generation.

So I have greatly modified my original beliefs. They came from Marietta Johnson and it was probably true twenty-five years ago that education is not preparation for life, but living itself. Perhaps, on the other hand, all life is really preparation. Our best hours are spent in preparing something; the moments of fulfillment are not by any means the sweetest and I am sure that in this day one of the most important—I will even say the most important—duty of a school is to prepare the young for active, devoted, and enlightened citizenship. It is too late to do it when they are actually at the point of becoming citizens. Attitudes must be built up just like character, little by little. That we teachers do not know enough to do this adequately is self-evident; we can only devote ourselves to the task with humility and hope.

EDUCATION FOR CHARACTER—In regard to the development of character, we have changed our original concepts very little. We still think that it can be done effectively only through myriads of little situations handled, through actual living, as they arise. The essential idea of the child's integrity has only grown stronger with experience. I hope that our technique has improved through many trials, failures, and affirmations. The child's knowledge of your belief in his best self practically always brings him through his difficulties, provided the adult has patience enough to wait; when we seek to force progress according to our own standards of speed we spoil everything. Most of us in the beginning had a hunch that this was true; now we know it. Oddly enough I found this same idea recently expressed by Jung in his commentary on the Golden Flower. He says: "The key is this: we must be able to let things happen in the psyche. For us this becomes a real art of which few people know anything." Of course, he is speaking of the attitude towards one's own psyche, but a teacher often has to realize for the pupil more than the pupil is capable of knowing at first. Then, little by little, the reality unfolds in the consciousness of the child and then "things happen in the psyche."

RESPECT FOR THE COMMON GOOD—When we began we wanted all the potentialities that had been smothered in other schools or by crass parents, to emerge from the chrysalis and fly forth as youth triumphant. That really happened. The first few months of unfoldment was an experience forever to be treasured by those of us who witnessed. As time went on—that robber, Time, that steals the bloom from every fruit—this rampant self-expression took on the nature of conflict with one's fellows. The self-expression of Mary butted in on the self-expression of Jane, and Timothy's concern with Timothy's inventions left him a dead weight for the group to drag along in other activities. So again we were defeating our pet ideas and we had to recognize that freedom for each individual can only exist within a social order, which necessarily sets barriers to the free range of the individual. Beyond these barriers he may not trespass without destroying the common good, which is as necessary to him as to his fellows.

I often feel that the aims of a progressive school could be summed up concretely by the two ideals—individual development and social consciousness or conscience. I would depict them if I could draw, each on one side of a scale, and they should perfectly balance. That this idea has grown amongst us (and incidentally, it is the conduct or character counterpart of the intellectual preparation for citizenship), there is no question. This is apparent in the fact that there are practically no fights, either between faculty members or children; the children only rarely deface the walls with writing or cut initials—they used to do it constantly. In the beginning we hardly dared leave nicely made objects around because they would have been destroyed. A month ago we had a collection of graduates' work in the central room for over a week; the children hardly touched a thing; they have learned to respect the work of others.

There is much more that can be done along this line to deepen and intensify the sense of social responsibility and social fellowship. A beginning at least has been made and the children themselves, to a large extent, carry it on even to the point of educating the newcomer, who may not have had previous experience with this type of group solidarity.

CAN THE "PIONEER" SPIRIT BE SAVED?—The pioneer days are the best days. I'm quite sure of that. In those first two years when we were all adventuring together there was a heightened pulse to every hour of the day that was quite without parallel in most of our lives. To give everything you've got to one purpose, and to that purpose alone, insures a profound happiness; and when you do it in company with others it does really become a sort of exaltation. We had that in those early days. It couldn't last. How could it? Useless to regret because to anything that is alive growth must come—otherwise stagnation. I am glad we all had that together; I cannot regret its passing.

But although we are no longer crude, though we are less noisy, though we have manners and though our faces are even usually clean, we must ask ourselves honestly—and often—if we have lost the ability to pioneer, whether we are still sensitive to the challenge of new situations, new factors, new discoveries? Not very long ago one of the members of the staff questioned a certain song we were planning to sing for a celebration. She said: "I don't like the sentiments in that song. Do we have to have it?" Immediately two or three voices piped up in outraged tones: "But we've always sung that." So easily does tradition seize us in its deadly grip and close over the open mind! The radical of today bcomes the conservative of tomorrow and nothing is easier than to slip into the self-satisfied·complacent belief that what we have once decided to do is the pattern for all time. We can be forgiven our orderliness, but never the taming of the free spirit of inquiry, nor the loss of enthusiasm, nor the dimming of the vital spark of faith in our free ideals.

In the course of human events you see this happen to institutions again and again. Institutions of themselves are nothing without an in-forming desire, an objective for which to strive and sacrifice. Isn't it possible to foresee the advance of senility and somehow or other to infuse new life before the struture becomes empty? Perhaps it is too much to hope that we can become ever more civilized and at the same time conserve the open mind, the willingness to experiment, and the flexibility of method which characterized the early years. We can at least exemplify the latter by trying it out.

ADULT EDUCATION—Since the beginning the school has been helped in so many hundreds of ways by so many people that there is no counting the gifts. Also there has been a belief current among us that the adults concerned in the venture also had a right to progress. This sometimes entailed difficult periods of adjustment of person to job, or job to person. In ordinary schools the adjustment is all one-sided and does not present the give-and-take of actual living. Just as with the children, so with the teachers and the parents the growth of each individual is deemed important because thereby the whole corporate life is enriched. Many found themselves through their giving. I think that is really why it has survived—because a purpose to which you give of yourself means something to you.

In most schools you pay for what you get; here you pay if you can and you give anyway.

WHAT OF THE FUTURE?—A progressive school should keep pace with the times. If it is worthy of its name, should it not perhaps even lead the way in encouraing "the ancient order to give place to new?" Surely it all presents a fascinating turning-point, the more so because it typifies in miniature the larger problem of all contemporary society. While we have this challenge to meet, I do not think we need to be afraid lest our days of pioneering are ended, nor that this particular human adventure has as yet run its full course.

The above analysis was written in 1934. It is amazing to me that Peninsula School has been able to continue ever since that hope was expressed more than four decades ago. Over the intervening years, staff members, pupils and parents have come and gone, and the standards and effectiveness of curriculum have varied with the quality of the administration, but the central guiding principles have continued. What saved the institution from the start was the stipulation that ultimate authority should be vested in the people most directly concerned. The fact that it was a *cooperative* organization, owned and operated by parents whose children were *currently* enrolled, assured a continual flow of new life and deeply concerned participation in its development.

For the last seven or eight years, since 1968, Barney Young has been headmaster. The old mansion has been renovated and modernized. Around its massive solidity, a flock of new, smaller buildings have been built, with the labor of parents and children, to house individual classes or special activities. The property has taken on the aspect of a village surrounding a baronial hall. The population has increased to two hundred and fifty pupils, augmented by some forty teaching personnel, who are full-time or part-time, professional or volunteer. The same creative exuberance and loving fellowship I knew in the old days are still evident. All sorts of new and exciting projects are underway, reflecting innovative ideas in science and society. It has always been my concept of a "progressive" school that it should respond and grow with the changing times.

I was director of the school for sixteen years. Then, when my children had all graduated, I felt it time for me too, to pass out of the picture. I was asked to serve on the Board or on an Advisory Committee, but I resisted the temptation to linger on. I had seen too many schools handicapped by the "dead hand" of an original founder, and I wanted my successor to feel free to carry out his own educational objectives.

Those sixteen years at Peninsula afforded the most challenging experiences of my life. I really grew up during that period. My memory is stored with beautiful children, dedicated adults, fascinating projects and delicate human situations. I learned more than I ever taught about subject matter and the organization of material and the techniques of study. But most of all, without academic training in psychology, I developed intuitive understanding of children's needs and desires. I learned when to wait and when to stimulate, how to allay fear and insecurity, how to disarm hostility and aggressiveness, and how to overcome hesitancy and failure. Children trusted me. I loved being with them and gave them all I had. It was more difficult for me to create a similar rapport with adults.

For my family, from 1925 to 1940, the school and the ranch represented the main focus of our activity. All the children went to Peninsula School (they had to—no choice!) but they gave me wonderful cooperation. I treated them in class like any other pupils, and they never took advantage of their positions. I found their judgment in ticklish situations invaluable. They never "tattled," but if something really destructive was going on, which might prove detrimental to the school, they would tip me off. I was careful not to disclose my source of information, but I quietly heeded their advice. Frank was on the Board, too, in addition to his teaching of mathematics and shop and his invaluable help when stage properties were in demand, or when problems of maintenance became formidable.

I tried very hard not to bring school problems home, but to save weekends for other interests and activities. Sometimes the children thought I did not give them sufficient individual attention, but I am not sure about this. I have an idea that if they had been the sole recipients of my solicitude that their individualities and independence would have been smothered. As it was, in spite of the demands of the school, Frank and I were pretty much on the job. For years, until our children were through school, we never were absent from the home at the same time. Evening meals were considered an obligation to everyone to be on time and to be reasonably clean, combed and clad. "Tucking in bed" was an important nightly ritual which involved stories and songs and sometimes relaxing back rubs. We all loved music and singing, and we enjoyed gathering around the Steinway piano. The celebration of holidays and holy days tied us together with gradually evolving traditions, many of which still hold in the younger generation. I know we made many mistakes with our children, but as I see them now in adulthood, they impress me with their ability to adapt to changing circumstances and to maintain integrity and right-mindedness in both fair weather and foul. Apparently, whatever obstacles we put in their paths were not so hampering that they were unable to surmount them. I believe that as a family we are motivated by pretty much the same objectives, although our vocations vary widely. Affection between our children and grandchildren seems to be deep and abiding. There is a sense of tribal affiliation also between the "married-ins" and the cousins which gives us a feeling of support and kinship that seems often to be lacking in fractured American families.

XVII

Quest (Two)

Unitarian Church; reading and spiritual growth; poems.

In the last few chapters I have been following the course of my life from marriage through childbearing, the creation of a home and the development of a series of mature relationships, including career commitments. What was happening to my inner consciousness during this period? First of all, the release from parental domination was like opening of the door for a caged bird. Freedom to be myself, and to share with another human being the fundamental realities of life, cleared the way for the woman part of me to mature. Intense emotion of either sorrow or joy deepens the understanding. Happiness has a mellowing influence. Fortunately, Frank and I had a really good time together. Coming from a similar background, we reacted in the same way to most social contingencies: we enjoyed music and outdoor excursions; we laughed at the same jokes, and we relished meeting odd and unconventional acquaintances. Of course, we also had strong interests in widely different fields—science, engineering and mechanics for him, and the humanities for me. These specialties enriched our mutual outlook on life. We respected and learned from each other's predilections. We did not always agree on minor issues—that would have been boring—and we could argue and become irritated, but still there was a basic understanding that produced emotional security in spite of different points of view. Romain Rolland described this situation well, saying, "Mysterious is the fusion of two loving spirits. Each takes the best from the other, but only to give it back again enriched with love."

It is difficult to recall now how incredible World War I seemed to a generation born at the end of the 19th century. To come to grips with this new and fearful manifestation challenged all our preconceived notions of the world and man's depravity. I had loved and admired Germany, its music, its philosophy, its poetry and its people—especially the Bavarian peasants. I had never realized how ruthless a so-called 'civilized' people could become. I found it very hard to adjust my concepts to recognize aggression; not only to recognize the bitter fact, but also to make an individual response to what had become a national emergency. I had never realized before that private lives could actually be subject to obligations to the state. I had read about this in history and fiction, but such situations never seemed to be related to my own condition.

The separation and the hazards entailed by Frank's going off to war, my encounter with the sickness and death of his father, and all the disciplines of child care and the responsibilities for family continuance, certainly had a profound effect on my thinking and my motivation.

There is an old German saying that summarizes the function of women, "Kinder, Kuchen und Kirche"—children, cooking and church. I have described the "Kinder" of which the "Kuchen" is an obvious adjunct. What about the "Kirche"?

The church Frank and I were married in, King's Chapel in Boston, had represented the Church of England in the Massachusetts Colony before the Revolution. By our time, it had been transformed into a Unitarian church, which, oddly enough, retained the Anglican or Episcopal prayer book (with deletions regarding the Trinity and a few minor doctrinal phraseologies). The pews in the church were like little enclosures that you entered by a door and closed against uninvited worshippers. The Lyman family had been pillars of this church for several generations, and when my mother lived in Boston, she transferred her membership from the Brookline Unitarian fellowship to King's Chapel.

After Frank and I had settled in California, we thought we should seek church affiliation for our family. We learned that there was a Unitarian church in Palo Alto, one that had an interesting origin. It was the outgrowth of the spontaneous efforts of Stanford faculty and a few Palo Alto townspeople, all of whom found the Stanford Memorial Chapel too ornate for their taste and the chaplain too ritualistic for their convictions. They desired a simpler building and a less orthodox ministry. Accordingly, they purchased two lots at the corner of Cowper and Forest Streets, which were then at the edge of Palo Alto, and which were both unpaved. The church was constructed of unpainted redwood shingles and was adjoined by a good-sized meeting hall with a built-in stage. The L-shaped building was designed by a noted architect, Maybeck, who slyly planned that the sanctuary floor should be gently slanted "so that it could never be used for dancing." The space outside the auditorium was filled by a little garden with gravelled walks, a palm tree and a fountain. Sunday School was conducted there.

The first pastor was Sidney Snow, then a recent graduate from the Pacific School of Religion in Berkeley. This was his first assignment. He was young and ardent and dedicated to liberal Christianity. Naturally, the Palo Alto group proved a fertile field for his ministerial apprenticeship. He related happily to the group and they to him. After only a few years, news of his success spread to Unitarian headquarters in Boston, where the position of assistant minister at King's Chapel was open. They wanted a young man who would appeal to young people to assist the aging Reverend Howard Brown. It was a prestigious offer, but the milieu was radically different from his previous experience. The Reverend Bradley Gilman from Canton, Massachusetts, was sent to Palo Alto as a replacement. Mr. Snow did not fare well at King's Chapel, and Mr. Gilman did not respond happily to his new responsibility in California. Coming as he did from the Atlantic Coast, where the ties to England were still binding, he was a strong proponent for the entry of the United States into the allied action of World War I. But in California, he found considerable resistance to such involvement. The moving spirits in the church to which he came had been born in Germany and found themselves caught in a distressing conflict of loyalties. Several of them were religious pacifists and were deeply opposed to violence. In his sermons, Mr. Gilman stressed patriotism and upheld the church's obligation to participate in the "holy war." He condemned those who were reluctant to take up arms and those who did not contribute to war bonds. He even went so far as to denounce certain members of his congregation, reporting them to the Federal Bureau of Investigation as dangerous subversives and enemy spies (which they *never* were). Naturally, such ministerial propaganda destroyed the hitherto harmonious fellowship. At least half the members withdrew altogether and the rest carried on half-heartedly. Mr. Gilman resigned and departed from California. In his place the remaining members arranged for a part-time minister, Reverend Elmo Robinson, to fill in the gap to the best of his ability.

This was the situation when Frank and I started to attend the church. There we met some of the faithful who, in spite of the tragic upheaval, still supported it. Among these were William Carruth, poet and head of the Stanford English Department, Percy Davidson from Education, Karl Rentdorff, head of the German Department, and Cornelis Bol, a visiting Dutch scientist. Later, just before Hitler marched into Holland, Bol would return to the United States with his wife and six sons. This was a wonderful group of people, and it seemed a great privilege to belong to their fellowship and to have them as Sunday School teachers and friends. However, it became evident that Mr. Robinson could not afford to remain on the salary available to him from the small congregation. After his departure, we tried to conduct the services ourselves, using lay persons both from within and without our group to deliver Sunday sermons. I became deeply involved in this effort and found inspiration working in cooperation with such dedicated people. But there were too few of us. The recurring weekly responsibility required more thought and time than volunteers with other pressing duties were able to give. Thus the church disbanded and the property was sold. Only a few precious friendships remained. Palo Alto Unitarians had to be content with other denominations, for it was only after a lapse of about twenty years that a new set of believers revived that religious body.

Having lost the corporate channel of worship through the elimination of the church and its fellowship of attenders, I began again to search on my own for deeper assurances. My patterns of being a wife and mother and teacher were by this time pretty well established and were moving along on a relatively steady evolutionary progression. But I was not satisfied. The deeper realities seemed to elude me. I remembered the glow I had experienced in the great European cathedrals. I recalled the peace of evensong in Christ Church Cathedral in Oxford, and I thought wistfully of the little chapel of the poor in the Boston slums.

Our home was such a beehive of activity there was no place where I could be alone and undisturbed. I ventured into some of the Catholic churches in the nearby towns. The only beautiful one was the chapel of the cloistered order of nuns in Santa Clara which was set in a garden isolated from busy streets by a long driveway and a high wall. It was an exquisitely simple retreat, fragrant with incense and quietness. Sometimes there was chanting by the unseen sisters, and there were never more than two or three suppliants beside myself. But I found it too far away and too impersonal.

Then it was that I began to read the Christian mystics. St. Augustine, Thomas à Kempis, Saint Teresa and Saint Catherine of Siena, Meister Eckhardt, St. John of the Cross, Jacob Boehme, Brother Lawrence, Loyola, William Law, Pascal and any others—when I could find their books. William James' *Varieties of Religious Experience* and Evelyn Underhill's *Mysticism* clarified my thinking. These books gave me the clues I needed to understand the age-old search for the eternal values undertaken by hundreds of people in many different lands and at many different times. In attempting to describe the indescribable, religious writers use symbols and vocabularies reflecting their own backgrounds and heritage. But whatever language is used, one finds that the mystic way follows a consistent pattern. The development of the psyche is not just the haphazard wandering that it often appears to be, but a steady purposeful progression, step by step up a lonely road into the high mountains.

Having studied the records and analyzed the incentives of the great initiates, I felt more assured that my humble aspirations were on the right track. But to move from a purely intellectual concept to the actual practices of inner dedication was a different matter. I kept a diary during this period, but now I have only a very dim recollection of the struggle and travail recorded there. How much aspiration and discouragement transpired under a relatively smooth worldly exterior! I wanted desperately to retain consciousness of God not only in periods of meditation but underneath all the day's activities, a constant background of remembrance. But I kept forgetting and breaking the thread. A poem I wrote at that time seems to express the intensity of my frustration.

DE PROFUNDIS

When you are come down so low you can go no lower,
When the waters close overhead and the tide resurges
When love is a hollow farce in the toils of delusion
What happens?

Is it that strength is built from the clay of weakness?
Out of the agony cometh a child to birth?
First must the reed be stripped and dismembered
Before it can sing?

Need the vessel be utterly drained before its refillment
With living water of life from the hand of the Master?
When I am come down so low, I can go no lower,
Will it be death or redemption?

The prevalence of my inner life was reflected in my thought and planning for the school. In one of the printed brochures I wrote, "Increase of good will lays the only lasting foundation for peace between individuals or nations. It is not too soon to start building such an attitude in the kindergarten, nor too much to hope that when they graduate the children will be committed to work for its realization."

And again,

"A deeper sense of spiritual values is one of the most pressing needs of our time. The school is in a position to stimulate young people to work towards a clearer understanding of themselves and of their human relationships. It is not enough to train the intellect. Where there is no vision the people perish."

The above objectives activated my ideals for Peninsula School. My own discoveries of invisible powers filled me with a deep sense of responsibility to infuse these ideals into the basic patterns of education. It was true that I went through barren stretches when I was filled with doubt and despair and the Heavenly Visitor eluded me. But at other times the warmth and joy of communion made me feel that my soul had been given wings. When I rejoiced in this mood, I felt a sense of mission to pass on the revelation to other people—children and adults alike. Although I do not think that I proselytized directly, I am inclined to think I became very dogmatic and intolerant of those whose ideals and ideas did not measure up to my expectations.

In planning programs for the school, my main incentive was to instill ethical and religious values. The songs we sang, the poems I read at morning assembly, the celebration of holidays (holy days), the plays, all contributed to the atmosphere of excellence. When personality conflicts arose, I tried to help the youngsters find solutions in forbearance and understanding and honest cooperation. I was always amazed at their willingness to face their own limitations and to live and let live and let bygones be bygones. Children are naturally intuitive and from them I received the response that I so much desired. With adults, it was a different matter. They were not so easily enthused, they had to put up defenses, and there was scepticism, incredulity, or a lack of imagination to overcome. Sometimes there was even hostility.

The Peninsula School staff held weekly sessions in which everyone participated on equal terms (at least I thought so) both to solve the latest problems and to plan long range objectives. I considered myself just a moderator at these meetings but, unobtrusively, also a missionary. One day as I turned a corner in the hall I overheard one teacher say to another, "I don't know why she thinks she knows it all. She seems to think her taste is better than anyone else's!" I knew she was referring to me. I took the thought home with me and tried to re-estimate my dealings with the staff and with other older people. It is so easy to delude oneself into assuming that all one's motives are dedicated to the improvement of a given circumstance and that there is no desire for power lurking in the decision. I began to watch myself in action. I had to admit that I did feel that I knew better than anyone else and that I tended to override disagreement in an autocratic way. I sensed that my ideas were good, but my methods of working with others to accomplish those ends were domineering and didactic. It became clear to me that there was indeed an enormous discrepancy between my ideals of democracy and my arrogant behavior in pushing through my own theories. I thought of Robert Burns' lines from *Holy Willie's Prayer*:

"O would some pow'r the giftie gie us
To see ourselves as ithers see us"

It is probably impossible to turn the searchlight fully into all the crannies of one's own personality. Too much is hidden in the subconscious. It is possible to examine the more obvious performance in relation to other people. But that is possible only to the extent that one can hold oneself to rigorous honesty. I became aware of overriding the opinions of my co-workers by my self-assurance and by continually violating their ways of achievement. The realization of my arrogance in the manipulation of people intensified my feelings of guilt. I found myself in a deep valley of humiliation, in a barren place where no light shone through. I don't know how long this "dark night of the soul" lasted. I could not find God. His face was completely turned away from me. I don't know how to put words together to describe such distress; still less can I explain the sequel. In the writings of the mystics there is always a tense moment or crisis in purgation to which they allude in seemingly exaggerated and irrational terms. I could not claim to experience the initiation they underwent, but I was the recipient of an overpowering manifestation of something beyond belief.

It happened in the night. I was at a very low point. I was sleeping out of doors on the porch close to the hill. A light breeze rustled through the overhanging branches of a great walnut tree. I was very tired. I looked up at the stars edging over the hill in my mood of great despondency. I said to God, "It's no use. I've tried all I can. I can't do anything more." All of a sudden I seemed to be swept bodily out of my bed, carried above the trees and held poised in mid-air, surrounded by light—a light so bright that I could hardly look at it. Even when I closed my eyes I could feel it. A fragrance as of innumerable orange blossoms inundated my senses. And there was an echo of far-off music. All was ecstasy. I have no idea whether it lasted a minute or several hours. But for the rest of the night I lay in a state of peace and indescribable joy. How impossible it is to explain such a phenomenon in everyday language, but whatever it was *changed my life*. It was not a passing illusion. I never was the same again. I felt a kind of new humility which swallowed up my need to dominate. For days I was terribly happy. The whole world seemed to be illumined, the flower colors were brighter, bird songs gayer, and people were kind, friendly and loving. This exaggerated brilliance faded somewhat with time and the intense sense of communion fluctuated. Later on there were, of course, low moments amidst the high peaks, and there were failures, dry seasons and the recurring need for patience and perseverance. But I never lost the clarification of mind and spirit that was revealed to me on that night. Near the end of his life, Carl Jung was asked, "Do you believe in God?" He thought for several minutes, then replied, "I am not sure about whether or not *I believe*. But I *know*."

During the following months I wrote a series of poems in which I tried to delineate different aspects of worship. The series is based on the medieval idea of the "Book of Hours." Each hour of the day and night presents another aspect of the divine colloquy, and I called it *Circle of Hours*.

FOUR O'CLOCK

The first hour of the day
Breaks tremulous
With whispers of tiny waking birds
And the swift droning of an early bee.

Like the softly surrounding dawn
Is the peace I would send to you,
So that whatever you do,
And wherever you go,
All the day long

Your world shall be filled
With the music of dawn,
And the sweet white light of the morning.

FIVE O'CLOCK

When I awaken in the morning
The sunlight is just touching the highest treetops on the hill.
The valley is in shadow.
And my thoughts so deeply plunged in the abyss of sleep
Are edged with sentiency,
And gently as the sunlight floods the hill
Lower and lower till the canyon glows,
So through all my senses the beauty of the morning flames like a fire.
And once more the miracle of life
Is renewed to my mind
Returning to its own.

With this ritual of daybreak, oh my God,
I come consciously into Thy Presence
To worship Thee in the light on the hill,
And in the spirit-light of my awakening.

SIX O'CLOCK

At the beginning of this new day, oh God,
Before the labors of mind and body claim me
I would give myself up utterly to the wonder of Thy Holiness.
O everlasting, uncreated light
That shines throughout all the world,
I pray that in this moment
My eyes may truly be opened to Thy Radiance.
And having seen,
May I carry with me all the day long
That shining memory
To illumine the dark places of my soul
So that through Thee, the pattern of today
May have significance.

SEVEN O'CLOCK

O God, I dedicate this day to Thy service;
Grant me to live it through
In the unbroken consciousness of Thy Presence,
So that the thread that binds me to Thee
May not for one instant be broken—
Every minute, every second,
Let me feel in my heart of hearts
That close unbearable pressure of Thy Immanence—
Though it crush with its weight
Or burn me with fire,

Yet all these things will I gladly endure
Rather than be separate from that ecstasy
Which is Thy love—
I dedicate this day to Thy service
Spare me not;
Grant that I may live continually
Under the shadow of Thy abiding word.

EIGHT O'CLOCK

Dear Lord, my body is wrapt with Thee.
Eyes that see nothing, see Thee.
Empty hands are clasping the folds of Thy garment
Deaf ears ring with Thy music,
Mute lips chant of Thy glory—
Oh Lord out of nothing, in completeness of loss—
Transfusion.

NINE O'CLOCK

After rain
The dust smells sweet
In the lane—
After rain
The dry grass
Is so fragrant with the wet
Almost I forget
As I pass,
'Tis not in bloom.

If Thou but send Thy rain
Into my heart
To cleanse its stain,
Perchance beneath Thy blessed feet
That dust sweet perfume might impart
To yield Thee praise.

TEN O'CLOCK

Warm sky,
Cool shadows of earth,
I lie
Snug on the sod
Conversing with God.

He is the breeze
That blows on my back;
The trees
And their laughter
Him answering after.

The spider and bee,
What are they
But He,
Taking delight
In climbing or flight?

Atoms of ground,
Wee midgets of sound
And all this sweet seeing
All part of His being—
The frieze of His dress
Shall I, then, be less?

ELEVEN O'CLOCK

How precious all the little moments are!
Each one might be a bowl to hold a star.

Firm fashioned in the flowing of the clay
I trace the rhythms of the night and day.

Leviathans, though large, may yet remain
Not so significant as drops of rain.

I would that I could serve Him with the sense
Of each thing's cosmic permanence,

With welcoming heart that goes ahead to meet
The stranger as he passes on the street,

Nor seek to bind in greedy futile clutch—
Knowing enough is better than too much.

TWELVE O'CLOCK

Thou hast filled my heart with sweet stirrings;
In the dark places of my body
Obscured by outer walls.
The light shines.
All within is suffused
With clear white radiance
Transparent yet glowing.

This giving Thine ownself in light
O ineffable One—
Why should it come to me,
Who have done so little?
I ought to feel ashamed,
I should be downcast because of my unworthiness,
But instead

My heart sings with gladness;
I can only accept Thee
O shining Presence,
Unquestioningly, like a happy child,
For whom his father has prepared
Some unforeseen surprise.
I beseech Thee to accept
My sacrifice of joy.

ONE O'CLOCK

At the middle hour of the day, O Lord,
Even in the midst of labor
Beneath the surface on which I move and speak and act,
I embrace yet another surface—part of the whole
But detached from action—
On that plane life is really lived
In its entirety—
Despite the blur of coming and going
And the agitations of people
And the noise of their mental conflicts
And my own hope to do the job a little better this time,
Here, even here,
In the midst of activity there is peace.
In the throb of desire there is rest,
For desire has become fixed in allegiance,
Even as the earth in infinite space
Holds to its orbit and does not chase the wandering planets.
So the soul, once polarized, cannot escape,
Nor entertain one dream
Outside the magnet of reality.

TWO O'CLOCK

O beauty of the inner life,
Like a deep pool where stars are mirrored,
Why must I continually ruffle thy surface
With pebbles of irrelevancy picked
From out the dust of a too-mortal mind?

So much I love, yet seems it not enough!
Oh blessed concentration of the saints,
Inform my errant and unruly thoughts
With longing so intense that there may be
No place therein for other urgency!

THREE O'CLOCK

From whence does it come,
This fog, this mist between me and the mountain?
Is it smoke from the fires, licking with scarlet tongue

Into the depths of the canyon and up to the skyline?
Or breath of the sea, sending its cool salt touch
To sweeten the valley?

If smoke—the symbol of self
Consumed in the flame of truth.
If fog—the sign of His mercy
Laying cool fingers that heal
The deep dark scars of the fire

Fire and mist—oh Lord
For both I have need.

FOUR O'CLOCK

If through this poor body of mine
Fragments of heavenly radiance should stream
Grant that I may never take unto myself that glory
Which is Thine.

I would be as a window
Letting in the light;
And I tremble lest the glass be tarnished with pride
And the vision dimmed.

FIVE O'CLOCK

Why must I always wait upon my Lord with time?
Eternity were not long enough for me to praise Him!
Why must I ever be counting off the niggardly hours
And taking myself away from the rapture of His presence
To service of hand and mind?
Always my soul thirsteth
For the infinite depths of the soul
Where nothing is but the All,
Where fire and water are identical
And opposites meet,
And the self is not different from God.

SIX O'CLOCK

Already the sun leans to the Western hills.
Oh day, passing so soon,
Have I fulfilled my pledge of the morning?
Still there is time for a deed of pure beauty,
Something so rare and refined in its chiseled proportions
That even the angels might smile
And ask for a copy.

Oh why must the clumsy tool
Forever betray the impulse?

And the drone of the lagging string
Distort the voice of one's yearning?

Oh God, does it never come,
The one great act of completion?

SEVEN O'CLOCK

The day is passing,
Beautiful day that will never return.
All the hills are on fire.
With the glow of thy last embrace.
The wind no longer blows,
But the hush of parting is in the air—
Beautiful day that will never return.

Just now I would not think of this day's use,
Whether for good or ill,
Pleasure or pain—
But only stand on this little knoll
Watching with hazy eyes
The form of the beloved light
Fading into shadow
And listen to the last retreating echo of its footsteps,
Beautiful day that will never return.

EIGHT O'CLOCK

Dear Lord, the hours of my day
Are almost spent,
I gather them together
And, caressing each one for its tender memories,
I weave a garland for Thy altar
So I return to Thee what is Thine own.
If there be aught of good, it came from Thee.
Forgive each blundering touch, each unseeing gesture.
Teach me to do better.
Absorb me in the flood of Thy immediate Presence
That with the coming of night
I shall not be separated from the love of God
Wherein I take my rest
And find my peace.

NINE O'CLOCK

From the joys of Thy kingdom, Oh my Master,
Only my own offenses hold me back.
Thou hast thrown wide the door
But I, who have fallen in the dust,
Am stained and unclean.
I am ashamed to join the guests who walk within,

Wearing such shining raiment,
Let me kneel for a little at the threshold
To worship the feet of those who enter;
Only suffer me to listen to the music
Which Thou hast provided for their entertainment.

TEN O'CLOCK

I sometimes wonder, is it right,
To be so happy in the night?

For other folk do often weep
And sob themselves away to sleep,

While I, with adoration blest,
Float gently off to blissful rest,

And find, in slumber clearer still,
The message which my days fulfill.

What can I give to men for this
As compensation for my bliss,

Who am not worthy to receive
This gift of faith, while others grieve?

How, with an utterance so weak and thin,
Can I make manifest the truth within?

XVIII

The Growing Years

*Los Altos ranch life; childrens' growth;
refugees.*

It is hard today to recall the transcendent beauty of the Santa
Clara Valley when we first settled in our new home in 1930. With the
exception of half a dozen small towns, the valley floor looked like a huge
checker board of fertile fields producing all manner of root crops, grain
and hay. Occasionally there was an acre or two of gladioli or
chrysanthemums tended by Oriental gardeners for the wholesale
market. The cultivated area extended from the bay to the mountains. In
the springtime, as far as the eye could see there was a fairy-land of
blossoms spread like a huge flowery fan all along the foothills. The
almonds came first, then the apricots, both delicate shell pink, followed
by peaches of a slightly darker hue, and finally the snowy white pear and
prune trees, bursting out like popcorn on the rows of slim gray
branches. As you drove along, the fragrance of the blossoms and the
murmur of bees almost overwhelmed you. In March or early April
"Blossom Tours" were organized to bring city dwellers out to Saratoga
and Los Gatos to enjoy the beauty of the orchards.

Los Altos was then an unincorporated town, whose population was
about 1000, with homesites widely scattered from valley to foothills. The
"business section" consisted of two streets—Main and First Streets.
There were three stores—groceries, hardware, pharmacy—a post office
(about the size of an 8' × 10' room), laundry, a gas station, a feed store,
a depot and a railroad storage shed. Our ranch was four miles from
town. All around us were open fields or orchards. There were no fences.
We could ride our horses across property lines and no one objected. It

was a temptation, when riding through an orchard during fruit season, to reach up from your saddle and help yourself to a few fully ripe, juicy, sun-kissed apricots. So delicious! The farmers dried the fruit after sulphuring it on large wooden trays spread out in the sunshine.

We knew the names of all our neighbors and stopped to talk with them about the weather, the crops, the town gossip and county politics. We especially enjoyed "Old Man Skinner," who ran cattle on the Blanco Ranch. He called me the "Buckaroo" because I once pulled a calf out of a swamp for him. He had aleady lassoed the little creature but wasn't strong enough to drag it out. A turn of rope around the horn of my saddle and a few slow backward pulls by my horse did the trick.

Another interesting neighbor was Dr. De Niedman. He came originally from Holland but had served in the United States Navy under Farragut. Later he became an assistant to Asa Gray, the Harvard botanist. I don't know how he happened to settle on Moody Road in Los Altos, but he planted all manner of trees and shrubs on his property there. I remember the blood peach from India, which was especially rare. It had an unalluring dusky gray skin but the meat was a deep carmine color, and was rich and juicy in texture. Frank made a cutting and grafted it onto one of the old pear trees at the ranch, but it never did very well. The pistachio tree has remained in the De Niedman's yard to this day and is certainly a fitting memorial for the old man. In October it fairly blazes in vibrant red glory. People come from miles to look on it and marvel. At Christmas time Dr. De Niedman cut a native bush, usually a toyon, which he set up in the corner of his living room. He used only native live ornaments to trim it, such as wild berries, thistledown, buckeyes, prickly wild cucumbers, feathers and keys from the broad leaf maple. As a family, on Christmas eve we used to go caroling to our neighbors' homes, and Dr. De Niedman's was always a way station. He explained each of his natural decorations and told stories of his early exploits. After we sang carols, his wife served us herb tea and sesame cookies. She was a rather dour, tightly-laced lady who eyed our muddy boots with disapproval.

The property adjoining ours on Moody Road is now known as Adobe Creek Lodge, but it was originally owned by Mr. and Mrs. Roberts. She was a diminutive but redoubtable lady, who tended her garden and her dogs with tender care. She used to take sun baths on the bit of lawn in front of her house. Sometimes people, intrigued by the woodsy entrance of their driveway, would drive in to see where it led. She resented such intrusions. One day when a big, expensive car filled with opulent city dwellers drove in and stopped by the house, she rose from her siesta and marched over to them, four and a half feet of suntanned nakedness, demanding, "Will you get the hell out of here? It's private property." They were startled by the apparition and sped away. "I embarrassed them all right," she said, "They won't come back."

Colonel Austin owned a hilltop of open, grassy land. A long driveway following the contour of the slopes led up to his elaborate manor house which had portico and patios and was surrounded by beautiful gardens. Gravelled walks led past statues and fountains and ended in a grape arbor. Colonel Austin had two daughters about the ages of my girls. He rode a fine horse and the girls had spirited ponies. Some years later, the Austins moved away and the house was bought by the mayor of San Francisco for a "country seat." The house caught fire under somewhat peculiar circumstances and burned down, leaving only a few arches, concrete walks and terraces. The ruins of the house still lie there just as they fell. The grape vines, old rose bushes, iris and clematis twine themselves rampantly over the rubble, which no one has disturbed. It reminds me of one of the ruined castles in Ireland. It would be a most marvelous playground for children to enact stories of knights and ladies amidst the ruins. On stormy evenings the huge eucalyptus trees tossing in the wind seem to invoke all manner of ghosts and hobgoblins.

In recalling early neighbors, I should not forget to mention "Stinky" Hughes, who lived in a small shack on one of the back roads. He had eleven dogs whom he left shut up in his house, who barked furiously whenever anyone passed. You could see them leaping up at the window trying to get out. The man who ran the local water company told us that "Stinky" paid an average bill for only 30 gallons of water a month; he was well-named.

In the early days, the only fire protection in the community was one rather ineffectual vehicle stored near Main Street in Los Altos and manned by a brigade of volunteers who were summoned from store or office or home by the mournful wail of the town siren. A speedy response could seldom be expected of them. Whenever there was a fire in Los Altos Hills, someone would call Hidden Villa Ranch. Whoever answered the telephone rushed out and pushed frantically on the horn of the "Banana Wagon," our yellow Ford Station wagon. At once, from all directions, Hidden Villa-ites would appear on the run, load the portable water tanks, hoes and shovels and burlap sacks into the back of the car, scramble in themselves and dash off down the road, usually arriving at the scene long before the town firetruck had even started. The Hidden Villa crew put out a number of brush fires, once led some horses out of a burning barn and by its speedy arrival actually saved a small house. The "Hidden Villa Fire Fighting Service" was much appreciated by our neighbors.

After our new house was finished and we had moved in, the landscaping presented Frank with a problem much to his liking. As a child, he had been on many walks with Possie in the old garden at Waltham. Now he had the opportunity to create something akin to that around his own home. A background of bay trees already existed to enclose the lawn, but Frank had a passion for trees and he could not resist planting deodars, Monterey pines and even redwoods. Colorado blue spruce, given to us by friends moving from Palo Alto, responded to resettlement and flourished happily, providing a contrasting background for a Japanese flowering cherry and a Siberian dogwood. Three little white birches at the end of the lawn shimmered in the sun like dancing maidens. Three pools at different levels harbored white, pink and blue water lilies. Over the largest of these pools one could cross a miniature waterfall by a wooden bridge and find oneself in a bamboo forest. Every year at Christmas time we bought a living tree to use for our indoor Christmas tree. At the end of the holidays, it was planted on the hillside behind the house. As the years went by, the Christmas tree grove grew to enormous proportions. New gardeners in California do not realize how fast and luxuriantly things grow. When we first moved into the house, we could see the mountains from almost any window, but gradually the vistas were closed by the expanding arboreal density. This has been a source of disappointment to me, for I love a wide open space and the lift of a canyon reaching up to the sky. Frank, on the other hand, likes to feel enclosed and screened, and he delighted in the mammoth evergreens that limited his horizon. We have one redwood tree so high in the heavens, it almost seems that if God lives up there, it would certainly be poking into His private office. I may not appreciate all of our towering enclosures, but the garden has unexpected nooks and crannies where rare, tiny plants are tucked away to be discovered in the Springtime. Crocuses and snowdrops, lilies of the valley, cowslips, Solomon's seal, even a fringed gentian will appear as if by magic in places where you least expect to find them. More obvious by color and fragrance are daphne and lilacs, tulips in the spring, begonias in summer and red salvia to linger on until frost. Planning for next season's flowering is a recurring pastime for Frank on many a winter evening by the fire, surrounded by intriguing catalogs. Carl Purdy's wild flower list used to be a favorite. With all this garden activity, a green house, potting shed and lathe house were necessary requisites, and they were added soon after the house was finished.

Another dream of Frank's childhood, which he was able to realize, was a spacious shop with work benches, storage space and wood working machinery. When he was a little boy his main interest had been in finding out how things work, but in the Lyman household there had been practically no tools in evidence, except perhaps a screwdriver and a pair of pliers. In spite of such meager equipment, he had constructed little models of farm machinery, household appliances, and other inventions that actually worked, using pins, wire, cardboard, match sticks and glue. Whenever any renovation of our home equipment at Hidden Villa took place involving building, plumbing or electrical skills, Frank was on hand to observe the workmen. His spacious and well-stocked shop brought him enormous satisfaction, and he shared it with countless other people, including his kids and their friends. He was generous in lending his tools, provided they were returned soon after use. But woe to the individual that left a clutter in the shop—or worse, the borrower who failed to return the special tool entrusted to him on a temporary basis! Our boys, and girls, too, for that matter, learned a tremendous lot by watching their father repair anything that went wrong as well as create all manner of delightful and useful objects. I remember especially the boats and steam engines, the tiny doll houses and tea sets, and watering troughs, gates and trellises for the ranch. Frank was carpenter, plumber, blacksmith, electrician and mechanic. He could fix anything. The availability of this well-equipped workshop and the skills learned from their father gave our boys and girls a fundamental knowledge of what to do and how to do it when faced with practical problems of all kinds. No "do-it-yourself" kits were needed, and no amateur messing round was acceptable. It proved a most valuable asset in their lives.

Frank had been teaching in the Peninsula School shop class once or twice a week, and had encouraged the building of miscellaneous boats. Our son Francis of course knew something about steam because of his father's interests, and his project was a four foot steam boat. We had a song we sang at school, "A Mighty Ship was the Gundremar," which was the name of Francis' ship. It had a Sterno canned heat boiler. When we launched it on the duck pond at the ranch, everybody from a neighboring grandfather to a two-month-old baby gathered in breathless anticipation. Francis applied a match and shoved the vessel away from shore. All at once the thing began to sputter and choke and blow steam off from the fly-wheel; finally, the diminutive tin can propeller began to spin, the exhaust pipe to spit, and off went the good ship Gundremar, chugging across the pond to the consternation of the duck population and the jubilant shouts of the onlooking humans. Great moments in little lives!

Horses were of importance to us all in the growing years. I taught Frank to ride and each of the children had a horse of his own. We had built trails up into the hills around Hidden Villa. The roads of Los Altos were still unpaved, and few fences offered any impediment to cross-country exploration. There were no "Keep Out" signs. As our ranch foreman during that epoch we had the services of Ben Piggott, one of the most "unforgettable characters" I have ever known. He had grown up in the San Joaquin Valley with very little formal education, but with a great deal of ranching experience and the equivalent of a master's degree in the care and training of horses. He combined the services of caretaker, riding instructor, medicine man and tutor. He was infinitely patient with kids and colts. He was a natural psychologist but also a good disciplinarian who wouldn't stand for any nonsense. His language was often colorful, but when the girls were around he was most circumspect in its use. He taught my children much horse-sense, but in addition, many lessons of honesty, persistence, hard work and self-control. He never let anyone abuse a horse or take unnecessary risks. He knew all sorts of tricks to overcome bad habits in horses, and

Duvenecks and friends

he used many homely remedies such as turpentine dressings, flax seed, and manure poultices. He would not tolerate sloppiness in saddling nor carelessness with equipment. Under his direction the kids all became good riders. In San Jose every June some organization put on the *Fiesta de las Rosas* to which all the horsemen in the county were urged to ride. The parade assembled on the Alameda in Santa Clara and progressed from there into San Jose. That was before the trees that grew in the middle of the avenue were cut down to allow for four lanes of traffic. I think we all went in costume, but now I only remember Elizabeth riding side saddle, wearing a Spanish dress, her hair fastened with a high comb and draped with a black lace mantilla. All the horses in the cavalcade were decorated with flowers, and there was music from the High School band.

On another occasion, in the early 1930's, Ben Piggott and Francis took two horses to the Salinas Rodeo. This rodeo is the largest and most exciting one in Northern California. It lasts four days. Francis had his special horse, Charlie, and Piggott rode our black and white pinto stallion, Apache. Each day they rode in the procession of riders a mile long that filed through the town and out to the fairgrounds where a big crowd assembled to watch the day's events. Of course the rest of us were all there to see our horses and boys perform. It was an amazing sight. A magnificent horse led the procession, and its rider, dressed in an embroidered Mexican cowboy costume, carried the American flag. He was followed by several hundred riders. There were old men in seamy overalls, young buckaroos in brilliantly colored silk shirts, girls in fringed leather outfits, children of all ages. Their mounts ran the whole gamut of horseflesh: ponies, plow horses, race horses, stallions, strawberry roans, Arabians, pintos, Palominoes, half broken colts, even a mule and a donkey or two. It was most exciting and colorful. Francis rode in the Boy's Race with about twenty contestants. He made a slow start, and was shoved out of a favorable position by a more aggressive youngster. He did not win a ribbon, but neither did he come in last, and I was pleased that he had the courage to compete. Ben Piggott and Apache showed themselves off very nicely in the stallion class. The winner of the trophy was a stunning Arabian, laden with silver mounted equipment and ridden by an equally showy Mexican *vaquero*. Against such magnificence it was hard to compete, but Ben Piggott maintained that Apache had received the most applause from the audience. Apache was indeed a charming little animal, full of high spirits, who did tricks at Piggott's bidding and showed such perfect manners that everyone wanted to pet him. They offered him apples and popcorn, which he crunched up, and caramel candy, which he spat out.

Piggott was an inveterate horse trader. I, being my father's daughter, enjoyed this form of gambling. Piggott and I had lots of fun going to auctions and figuring out what was wrong with the horses up for sale; and once in a while striking a bargain among the duds and mavericks. I remember trading one dangerous but handsome animal for three non-descript new ones. One of the three turned out to be a thoroughly reliable and useful mare, although her gaits fluctuated between single foot, pacing and square trot. Piggott liked to name these new acquisitions. They often followed sequences such as Mope, Dope, Lope, or Lop, Slop, Drop, etc. His most impressive name was *Dirigible*, which was inspired by a Zeppelin-type balloon that the army sheltered in the Moffett Field hangar in Mt. View and which eventually exploded in mid-air.

We all loved and trusted this man completely who taught the children so much in the matter of responsibility, patience and self-control, as well as their skills with animals. Ben and his wife and three children, the last one of whom was born on the ranch, were like members of our own family. His children went to Peninsula School with ours and partook of all the ranch activities. When the war came along, Harold, the oldest, was drafted and sent to the Pacific area. He was taken prisoner and placed in a prison camp, in the Philippines where he was when the armistice came. He was among a group of released prisoners who were on the way to a gathering in the Philippines to celebrate the Armistice, when an American truck rammed into them. Several GI's were killed, among them, Harold Piggott. This sad news came just a day or two after the Piggott family had heard from the Red Cross that Harold was alive and would be returning home shortly. His father, Ben, who had been suffering from acute arthritis, took this blow very much to heart. The combination of arthritic pain and grief from the loss of his son caused him to start drinking heavily. Early one morning I heard a shot. I wondered if someone had been trying to get the raccoon that upset the garbage cans, but about an hour later, the telephone rang and Mrs. Piggott screamed, "Come quick, Mrs. Duveneck, Ben's shot himself!" I got dressed and hurried over to find him huddled on the back steps of the ranch house. It was a great shock. It was the first time I had seen anyone dead. I called the coroner and the undertaker and Mrs. Piggott's sister, and then I had the hard task of telling his daughter, Jane, who was working as a nurse's apprentice at the Children's Health Council in Palo Alto. Such a brave little girl, and so understanding of her father's experiences. Mrs. Piggott lived on for many years and the two surviving children were married. They still come to visit us frequently. Jane especially considers herself a child of the ranch.

As a horse-related interest, our kids—especially Francis—became interested in old wagons. We had a couple of horses broken to harness and, in the countryside round about, many an ancient surrey or discarded buggy, having been superseded by the automobile, could be removed for the asking. With the help of string and baling wire, the harness was pieced together, the spokes tightened in the wheels and the equipage could be on the road again. One such ancient conveyance collapsed like the One Hoss Shay, while it was being driven up on

Skinner Lane now called Moody Court. It just disintegrated, scattering its component parts all over the lane. The boys salvaged the wheels and a few other usable pieces and just kicked the remainder into the brush. Later, a "covered wagon" was constructed from an old farm truck, with the help of curved saplings and pieces of discarded canvas. A journey across the plains was enacted by suitably dressed pioneers. They encountered many privations enroute, including hostile Indians who appeared out of the woods on galloping horses. (I became adept at making head bands of turkey feathers.) Little by little, these salvaged, improvised vehicles petered out until there was only one old frame held up by four rickety wheels. One day this contraption, with tremendous efforts on the part of all hands, was hauled up to the top of the knoll, a very steep little hill on the ranch. The crew of a half-dozen youngsters piled on to the frame and started it down over the edge of the incline. Gathering momentum, they went tearing down the steep hill. As the strange vehicle rushed on, however, the spokes of the wheels started flying out in all directions; one whole wheel spun off separately and rolled on down ahead and the whole affair ended in a great debacle of spokes and hubs and rims and children and pieces of iron. Our kids survived unscathed, but one of their visiting friends suffered a minor concussion. If you know where to look, you can still see the rim of one of the old wheels in the brush at Hidden Villa.

Other creative pastimes devised by our gang consisted of a high bag swing which you jumped onto from the roof of a storage shed and swung out over the horse corral. Then there was a steep slide down the mountain which was negotiated by drawing a burlap sack up over your legs and backside before sitting down to go shooting downhill between rocks and clumps of chaparral. Tree houses involved many weeks of construction, dams in the creek and trails to isolated hideouts were always being developed.

To keep my juvenile activists from overdoing, I instituted a post-luncheon siesta. They seldom slept, but they lay under the big walnut tree on folding cots for about an hour while I read aloud to them. *Treasure Island, A Tale of Two Cities, Gulliver's Travels, Robin Hood,* to mention some of the books. I think, perhaps, the most memorable was the *Three Mulla Mulgars* by Walter de la Mare, a unique and enthralling romance of three little monkeys traveling in search of the wonderstone. This book antedated *The Hobbitt* and the *Lord of the Ring* series. I don't know why it never gained popularity. We all loved it and could hardly wait for the next chapter's adventure.

For me these sessions of sharing beautiful literature with young people are among the happiest memories of being a parent. The books I chose were a little bit ahead of what they could read to themselves, but were not beyond their understanding. We did not have a radio and TV was, of course, not yet developed. Reading and home-made music are family experiences in which the differences in age are absorbed by common interest. Great books can have a profound influence on a person's conception of life and his ability to analyze human relationships. They stimulate imagination and provide hero images not often encountered in every day living. They constitute a precious heritage from the past from which the culture of the present derives its significance.

As the children got older, the inevitable shift of their interest from horse power to motor power took place. The wrecks of Model T Ford cars could be purchased for a few dollars. Spare parts could be picked out of the dumps at no cost but for the time and labor of obtaining them. Francis was especially preoccupied by these old cars, and the first of the species he revitalized was the *"Rambling Rosie"*, a Model T chasis with a couple of improvised seats fastened to it with baling wire. Soon there was a Rambling Rosie Club. The Rambling Rosie Club membership depended on the completion of a trip across the volcanic terrain of one of our lower fields, where grapes had at one time flourished. The field was still characterized by ridges that provided an incredibly bumpy corduroy transit. If you could negotiate the journey without getting seasick or falling off the precarious perch, you were admitted to the fellowship and entitled to wear the special, colorful RR badges which were made by Elizabeth. I managed to qualify but our babysitter only got half way and was sick for two days afterwards. The kids decided she should be granted membership, even though she had failed the test.

I have forgotten all the subsequent jalopies except two. One was Bernard's refuge—a house trailer utilizing an old tool shed and mounted on a chassis, equipped inside with cot, table, chair and second-hand radio. When he could no longer stand the sight and sound of his family, he could run his ambulatory bedroom off to Silver Creek, his hideout in the lower field. This provided a respite for him—and for the rest of us.

The other contrivance that I recall was Francis' creation. He had worked for weeks at Peninsula School shop fashioning a five-foot propeller out of wood. It was a beautiful job, sanded and polished like velvet to the touch. He brought this home and fastened it somehow to the front of one of his old cars. The trouble was that when he started the car running down the driveway, the wind from the fast-turning propeller picked up all the gravel and dust of the road and hurled it back into Francis' face.

When the children were growing up I always made a practice of celebrating important days of the year—Valentine's Day, Easter, Washington's Birthday, St. Patrick's Day, the Fourth of July—as well as all the family birthdays. They provided welcome breaks in the routine of everyday life. Most important of all was Christmas, a time of loving and sharing and forgetting the irritations and resentments inevitably caused by living closely together with several other dynamic characters. In one of my "Christmas Chronicles" I wrote a description which recalls some of these occasions.

About a week before Christmas or when vacation begins, we go and get a living tree from one of the nurseries. We used to go way up in the woods and cut a Douglas Fir, but I always felt so badly when it withered and had to be thrown out and burned, that we decided not to destroy but to plant. So now at Twelfth Night we have a tree-planting ceremony after dismantling the living branches of their balls and trinkets. Last year we had a Deodar cedar which is prospering beautifully on a side hill near the house. Someday I hope to have a Christmas tree grove.

The children trim the Christmas tree. At the top there always hangs a little wax cherub which came from Germany long years ago. He is always in the same high place. One of his wings is slightly shirred off because one year he was too near a light and the heat melted the edges of his wax feathers. Francis has now taken his father's place as electrician and straightens out the electric bulbs and the switches which seem to have to be done over every year.

About the same time we take out the creche which has been packed away all year. Edith Storer sent us the figures years ago and Frank made a stable from a wooden packing box. Some of the figures have to be renewed occasionally but the three kings and Joseph and the shepherds and the ox and the donkey and the sheep have survived intact. Bernard has the responsibility of setting these up on a table and we have little red candles on either side. The Madonna from Nuremburg is scrubbed and repainted if she happens to need it.

We make an expedition into the woods and bring down big bundles of bay and wild cherry and toyon and Frank makes wire hoops and we have spools of soft copper wire with which to wind the greens into the hoops to make wreaths. The wild cherry has a shiny dark green leaf with a prickly edge. It looks like holly only it is smaller. The bay is shiny too and very fragrant. The toyon is sometimes called California holly. The berries are in bunches and very vivid red. I usually add tangerines and crabapples which I paint with orange shellac. It makes the wreaths look like Luca della Robbia's. I finish them with a big red bow and deliver them a few days before Christmas to certain families who have come to expect them as holiday decorations for the mantelpiece or the front door. One year the Webster's wreath served as Christmas feast for their goat which came up on the porch and enjoyed bay and crabapples and berries and all. Contrary to the legends told of goats, however, it did not consume the wire but considerately left that hanging in circular nudity.

After the wreaths are made we decorate the house and then we sweep up!

On Christmas eve we light candles in the windows true to the good old Beacon Hill custom and about dusk we sally forth to sing to a few old people in Los Altos. The distances are rather great so last year we went by automobile although the year before we were on horseback and it was without exception the darkest night of the winter. Last year two groups of carollers came to us all the way from Palo Alto and we served chocolate and cookies steadily from 8:30 to 10:30. The children still hang up their stockings ceremoniously on the mantel-piece and after they go to bed I usually go to San Francisco for Midnight Mass at St. Francis Church which has wonderful music and is quite a beautiful old place.

Christmas morning I make pancakes and then stockings are opened by the hearth. Soon afterwards we tidy up the mess and start setting tables for dinner. We try to carry on Mama's custom of gathering in people whose families are gone or scattered and ask them to share our Christmas cheer. Last year twenty-five of us sat down to Hidden Villa goose and chicken pie. The children wait on table and it is jolly. Frank always makes a toast to all those whom we love and who are not with us and then my mind always flies quickly to all the dear far-away people. It sort of goes the rounds wishing each one joy and peace.

After dinner—coffee, of course, and cigarettes and usually we have some little present for each guest. Sometimes we talk and sometimes we play a game and then usually we sing carols in which everybody who wants to joins. Last year Mrs. Lucas read the Saga of the Building of the House which I sent you all. This year we're going to have some music—a quintette. Elizabeth and Bernard playing the violin, Hope cello, Francis flute and myself at the piano. This is the first time that Bernard has been able to get in on the "chamber music."

When the guests depart, anybody who wants any supper goes and rustles it for himself. I usually send them all to bed pretty early and then the old folks—Frank and I—open our bundles in front of the fire and talk over the day and other days and sometimes I go to sleep in the middle of our conversation, and after awhile we put out the Christmas tree lights and the candles and push the logs back in the fireplace and toddle up to bed, thankful for all the blessings that the day has held.

And that's Christmas!

I have already said a good deal about the influences that Ben Piggott exerted on our lives. But he was not the only person to be associated with us intimately. Our children never knew any of their grandparents, but Frank's Uncle Charlie proved to be a good substitute. He was a younger, half-brother of Frank Duveneck, Senior, and he was born when the artist was already studying in Munich. Aging Uncle Charlie was hard hit by the Depression in the early 1930's; his health had deteriorated and he felt much alone. We invited him to visit us to escape the rigors of a Middle West winter. He became so enamoured of California that we urged him to join our family. He grew to be greatly attached to the children, especially Hope, and they all became great pals. He enjoyed growing flowers. We let him take over the gardens round the house. The lawns, paths and hedges were never so well-manicured, before or since. He had never had much contact with children before coming to us and he tended to be over-protective. Once, when the old barn was being reshingled, the youngsters were all up on the roof watching the workmen. Uncle Charlie came hurrying to Frank to tell him, "Those kids are all over that roof. I'm afraid they'll fall off." "Oh, well," Frank replied, "if one gets killed there are three more." Uncle Charlie had always been a Republican and a very conservative one. Some of our friends and our activities must have seemed very questionable to him, but he never aroused any controversy. He went his own way quietly and let us be as subversive as we chose. He lived with us until he became somewhat senile. Then, whenever the young people became a bit boisterous, he would pound on the floor with his cane and I found that I could not cope with the divers needs of both old and young. It was a hard decision, but we found a suitable retirement home and moved him there.

Our household helper for a number of years was Felix Ringor, a young Filipino who came to the United States to go to high school. He had stayed on, earning money by housework, with the hope of returning home one day to retire as a plutocrat. He was always pleasant and agreeable, and he was a good cook. His specialties were Brownies which he used to hide until mealtime, and a dessert called Bavarian Cream. The Filipinos apparently have no sound for v, and he always called this dish "Barbarian Cream," much to the delight of Bernard, who used to ask him what it was just for the sake of hearing his pronunciation. When the war came along, Felix enlisted in the Filipino regiment (thereby earning his citizenship), and went off to Fort Ord for training. He was careful not to reveal that he knew anything about cooking. He got the job of taking care of the guns and ammunition. He could not stand long hikes in the hot sun, and he was such a gentle soul that I don't think he could ever have brought himself to shoot anybody. When the war was over he returned to us for a few months, and we insisted that he should eat his meals with us instead of by himself in the kitchen. He made a trip back to Manila and found himself a wife whom he brought home to us. She was terribly shy and almost passed out at the idea of joining us for meals. It was a real agony for her at first, but gradually she got accustomed to us. Later she and Felix had a daughter who was born about the same time as our granddaughter, Weegee Dana. They used to play on the lawn, in and around a wading pool, the fat, dark-skinned little Linda and Weegee, who was slim with almost white blonde hair. It was fun to watch them. Later Linda had a brother. When a third child was anticipated, we decided that the two-room apartment off our kitchen was too small and that pretty soon we would find ourselves living with the Ringor family instead of they with us. So we helped them arrange to purchase some land in Mt. View, using his veteran's benefits. Felix worked for many years for the City of Palo Alto maintenance department. All three of his children went to college, and his family was very much respected in the community.

Early in the period while Hitler was coming to power in Germany, we provided a foster home for Peter Neumeyer, the seven-year-old son of Dr. Fred Neumeyer, who became head of the Art Department at Mills College. Dr. Neumeyer was a noted art historian in Munich, and he and his wife had come to California expecting to stay only long enough to give a summer course on History of Art. Peter had been left in Germany to study with his grandmother, but when the situation of the Jews worsened, the Neumeyers decided not to return to Europe. Luckily for them, a secretary at the U.S. Consulate had slipped an immigration quota number in with their temporary passport visas. A grandmother brought Peter on the long journey across sea and land. Peter spoke no English, and because his parents were still living in temporary quarters in Oakland, they felt an American home experience for Peter would be a god-send for them, as well as for him. Since I could speak German, I was able to help him get adjusted to his new environment. What a sweet little personality he was, dressed in his Bavarian boy's costume, with his formal manners and his eager responsiveness and yearning for affection. He had been brought up a Catholic and at bedtime he said his prayers in Latin and German. He had been to school just before the time when Jewish children were banned, hence he was thoroughly indoctrinated with Nazi ideology. He made himself a swastika flag and set it up on our lawn, inviting the eight year old Piggott boy to learn the manual of arms. He told me that Adolph Hitler was the greatest man since Jesus Christ. I did not try to disillusion him. Soon, with the help of our horses, his hero worship was transferred to cowboys and Indians. At Peninsula School, he learned English and also found out how to play games instead of how to march. I remember vividly the day when the portrait of Hitler that he had tacked up on his closet door disappeared, and a poster with Franklin Roosevelt's photograph on it took its place. After nearly a year, he moved in with his parents in their new home. By that time, he was well on his way to being thoroughly Americanized. I think it was a bit disconcerting for them as well as for him, when he had to revert to a European atmosphere.

After Peter left, we adopted another refugee, Walter, an older boy who went to high school with Bernard. It did not take him any time at all to adapt himself to his new country. Bernard and his friend, Nye, used to teach Walter words and phrases slightly off-color and watch their effect on uninitiated acquaintances. But Walter was soon on to their tricks, and after six or seven months, except for his slight accent, you would not suspect him of being foreign-born. He became a warm and faithful friend, and today he and his wife, Marie, live nearby. He and the Peter Neumeyers were the first members of our so-called "extended family", and we have had precious association with them and their families over the years.

Two of my nieces from New England stayed with us and worked as teaching apprentices at Peninsula School. It so happened that when Happy stayed with us, we also had a graduate student from Stanford living here. There was nothing premeditated about this, but the power of propinquity prevailed. Happy's marriage to Stanley was the first of a score of weddings to take place on our lawn. Although Frank and I had moved a long way from New England, family ties continued to hold, only now our home represented the center for "western expansion."

As I look back to the period of the growing years, it seems to me that it was one of the happiest periods. The unfolding of the personalities of

Hope, Elizabeth, Francis and Bernard by the family fireplace; Josephine and Frank Duveneck; Bernard's retreat.

our four children was a fascinating drama. They continually surprised us by their reactions to the world around them and to the people they met. They seemed to progress so fast from babyhood to adult personalities. As their minds developed, new incentives emerged and were expressed in creative ways. Sometimes the genetic pattern was obvious, but then again there seemed to be no clear connection with anything that had gone before. The pre-adolescent stage is such a delightful time! As a teacher, I preferred it to all other ages, and as a parent I found it most comfortable. At this stage, the young are in possession of their intellectual faculties, they have a great curiosity, and yet they are still naive enough to welcome adult guidance. This is the time when you can have fun together with a minimum of discord. It does not last long. The closeness and intimacy of the family group must give way to wider relationships and to a reassessment of inherited values. The search for personal identity usually means tough going for both generations.

"I love you"
Said a great mother.
I love you for what you are
Knowing so well what you are
And I love you more yet, child,
Deeper yet than ever, child
For what you are going to be
Knowing so well you are going far
Knowing your great works are ahead
Ahead and beyond
Yonder and far over yet.
—Carl Sandburg

XIX

Europe and the Near East, 1935

Egypt, Italy, the Mediterranean, Palestine and Turkey; Germany at the start of the Nazi era; travels abroad with our children.

In 1935 Frank and I were moved to undertake a European journey. We had not been there since 1914. We longed to revisit the places we had enjoyed in previous years, and we wanted to introduce our children to the sights and scenes of the Old World. I had long desired to see the Near East, especially Greece and the country then known as Palestine or the Holy Land. We took Hope and Bernard out of school and Elizabeth out of college, but Francis was in his last term of high school, preparing for college entrance requirements, and we thought we should not interfere in this part of his career. I think we made a mistake not to take him along even though he made up for this omission in part by a bicycle trip through Central Europe with Elizabeth in 1937. Travel is the most penetrating method of education and excels the most inspired classroom.

My "Christmas Chronicle" of that year, which was written shortly before World War II, describes conditions prevailing in the countries we visited which were to be drastically altered so soon afterwards:

"February 7, 1935—Here we are, all five of us, actually and unquestionably and unequivocally on the boat and on the way. We arrived in New York just as we should on a freezing cold morning and Elizabeth met us and took us down a street or two to breakfast and we just gasped for the cold.

An old friend came to our assistance with her banana wagon like the one I drove East three summers ago, only more modern—and into it we all got, we with our bags and about a million books and boxes, and then Elizabeth and Hope perched on the bags—and we went roaring over to

Hoboken. It was so nice and familiar and everybody simply shrieked with laughter when we drew up at the dock surrounded by imposing limousines. We kept pouring out of the banana wagon. Elizabeth with her viola and Bernard with his cowboy hat which he insisted on wearing, adding color to the picture.

March 15, 1935—We have just had five most interesting days in Egypt. It seemed so wonderful to be visiting the places which we have studied about and which we never expected to see any more than you might expect to see the country of Ali Baba or Aladdin.

I found the Pyramids were a good deal the way I had always imagined them, but the Sphinx was quite different. I had her in a somewhat different location in relation to the Pyramids and at first she seemed a lot smaller. As I kept looking at her, however, she seemed to be growing and before long I felt overwhelmed by her size and by the mystery of her wonderful face, battered and scarred and worn with wisdom. I can't believe the eyes do not really see—much more than any of the rest of us can.

The children climbed up to the King's Chamber, which is in the middle of King Cheop's pyramid half way up. I decided to be content with the Queen's Chamber that's only a quarter of the way. In order to get there you have to go along a dark low narrow passage; we looked like a lot of dwarfs—all hunched over, scrambling along in the half darkness. It's frightfully steep, too, and rungs were put on the incline instead of steps. And it was hot and close and strange smelling.

Cairo has a king now and has had since 1922 when the English declared it to be an independent country. We notice, however, when we went up to the citadel that it was guarded by Scotch soldiers—kilts, sporans and all, so I judge the independence is still "protected." The poverty and dirt everywhere is quite unbelievable. People who work in the factories are paid about thirty cents a day, and children who are apprenticed to craftsmen earn about five cents a day. A graduate of the University starting in a profession or in some business, gets $35.00 a month and considers himself fortunate.

It's a very uncomfortable country to travel in for everybody is begging for "baksheesh" or trying to sell you something you don't want or trying to black your shoes or trying to be your guide when you don't want a guide, or to make you get onto a donkey or into a carriage or into a wheezy auto or on a camel when you prefer to walk. You have to fight your way through and it's very unpleasant, especially as you are all the time conscious of how desperately they need the money.

Everywhere the Nile runs and where the government has put in irrigation the land is wonderfully fertile—clover, beans, cotton, artichokes, cucumbers, watermelon—just as luxurious as California. But the most primitive methods of agriculture still prevail. The old wooden plow, just a tree trunk sharpened, the old wheel turned by a donkey, camel or buffalo which lifts the water from one level to another (when they water the road they do it by man power, dipping the water out of the canal in a bucket and sloshing it onto the road). You look at a landscape in Egypt with all these people at work and it's just exactly like the old bas-reliefs on the tombs which show how the ancient Egyptians worked. I might add that the sacred Ibis, a sort of crane, and geese are quite prevalent, and hawks go circling all day, even over Cairo. It's easy to see how the hawk became identified with the Sun God.

The Egyptian twilight is such a tender interlude. It has something so gentle and caressing about it—first a golden light over the tawny desert, then a fading into cool mauve and the sky fades out and the sun fades out. The sky is almost greenish and then the night gets gradually deeper and deeper blue. I wish I could go with a caravan into the desert to see the sun rise and the sun set and starlight come and go for several times.

May 4, 1935—Florence Italy—We are living in a delightful pension just outside the Porto Romano. It has a lovely garden, a tennis court, a large fuzzy white dog, and other young people. Bernard takes the dog to walk every afternoon. Elizabeth and Hope, by enrolling for a course in music at the University (cost $5), each get a ticket entitling them to enter free into any of the museums and galleries. Also they receive a reduction on rail and bus fares (in addition to the 50% allowed to foreigners). Elizabeth goes to the galleries every morning and usually paints in the afternoons. Frank is happy to be on his native heath. He went out to the old villa where he used to live and the Marchese who lives there now invited us all to tea. The view is lovely, overlooking the Arno and the country round Florence, with the orchards of olives on the slope leading up to it. We saw the cypress tree that was planted when "Frankie" was born. It is a pretty good sized tree.

We also visited the English cemetery where Frank's mother is buried. The bronze figure made by Mr. Duveneck is there and it is very beautiful and peaceful and serene. Frank had a little work done on the masonry and one afternoon Bernard and I went out and planted forget-me-nots and pansies around the edge and put in a few bulbs. He was deeply impressed by the monument and tremendously absorbed by "fixing it all up" as he called it.

It is very noticeable how soldiers constitute a large part of the population. There are compulsory military organizations in every school, and even little tots of three and four are enrolled in the Junior Corps. You see them with their proud parents out walking on Sunday in the green uniform and hat with a minute toy gun slung across their backs. It gives one the creeps.

May 5, 1935—The day before we left Florence big placards were stuck all over the buildings, calling on all the Fascisti organizations to appear at 5:30 in uniform with banners, etc., in one of the big squares in the center of town, and other placards urging all citizens who loved their country to attend the parade and departure of the 31st (?) regiment for Africa (Ethiopia). Accordingly, Bernard and I (the others had gone to Venice for a second visit with Dr. Leigh, President of Bennington and his family, who were in Florence), considered ourselves citizens and decided to heed Mussolini's request and went to the station to see the troops march down. We followed them into the station by the back way and watched them get into the troop train. After waiting an hour or more, we saw them actually off for Abbysinia (via Naples). Most of the men looked between the ages of 20-25. They wear green uniforms. Their packs are wrapped in waterproof coverings with camouflage markings on them. Each man had an extra pair of shoes strapped on to the sides of his pack. In addition he carried a canteen. They marched through the streets with fixed bayonets, but very sloppily. Their brothers, fathers, wives, sweethearts or children marched with them. The band was not very good, and the whole performance was done with little style or enthusiasm. Several women fainted as the train pulled out. Just before it left an officer, one perhaps who had trained this regiment, for he seemed to know them well, went down the train, stopping at each compartment where the soldiers were leaning out, and kissed on both cheeks all he could reach and shook the hands of the others. It seemed very democratic—all brothers in Fascism.

Our stops in the Mediterranean included Majorca, Algiers, Spain, Malta, Rhodes, Egypt, Palestine, Istanbul, Athens, (we were the first boat allowed in after the Revolution), the Dalmation Coast, Taormina, and Venice. None of us had ever been to most of these places so it was terribly interesting.

To me the most interesting place was Palestine, especially Jerusalem which is dirty and squalid, of course, but every inch so pregnant with human history and drama!

This Christmas time I shall be able to visualize the rise in the ground leading up to Bethlehem and the fields afar off known as the "Shepherd's Fields." And I have a quite indelible picture of the Garden of Gethsemane, which is cared for by the Franciscans who do everything with grace, in which grow olive trees so old that they may well have been standing for two thousand years. The paths are lined with the most enormous violets you ever saw. Each visitor is allowed to pick two. Somehow I couldn't bring myself to do it. I didn't think they would like it.

The Wailing Wall and the Mosque of Omar and the Via Dolorosa are all within a small radius, making this rocky high place the most sacred place in the world because three great religions so consider it. The market place is just as it must have been when Abraham lived, with sheep, goats, and goatskins of water or wine and we saw camels coming in caravans, bearing rugs from Persia.

The new parts of Palestine interested me too. Wherever they have irrigation projects, the "desert blossoms like the rose." The Zionist Colonies are places full of hope and industry and idealism. Everyone has always thought the Jew could not farm but he seems to be doing it. If I were a Jew living in Europe, I should make tracks for Palestine so fast that you wouldn't know where I'd gone for dust. I like the country, too, partly perhaps because it reminds one of California, and the things that grow there are similar to our trees and crops. The little village of Bethany, ruined, of course, is still a touching place, not very far from Jerusalem. They show you Martha and Mary's house. The goats in that little village wore particularly musical bells.

It is strange, but I would not care very much if I never returned to Europe. Somehow it seems as if it were hopelessly in an ebb tide and as if it would take years for the flood tide to carry them out of all the messes and entanglements that they are caught in. But the Near East intrigues me. So much is stirring there. A new spirit and new life. Even Turkey is no longer asleep, not even in the yawning stage, but well awake and standing up. I had the same feeling about Syria and Palestine. Not that there are not problems, knotty ones, before all those countries, but somehow it seems as if they were entering on some kind of new cycle and that perhaps the dormant years have given them a vitality that will lead to something. I should have loved to go on to Persia and of course India.

After leaving Italy we had a month in Germany. We went to Munich for our headquarters. You remember, some of you, that it was the first place where Frank and I kept house. I dare not say how many years ago. We found lodgings not far from where we used to live near the English Garten and we all rented bicycles which are very generally ridden there. I

Hope, Elizabeth, Frank, Bernard and Josephine Duveneck in Munich, Germany, 1935.

felt very queer when I first began to pedal along and the first automobile that whizzed by me scared me so that I fell off. Luckily the children were ahead and did not see this mishap. We took a ten day bicycle trip south of Munich to some of the fascinating little villages, such as Partenkirchen—Garmisch where the Olympic games skiing is soon to take place. When we arrived at Oberammergau, weary and cold, from much hill pushing in the rain, we had a hard time finding quarters because it seemed as if the whole German army had moved in just ahead of us. They were having manoeuvers in the hills. It didn't seem very appropriate for that peace-loving little village, but "Heil Hitler!" We finally managed to get two beds and a cot in a funny little house where the beds were as damp as wash cloths and the only warm place to sit was in a little tiny room where the officers and the host sat drinking beer and smoking, and where a fire just raged in the cockle stove. One of the nice places we visited was Mittenwald where they make violins and we saw the instruments in all the different stages of being built. We found the people friendly and terribly interested in the "Amerikaner" who preferred bicycles to automobiles. The only blots on the landscape were the forbidding signs at the entrance to every little town, "Here Jews are not wanted."

To the above observations about Germany I might add memories which did not seem important at the time, but acquired significance in relation to subsequent happenings. I remember coming into Munich from the countryside one afternoon and hearing a strident hysterical voice shouting above the traffic. It came from a huge outdoor auditorium packed with people and it was the voice of Adolf Hitler. We dismissed the oratory as a crackpot demonstration then, but it made me so uneasy that to this day I can still hear it—the most concentrated blast of evil I ever listened to. At another time we were in the Marian Platz and noticed across the plaza a group of soldiers at the doorway of a store, apparently arresting someone and pulling the iron bars across the store front as if closing it. Later we realized what was going on. It was the elimination of a Jewish business. Every morning the telephone poles in Munich were plastered with little white stickers, stamped with opprobrious remarks and stories about Jews. We used to tear them off when no policemen were in sight. But the next day they reappeared. We realized it was no use. It seemed ridiculous to predicate everything you said with "Heil, Hitler." At the postoffice, "Heil, Hitler, give me an airmail stamp," or at the grocery store, "Heil, Hitler, I want five pounds of flour." At the Feldhalle there was always a sentinel standing guard at the corner. All passersby gave the Nazi salute as they passed by, but there was a back alley where those who did not want to salute could make a short cut. We always went that way. One day Bernard said, "I wonder what it feels like to salute those guys?"

"Do you want to try it?" I asked. He decided he would like to see how it made him feel. I agreed to go with him. (Frank and the girls said, "Nothing doing!") Bernard and I stalked by the sentry and thrust our arms out properly as we went by. Bernard's only comment was, "Let's not do that again."

One other incident is worth recounting as a small personal experience of a historical epoch. Bernard had worn his cowboy hat everywhere until we reached Egypt where he bought a red fez with a black tassel. On landing at Istanbul, we got off the boat planning to go exploring on foot. We had not gone half a mile before we were stopped by a burly Turkish policeman who seemed to be very annoyed with us. He talked very emphatically and kept pointing at Bernard, who at that time seemed innocent of any unseemly behavior. The policeman became more and more excited while we became more and more mystified. Just as the policeman seemed to be about to collar Bernard and take him off to jail, a passerby who stopped to observe the altercation and who spoke English, intercepted the policeman and explained to us that it was illegal to wear a red fez anywhere in modern Turkey. This was one of the decrees of Ataturk who, in the capacity of dictator, revolutionized the whole structure of Turkish society. He made the fez taboo along with the veils covering the faces of women and substituted European script for Islamic characters. After Bernard exchanged his fez for his cowboy hat, we were no longer molested.

Homecoming after the trip was an experience in itself. In those days the transcontinental train deposited you at the Oakland Mall where you transferred to a ferry boat. On the ferry, passing Goat Island and the small craft in the bay, looking across to the Ferry Building, (then the tallest landmark on the San Francisco waterfront) and seeing the San Bruno Hills beyond, gave us a wonderful feeling of coming home. The beauty of the bay and the picturesqueness of the hills with their clinging buildings gave us such a thrill of recognition. We drove down El Camino Real past the little towns of San Carlos and Belmont, and finally along Moody Road to the ranch. As always, whenever I came back from a trip, the sight of the olive grove just inside the gate stirred something very deep and very intense in my consciousness. It usually brings tears to my eyes. I don't know why this is so, but there is a serenity in those ancient grey trunks with their closely interwoven branches overhead and the exquisite pattern of sun and shadow on the ground underneath that seems to produce an inexpressible feeling of peace.

The European trip was one of the ways that we tried to broaden our children's horizons. We had all been so very close, what with our involvements in Peninsula School and our sharing in the development of the ranch, that it seemed to me that they might become ingrown. It is always possible that too tenacious a family solidarity may handicap the normal development of outside relationships. Our children did not take very kindly to summer Scout camps; they were already completely at home in woods or mountains, and they had acquired many manual skills which made them self-reliant and resourceful. On the other hand, independent non-agency camps did much for both girls. Hope benefitted from finding her own way in a group of girls, away from the domination of her older sister. Elizabeth, interested in dancing and riding, blossomed at the Perry Mansfield Camp in Colorado. And the boys each spent two years at Thacher School in the Ojai Valley. For several years it seemed as if our lives consisted of a series of good byes, brief sojourns at home and then good-byes again. Every time one of the children went off by car or railroad or plane, it seemed as if a little piece of me went along with them.

It isn't any wonder that some parents make the loosening of the apron strings so hard for themselves and for their offspring. A Mother's life has for so long revolved in and around the young generation that letting go is too much of a wrench. She finds herself dependent on the dependence of her children, and closes her eyes to the fact that they no longer need her ministrations. Unless she has managed to keep other interests alive, her function in life seems to have disintegrated, and she is at a loss to know how to fill the long hours of the day and night.

I found that adolescence is like April weather. One minute I was dealing with an emancipated adult, but the next minute the adult turned into a child hungry seeking comforting or reassurance. I learned that if I could play it by ear and be sufficiently flexible to whichever mood prevailed, I could get by without making too many wrong responses. Above all, the mother-hen behavior had to be concealed, although, of course, it still operated under the surface. I remember so well, after the youngsters acquired licenses to drive, lying awake into the wee small hours waiting for the sound of the returning automobile. I could hear it first coming up the road passing the hostel. Then the lights would flicker on the ceiling of my bedroom, and soon I could hear the back door open. Presently, a cupboard door or the refrigerator would slam, and I could turn over and go to sleep while the late-comer crept up the stairs in stockinged feet "so as not to wake Mother."

A little later, when they had been to college and the mating season overtook them, is when I think I went through the most acute suffering of any time in my life. It is said that "the course of true love never did run smooth." That is easily accepted, but how can you tell if it is *true* love or just an imitation? You can't interfere, you dare not criticize, you watch anxiously all the little signs that indicate what is happening, but you have to maintain an impersonal and objective attitude—even when you are worried crazy over the latest developments. When disappointment or rejection occurs, then you feel torn apart with heartache for the child you love, yet you are powerless to do anything about it. I remember some nights standing in the hall, hearing sobs from one of the bedrooms, and wondering whether I should go in and cradle the sufferer or if it was a crisis that had to be met and worked through the whole bitter way without outside intrusion. Like the Negro spiritual:

> "You must walk that lonesome valley. . .
> Nobody else can do it for you.
> You have to walk it by yourself."

That is a time I should not like to live over again, and I am glad that it took place before the current era of frustration, marijuana and violence. I don't know how I should have managed to reconcile myself to that upheaval. As it is, my children seem to have survived the vicissitudes of growing up and marriage. I feel close to the people they married, and my life has been immeasurably enriched through the flowing pattern of their lives in which I am privileged to participate.

When our children had completed their formal education and were looking for real jobs, all four of them were drawn into liberal forms of service—the Farm Security Administration, Red Cross, Occupational Therapy, the Cooperative Movement, Low Cost Housing, and the American Friends' Service Committee.

XX

Youth Hostels – Then and Now

*Their origins in Germany; their
beginnings and future in California;
Hidden Villa's part in the enterprise.*

Before we went to Europe in 1935 we had heard something of the youth program that had been developed in Germany a few years after World War I. In a period of severe economic depression, when the younger generation found it almost impossible to obtain employment—and still more difficult to find recreation to their liking—street gangs developed, vandalism increased and family morals were at a low ebb. Even in Bavaria, formerly the center of song, folk art and festivals, life had become grim and monotonous. Most adolescents grew up in fatherless homes; their mothers, hard-pressed to provide the daily bread ration, had no time to engage in social amenities.

A high school teacher, Richard Schurmann by name, realized the deprivations of his students, especially during vacation time. He decided to take them on trips to the country. Although they lacked funds for transportation, some of them had bicycles and all of them had two legs on which they could travel. He took them in groups to visit historical monuments and places of scenic beauty. They made friends with country folk and were allowed to sleep in their fields or share the barns with the sheep and cattle. They had unexpected adventures along the way as travelers always do. Among themselves and with their leader they developed a camaraderie that helped to dispel feelings of frustration and defeat. The idea spread fast throughout Germany, and the young travelers became known as the *Wandervogel* (birds of passage). It was beautiful to see them clad in *lederhosen* with *rucksacks* on their backs, swinging along in groups of ten or twelve, singing as they went. Soon their numbers multiplied to the point of making it more difficult to count on free hospitality. Shelter from rain and snow could make a vast difference in the enjoyment of the outing, and it became desirable to find new ways to provide something dependable.

Richard Schurmann had inherited a small mediaeval castle which he donated to the cause, and he persuaded other landowners to join him in setting up a series of simple accommodations a day's journey apart to be known as *Jugend Herberge* (Youth Hostels). There, for a small fee, the young people could stay overnight, cook their own meals and tidy up before continuing their journey. Soon they began to extend their trips to neighboring countries, and this resulted in the formation of the International Youth Hostel Association.

Unfortunately, when Hitler started to build up his political power, the *Wandervogel* provided a readymade, already well-organized group of vigorous young men whom he could subvert. By getting rid of the idealistic leaders and replacing them with military disciplinarians, the *Wandervogel* were tragically transformed into the Hitler Jugend Corps.

But previous to this, in 1930, two Americans, Monroe and Isabel Smith, had made a trip to Europe and witnessed the flowering of the movement before it was destroyed. Monroe, a national YMCA executive, was impressed by the possibilities it suggested for American youth. Filled with enthusiasm, he followed Richard Schurmann's example and donated his home in Northfield, Massachusetts, as a center for the development of the program. Many students from colleges in New England, enthused by his ideas, volunteered their services in the summer to extend the facilities and to recruit participants. The small towns adjacent to one another and the multiplicity of country roads in western Massachusetts were conducive to the establishment of hostels a day's journey apart.

In San Francisco, Josephine Randall, Director of the city's Recreation Department, was concerned during the depression years 1929-1935 to find challenging inexpensive activities for teenagers. She felt that the beautiful open country down the Peninsula should somehow be made available. Because the Loma Prieta Chapter of the Sierra Club knew the area, she asked their help in planning a series of trails and shelters by which trips could be carried out. My husband Frank was on the Loma Prieta Board of the Sierra Club and was on the joint Committee that made a survey of possibilities. Miss Randall heard about the Hostel Program that Monroe Smith was developing and invited him to come to the West Coast for consultation. There were some difficulties in the way of joint promotion, but while he was here, Monroe Smith organized a tentative group with Frank as chairman and Bill Silverthorn as field worker. Frank made a trip to Northfield, and on his return he brought one of the Northfield staff with him to become field worker for California. Her name was Betty Blodgett—and later she married our son Francis.

Betty was able to set up a loop comprising seven hostels to provide a week's trip out of San Francisco and back. These stops were in Montara, Purissima Creek, Soquel, Saratoga, Los Altos, Skyline and San Lorenzo. In those days there were relatively few automobiles infesting the roads so that bicycle travel was not as hazardous as it is at the present time. There was also an isolated hostel at Colfax in the Sierra foothills which provided for skiers and mountain climbers.

Here at the ranch we had a few cabins originally used on weekends by a San Francisco pediatrician. These provided temporary quarters for hostellers but were inadequate for constant use. We built a new building under circumstances I shall relate in the next chapter, describing the unexpected problems and radical adjustments entailed in this project.

The new building was completed, and it was the first hostel on the Pacific Coast. Between the years 1944 and 1964 it was the only one. Those set up by Betty elsewhere on the San Francisco Peninsula, and a few in the Northwest, all succumbed to the urgent need for housing at the onset of World War II.

For several years we were asked to be responsible for groups visiting California. They traveled across the country by Canadian railways, stopping at Banff, Winnipeg and Vancouver, transferring to American railroads in Seattle and landing in Oakland to begin their California tour. The boat trip across the bay was a welcome relief. But consternation was in store for them when they trundled their bicycles out of the ferry building and were confronted with San Francisco hills. They were really taken aback. Neither Boston nor Middle Western towns had prepared them for such a challenge. One boy explained, "Gosh, this isn't at all like Florida!" Sometimes we arranged for temporary overnight accommodations in San Francisco. On one occasion, using the Friends Service house on Sutter Street for the boys to sleep on the floor of the social hall, we bedded the girls down in an adjacent apartment at that time rented by a peace workers' co-operative. The house had originally belonged to a Japanese family who had been evacuated by the army in the spring of 1942. Their tenants had also left about the same time. After the hostel girls were comfortably settled, the peace volunteers were surprised to have their doorbell rung repeatedly by gentlemen inquiring if they might come in and be welcome. Gradually it dawned on the demure Quaker hostess what the former character of the apartment must have been and why the arrival of the bevy of charming young girls had raised such hopes in the neighborhood. The girls of course knew nothing of this and the episode was never reported to National Headquarters.

On looking over their travels and time schedules, we realized that the plans had been laid out in New England, using a mileage map without consideration of terrain or climate. For example, one day was allotted to bicycle from Fresno to the Yosemite and one day to return—a distance of

180 miles each way! In July heat what a catastrophe it would have been. We altered the Northfield schedules for mileage and allowed for three or four extra days of rest and rehabilitation at Hidden Villa. Our hot showers and our washing machine ran all day and part of the night. Sewing materials were laid out and clean bandages for blisters and scratches. Shampoo and face lotion were in demand. Usually some member of the team needed to visit a dentist or physician. Most welcome for them were three well-prepared and cooked meals a day, which they could enjoy seated at a regular table. Peanut butter and jam sandwiches, potato chips, chocolate bars, bananas and soft drinks had lost their appeal.

An amusing episode connected with our work for hostelling happened early in the war years. We had been given fifteen or twenty folding cots and mattresses which had been discarded from one of the Stanford dormitories. Frank collected them for one of the hostels we were then fitting up for use near the coast. Some busybody who saw his truck loaded with these beds and enroute to the ocean telephoned the F.B.I. to say that he was taking those beds over for enemy infiltraters who were supposed to land from submarines on a beach near Half Moon Bay. Even the F.B.I. investigator had a good laugh over that fantasy!

The fundamental ideas of hostelling always seemed to me reasonable and sound. Travelling on one's own steam by foot or bicycle or canoe, with possessions reduced to bare necessities, and having the chance to meet strangers from distant places, can be an adventure that provides a most valuable educational experience. The availability of shelter and cooking facilities and the presence of houseparents for some necessary but minimum supervision or counseling seems desirable, especially for the younger ages. However, in California the picture is somewhat different from other parts of the world. Most months of the year bring little snow or rain, and we have a large number of Federal and State parks and mountain trails where camping is available for a small fee or for free. However, the distances between towns, the heavy automobile traffic, and the scarcity of side roads limits safe bicycle routes. Population growth and greatly increased demands from the public for outdoor recreation have created pressures for preservation of open space and conservation of natural resources. It seems likely that facilities in Northern California, at least, will be developed to satisfy this demand. The hostel idea may be revived in some form suited to the needs of the communities and the availability of trails and byways. In some countries, notably England and Japan, the hostels are now financed by government subsidies. This is certainly a more constructive use of funds than the establishment of juvenile detention halls, but it seems hard for many American citizens to realize that prevention of evil costs far less than repairing the damages. We are disturbed by the increase of crime, but we fail to come to grips with the underlying causes. Communist regimes sometimes seem to deal more efficiently with such problems. Is democracy so cumbersome that it cannot find effective ways to control social inequalities? I sometimes wonder if our much vaunted "standard of living" may not prove to be our undoing.

The new enthusiasm for backpacking, camping and hiking has stimulated reexamination of the idea of hostels and the development of foot and bicycle paths in America. There is hope for a continuous trail near the West coast of Washington, down through Oregon and California to Mexico, with frequent shelter stations, which would enable travelers to make short or long trips under their own steam, in beautiful scenic country, away from cities, suburbs, and crowded highways. What a tremendous resource this would be for future generations!

XXI

Pacifists
in World War II

*Pacifists in California; their motivation
and treatment by the community.*

When you study history, you follow the course of massive
movements like the outreach of the Roman Empire, or the European
colonization of Africa, and the facts of these developments seem to
culminate in a logical conclusion. One does not usually consider history
in terms of slow-moving, individual experiences. On the other hand,
when you *live* history, you find yourself in the midst of turmoil, and it is
almost impossible for you to ascertain the direction of the winds of
change. What is really happening? Where are we going? What should
we hang on to or let go? How can we distinguish truth from hysteria?

The fifteen year period from 1935 to 1950 was an era of turbulence
throughout the world. Europe was restive under terms of a peace treaty
that imposed impossible restrictions. The great colonial empires were
breaking down throughout the world, and the natives of Africa and Asia
were beginning to discover their own potential for self-government and
freedom. As frontiers were violated and maps became obsolete, so
political institutions appeared to be inadequate. Guidelines of accepted
behavior no longer held.

In the United States, we were pushed out of isolation by World War I
and shaken up by the Great Depression of 1929-30, but we were
fortunate to be able to adapt to change because of the leadership of
Franklin Roosevelt and the various imaginative panaceas of the New
Deal. In California, because of our advantages, we had a great increase
of population. Also, the growing threat of war in the Pacific and the resulting demand for military supplies and ships brought us workers from
every state in the union.

During this turbulent period, I found myself forced to rethink my conception of the world and to re-evaluate my social ethics. Living in California had been an easy-going, self-indulgent manner of existence, far away from industrial pressures. I was reluctant to admit the shattering of the dream, and at first I found it hard to welcome the immigrating hordes. But I realized that unless I could revise my frame of reference, I would be unable to function in a changing society.

Having close contacts with many young people and seeing through their eyes made it easier to modify some of my old convictions than it would have been otherwise. My children, who were just at the threshold of adult life, were confronted with the necessity of making important decisions before they had even had the opportunity to experience much of life, and little time to develop their own philosophy and objectives. The shadow of approaching war hung over all our lives in the 1930's. It was like the tule fog in the San Joaquin Valley which is so confusing to night drivers. One moment you can see the traffic lines and the next moment they disappear and merge into the impenetrable mist. We tried to pretend to ourselves that somehow war would not happen, but when Hitler marched into Poland in 1939 pretense was no longer tenable. The monster had to be faced.

In 1914, at the beginning of World War I, the conscientious objector in England, and a year or two later in the United States, faced a bleak and uncompromising situation. The refusal to bear arms almost inevitably landed a young man in jail. Because war had seemed obsolete for so many years, peace was taken for granted as the natural climate of civilized nations, and very little had been done to prepare citizens to meet the crisis. It was in 1917 that the American Friends Service Committee first came into being. It was designed to permit volunteer service under civilian leadership as a substitute for military duty. The first team of twenty or thirty volunteers went to France to help rebuild French villages destroyed by the Germans. As the lines of battle swayed back and forth due to fluctuating attacks and withdrawals, these boys were very close to action and often caught in lines of fire. When the war ended, they were on hand in Europe to participate in relief work carried on in Belgium under Herbert Hoover's direction. Joined later by additional personnel, they worked in several other destroyed areas and developed a massive feeding program for the children of Germany who were starving. A whole generation was kept alive by *"Quaker Brot,"* and it was not till long afterwards that they found out where it had really come from. They thought *Quaker Brot* was a trade name like Langendorf or Bonnie Hubbard.

During the years between World War I and World War II, all Quaker groups, as well as the other Peace churches such as Mennonites, Brethren, Jehovah's Witnesses and innumerable lay groups, laid great emphasis on the analysis of war and peace. Study groups, seminars, work camps and communes enlisted the idealism of high school and college age boys and girls. Mohandas K. Gandhi's campaign in India, which opposed British control by every device short of physical force, caught the imagination of the young. Gandhi became a sort of patron saint for all war resisters. And as the leaders of youth stressed once again the teachings of Jesus "to love thine enemy and to do good to those who despitefully use you," the discrepancy between faith and practice became more evident. Whereas in 1914 armed conflict had seemed a remote possibility, from 1918 on there was never a time when war was not going on somewhere in the world. A host of new organizations were born to further the cause of peace. The Fellowship of Reconciliation, the Committee for the Study of Non-Violence, the War Resister's League, and many more preached the philosophy of peace and provided situations in which the practice of conciliation and brotherliness was the guiding motive. The idea of Work Camps for young people, organized to assist under-privileged groups at home or abroad, originated with the Friends. They thought that the experience of working as a group to assist a low-income, unfamiliar minority to achieve a definite improvement in living conditions would provide training and discipline in loving human relationships. Such projects as digging wells, draining swamp areas, repairing homes, and developing health clinics, play-ground facilities, and child care centers were organized. The effect of these summer projects on the participants themselves was far-reaching, even if the project itself was not entirely successful, as sometimes happened. We had two such work camps on the ranch. The first one centered on migrant agricultural workers' camps, the second one built a playground in a Mexican-American neighborhood in Mountain View. The depth of commitment that took place depended on the leaders. In the two I have just mentioned, Frieda and Irwin Abrams were outstanding as inspirational and co-ordinating directors.

As war appeared more and more imminent during the 1930's, possible forms of alternative service became pressing. Because of my involve-ment with the Friends Meeting and the Service Committee and contact with young people through my children's friends, my former pupils and youth projects at the ranch, I found our home in constant demand for discussions, committee meetings and individual consultations.

I think I would like to pause here and refresh my memory in regard to the background of conscription in our country. When war is over it is so easy to forget the past problems. But in the late 30's, conscription loomed ahead of every family as an inescapable reality that had to be faced by the young people themselves, their parents and teachers, their leaders and priests. Only the very old and the very young were immune.

The last draft call of the Civil War was made in 1864. Until World War I, recruitment for Army and Navy was on an entirely individual and volunteer basis. In April, 1917, the issue of compulsory service met with intense opposition in Congress, but after war had already formally been declared, a selective service law was adopted in May of that year. The term *Selective Service* is based on the assumption that in a technological economy, many men are needed for industrial and agricultural purposes: these men are not conscripted. Others engaged in less essential work are *selected* for military duty. It was applicable to male citizens between 21 and 31. In August, 1918, it was extended to include ages 18 to 45. When peace was declared, the law lapsed.

However, during the 1930's, as the Nazi power developed in Germany and threatened to overrun the world, considerable propaganda was spread by the joint Army and Navy Departments to establish Universal Military Training (U.M.T.). Already in 1936, planning for the next war was well underway. In 1940, the Selective Service Conscription Act was passed and put under the direction of General Lewis Hershey. In this mandate, conscientious objectors were permitted to substitute "work of national importance" under civilian management, provided that their objection to war could be proven to be due to religious belief and training. The original act of 1940 applied for one year only, but as war became certain, the Selective Service Extension Act of August, 1941, was adopted. That there was strong opposition is evidenced by the endorsing vote which was 203-202 in the House of Representatives.

The process of carrying out this vast program of registration was rapidly executed. Information media—radio and newspapers—and public institutions, such as schools, colleges, churches informed the public. All men were required to fill out a form to be filed with the government. A draft card "to be carried at all times" was received by the registrant, and he was notified of time and place for physical examination. Recruits were assigned to certain categories. I cannot remember all of them except *1A* which meant immediate enrollment in the army; *4F* which indicated physical disability, and *1AO* which was the conscientious objector designation.

Among the boys I knew, there were several degrees of pacifism and several possible avenues of escape from the killing of other human beings. The Merchant Marine, The Coast Guard and the ship building crews offered solutions to a few. Service in hospitals and mental institutions and enlistment in the army medical units (with the proviso that the ambulance workers would not be required to carry weapons) satisfied others. Those unwilling to register at all went to jail. I myself, like the young people who came to consult me, felt pulled apart by conflicting ideas. On the one hand our ethical standard "Thou shalt not kill" implied that the taking of life was wrong; on the other hand, considering the ruthless power then destroying thousands of innocent victims, how could that be arrested? Obviously, not by prayer nor offers of arbitration. Such force could only be restrained by force. Was it not my duty to join this cause and give up my life if necessary for the sake of humanity? Hitler had to be stopped. And yet I could never bring myself to shoot a German soldier. My enemy, perhaps, but still a human being. I could not violate my soul. But here was my friend who hated war as much as I did who felt impelled to enlist. Was it fair for me to avoid carnage while he sacrificed himself? These soul-searching questions were uppermost in all our minds. To older people the resulting judgments were philosophical, but for the younger generation their decisions led to drastic and immediate actions which might well shape the course of their whole future lives. My two boys wrestled with these alternatives. I agonized over their struggles. I listened and I watched. I tried never to advise or influence. Francis chose Alternative Service in a Friends CPS camp. He spent all one night from dusk to dawn writing his reasons on the selective service form requesting exemption from the draft. Bernard couldn't feel justified in setting himself apart. His decision was to go into the Army Medical Corps as a conscientious objector with the understanding that he would never be asked to bear arms, but would serve only as an ambulance driver or hospital orderly. I felt their decisions were right for their temperaments, and Frank and I respected their positions. Both boys accepted each other and I don't think they ever were critical of one another's sincerity and good faith. It distressed me that some Quakers were so intolerant of any boys in uniform that they did not want them in their homes or in their meetings. Some were actually read out of meeting. I remember one elderly peace fanatic who would arrogantly question any soldier he met by asking, "Why do you wear the uniform of a murderer?"

The American Friends Service Committee made an agreement with the military authorities to establish a series of Civilian Public Service camps (known as CPS) where conditions would parallel the soldier's assignment in terms of duration, hours of work, furloughs, health insurance and monthly pay. The actual work was directed by a federal agency such as the Forest Service, Public Health Agency, or Hospital. Living quarters were in barracks. The organization of the group life, the administration of food preparation and household chores, the social relationships, hardship cases and disciplines of communal living were the responsibility of the Friends. It proved to be a somewhat cumbersome dualistic arrangement complicated by the variety of dissenters involved. Quakers were in the minority. There were Mennonites, Brethren, Jehovah's Witnesses, a few Methodists and Catholics and a group of rank individualists incapable of accepting any rules or restraints contrary to their personal prejudices. These individuals and a lunatic fringe of psychologically disturbed persons became a burden for the work crews and for administrative programming. The Friends' manner of conducting business, entailing unanimity of decision on even trivial matters, was well nigh impossible with so divergent a constituency.

To be eligible for one of the Friends' Camps, the candidate had to fill out a detailed form describing his religious training and background. He was required to present two or three letters backing up his statements and attesting to his sincerity. He also had to write a *resume* of his belief and how he had arrived at it. In preparing this statement, a good many boys wanted to talk about it, what words to use, what to put in or leave out. One youngster brought in 20 pages for me to criticize. "But Tom, you can't present all those pages to your Draft Board. They would never read it. Condense it into a page and a half, or at most two pages."

"I already broke it down from 50 pages. I can't explain God in two pages."

"The Draft Board isn't interested in God. All they want is your reason for not using a gun to kill people."

The Draft Boards, organized by counties, represented prominent citizens who served gratis and held hearings once a week to interview protestants and decide their destinies. For the most part they were decent, Rotary-type individuals who did their best to decide fairly even though they were not in sympathy with the pacifist point of view. The key question—"Do you believe in a Supreme being?"—required a 'yes' or 'no' reply. Many registrants felt it necessary to qualify or enlarge this statement but were not permitted to do so.

The first camp to be established in California was at Tan Bark Fire Station in the mountains east of Pasadena. Francis was among the first contingent of nine Californians who started there. They were joined by other C.O.'s from the East and Middle West, and some months later a second camp was set up at Coleville in the Owens Valley near the Nevada boundary.

I visited both these camps and noted similar arrangements in both. Three or four members of the group were assigned to work in the kitchen. At meal time long bare wooden tables and benches were quickly filled with hungry young men in shabby work clothes, many unshaven or with astonishing beards. Everyone picked up plates and utensils cafeteria style and hurried unceremoniously through the meal. There was a library and a common living room furnished with a few nondescript sofas and overstuffed chairs and an out-of-tune piano. These were the only amenities of living, and there was no YMCA or Ladies Defenders' Club to provide recreation. Of course, both camps had beautiful mountains to look at, but scenery is very impersonal. At Coleville where the surroundings were desert land, the prospect was less pleasing. The presence of a woman, even an old one like me, seemed to please the boys. Many came up to be introduced and seemed glad to chat with someone "from outside." On one of my visits I brought along my sewing basket and announced at breakfast that I would mend or darn any garments that needed attention. I received some ghastly specimens which I did my best to redeem, not always very successfully. The half hour of worship held before work, not compulsory, was attended by a small, dedicated group. I remember going outside the mess hall one Sunday morning and looking down into a great sweep of tree-covered canyon and suddenly hearing out of the distance a tenor voice shouting hymns that echoed from mountain to mountain. It was Peter, a Jehovah's Witness, witnessing to the wilderness.

The boys in these camps encountered a good deal of outside criticism. Especially after Pearl Harbor they were stigmatized as "slackers, yellow bellies, milksops, etc." It was not always very pleasant for them to do business in nearby communities. In some cases they were not even welcome in their own homes if their families and neighbors had not been in sympathy with their convictions. So it happened that when they had a few days furlough, many of them came to Hidden Villa, where they were sure of a welcome, plenty of hot water, civilized meals, a chance "to sleep in" and the society of two young and attractive daughters of the house. The boys at Coleville used to refer to the ranch as the "CPS Country Club."

When the war ended some of the young men had considerable difficulty in reorienting themselves in normal life. The returning soldiers also encountered this problem, but they had earned certain benefits of subsidies and educational opportunities denied to C.O.'s. Employers were often prejudiced. The transition was hard. I asked one of the boys who had survived nearly four years of camp experience if he felt the time had been wasted. He said no, that he had learned so much about all kinds of people and how to get along with them; he had found out how few possessions were really necessary to survive; he had been confirmed in following his own inner convictions by having to encounter disapproval and criticism; and, in addition, he had acquired specific skills which proved valuable in his later life.

One of the subsidiary experiences that grew out of my contacts with the War Generation consisted of interviews with Army and Navy Intelligence and the F.B.I. They came to the door, flashed a card of identification and said they wanted to inquire about so-and-so who had given my name as reference. These men interested me. The F.B.I. men were courteous, direct and well-informed. They knew about Quakers and they understood that all pacifists were not motivated alike. I became quite friendly with one man who came more than once. One day I said to him, "I suppose you really come here to find out *about me*. The boy you're inquiring about is just a means of entrance."

"No," he said, "Mrs. Duveneck, if we had to investigate you it would take at least four people to follow your trail in all the different organizations you are connected with."

"So you know already," I said, and we both laughed. The Army Intelligence snoopers were quite different from the F.B.I. agents. They were stupid, narrow-minded, rather arrogant men with very limited backgrounds. The Naval investigators were formal and business-like. They checked the bare facts and didn't bother about personality complications.

The Civilian Public Service Camps were opened early in 1941. This was several months before Pearl Harbor. In my Christmas Chronicle written December 14 of that year I had this to say about the crisis:

A week ago at this time the first news of the Japanese attack on Hawaii was flashed over the radio. We had, of course, been expecting a declaration of war for many days as "negotiations" proceeded in Washington and tension grew throughout the Pacific area. But while there was a flicker of possibility left, one continued to hope that armed conflict might be avoided. Already it seems as if the war had been going on for months and months instead of one short week, so quickly and so completely does social psychology change thought and habits under pressure of crisis. American people are very adaptable. It has taken San Francisco only a few days to learn the techniques for complete blackout, with wardens for every block. Smaller communities functioned also without hysteria (with some exception I must add). The more well-to-do people are, the more frightened they become. The wealthy have more to lose, and privilege does not by any means always increase fortitude.

My letter went on to tell of our concern for our Japanese friends and our fear of reprisals if any bombs are dropped along the coast.

Meetings were hastily called in all the towns between San Francisco and San Jose to arrange for the evacuation of women and children in case of air raids on the city. How many beds could be made available, how many nurses and doctors, how many emergency kitchen facilities, how many blankets, cribs, wheel-chairs, etc., etc.? Having a fully equipped hostel and large fields suitable for the installation of tents, we were drawn into the planning for the mid-Peninsula. Everybody had ideas to contribute at these meetings, most of them impractical. There was much oratory, but very little coordinated planning. I remember one man who kept popping up, reiterating, "Yes, yes, but what are we going to do about the pregnant women? We must decide how to deal with the *pregnant women!*" An official from one of the emergency patrols described the necessity for blackouts of lighted windows and doors in all stores and private homes. The window shade people did a rush business. Black paint and black paper of all kinds for lining window panes was in great demand. In the evening an airplane flew low over the county. If any light was located, the owner had to pay a heavy fine.

My letter of December 14 ends thus:

I wish we had special Christmas carols to sing in war-time. It seems ironical now to chant about "good-will towards men" and "the coming of the Prince of Peace to the world" . . . A wonderful thing happened in our garden last Monday, the day after war was declared. Nothing much is growing there now but one little shrub that has never done anything interesting before suddenly burst into bloom. It was a Japanese flowering cherry, a symbol of all that is lovely and sacred in the soul of a people gone astray.

During the war we became acquainted with a group with whom we had not had previous contact—the Dutch seamen. After the Germans had occupied Holland, none of the Dutch ships could return to their home ports. They had considerable business in the Pacific because of their colonies in Indo-China and one or two South Sea Islands. Their home port for the duration of hostilities was San Francisco, and it was there that the crews were granted the first shore leave that they had had for many months. The people of Dutch descent living in the Bay area organized a club to offer hospitality and welfare services for these involuntary exiles. They asked us to invite individuals to stay for a week or two just to get away from their boats, relieved from the tension of avoiding Japanese ships in the Pacific. I remember one young officer for whom I made a picnic lunch every day for a month so that he could go for long walks up the mountain all by himself. He told me that the opportunity to be alone saved him from a nervous breakdown. We also had an older man, a cook who could speak very little English, who was deeply disturbed about his wife back in Holland. He had not heard from her for over two years. No mail could get through. We arranged for him to send a letter through the International Red Cross but it took six months to get an answer back. And then only if the address was the same as it had been when he left. He was afraid she would not wait for him to return before taking another man. "Woman alone, no good. Find man," he said, with tears running down his troubled face. The day he left he baked us an enormous gaudily decorated cake. It looked magnificent but the taste was disappointing. Felix, the youth who helped in my house, made another cake the following day, not so resplendent, but more palatable.

Then there were two quite young men, Florian and Adrian, who came together and played volleyball by the hour. They were here for nearly three weeks and they both talked about remaining in the United States after the close of the war. I used to tease them about finding American brides. "No," they insisted, "We'll wait and go back to Holland and find ourselves some nice wholesome Dutch girls who won't expect too many favors." What was my astonishment to be called to the telephone by Flori a couple of months later and told with a little giggle how he and Adrian wanted to come down for their honeymoons. "So you *did* find some American girls?" I said.

"Uh-huh. Can we come for a week before we have to go back on boat?" I have two sofas in my living room and during the next week at any hour of the day you could see one couple "necking" on one davenport, and on the other one a close-up cuddle. I should have taken a photograph of this conjugal bliss.

At the close of the war we had high hopes for a peace treaty that would lead to conciliation among the world powers. It was tragic that Woodrow Wilson's dream and his Fourteen Points met with failure after World War I. A similar ordeal was encountered by Franklin Roosevelt, also a sick man baffled by wily European politicians at the close of World War II. We were strong supporters of Roosevelt. We never missed any of his

Fireside Talks that came over the radio at times of crisis. He always began "My Friends," and the content and delivery were beautifully coordinated. Sometimes now on a TV program the station will introduce part of an old Roosevelt speech. The voice is recognizable at once. My eyes fill with tears because, in spite of some shady episodes which have come to light in recent times, I feel that F.D.R. was a great man and an inspiring leader. I shall never forget the shock of hearing Truman's first speech as President. His dry, rasping voice and matter-of-fact remarks were in such great contrast to the sonorous cadences and the cultivated diction of his predecessor.

"The war is over. We can all return to normal living," the radio told us in 1945. But normal living in 1945 was very different from normal living in 1935. And by 1975, the only "normal living" seems to involve uncertainty and change. Who at the end of World War II anticapted thirty years of United States aggression in the Far East? However, in 1945 when World War II ended, great hopes centered around the promise of a World Conference to establish the United Nations. The discussions of where this momentous convocation should take place surged back and forth across two hemispheres. The decision to hold the organizational meeting in San Francisco brought great excitement to the West Coast. Los Angeles and Seattle were disappointed. But San Franciscans said, "Of course, our city was chosen! Isn't it the most beautiful setting in the world? Aren't the inhabitants the most cosmopolitan? It's the gateway to the Orient."

You can imagine the reactions of the Chamber of Commerce when San Francisco was finally chosen as the site for this world-wide assembly! And we, like all West Coast citizens, were equally elated at the prospect of being close to such a momentous international gathering. Peace! Peace at last for the whole world. What a beautiful dream!

XXII

Quest (Three)

Oriental religion and La Crescenta Ashram.

The Great Experience which I tried to describe in Chapter 17 transformed my inner life. I experienced a new frame of reference. Whereas I had formerly been travelling through life as if I were in a great, dark forest, feeling my way from tree trunk to tree trunk, stumbling over rocks and rubble, frequently falling, now there was a luminous beacon clarifying the pathway. The obstacles still existed on the trail but the far away light burned clear and never wavered. I could not explain why doubt and indecision no longer hampered me, but the authenticity of the revelation could not be questioned. It was different from any other type of knowledge. It was absolute, implicit, complete. "And ye shall know the truth and the truth will make you free." No one has ever been able to explain the validity of this kind of mystical certitude.

Still I had a lot of work to do before my daily living would be in harmony with my inner conviction. I find it hard to reconstruct the two levels of my life during this period, because it was a time of extremely active social involvement on the one hand and no less active psychic endeavor taking place below the surface. It was similar to my experience as a child. I functioned simultaneously in a secret dream world and in the actual world. A great change had taken place in my attitude toward other people. The desire to dominate dropped away; instead, the desire to understand the needs and the capacities of other human beings and to further their aspirations became all-important. I was increasingly successful as an organizer during that time; perhaps there was more

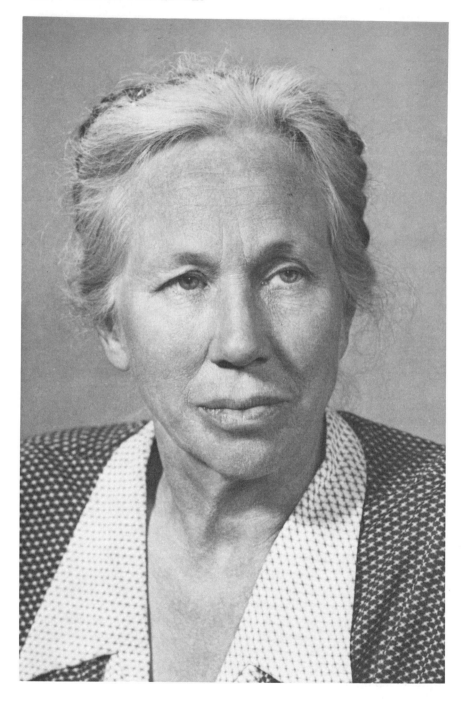

connection than I realized between the invisible and the visible performance.

The Christian tradition of the mystic way did not completely satisfy me. The Jewish notion of a chosen people and the Christian theology depending on salvation through Jesus Christ alone, seemed to me to cut off half the people in the world. To believe that revelation occurred at only one time in the history of the human race and that this event constitued the only valid truth for all mankind seemed untenable. It implied a superiority of favor for those born within a certain geographical radius. If there is a God, He must be universal—approachable by all men anywhere. I was led to explore other world religions and other symbolisms. William James' *Varieties of Religious Experience* and Edouard Schure's *Les Grands Inities*, clarified the fundamental essence of religion manifested in so many different beliefs and forms. Years before, when I travelled in the Orient, I had visited temples where monks with shaven heads and saffron robes sat cross-legged in the shrines oblivious to the passerby. I wondered then what their prayers were. Schure's book said, "Yes, there is a mother-doctrine, a synthesis of religions and philosophies. It develops and deepens as the ages roll along but its foundation and centre remains the same. . . . The unity of truth will appear in the very diversity of its expression."

At this point the Oriental religions offered me new insights for the cultivation of the spirit. I don't remember just how I got started, but Gibran's *The Prophet*, Tagore's poetry, Romain Rolland's *Prophets of the New India*, Paul Carus' *Life of Buddha*, Max Muller's translation of the *Vedas*, and *Gita* and many other books I discovered in the Metaphysical Library in San Francisco, opened up marvelous vistas of spiritual exploration.

The idea of self-perfection as an end in itself was a new concept for me; I had always felt that working actively for other people was the primary aim of a good life. To justify one's existence by the attainment of perfection within required a radical readjustment of values. I found that it was one thing to grasp the idea intellectually. It was not unreasonable. But the psychological acceptance was much more difficult. I found that I needed longer periods in which to experiment with the control of my thoughts. Trying to follow through on techniques of meditation described in the books I had been reading required uninterrupted hours of concentration. I found myself in a dilemma that I had struggled with before, but never on such an insistent level. I could withdraw into a secret arcanum shutting out actualities, but worldly obligations kept pulling aside the curtain. On the other hand, in the midst of busy occupations there was always a shadow in the background, reproaching me for unawareness. Life on two levels was uneasy. A dual personality never satisfied me, and I felt that it was imperative to develop some sort of harmony between the two aspects of reality which pulled in seemingly different directions. I was convinced that it should be possible to achieve a sense of unity between the inner and the outer motivation, provided that the inner was in command and undergirded and dictated the action. I had the inner certitude established for me that memorable night under the stars, but its relationship to the daily routine was not yet truly operative.

I was very fortunate to have a husband who, in spite of not entirely understanding my inner compulsions, was generous enough to accept the urgency for me. He built me a charming little cabin high on the hill behind the house where I could overlook the valley and the mountain and open sky. He never disturbed me there and he so impressed everybody on the ranch, that no one else ever dared approach it. It was a beautiful sanctuary and it served me well through some difficult years.

He also cooperated in letting me go off to the Lake Tahoe region for a solitary week every summer. Near the little town of Meyers I rented a small cabin isolated from traffic where I slept outside at night and spent hours each day exploring alpine meadows and sunny mountain slopes, where chipmunks skittered among the rocks. For a whole week I spoke to no one. Time became unimportant—dawn, daylight, dusk, night punctuated the rhythm of my days. Long hours of deep meditation led to an incredible expansion of consciousness. The weeks that I spent in that mountain retreat during three consecutive summers left me unforgettable memories of beautiful scenes visible in sunlight and shadow often accompanied by flashes of insight and deep happiness. I began to appreciate the unity of all things. The earth and its myriad manifestations, man and all the complexities of his being, not separated but all part of a tremendous synthesis of creation. I had come to believe that the Divine Image can be encountered in many different forms throughout the whole Universe. All things are mirrored in that transcendent reality. Even the tiny individual soul can reflect the glory. During meditation it is not difficult to sense this Power, but the question remained: How could I live continuously in tune with the inner light?

I felt the need of some guidance other than my own prompting or the guidelines laid down in written testimonies. I seemed to crave some person wiser than myself to teach me the techniques of concentration. If this search had originated today (1974) I would doubtless have had little difficulty in finding the answer. The present "younger generation" has imported Oriental religion. There are hundreds of small groups practicing methods of meditation in the manner of Zen and other forms of Buddhism, disciplines borrowed from the Sufi and Moslem masters and the ancient Yoga seers of India. The term Yoga is used to define the revolutionary trend responsible for this new awakening. The real meaning of the word Yoga is Yoke. The purpose of all the different manifestations is the linking of the soul to God through contemplation and self-discipline. But before the Second World War, access to such knowledge was much harder to come by. I explored Bahai and Quaker fellowships, but they did not seem to offer exactly what I was looking for. I read about Ashrams in India, but they were too far away. I stumbled on the Vedanta Society and obtained some of their pamphlets describing the extraordinary life of Sri Ramakrishna, Indian prophet of the 19th century. Ramakrishna was born in 1836 of a Brahmin family and followed the age-old traditions of his country by joining a monastic order at a very early age. He, like the Persian Baba, accepted the validity of all religions. He considered Jesus and Buddha and other spiritual leaders as incarnations of the Godhead. He won many disciples and accepted about twenty young men to help him to estabish the Vedanta Fellowship. Vedanta signifies "The Way." One of these monks, Swani Vivekenanda played a role similar to Saint Paul who had proselytized so effectively in the Christian cause. After traveling in Europe, Vivekenanda pushed his way into the Congress of World Religions held in Chicago around 1890. The leaders of the Congress were reluctant to even admit him into their august gathering. His credentials were almost unortho-dox. But his insistence and his vibrant personality won a begrudging acceptance. Somehow or other he obtained permission to make a short speech—ten minutes or so—but once started, he became so carried away in presenting the life and teachings of Ramakrishna and the audience was so spellbound by his eloquence and spiritual power, that they listened enthralled for nearly half a day. The decorous complacency of the theologians was shattered by the bombshell of this stranger from the East. No one could resist his eloquence nor doubt the authenticity of his inspiration.

The impact of the new doctrine led to the establishment of centers in New York City, Boston and other cities. I heard that the movement maintained an Ashram just outside of Los Angeles in the hills of La Crescenta. I found my way there and was invited to remain as a guest if I so desired. The Ashram nestled in a sloping, open ravine, in the midst of an old orange grove. A large building with meeting hall, dining room, kitchen and living quarters for the members of the order, a dormitory for visitors, a sanctuary, and a lathe house, a garage and a few miscellaneous sheds housed the community. Swami Paramananda was the leader. There were five or six Sisters and two young men disciples. One of the Sisters was responsible for all the business and financial arrangements. She drove the car and did the shopping and answered the telephone. Another Sister prepared the meals, another took care of the garden and the bees. Sister Devamata was a sort of Mother Superior. She came originally from Boston, had been converted by Swami Vivekananda when she was about 18 years old, worked with him in New York and India, wrote a number of books and was a spiritual understudy for the Swami.

She was dressed in snowy white robes, her face as pale as her dress, framed in filmy veil. She was frail like a delicate flower and seemed like a spirit moving among us. Yet she was firm in making decisions concerning rituals and the lives of the younger women. I was amazed to have her ask me about Boston and some of the old Boston families like the Hallowells or Lowells whom she had known in her girlhood.

It was an idyllic environment. The air was saturated with orange blossom fragrance, birds sang, bees sifted in and out of the branches. One could walk back into the canyon or wander into the temple where the doors were all open for the fragrant breezes to flow through. In the evening one could sit on the terrace and watch the lights of the city on the other side of the canyon. The lights seemed so far away. The moon when it rose a tiny arc in the overreaching heavens, became a symbol of serenity. The day's routine began with worship in the temple. Silent meditation was interspersed with chanting by the Swami or Sister Devamata's offering of a tray of fruits and vegetables which were fresh from the garden and were placed on the altar to be blessed and later used during the day for the community repasts. After a simple breakfast of fruit, bread and honey, the morning hours were spent caring for the house and gardens. In the afternoon, there was reading or meditation or walking on mountain trails. At sundown came the evening worship, the benediction of ingredients of the supper and a sustained period of silence, sometimes chanting of the symbolic word *Om-m-m*. After supper, we had an hour or two of friendly talk on the terrace, some music, perhaps, or a game and enjoyment of the cool breeze, the distant city lights and the star-studded sky. A deep sense of fellowship with the other seekers and an atmosphere of joy made the gathering an integral part of the spiritual continuity of the corporate life.

The presiding genius of this Ashram was, of course, Swami Paramananda. When you first met him he appeared like a young boy, tall, slim, moving with the grace of a deer or a panther. His face was unlined and the warm smile on his lips and in his eyes seemed to envelop the stranger with an encompassing welcome. He was in reality no longer very young for he had been active in the Ramakrishna Mission for at least thirty years. He was one of those people who seem timeless, who do not age, but live in a perpetual springtime of love and service. With all his profound wisdom and spiritual insight, he retained a child-like quality. He liked to make kites, he liked to prepare special dishes, he liked to drive a car. He told me "When I first came to the United States I imagined that people expected me to talk philosophy, but I found out that automobiles create a quicker point of contact. As soon as I learned to drive a motor car I had an unfailing topic of sympathetic conversation with everyone I met."

I talked alone with him twice. He knew exactly where I stood, how far my inner consciousness had developed without my telling him. I felt that it was not so much what the Swami said but the validity of his whole being that had meaning. Tagore said in one of his poems, "He who opens the flower, does it so simply." To be totally immersed in the

Divine Presence results in simplicity—there can be no barriers to the flow of love from that source and he who has become part of this Reality becomes an instrument for its fulfillment. Herein lies the mystery of incarnation. "The word was made flesh and dwelt among us." From the Swami I learned the joy of the sacrificial life, and that I should not worry about unworthiness and shortcomings, but just go ahead and really renounce the world, the flesh, and the devil by becoming a child of God, rejoicing in His manifold appearances and revelations. He suggested a prelude of recollection by which I could quickly enter the threshold of communion, and negative considerations of past short-comings melted away in the positive sunlight of adoration.

The brief stay at the Ashram gave me a great yearning to remain there and become part of what seemed an idyllic community. If I had been free to do so, would I have found satisfaction in such an ingrowing group? At the time I thought I would, but I doubt if I could have been satisfied indefinitely.

However, the brief experience of the cloistered life penetrated deeply into my consciousness and seemed to take root there. The main difference between Christian theology and Hindu doctrine lies not so much in the definition of Deity, as in the conception of man. The Judea-Christian believes in original sin, that each person is unregenerate until rescued by redeeming grace; the Hindu on the other hand perceives man as essentially good, born bearing within himself a seed of the universal spirit which he must seek to discover and nurture and cultivate. By the practice of devotion, grace comes. Swami Paramananda was the most joyous and simple person I ever met. He said to me, "No single soul has ever found happiness or peace or lasting contentment in the outer world; but after one has found it within, one can carry it to the outside. When we cease to follow our lower instincts and obey only our higher intentions, life becomes so rhythmic that everything runs along harmoniously and we can live in the world, or out of it, without danger."

My mind seemed orderly, my spirit lightened, my strivings centered in one direction. A state of blessedness. And so I left La Crescenta with great peace and thankfulness.

XXIII

American Friends Service and European Refugees

Involvement with the Quakers; European refugees at Hidden Villa; the Baker Street house in San Francisco.

In the years prior to the outbreak of World War II, I became more and more closely connected with the Society of Friends. I found myself in sympathy with their religious convictions and also impressed by their manner of carrying out moral ideas in everyday living and in human relationships. For them, peace was not just the absence of war, but the practice of goodwill in all controversial situations. They also involved themselves with community problems. Young men faced with conscription, migrant workers in the fields, and refugees escaping from Nazi terrorism in Central Europe, all these were urgent issues that were not being adequately met by government or philanthropic agencies, which stirred Friends to seek remedial solutions.

There were several worship Meetings in California, the largest group being located in Pasadena and smaller ones in Berkeley, Palo Alto and San Jose. Members of these groups, acting individually, responded to the growing community needs. The American Friends Service Committee, an entity separate from Meetings, was organized to implement social concerns, and operated chiefly in the eastern states with headquarters in Philadelphia. The American Friends Service Committee had considerable success in conducting seminars for the study of international relationships in Europe. As emphasis shifted to the Pacific, because of the increasing militarism of Japan and the rising tide of hostility on the part of West Coast residents, it seemed expedient to arrange such seminars in California. The first two California Institutes were held in 1935, one at Whittier College headed by W. O.

Mendenhall, and one at Mills College with Dean Rusk as leader. Such topics as "Economic Problems of the Pacific," "Post-War Efforts at World Cooperation," "Effective Peace Programs for Local Groups," and "Latin American Affairs" were subjects under discussion. The Institutes lasted ten days and were well attended by many non-Quakers.

Student participation was encouraged and opened the way for the future recruitment of young people for work camps and seminars and for the counseling of pacifists who were soon to face the draft in World War II. Joseph Conard, a Friend from Philadelphia, was the secretary responsible for the success of these gatherings. I think it fair to say that through the Institutes many people in this area first became acquainted with Quaker testimonies and Quaker methods. They became, therefore, more inclined to accept action programs which a few years later needed their financial and ideological support. The pressure of the Nazi campaign against the Jews first became evident in San Francisco in 1937. The English and American Friends living in Europe had already been involved in heart-breaking efforts to alleviate the sufferings of the despised people. The Philadelphia office was deeply involved in providing hospitality and reorientation for emigres. Hostels were set up in many places, and all Meetings were being urged to provide affidavits and housing for displaced people. A special committee was established by Bay Area Meetings to deal with these problems. Mary and James Kimber of Berkeley gave many hours of service in seeking sponsors, temporary homes, and job offers. Such cases were processed in Philadelphia, and then we of the Pacific Coast waited eagerly for the arrival of our guests. Delays were frequent; some guests never arrived; sometimes a completely different family turned up with completely different qualifications. It was a little disconcerting to some Friends who had offered hospitality expecting to meet a professor and his wife and two high school children, to go to the depot and find themselves welcoming a business executive with four youngsters under twelve. It required considerable mental readjustment, not to mention the immediate rearrangement of living space (beds, cribs, play yards, meals). While many Friends are notably flexible, some are not. And the Committee endured some stormy sessions trying to justify the frustrations unavoidably encountered in the dilemmas of sudden exile. The California Branch Office of the Service Committee was located in Pasadena, for in that area there were many Friends. But it became apparent after 1933 that a closer contact was needed in the San Francisco area, which would make it possible to deal more directly with problems than was possible through an office four hundred miles away.

Aside from the International Institute at Mills College, perhaps the earliest direct involvement of the Service Committee in Northern California took place at Hidden Villa Ranch. A Vermont man, Donald Watt, the originator and Director of the Experiment in International Living, had organized a teenage group to spend the summer of 1940 in

Germany. The kids were all signed up for European travel when the war broke out in September 1939, and the trip to Germany became impossible. Donald Watt conferred with Hertha Kraus, who headed the refugee program working out of the AFSC office in Philadelphia. Together they conceived the idea of a camp staff consisting of recent European arrivals capable of introducing German culture to the students. In return, the students would introduce the foreigners to American ways, and both groups would cooperate in carrying out work projects at Hidden Villa Ranch. It was a neat plan, and we agreed to help carry it out. About twenty teenage boys and girls traveled across the country from East to West in station wagons. The European staff, all Jewish refugees, consisted of a photographer, a poet, and art historian, an international lawyer, an expert on South America (especially, it seemed, on the feminine population)—these all male—and two females, an opera singer and a teacher. Julius Wahl, formerly house father at the Northfield hostel headquarters, had come to California to stay. He was work director, assisted by my daughter Elizabeth and husband Frank. Julius's wife, Lee, was in charge of cooking. Either Donald Watt or Hertha Kraus selected as overall camp director a missionary who was born and raised in China and who had been displaced by the Communists and needed a job in the United States. Naturally, he and his wife were out of touch with American youth and likewise with European Jewish intellectuals. It would be hard to imagine a more impossible conglomeration of personalities to mould into a "beloved community." One of the first projects involved putting up a new building, as I mentioned in the previous chapter. The construction work, under the direction of Julius Wahl proceeded slowly, because practically none of the participants either old or young ever had any previous experience with tools. I overheard a typical dialogue between Julius and the Austrian poet.

Julius: "Do you think you could saw this piece of wood into three pieces?"

Poet: "That's very hard work."

Julius: "Oh, not really very hard. You need to use your muscles so you will get strong."

Poet: "But why should I want to be strong?"

Another time, after new windows had been installed, the art historian was asked to clean them. One of the panes had a small round factory label stuck on it. When Wolfgang polished the glass he was very careful not to remove the sticker, and this created a further "incident".

If their physical ineptitude presented problems, their two-way indoctrination was even more laborious. Every day brought new misunderstandings arising out of such divergent cultures. The missionary director was in no way qualified to resolve them. I had not expected to have anything to do with the running of the project, but after two or three major explosive incidents it appeared that the whole project was in danger of complete disintegration. Therefore, I decided to pitch in and try to assume some control of the emotional chaos. I was able to talk to the Europeans in German and arranged sessions for them without the students and without the Christian zealot. I also could communicate with the youngsters, having been involved with teenagers in my own family and in school. Having visited China, including some of the Christian missions there, I could appreciate the missionary's dilemma. So it was my function to interpret for each group the attitudes of the others. For the refugees I arranged some evenings at our house and outside adult community contacts for them. For the teenagers, I developed a program in two migrant workers' camps where they could spend mornings or afternoons teaching arts and crafts to camp children, and playing games with them. This really appealed to our young people, and it gave them a purpose and sense of accomplishment which they craved. Supplies for this program were not hard to come by, and I assumed responsibility for transportation and helped plan each day's activity. Guidance to the missionary "director" was a more delicate matter, and I never succeeded in explaining to him why he was so ineffectual. I did, however, persuade him not to bring his *New Testament* to breakfast and insist on reading a chapter before anyone could spoon out the oatmeal.

One evening, I had invited some good Quakers from Palo Alto Meeting to meet the members of the group. After a buffet supper, we gathered in the living room and I planned to ask each member of the staff to tell a little about their own lives before and after evacuation. I began with Mr. A, the supposed expert on South America, who had an unpleasant little Mexican hairless dog who accompanied him everywhere. This animal's name was *Gummi*. As Mr. A. talked, he held Gummi on his lap and slapped the naked grey body of the dog with resounding love pats. Mrs. M., the wife of the missionary, and Mrs. T., a straight-backed prim middle-aged Quaker lady of the old school, sat side by side in front of the big window. Mr. A., telling about his explorations in South America, kept emphasizing the beauty of the women there. He said, "I came into the village of —— and in a garden by the first house I came to was the *most* beautiful girl I ever saw. She was in a swing. So *beautiful*. I stayed with her a long time." He went on with detailed descriptive analysis to the delight of the kids who were present—and the evident disapproval by the two ladies in the window. Anxiety on my part moved me to interrupt and say, "Where else did you go, Mr. A?"

"Oh, yes. I went on to the next village and here I found an even *more* beautiful girl. *So* beautiful!" More lingering details by Mr. A., more giggles from the youngsters, and more horror on the faces by the window. With growing consternation, I finally said, "Mr. A., how about the arts and crafts of South America? I understand they do wonderful work there."

Mr. A. replied, "Arts and crafts? Oh, yes, they are nice. But the women! I must tell you about the most beautiful of all . . ." At this point, to the hilarity of the members of my family who were present, the regret of the other kids and the relief of our guests, I decided it was time for more refreshments. (I always suspected that Hertha Kraus, in the AFSC office in Philadelphia, had chosen to send as far away as possible those most difficult to place in the East.)

At the close of summer, after the director and the students returned to the East coast, most of the refugee staff decided to remain in California. Their situation of dependence pointed up the need for Bay Area Friends to create some sort of organization to deal with the Germans and Austrians who were escaping from Central Europe and arriving here in increasing numbers. The Jewish organizations were overburdened; many newcomers had already been helped by English and American Quakers in their own countries; many not Jewish in religion preferred dealing with Friends rather than with other denominational groups.

In the Spring of 1940, Gerda Isenberg, Dorothy Murray and I (from the Palo Alto Meeting) opened a Newcomers' Evening at the Presidio Hill School on Washington Street in San Francisco which I was principal of at the time. We welcomed from 12 to 40 of them each Wednesday evening. Gerda and I spoke German, so we were able to communicate more readily than many other Friends with new arrivals whose English was scanty or non-existent. At Christmas time we arranged hospitality for some 50 couples and individuals in the Peninsula area. In the summer the Presidio Hill School Board authorized us to establish a hostel for displaced persons. Mabel Pound Adams from Sacramento, a member of College Park Meeting, agreed to act as volunteer hostess. We gathered some cots and other housekeeping appurtenances. Our first tenant was Theodore Kann from Vienna, who afterwards established himself as a photographer in Oakland, where he lived for many years. An event that contributed greatly to the development of Friends' activity was the revival in March 1940, of the San Francisco Meeting for Worship which had been discontinued for lack of attendance. Clarence Pickett and Ray Newton from Philadelphia were present at the meeting which was held at the Presidio Open Air School at 3839 Washington Street. Others who attended this important occasion were: Elizabeth Owen, Hanna and Andrew Erskine, Peter Gulbrandson, Anna and William James, Virginia Perkins, Joseph Conard, Florence Thomas, James and Mary Kimber, Phoebe Seagrave, Isabella Perry, Elton Trueblood, Skoras, Arthur and Katharine Hall, and, of course, myself. Elizabeth Owen was chosen clerk of the meeting, and Arthur Hall, secretary.

As a symptom of the increasing activity among Friends, it is interesting to note that the first Pacific Coast Yearly Meeting was held at Hidden Villa in the summer of 1941. Because of increasing pressures involved in serving newcomers, migrants, young men facing conscription, as well as the upholding of the peace testimony, the need for a permanent headquarters became evident. The newly organized San Francisco Meeting continued to use the school as a place to hold First Day Meetings, but its use for other Friends' concerns was of necessity limited by the obvious weekday needs of the school.

Therefore, in September 1941 a house on Baker Street was rented, and Joe Conard, who had been a liaison person with the national AFSC office through his involvement with the International Institutes at Mills College, was asked to work out financial arrangements for work in San Francisco. As usual with Friends, considerable discussion took place before there was agreement on the advantages setting up such a place and entitling it "Friends Center". Many felt that "autonomous groups in various localities should form nuclei" and localize their efforts. Many were skeptical about a Friends Center. Some felt that it was a risky project which might be abused. But the need for a coordinator became obvious because of distance between meetings and the danger of duplication. And their minds were partially relieved when a minute was inserted stating that "smoking, card playing and dancing should not occur on the first floor of the center!"

The financial arrangements that Joe worked out were a little unique, as Friends' financing tends to be. Here again, I was able to merge several of my concerns into one conglomeration. Development of Youth Hostels in California was one of our objectives. The California Hostel had a part-time secretary, Betty Baker, who later was married to Joe Goodman. She was transferred to Baker Street where one-third of her salary, and one-sixth of the expenses of the center were paid by the Hostel Committee. The balance came from Palo Alto and Berkeley meetings and the Berkeley Friends Church. Mrs. Edward A. Heller, Sr. donated liberally because of her interest in refugees, and many other individuals gave generously. Furnishings were scraped up hither and yon. Gerda Isenberg donated an elegant dining room table and eight chairs; beds showed up miraculously, and nondescript sofas and large, upholstered, dilapidated "easy armchairs" appeared from unidentified sources. Julius Wahl made window seats. A house committee with Clara Brown and Anna James scrubbed, made curtains, and spreads. Betty Baker was in residence and brought her own furniture, including a thousand books. Joe Conard was there and his sister-in-law, Florence Thomas, who took care of Joe's little son, was housekeeper and hostess. Various people used the guest rooms from time to time, sometimes passing through, sometimes staying longer. Among our most frequent guests might be mentioned Eleanor Polturak, Dr. Goetzel, a well-known physician from Vienna, Robert and Nuschi Plank, Meta Hendel, and two Dr. Loewensteins (male and female). Outside helpers included Sheila Bessemer, Dick and Elsie Richlefs, and Mark Luca and his wife, Anita Levy, a San Francisco librarian, gave us all her spare time to take the young children of refugees to the zoo and playgrounds on Saturday; she also furnished three turkeys for Thanksgiving dinner. We had some unexpected visitors, too, such as a Dutch sailor who wandered in and demanded a meal because "my grandmother was a Friend"—and of course we gave it to him.

Residents came and went, and two of our more permanent residents shared an amusing experience. Their names were Joe Goodman and Ken Stevens. They met at a conference, and they talked about common interests and public affairs for some time before discovering that they were sharing the same bedroom! Ken worked at night and arrived at Baker Street to sleep just after Joe had left for California Academy of Sciences. By the time Joe returned in the late afternoon, Ken had left. So they never had met before, even though they had been sharing the same bed!

A visit from Emma Cadbury was a highlight of the first winter. Because of the war she had recently left the Friends' Center in Vienna. Emma knew many of our refugees personally and had laid the ground work for their escape. We held a special reception for her when she arrived, and the Newcomers welcomed her with tears of gratitude. It was a touching reunion—this tiny little lady with spectacles, dressed in black with flat shoes, quietly smiling as she received the flowery exuberances of her friends, voiced in exotic basic English.

With the outbreak of World War II, the activity at the Friends Center increased enormously. Since the United States was now at war with Germany most of our Newcomer friends became "enemy aliens" overnight. They crowded into our office for advice and reassurance. Some of the neighbors in our block had become somewhat suspicious of the "goings on" at the house where so many German people congregated. Joe Conard and I considered it advisable to talk with the F.B.I. and explain what we were up to. We had an appointment with the head of the San Francisco office who, by the way, had the appropriate name of "Nat Pieper." We found him a most intelligent and knowledgeable gentleman who knew all about Friends and their peculiar ways and was not at all disturbed by our operations. Just around the corner from our Center was a fire house. At many times during the day and night a siren—a practice signal—would go off with a deafening roar. But you always wondered if it really was just practice, and it terrified some of our refugees who had been through bombings. We also had blackouts, with all windows darkened and only candles inside. One night when there was a blackout, and the staff was sitting in the gloom, there came a knock at the door. When we cautiously opened it, there were the two Wolff sisters, one of them carrying a violin. "What are you doing out in the blackout?" we asked.

"We come for rehearsal."

"But don't you know it's blackout?"

"Oh, yes, we haf it too in Berlin. We are not *ängstlich* —we know."

One incident which comes to my mind illustrates the more serious difficulties encountered by some of the recent arrivals. An Austrian woman, Mrs. F., who was a cook, made delicious little cakes and *tortes*, for which Vienna is deservedly famous. She and her husband were both Jewish. They developed a small business in which she baked cakes and her husband delivered and sold them. Their best customers were members of the Nazi German consulate and their entourage. When war was declared, this group was immediately picked up by the F.B.I. and shipped off to Bismarck, North Dakota. Their personal papers and bank accounts were confiscated. Among the latter were numerous checks from the consular staff made out to Mr. F. Because of this, he was suspected of being a spy and shipped off to Bismarck along with the Nazis. On arrival he found himself surrounded by unfriendly countrymen who, in keeping with their party philosophy, amused themselves by persecuting the poor little Jew who had been provided for them. His wife received a letter from him and tearfully brought it to the Friends. We were able to explain the situation to the authorities and, fortunately, arranged to have him released from this unpleasant predicament.

In February, 1942, all persons of Japanese ancestry were moved out of Pacific Coast areas to temporary "security" centers. I shall have more to say about this in a later chapter, but their exodus made available a new location for the Service Committee. A large number of Orientals lived in "little Tokyo" between Van Ness Avenue and Fillmore Street. The Japanese Y.W.C.A. building, specially designed by Julia Morgan, had great charm and openness. When the Japanese were evacuated, it became available to the Service Committee. We found it admirably suited to our needs. A large assembly room, offices, kitchen, upstairs bedrooms and basement storage space could accommodate a variety of activities. Best of all, the bus stopped at the corner two doors from our entrance. I spent three days a week in the office and handled most of the work with the refugees, cooperating with the Jewish agencies and the International Institute. We dealt with a truly wonderful group of people. Most of them had already attained professional standing in Europe. To be suddenly uprooted, separated from family and social ties, and shuttled into a foreign country was a traumatic experience for them. Handicapped by lack of language facility, totally unprepared for the only kind of employment open to them, and frustrated by the disregard of status to which they were accustomed, each case presented unique problems. The young ones were not so difficult. They could fill in places left vacant by defense workers or army recruits in stores or businesses. Being young, they learned English quickly. Professors were not too difficult to place, and for a while, doctors could get into San Francisco hospitals, until a law was passed requiring two years as an intern before licensing. Lawyers were really impossible because Germanic and Anglo-Saxon legal systems are quite different and most lawyers were not skilled as dish washers or gardeners. Many of the women, who had formerly been employers of servants, were hopeless as housekeepers or seamstresses. Often I brought some of these poor souls home with me to give them decent food and a quiet place to reorient their lives. I presumed on the good nature of my friends to invite strangers to stay over weekends or on holidays at their homes.

There were many memorable incidents in finding jobs for uprooted people. An Austrian lawyer, for instance, whose legal training in Germanic law did not qualify him for the American bar, did learn to be a gardener. A surgeon of twenty years' experience who was forced to begin his internship over again, did obtain the California medical license. A newspaper reporter from Vienna set up a photography shop; a banker ran the service elevator at a hotel. One young golden-haired dilettante acquired the job of hospital orderly in what he called the "matrimonial ward." Some women worked in restaurants, baked fancy goodies, cleaned house, wrapped packages in department stores and did similar tasks—nothing too menial for them to undertake. Extraordinary readjustments for displaced intellectuals to make in middle life! Yet within ten or fifteen years nearly all of them had reestablished themselves in the new land as functioning members of the community. It was my privilege to attend several citizenship ceremonies, and it was inspiring to share their enthusiasm on becoming bonafide Americans. Many of them pinned small American flags in their button holes. The Pledge of Allegiance they gave was no hollow repetition but a deeply moving dedication. It made me feel very proud of my country that we could offer freedom to so many victims of tyranny.

Some very dear friendships evolved from these emergencies, and several of them have lasted all our lives. For instance, there are Robert and Nuschi Plank, who came from Vienna. He was a lawyer, she was a Montessori teacher. At first she worked as an attendant in an orphanage in Oakland. Someone introduced her to me, and I was fascinated by her description of the school she had conducted in Austria. I was familiar with the pre-school material developed by Mme. Montessori, but I had never seen the elementary devices which seemed to me of great importance (antedating "new math"). It seemed to me preposterous that a woman of her dynamic personality and achievement should be making beds and srubbing pots and pans. Although her English was pretty scant, I persuaded her to talk to a group of teachers and show her educational materials. Then I offered her a teaching job at Presidio Hill School, where she later became principal. Her husband took training in social work and both followed successful careers in California. Eventually, they moved to Cleveland, Ohio, where they live now, but we still see them once or twice a year.

The Germans and Austrians were the first "displaced persons" that I came to know about. I had been familiar with Irish and Italian emigrants in New England earlier, but they had come of their own volition.

Although they had problems, they had not been forced to emigrate in order to escape annihilation. Not since the Middle Ages had there been such a procession of dislocated persons in all parts of our world. White Russians from the Soviet Union, Jews from Germany, Austria and Poland, Arabs out of Israel, Greeks out of Egypt, Moslems out of India, Buddhists out of Afghanistan, Belgians out of the Congo, Dutch out of Indonesia. The list goes on and on.

One group that was relatively small and unknown was the Russians, who experienced exile twice in one lifetime. At the time of the Russian Revolution, a number of these people escaped to China. Due to the unstable political status in Mongolia and Manchuria, they ventured further south and established a fairly large colony on the outskirts of Shanghai. Here they set up new businesses and led a reasonably prosperous existence. They were more or less isolated from both English and Chinese neighbors, but within their small domain where Russian was spoken and the old culture adhered to, their lives were quite secure. When the revolution in China came, however, their security was immediately at stake. There was little doubt but that they would all be liquidated when the tide of conquest enveloped the Shanghai settlement. I do not know just what arrangements were carried out by the U.S. Government, but I do know that most of the Russians from Shanghai were brought to San Francisco for resettlement. Our city had already absorbed a few white Russians in the 20's, many of whom lived in the neighborhood of the Friends Center. They had a Russian church and they ran restaurants and served as waiters or lady's maids or married wealthy American girls. By the time the new influx arrived, they were well established as U.S. citizens. The later group consisted almost entirely of older people, people who knew no English and who represented a non-soluble mixture of old aristocrats and scarcely literate peasant types.

Although all entering immigrants are supposed to have affidavits of support from U.S. citizens, it seemed that the assurances in the case of this group of people were largely fictitious, probably due to the haste of their removal. The sponsors designated on their forms of entry did not realize their obligations beyond just signing their names. Normally incomers would have been subject to deportation but in this case they could not be "returned to country of origin." So they remained to worry along as best they could. Someone told them of the Friends and they appealed to us for assistance.

The language barrier seemed insurmountable until Dr. Yavden came to our aid. She was a professional woman from China who had been in the Bay area for some years. She volunteered her services one day a week for conferences, counseling, help with employment, referrals, or just plain listening to tragic and heartrending stories of disjointed twice-uprooted lives. Between January and September 1953 she served about 80 clients. If you had walked into the lobby of 1830 Sutter Street of a Monday afternoon, you would have seen rotund old ladies wearing scarves over their heads, real live *Babushkas*, or stately gentlemen with whiskers and canes, ex-generals perhaps, waiting for Dr. Yavden and her friendly, realistic help. We served them tea and cookies and offered English lessons. One had to take care not to offend their dignity by brash American manners. A major crisis over presumed loss of status could develop, for example, when one English class was conducted in the basement while another was on the main floor. One can smile at these little idiosyncracies, but how would *we* fare if transplanted into social circles alien to our heritage?

All in all, it has been a wonderful thing to see how alien people have surmounted dislocation and have been able to put forth new shoots in American soil. It renews one's faith in the future of our country, and we must never forget that ours is a nation of immigrants existing as a unique experiment in democracy.

XXIV

Evacuation of Japanese from California

Helping at the evacuation center in San Francisco; visiting the camps at Tule Lake Resettlement; after the war.

In the 1930s, before so many houses were built, the fields of Los Altos were covered with California poppies. If you had chanced to be passing through town, a little before nine o'clock of a spring morning, you would have seen the Japanese children walking across these fields on their way to the San Antonio School. The girls, dressed in their gay flowered kimonos, looked like flurries of butterflies hovering over sheets of orange gold.

The teachers loved these children. They came to school immaculately washed and combed, they were courteous and well-behaved, always smiling and eager to learn. Many of their parents did not speak English. They worked in homes or on ranches, operated laundries, grew flowers and vegetables and cleaned the streets. They were not allowed to become citizens, but their sons and daughters, born in California, could look forward to that privilege. The parents saw to it that the younger generation availed themselves of all the opportunities this country had to offer its immigrants. No alien group in the United States ever worked harder than the *Issei* (the foreign-born Japanese). They leased land because they could not own it, but by their diligence and incredibly long hours of work in the strawberry and tomato fields, in the fisheries of southern California and truck gardens in the valleys, in little shops and laundries in the towns, they competed successfully with white farmers and business men. As they grew wealthier, they were able to purchase property in the name of their native born children, the *Nisei*. These young people, who were educated in our schools and who spoke

English perfectly, had become completely identified with American ideals and practices, but were looked upon with jealousy and distrust by some older community groups who felt threatened by their competence.

When the attack on Pearl Harbor precipitated the Pacific War in December 1941, the American-Japanese in California were as shocked and outraged as any of the rest of us. Like the German-Americans in the First World War, they were called on to relinquish all ties with the country of their birth and with relatives who still remained there. Although they were troubled, the loyal response of the Japanese group was instantaneous, with the exception of the nationals representing the government who were immediately picked up by the FBI and a few who chose to return to Japan.

On December 9, two days following Pearl Harbor, Attorney-General Biddle stated, "There are in the United States many persons of Japanese extraction whose loyalty to the Country even in the present emergency is unquestioned," and President Roosevelt, referring to these persons, declared, "Americanism is a matter of the mind and heart. Americanism is not and never was a matter of race or ancestry." Many Japanese-American boys were already in training for service in Europe, and Japanese-American civilians responded loyally by purchasing war bonds and providing food in the national emergency. In February 1942 Attorney-General Warren (later Governor of California) assured the public that "we have had no sabotage and no fifth column activity since the beginning of the war." Despite these statements from responsible officials, certain California groups, long antagonistic to the Japanese, used the occasion to fan the flames of hysteria and hatred. The American Legion, the Associated Farmers, the Native Sons and above all, the Hearst Press, worked fast and furiously, and a group of California Congressmen headed by Leland Ford urged the President "to move all Japanese, native born and alien, to concentration camps." Soon that authority was given to the Army by executive order, and on March 2, General DeWitt ordered evacuation from California, Oregon and Washington, and part of Arizona. On March 18, the War Relocation Authority was established. It all happened so quickly and so conclusively that the people who knew and loved the Japanese were caught napping. Church people, teachers, university presidents (like Sproul at Berkeley and Wilbur at Stanford), social workers, county and city officials, YWCA, YMCA workers protested by telegram, letters, meetings, newspaper articles. But it was too late. "The caissons were rolling." The largest single forced migration in American history was under way.

What was my horror when I went to the Service Committee office on March 30, 1942, to see signs on all the telephone poles in San Francisco stating that all persons of Japanese ancestry were required to leave the area before the end of the month. It was a shocking reminder that what had happened in Nazi Germany could also happen in democratic America. It was a bitter disillusionment, and it reminded me of our trip to Germany in 1936. Frank and I and three of our children had rented bicycles in Munich and had gone for a trip through the Bavarian Tyrol and saw signs in every village: "Hier sind Juden nicht Gewunscht." (Here Jews are not wanted.) This expression of bigotry had made me want to tear the signs down, but I was stopped by Frank who warned that such an act might lead to trouble. So I desisted, but the signs were a sad note of discord in that lovely rural paradise, just as these were now.

Since there was no recourse from General DeWitt's evacuation order, the next question was what could be done to help in the sudden emergency confronting the Japanese residents. A few with contacts in other states, had left voluntarily, but the balance of 110,000 faced complete rupture of their lives within a few weeks. They were to be allowed to take with them only what they could carry. They had to decide how to dispose of their household furniture, their houses or apartments (owned or leased), their businesses, their automobiles, their debts and any moneys owed to them. It was a mad scramble. Many people came forward with offers of temporary stewardship of property, help in disposing of goods, providing legal advice, etc. Unfortunately, there were others who used the occasion advantageously to themselves. Many Japanese-American families lost all they had so laboriously accumulated over the years.

Certain spots in the city had been designated by the army as reception centers from which the evacuees were to be taken to temporary barracks to wait until the nine relocation centers were made ready on out-of-state government land. I shall never forget the morning when I went to work at the Japanese-American League building on Post Street. On all the streets in the vicinity and from the hills above little groups of people were hurrying laden with suitcases, bags, cartons and all manner of impediments. One carried a bird cage, another a hundred year old dwarf tree in a pot, blanket rolls, baby baskets, toy animals, dolls, packages of books, heavy coats, umbrellas. An incredible sight converging on the place of assembly. It was guarded inside and out by soldiers with fixed bayonets. Some of the Friends had organized a canteen with hot coffee, tea, chocolate, doughnuts and sandwiches. Each individual, even the babies, had to have a number. We helped fasten on the degrading labels. We provided extra twine to tie up sagging bundles. We offered tags and letter paper and stamps, and a box of bandages for bruised knees. We had a little stove to heat baby bottles and kleenex to wipe the tears off the faces of frightened little children. We had several private cars in which to run errands. Gerda Isenberg took one old man back to his apartment to recover his false teeth which he had left on a shelf in the bathroom. The families huddled together, surrounded by the pitiful bundles and bags they had salvaged. Most of them had no idea where they were going and believed they would never be able to return to California. At last the chartered buses arrived, and

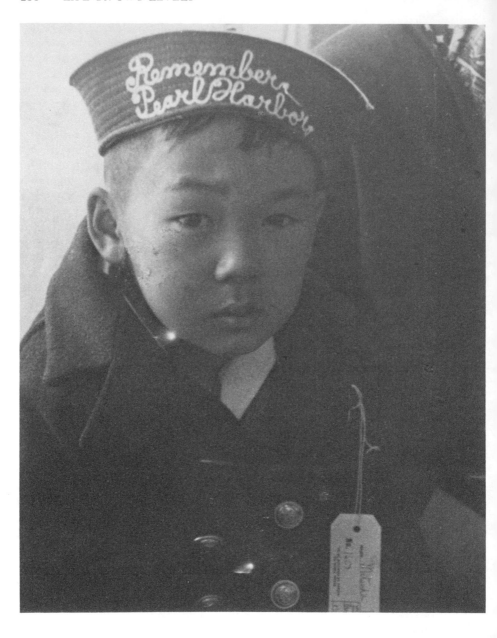

the little groups gathered themselves and their possessions to climb aboard, supervised by soldiers. We helped get the luggage in and lifted the children onto the steps of the bus, watching as they found their seats inside, and waving goodbye when each bus was full. As it moved away we had tears streaming down our cheeks. "Wipe them away quickly, girls," we told ourselves. "We have to go in and cheer up the next group."

Frank wrote down his own experience on this day.

"I walked around with a strange feeling that this could not be the America that I had fought for in 1918. And then I saw among the crowd an American Legion cap. I went over and talked with him. He was pretty discouraged and a little bitter as he told me how he had thought that his record of service in the first World War would have entitled him to remain in his home, or at least to have an investigation. There wasn't much I could say, but I stayed with him until he left. He told me of one other Legion member who had rented a room in the hotel the night before and blown his brains out rather than be evacuated."

The temporary destination of these San Francisco residents was the old Tanforan race track on El Camino Real near Millbrae. Not only the booking areas and employee dormitories, but the horse stalls had been cleaned out and set up to house the incoming families. As the bus loads of evacuees arrived, they were dispatched by soldiers to the accommodations corresponding to the numbers pinned on their clothing. Mattress bags collected from army surplus to be stuffed with straw were supplied to all residents to be placed on iron bunks. Most outsiders were not admitted to the quarters, but I was allowed to drive my car all the way in because I had three old people dependent on crutches or wheelchairs who were unable to board the bus and needed to be taken direct to their lodgings. It was a heartbreaking sight to see a family, surrounded by their meager belongings, sitting on the beds or on the floor of their 9×12 spaces—just sitting, wondering what was going to happen next.

Frank had his car at the Assembly Center also. He was delegated to deliver a psychotic female who was inimical to bus travel. A soldier was sent with him to guard his passenger. The lady in question started in at once on Frank, but finding him absorbed in driving and completely oblivious to her tender advances, turned her attention to the soldier in the back seat. He was a young nice looking chap who was enormously embarrassed by his assignment. He tried to be kind and patted her hand gently while withdrawing from her entwining attempts to embrace him. If the occasion had not been so sad, this episode would have been ludicrous.

I do not remember how many were located at Tanforan; Santa Anita outside Pasadena accommodated 18,000. The army allowed visitors in on one day in the week between 1 and 4 p.m. At Tanforan, the bleachers were used for visits with the inmates; at Santa Anita, you could only talk with your friends standing up with barbed wire between you and them.

We went every Thursday to visit Tanforan, taking with us gifts of homecooked foods or canned goods to vary the monotony of mass meals. We brought toys for the children, reading matter (censored at the gate) and other articles requested by the recipients. The line outside waiting to enter represented a cross section of the population. Young housewives, perhaps with a child or two, professional people, business men, professors, Negroes, Mexican-Americans, ministers and priests— every conceivable sort of person caring enough about the innocent victims of war hysteria to spend hours travelling and waiting in line for an hour's visit. I remember standing next to Mrs. Jordan, wife of the President of Stanford University. She was going to see the "houseboy" who had served her faithfully for twenty-five years. Another time I saw a prominent San Francisco lawyer beside a defense worker in overalls. This spontaneous protest and continuing demonstration of goodwill must, I think, have mitigated to some small degree the resentment, anger and frustration experienced by these uprooted people.

Between March and November 1942, more tar-papered barracks were thrown up, more barbed wire fences built in remote desert areas and the evacuees with their miserably few possessions were herded onto trains to be deposited in these crowded villages of barracks encircled by barbed wire and guarded by soldiers. Seven thousand to eighteen thousand in each bleak desert area swept by icy winds in the winter and roasted by unadulterated sunshine in the summer. The Japanese accepted the situation with a stoical forbearance which amazed me. I wonder what the Irish would have done under an equivalent provocation?

I knew a number of teachers who had volunteered to teach in the Relocation Centers and when I visited the Tule Lake Center on the Nevada border, I stayed in their quarters inside the barricades. I was free to roam anywhere, but not to take pictures—and I knew why. The images of what I saw remain in my mind, indelibly etched. The little children singing the songs and playing the games we used at Peninsula School, the High School students studying American history (not forgetting the Constitution and the Bill of Rights!), old people with folded hands sitting waiting and waiting, the alert young people in the offices and maintenance areas, the unbelievable little gardens around the steps of the barracks where trellises made from old packing cases were set up to guide the hoped-for sprouts, the huge noisy communal dining halls where three times a day food was served on thick white china plates on long tables with benches holding twenty to thirty people, first come first served. I think meal time was perhaps the greatest trial to the Japanese, used to their dainty bowls and ceremonious meals at low tables. The clattery meals and the lack of privacy in the toilets offended their sensibilities more than anything else. I think I found the watch towers armed with machine guns at each corner of the stockade the most distressing symbols. While I was present at one family's cubicle the mail was delivered. A letter from the son of the family fighting in Italy with the 442nd U.S. Combat team was opened by his mother living in an American Concentration Camp!

As soon as it was evident that there was no way to block the removal of Japanese, California Friends, the Council of Churches, YWCA, YMCA and other groups turned their attention to the young people whose schooling was being interrupted by the forced migration. The idea of Student Relocation was born at a meeting at Anna Head School in Berkeley but was soon transferred to Sutter Street Friends Service office in early summer. Because no adequate facilities existed in the Relocation Centers, the purpose was to insure outside training opportunities to the young people of college age. To do this it was necessary to screen applicants and determine their major lines of interest or talent, to obtain scholarships in eastern institutions, to arrange living quarters and means of transportation and to gain clearance from the Army. A national organization was set up in Philadelphia and in the course of a few months over 500 colleges agreed to accept applicants. Each case had to be processed individually. A tremendous volume of correspondence was required, often as many as 25 letters in a single case. It was necessary to arouse the student to make application, to determine his desired line of study, to get his parent's permission, to communicate his desires to the appropriate college, to arrange living accommodations, to receive assurances from college and lay hosts, to get military clearance and a transportation voucher, and to arrange for some Friend or Friends to meet the student on arrival to allay his fears and to help him find part-time employment and befriend him in his period of adjustment. I worked on this project for awhile, and I remember the bulging files that represented the details on each case and the maddening delays and revisions associated with each one. After two and a half years of intensive work, 3500 students had been accepted. The scattering of Japanese into so many communities was really a blessing in disguise for the young people. They were extricated from previous ghetto living areas and came in contact with a much wider social and intellectual milieu than they would have known if they had stayed in their original homes. Many of them remained in Eastern cities. All benefitted from wider contacts with college students and host families from different backgrounds.

Taken by surprise by the swiftness of the military action removing people of Japanese ancestry, more and more people grew concerned with the injustice of the whole affair. It became evident that racial discrimination was at the root of the matter and that presented a greater threat to the American way of life than the war itself. To deplore the Nazi persecution of Jews in Europe and find ourselves guilty of similar unchristian tactics towards a minority group in our own country, was a shock to many people previously unaware of what was going on. Church groups, especially Friends, Methodists and Congregationalists, the Civil Liberties Union, peace groups, lawyers, college presidents like Sproul, Wilbur and Millikan, lawyers including Earl Warren (later Governor of California), business men, YMCA and YWCA, and many, many "little people" rallied to right a wrong that belied the foundations of democracy. An organization known as the Committee for Fair Play and American Principles, because of its sponsorship by distinguished California citizens and its indefatigable field workers, Harry and Ruth Kingman, was able to instigate an effective publicity program using speakers, news media, pamphlets and sustained pressure on the War Relocation Authority to prepare for the orderly return of the evacuees when the war ended. I was a member of this committee. Much of the Friends' efforts during these years were in conjunction with its program.

Certainly strong forces were at work to discourage, even to prohibit the return of the natives to our state. Luckily we had individuals in our federal government who realized the importance of the rehabilitation of the Japanese-Americans. I seem to remember that righteous old warrior, Harold Ickes, blasting the opposition. Dillon Meyer, appointed head of the War Relocation Authority (WRA), organized centers in fifteen communities in California to arrange for the reception and oversight of the families returning to those areas. The first requisite was favorable publicity. To educate the average family to differentiate between the Japanese enemy and the loyal American citizen of Japanese ancestry was not an easy undertaking. The very fact that they had been removed increased suspicion. Pamphlets were circulated by the Fair Principles Committee, by the Fellowship of Reconciliation, by American Friends, the Japanese-American Citizens League, Civil Liberties Union, the California Alumni Association. An excellent illustrated brochure entitled "Nisei in Uniform," published by the Department of the Interior in collaboration with the War Department gave stirring accounts of their record in the war. These and articles in current magazines, newspapers and radio programs reached a segment of the population, but the down-to-earth problems of convincing city dwellers and rural inhabitants necessitated first-hand encounters to explain the procedure.

I think the War Relocation Authority did a good job in their approach to this vulnerable situation. As a preliminary measure they allowed representatives of the YWCA and JACL (Japanese-American Citizen's League) and a few business people to return temporarily in order to make arrangements for the influx to come. Teiko Ushida was one of the first to show up in San Francisco. She had a soldier escort to be sure she did not commit any subversive acts. He had to accompany her everywhere except into the ladies rest room. He slept outside her door at night. Teiko had some Caucasian friends whom she wanted to see in addition to her business contacts. How could they talk intimately with the G.I. right there? The girls discovered that if they went to a stylish and expensive restaurant the soldier was too embarrassed to join them at a table, so he sat by himself near the door and kept watch while they chatted intimately over Crab Louis and cheese cake. Kay Yamashita was another early emissary. We met her at the Ferry Building and smuggled her into our home. The next day she needed to go to the headquarters of the Army Control whose offices were located in Hotel Whitcomb on Market Street near Van Ness. The hotel management refused to let her appear in the lobby so she had to take the freight elevator in the basement to get to the eleventh floor. Here she interviewed Colonel Bonesteel, the officer in charge. At the conclusion of their conference he said, "Miss Yamashita, you talk just like an American girl."

"I am an American girl, Colonel Bonesteel," replied Kay.

Another person who stayed with us overnight was the owner of a Los Altos plant nursery. He was fortunate to find his house well-cared for by a former neighbor, even to the preservation of the miniature garden with curved bridge and tiny fountain completely intact. Another horticulturist in Mountain View was not so fortunate. He had two spacious green houses in which every pane of glass had been smashed.

The first returnee to obtain permanent transfer to the Palo Alto region was June Shiraki, formerly a secretary in the Oakland office of Education. Her husband was in the 442nd Combat Team in Italy. Her little daughter Jeanie, seven years old, was unhappy in the camp. A sensitive child, she hated living in a crowd and the food disagreed with her. The camp doctor advised getting her out of the environment as soon as possible. Mrs. Shiraki was one of the first to apply for return to California. Her mother and the Issei advised her not to go. "You'll be shot at," they told her, "when you cross the Bay on the ferry boat." But June was a determined young woman. Being assured of living quarters and a job, she demanded her WRA permit to travel and to enter California. To circumvent the prophecies of danger and doom which she knew would accompany her departure, she chose to avoid the sendoff by taking a train that left at 2 a.m. when everyone was asleep. We welcomed the two travelers into our household where they remained a little over a year. Little Jean with her sparkling brown eyes was a favorite with everyone in the ranch. The quiet atmosphere, good food, sunshine and freedom and love brought back health and the joy of living to this charming child. In the fall when she was due to go to school, I talked with the principal and the second grade teacher to insure her acceptance. I impressed on them the honor as well as the responsibility of receiving the first Nisei child. They promised to explain to the children and the staff ahead of time. I also talked to the President of the PTA who agreed to ask one or two of their members to send a special invitation to Mrs. Shiraki and to accompany her to her first meeting. Once the ice of fear was broken and they learned that June's husband was in service overseas just like their husbands, everything went smoothly. June and Jeanie made their own way easily after that.

Our experience with June and Jeanie illustrates the importance of the personal approach. We found that in communities where a well-respected individual would take the trouble to sponsor and befriend a returnee, there were no riots and no violent demonstrations. Those demonstrations could be very frightening. I was in the middle of one such in a home of a friend in San Francisco who had rented a room to a Nisei couple. The neighbors from two or three blocks charged into the house, threatening to break the windows and set fires. I shall never forget the hate-contorted face of one woman who looked around at the walls saying, "These would burn up fast, wouldn't they?" At that point I was standing up on a chair trying to make a speech but no one would listen. We thought we might have to call the police, but the hostess and I decided to make coffee and serve it to the intruders—with lots of sugar. We offered it first to the most voluble rabble-rousers, who spurned us. Their henchmen were not so adamant; a few accepted the offered cups and little by little, under the influence of the hot soothing potion, the tension eased. It was interesting to see how some of them began to feel a bit ashamed of themselves and slithered out of the door and down the steps. After they all left, the floors were tracked with mud, but only one flower pot in the front porch was broken. And there was no coffee for breakfast! But my friend—bless her heart—said, "Now that's over with, I shall keep the Akiyamas." And she did.

About this same time I went to Auburn, California to visit one of my former students who was in the Army Hospital. As I passed through the town, on my way I noticed signs in many stores, "Jap keep out," "No Japs wanted here," "The only good Jap is a dead Jap." In the hospital there were a good many wounded Nisei soldiers from the 442nd Combat Division and I thought how terrible it would be, if when those boys started to convalesce and would go downtown, to be confronted with such signs in the store windows. My young friend was in bed but some of his buddies were already ambulatory. I told him of my apprehension and he said he would call a few of them together and take care of it. A small group of white veterans went to the town and wherever the objectionable signs appeared in the window they went in and said, "Take that sign down. We've fought side by side with those guys. They're O.K. And we won't patronize your store if you have a sign like that up." Within a week the signs were all gone.

When the serious business of relocation got underway, between fifteen and twenty centers were established by the WRA in various towns. One of the largest was in San Jose, and the area to be covered was so spread out that Mr. Edmonston, the director, called for volunteers to help. The procedure was like this. Mr. Edmonston would be informed that such and such a family would be leaving Utah or Arizona on a certain date; they had a house, or a ranch or a store, but needed a place to stay for the first few days. It was his job to take care of them on arrival. He would have investigated the condition of the property and would be able to finance their initial expenses, but he lacked the time to go to the address and find out about the attitude of the neighbors. So he asked me to do that, and I would go and tell the storekeeper or the postman or the city council, or someone in the school or the church that the Japanese were coming back, and would ask them to please help to welcome them. I learned a lot from these conversations. The minister in a small Baptist church said, "If the dirty yellow bastards come into my church I'll shake my fist at 'em and they'll leave." A storekeeper said, "I'll be glad to see them back. They're real nice people. Worked hard, paid their bills better than most white folks round here." Responses ran the whole gamut between hostility and friendliness.

One day Mr. Edmonston telephoned that there was a rumor that a returnee, Mr. Hashimoto, had been hanged in his barn. Could I possibly go and find out? I did not fancy that job, so Frank went to the location. Here he found Mr. Hashimoto sweeping out his barn and getting ready to go to work. Frank asked at the General Feed Store nearby if there had been any trouble. "Heck no," said the owner. "He's been over here. I lent him some tools. Glad to see him back." So much for that rumor.

In San Francisco during the spring months of 1945, the Friends Center welcomed about ninety different individuals who slept for a night or two before finding more adequate lodging. The WRA desired to speed up the closing of the Relocation Camps but found it particularly difficult to dislodge some of the larger families. An arrangement was made with the Buddhist Church on Post Street near Buchanan to provide facilities in the large basement formerly used as a gymnasium. To prevent any profit motive from entering into the bargain, the WRA insisted that the church obtain a co-sponsor from some established American agency to cooperate in the management. The Friends Service Committee was asked to act in this capacity, and Joe Conard and I were appointed as their representatives. Every week we met for a long afternoon at the church with two of the Buddhist priests, a Japanese American businessman and a bi-lingual secretary. Our function was to check on the quality and cost of the food served and the maintenance of the facilities. We were to arrange referrals for health and welfare cases and to try and obtain recreation for children and adolescents outside the Center. From 100 to 150 people stayed at any given time, of which one-third were expected to turn over every week, allowing for a steady stream of new arrivals. Joe and I were often amused at these meetings. The head priest or Abbott, employed an interpreter because he said he did not understand English. When the latter translated, we of course were unable to know what he said, but we were quite sure that a typical dialogue went something like this:

"They want us to do so-and-so."

"Do you think we have to?"

"They seem quite insistent."

"Maybe we better agree."

"Let's hold out a little longer. Maybe compromise on the cots."

Downstairs each famly was allowed a space of 9 × 12 or 9 × 15 feet which was marked off by chalk lines on the floor. Here they slept, ate and existed till new housing was obtained. When I visited Hong Kong later on and saw the congested apartments for refugees in Kowloon, I was reminded of that huddled basement in San Francisco in 1945. The outcome of this tragic experience for the Japanese-Americans has always amazed me. In spite of a certain amount of restitution voted by Congress, many of the Issei never recovered from property and financial loss, but the younger people made an amazing comeback. In a very few years you found them in business, in stores, as teachers, in air lines and of course in flower stores and nurseries. This was due in part to the determined leadership of the Japanese-American Citizens League, and to the education many had received in Eastern colleges. Also, as the public became aware of what had really transpired and as the gallantry of the Nisei soldiers was publicized, a lot of people had guilty consciences and were ready to make amends. It was not a costly reparation. The charming ways of the Nisei secretaries and the skill and intelligence of the medical technicians and the efficiency of the strawberry farmer, just to mention a few, soon made them highly desirable employees and desirable co-workers. Only the Auto Mechanics Union continued to bar their membership for several years. They were probably correct in anticipating rigorous competition.

Many books and many photographs have been published since this chapter of American history was played out. Still, relatively few people under fifty have ever heard of it. Even many Japanese of the second generation now in college often ask about it curiously. The episodes from the Japanese point of view have been graphically described. It has seemed to me that very little has been said about the effect on some of us Caucasian people who shared in the disillusionment and shame. We learned how vulnerable our democracy is in the face of economic competition and military dictatorship. We also marvelled at the degree of patient acceptance and mental adjustment to harsh treatment these people showed and their spirit of forgiveness to their persecutors. The friendships made with those wonderful people during those sad days have enriched our lives enormously. And they never forget. Every Christmas packages of fortune cookies, dried fruit, children's photographs and innumerable cards recall rare moments of precious intimacy. We can only accept their love with gratitude and give ours in return.

XXV

Black Friends
and Civic Unity

*The arrival of Blacks to work in
shipyards; housing and social problems;
the interest and help of the Friends.*

In a previous chapter, I described the development of the
Friends Service Committee in Northern California and the location of its
offices in the YWCA building vacated by the enforced exodus of
Japanese residents. Their departure left many vacant houses in the area
which had previously been known as "Little Tokyo." Even before the
Japanese had all left, Negroes from the deep South and other parts of
the country moved into every abandoned apartment and room. They
were being recruited in great numbers to work in Bay Area shipyards
constructing "Liberty Ships." It was only a matter of a few months
before "Little Tokyo" became the "West Coast Harlem." And Friends
were right in the middle of it.

Before the war only a handful of Negro families lived in San
Francisco. They were well-respected by their employers and self-
sufficient unto themselves, maintaining selective social organizations
which never encroached on white dominance. There were one or two
Negro churches and the Booker T. Washington Settlement House. The
group pretty much took care of its own problems.

In 1942 the tension and confusion in San Francisco was frightening.
People were apprehensive that the Japanese might attack by air or by
submarine. The city was full of boys in uniform transferring to training
camps or embarking directly for the Pacific War theater. The Bay
Shipyards worked all round the clock in eight hours shifts. When bus
load after bus load of Blacks began to arrive, accompanied by a great
many children, the resources of the city were totally inadequate. Native

San Francisco families already had problems of their own, and the sudden influx of uprooted and unintegrated people caused a near panic in many neighborhoods. It all happened so fast. The newcomers squeezed themselves into every available nook and cranny, including old condemned houses listed as substandard and waiting for demolition. They crowded the buses, stampeded health and welfare agencies, disorganized the schools by the introduction of ill-prepared students, and crowded restaurants and bars with noisy, sometimes quarrelsome customers.

This invasion could not be turned away nor prevented. The Negro workers represented a crucial factor in the war effort. Hence it was everyone's patriotic duty to accept them with as good grace as possible. Unfortunately, the grace did not always extend very far. There were altercations, disturbances, even riots which assumed dangerous proportions. The older Black residents of San Francisco felt even more threatened than the Whites. It was hard for them to be identified with a group fresh off the corn patches of Mississippi and Alabama, whose manners and customs fitted a rural environment but were inappropriate in a sophisticated urban center. There were so many of these visitors and, to make matters more irritating, they were being paid salaries for unskilled work that far exceeded most incomes of established citizens.

The Young Women's Christian Association has had a long record of interracial endeavors. At this period of emergency one of their board members, Miss Johanna Volkman, donated a large sum of money to make a survey of problems related to the incoming minority workers and an analysis of community resources required to meet their needs. The proposal was described at a large public meeting to which all those involved were invited—business men, agency directors, school officials, ministers, Negro leaders, government representatives, press and radio and anyone interested enough to particpate. Mrs. Oliver Wyman, a member of the YWCA Board, accepted the over-all chairmanship. Dr. Charles Johnson from Fisk University, and his assistant Dr. Herman Long, were the experts chosen to conduct the survey. They invented a novel plan of fact finding which proved immensely effective because it not only collected data, but also dramatized existing conditions to people usually unaware of how the other half lives. The plan called for the enrollment of several hundred individuals willing to devote considerable time for a two-week period. They were to be divided into groups of twenty or thirty under the direction of a chairman chosen by the group. Questionnaires prepared by Dr. Johnson were given to each member to use for guidance. Training sessions were arranged to instruct the workers how to go about conducting interviews and what kinds of information were relevant. Certain blocks in the Fillmore area were assigned to a team. The members canvassed every house and talked to every tenant living there to find out the number in the family, where they came from, how employed, what problems bothered them most and to what degree they had availed themselves of services offered by community agencies.

Many well-to-do, cultivated ladies began to ring door bells, explained their purpose and interest, and penetrated into the dilapidated ghetto flats where the new arrivals had found the only accommodations available to them. They asked such questions as: "How many people live in this apartment?" "How many beds for this number?" "How many people use the same toilet?" "Is there a bath or shower?" "Are stairs safe for children?" "Where do they play?" "What about teenagers?" To many of these good (really good) inquirers, the glimpse of such sub-standard housing and such devastating poverty was a shocking revelation. It is one thing to read about slum conditions: it is quite another to see, with your own eyes, the peeling walls, the dirty sinks and the filthy toilets, to climb rickety stairs, to witness the over-crowding and sense the peril of fire.

The Friends' Center was a convenient meeting place for collecting the questionnaires and for the groups to classify the information obtained. Because of the participation of so many volunteer workers, a great many people were vitally interested in Dr. Johnson's findings. His report included an analysis of existing agencies, and recommendations for expanded programs and closer cooperation. It also pointed up the need for new concepts of integration. The report was widely distributed, receiving excellent publicity in the news media. As a means of arousing public opinion in a short time, I think Dr. Johnson's technique is unexcelled. It cut through ignorance and indifference and color distinctions by presenting first hand evidence to decent people unaware of actual conditions. Feelings and consciences were aroused, hostility gave way to compassion. What to do about it? The need for war housing was evident. The schools needed help. Welfare procedures must be speeded up. Subsidies had to be increased. For awhile constructive changes took place and creative energy poured into civic institutions, and a few individuals found a new direction for their lives. But that was not enough. The danger was that when the first impact of the disclosures wore off, people would tend to forget the implications and purpose of the whole endeavor, filing away the substance as just so much paper information "for future use." Mrs. Wyman was through with her job and it looked as if the committee would disband without further commitment. I was greatly concerned lest this should happen and due, no doubt, to my vigorous protest I was made chairman of an "interim committee" charged with following through the recommendations adopted by Dr. Johnson and the inter-agency groups. This phase resulted in the formation of the San Francisco Council for Civic Unity, which has continued to function for over thirty years—even up to this day. Soon after it was established, the Bay Area Committee for American Principles and Fair Play joined forces with it, and on the same floor at 101 Post Street, the National Council on Race Relations (which is headquartered in Chicago) opened its West Coast office, with Larry Hewes as regional director. Also, Franklin Williams worked on the NAACP program in the same building. This proximity led to a concentration of power.

The location of the Friends' Center in the heart of a ghetto neighborhood made a natural for neighborhood out-reach. In February 1943 I wrote, "We had a block party for everyone in the 1800 block (the Center was 1831 Sutter Street). It was a small but good group with which to begin. Our next plan was an Easter party for children to be worked out in collaboration with the Booker T. Washington Center behind us and the Filipino Mission just round the corner. In December another letter notes, "We are working to establish friendships between us and the colored people, to have meetings, discussions and fun. Not so much for them as *for* us and *with* them. We have a Mother's Club, a recreation club and several groups of black and white young people who try to overcome discrimination in restaurants and other public places, going in mixed groups. When refused, the white youngsters take the matter up quietly and courteously with the management. This tactic usually worked. Another practice was to go in a fairly large group, predominantly white, and fill all tables in a restaurant, refusing to order unless their Black friends were also served. Once a month we have a dinner for professional people (white and black) followed by a discussion of some pertinent issue. A recent development has been the establishment of an interracial Church of all Peoples, under the pastoral direction of Dr. Alfred Fisk of San Francisco State College, and Rev. Howard Thurman, a well-known Black poet and minister.

The Council for Civic Unity responded to a great variety of complaints. One issue was employment for women in the stores. I remember we finally succeeded in getting one of the department stores, I think it was City of Paris or Liebes, on Grant Avenue, to accept Negro salesgirls. We got several people to transfer their charge accounts from stores that refused to cooperate. I remember transferring my account to a new store, where I bought an expensive hat to express my approval to the store. It was a hideous hat which I seldom wore, and my family named it my "Race Relations Bonnet." I had no regrets when it was finally stolen from our Palo Alto house, although the camera and a sapphire ring that were stolen with it were quite another matter.

A tenant dispute I was involved in comes to my mind. An irate white woman complained to me about her neighbors on the flat above. The special object of her wrath was a very large Negro woman. "She has on a nigger pink blouse. You know the kind. It don't hide nothin'. All the men in the house can't keep their eyes offen her. Noisy—oh Lordy, and me right down below!"

I had met the Negro lady in question, and I knew she had no money to spend on clothing. Luckily, in the Friends clothing closet I found a large dress, size 44, royal purple in color, which I offered to her. She tried it on, and it *fit!* It was an elegant cover up. She was delighted. Over a cup of tea in the Friends' kitchen we had a friendly chat. She brought up the complaints she had suffered from her white neighbor. I tried to point out that spitting on the stairs, obstructing passage through hallways and talking loud was not conducive to neighborly tolerance. In the South "on the farm" she had lived in a cabin. City apartment—how different! She told me about funny things she had noticed about white people, and we chuckled together. Humor is like oil on a squeaky hinge, it smoothes away differences and establishes a subtle bond between people. I was able to make her realize why others complained about her. Later, in talking to her white neighbor, I was able to sketch the background out of which the Black woman had come. It must have helped, because some time afterwards I saw them sitting together on the steps of their apartment house deep in conversation—purple dress and all, their children happily playing together on the sidewalk.

As soon as the war ended many people thought "now the Negro people will all leave California and return to their homes in the South." But of course this was wishful and foolish thinking. Very few returned. In spite of their difficulties, life on the West Coast offered more opportunites than they could hope to find in Alabama or Mississippi. Many had enjoyed steady paying jobs at the shipyards and elsewhere. The shovel and the hoe held no fascination for them. Why should they leave?

It soon became evident that San Francisco (and Los Angeles) were not the only danger spots. On the horizon were many smaller towns in California whose inhabitants had hardly ever seen a Negro. When work on ships dwindled away, unemployed workers started looking for occupation elsewhere. Incidents of discrimination in housing, in eating places, schools, and elsewhere, led sometimes to riots or violent individual encounters. The emergency situation stirred up a lot of decent people also who believed in the democratic principles of liberty and equality. They worked hard to convince their less enlightened townspeople that the newcomers should be accepted and welcomed in their communities. But the opposition of the majority was strong and the going was rough. Because of prior experience, the San Francisco Council for Civic Unity had many requests to help out-of-town church or civic groups to organize their committees. I traveled around quite a bit, giving talks, participating in conferences and distributing literature and helping local groups to organize. I found it very fascinating to go into a community and in a few hours try to analyze the potential of the individuals or groups of individuals who had bound themselves together in a spur-of-the-moment association to deal with the emergency. The key figure who inspired the movement could come from anywhere: a teacher, perhaps, or a clergyman, a lawyer, a doctor, a club woman; it was a mayor in one case, and in another, a policeman. The Negro leadership in the community was a very important factor. To try to suggest ways of working, based on the particular issues, and taking into account the resources of the dedicated people involved was a challenge to one's quick thinking and discernment. What soon became evident was that these small, detached groups needed to compare notes with each other. They lacked the strength and prestige of a larger unit. To accomplish this interchange, a federation consisting of groups all over the State working for a common goal seemed desirable. Accordingly a conference was called at Asilomar, the Conference Center on the coast near Carmel, and the California Federation for Civic Unity was created. It was financed by the participating member groups and a few individual donations, and a field worker was employed. The business office was located in the San Francisco Council's headquarters.

This organization lasted for a little less than ten years. For many of us it was a great experience—a time of learning, of inspiration and dedication. I think the best people, that is the people with the deepest sense for democarcy and the most sincere desire for racial brotherhood, were gathered together in the yearly conferences we held at Asilomar. They came from all over the state. In 1948 fifty organizations were affiliated. Among the Directors one finds the names of Rev. Allen Hunter, Judge Isaac Pacht, Martin Luther King, Walter Gordon, Dan Koshland, K. Nobusada, Loren Miller, Earl Raab and many other leaders.

The Ku Klux Klan has always been considered an unpleasant phenomenon confined to the Southern states, but its activities were not always geographically limited. After the war and all through the 1950's manifestations of its presence kept cropping up in our urban and suburban areas. In 1929 Palo Alto was a sedate, well-mannered little college town, but even then Frank and I witnessed a scene that no other resident to whom we have spoken can believe. Late one night we were returning from San Francisco. Between 2 and 3 o'clock, as we neared our house on Hamilton Avenue, we noticed a red glow nearby, and we thought it was a house on fire. But when we went to investigate, in a large open lot on Channing Avenue near Melville, we saw that the glow came from a burning cross, which was surrounded by an assemblage of white-clad figurs moving around in the circle of light. They wore white-peaked hoods by which we recognized their identity. It was a weird and sinister spectacle in the midst of the dark and sleeping town. We never knew what the purpose of their gathering could have been, and we learned that even the Chief of Police was not aware of that meeting.

Later, in the 40's and 50's, the Klan surfaced again. On the sidewalks in Palo Alto, large capital letters KKK appeared in several localities. Crosses were set afire on front lawns in Richmond and Oakland; threatening letters were received by those renting or selling property to Negroes. In Redwood City, a new house under construction by a Black man was burned just before completion. Shots were fired at night into homes where Blacks moved in. The Civic Unity groups in many neighborhoods organized vigils to protect new residents, held block parties to get acquainted and provided legal assistance when needed. We found that it was expedient to be prepared ahead of time to act quickly when people moved to a new neighborhood. To prevent riots or confrontations, households were visited. Residents were given a small pamphlet published by the Federation which outlined the California Civil Code of Personal Rights, and the problems were discussed sympathetically with the white property owner. If a normal contact could be established, the barriers usually dissolved. I remember an instance in which a vicious movement against a Black couple was instigated by a white family. A member of the Civic Unity group, a person of some local prestige, asked if he might bring the new tenants to meet the objectors. They could not refuse a visit from that person. The evening revealed that the two couples were interested in the same aspect of life and had much in common. They had an interesting discussion over the coffee cups and by the time the visitors had left, arrangements to meet again to carry on the acquaintance had been made. Another instance that comes to mind concerned a family who moved into an old house on the edge of a new subdivision in Los Altos. A petition to oust them was in the making when it was discovered that the white children of the neighborhood had already been invited into the yard to play with the little Black children. There they had found all sorts of swings and games. They had much more space than anywhere else on the street. They had also found that Mrs. Smith's cookies were "out of this world" and so the kids were "keen." The bottom dropped out of that petition. Still another episode took place on one of the country roads in Menlo Park. There was to be a protest meeting of all residents to decide how they could get rid of the undesirable "colored element" that had intruded into their all-white community. A meeting had been called to discuss "Community Improvement Measures" and notices had been left in the mail boxes on both sides of the lane. The "intruders" also received the notice, and they attended the meeting, too. The organizers of the meeting quickly revised their agenda and substituted other business. It was discovered that the new residents were delightful, cooperative and eager to share responsibility for the improvement of the neighborhood. There was no further discrimination on that street.

XXVI

The Mexican-American in Town

Social conditions, votes, civic consciousness.

My first close contact with a Mexican-American family came about in 1942, when an old ranch house burned to the ground on an open field now occupied by the Mayfield Mall shopping center in Mountain View. The newspaper told the story of the family; there were thirteen children, three of whom had not been able to escape. The fire had just swept through the fifty year old house as the rooms upstairs and down had almost simultaneously exploded into flames. The whole family was stricken by the loss of the three children who were two, three, and five years old. I went to see what could be done for the remaining ten children, one of whom was a year-old baby who was rescued by her oldest sister. Some temporary arrangements were made by the Red Cross and County Welfare office, but suitable housing for a longer term had to be found. How could we get the money to buy an adequate house for twelve people? After searching the countryside, we succeeded in finding a suitable property in Monta Vista, a small settlement near Cupertino. The house had seven rooms, a yard and a carport. In consultation with the Welfare Department, we learned that if the first payment on a certain house could be met, the Welfare Department would finance the monthly balance from funds available from the Aid for Needy Children program. I have forgotten the amount of the down payment, but I remember writing a letter to the newspaper, and soliciting many of my well-to-do friends. This appeal brought in a sizeable amount. The Mountain View Catholic parish contributed also and we rustled up furniture and clothing from many sources.

In arranging some of these details I encountered Father Donald McDonell, an Irish priest, an activist assigned to work with Mexican-American families in Santa Clara County. At first I found him unexpectedly hostile towards my efforts—he seemed to resent my interference. I realize now that he had reason to question the motives of a white Protestant. In any case, one day I got angry with him and said, "Well, all right Father McDonell, I'm perfectly willing to leave the whole business in your hands and I won't do anything more about it." I got up to leave. But he stopped me, apologized and said, "Well, now, and what do you think we should do about the moving in?" From that point we became good friends and I had opportunities to work with him on subsequent occasions, in dealing with individual families, community conferences and even political issues. When I needed a reference to contact Chicano families, he always allowed me to use his name as an introduction. Once he told a woman, "Sure yo con talk to her. She's all right." I came to have the greatest respect for this priest. He was a real Father to his people. Knowing their sorrows and their joys, he helped them in a hundred different ways. He was their spiritual guide, of course, but he was also a practical down-to-earth family friend in times of hunger or sickness or other adversity, and a good companion at fiestas, weddings or other celebrations. He testified often at trials and police investigations. In County hearings on labor disputes he was right on hand to tell the truth about the police, the employers or hoodlums. At federal investigations Father McDonell and another Irish priest from the valley were about the only Anglos to really lay out the true conditions of the workers in opposition to the ruthless exploitation of them by the farmer bloc.

With the help of Father McDonell and others, the family moved into their new home in a friendly neighborhood. The children all went to school. Indeed, the younger generation is self-sufficient today. Although the father and mother spoke almost unintelligble English, the youngsters made it through school, and some of them went on to college. The boys have good jobs in the electronic industry, two of the girls are teachers. Only one of them got caught up in the drug trade. They look after their father since their mother's death. On his birthday every year they have a reunion at Hidden Villa picnic ground, a patriarchal affair which numbers between forty or fifty descendants. If every Chicano family could have a little bit of help at the time of need there would be more such success stories. They are wonderful people and very prolific!

In thinking about them as a minority group in our state, it seems to me there have been two groups originating in Mexico whose paths in the states followed divergent patterns. I have already spoken of those who came north to work on the ranches, remaining in rural areas near the sources of work in the Valley. But there was another group who migrated into the Southwestern U.S., lured by jobs offered by the Santa

Fe and Southern Pacific Railroads, when these lines were being built into the rapidly developing city of Los Angeles. The railroad provided box car habitations and tents in the early days. Rows of cheap houses for the families replaced these boxcar settlements and gradually developed into the *colonias* on the outskirts of town which sometimes became completely surrounded by the mushroom growth of Los Angeles and other southern cities. The story is told that in 1916, when a box car of immigrants arrived at the end of their journey, the immigrants looked out at Belvedere, a large area on the Eastside, they exclaimed, "Que maravilla!" (What a miracle!) The name *Miravalle* remained and by 1920 approximately 20,000 Spanish-speaking inhabitants lived there under substandard ghetto conditions. Hardly a Miravalle! This was the pattern repeated again and again, especially in the Los Angeles area where the building boom swept past and around their shacks, not ever really absorbing them. Out of this social ostracism a unique alien culture developed. The Mountain View family whose tragic loss by fire I told about at the opening of this chapter belonged in this category.

Another Mexican-American scenario made the headlines in the Hearst papers and, for a few weeks, had everyone in California, especially in the southern counties, looking at every dark-skinned passerby as a potential criminal. As a result of discriminatory practices restricting participation in theatres, restaurants, swimming pools and all other types of recreation available to white citizens, young Chicanos were forced to seek social contacts within their own restricted groups. Hence, gang associations became the major source of social life for the teenager and young adult. As a badge of status, the boys wore peg-topped high-waisted black pants, long loose coats, heavy boots and duck-tailed hair cuts. The girls sported black skirts and sweaters, black stockings and huaraches, crowned by a massive pompadour hair-do. In those days instead of saying, "You look like a Hippie," we said, "You look like a *pachuco.*" Interestingly enough, no one seems to know the origin of the word *"pachuco"* any more than they know the origin of *"Chicano."*

Within the colony, rivalry between gangs led, naturally, to encounters. Some were harmless, but inevitably some resulted in violence. The city police department and the county sheriffs utilized these sporadic disturbances to instigate shocking and brutal assaults. I don't remember the details, but on several occasions raids were conducted in the Chicano districts, young men were outrageously beaten up for no reason at all, and scores carted away to jail and railroaded through the courts on scanty or non-existent evidence. I remember reading that a group of suspects were denied bathing facilities and clean clothes before trial so that they would appear before the jury looking as disreputable as possible. In June 1943, twenty taxicabs carrying 200 sailors cruised into East Los Angeles hunting zoot suiters. Later in the same week a mass lynching mob of soldiers, sailors and civilians combed all parts of the city, dragging Mexicans out of restaurants, street cars, movie houses, etc. Eventually Governor Warren appointed an official committee to inquire into the situation and propose remedies. The bloody excursions were officially banned, but the heritage of resentment and hatred engendered in the minds of hundreds of young men and women still rankles. It cannot help but impede, even now, their relationships with the white community. We reap what we sow.

News of the turmoil stirred the American Council of Race Relations in Chicago to send a representative, Fred Ross, an experienced and skillful grass roots organizer, to the West Coast to alleviate the antagonisms. Unity leagues had been started sporadically in several places, but never got very far because of limited resources. The League of Latin-American Citizens (Lulac) organized earlier in Texas, represented the more or less established middle class, but did not concern itself very much with the poorer elements. Fred's efforts were directed to reinspiring the League movement and emphasizing the importance of the ballot. So effective were his efforts that the Mexican-Americans were able to elect Edward Roybal, one of their own numbers, to a place on the Los Angeles City Council. (Years later, in 1963, he was elected to the House of Representatives in Washington.) Tremendous progress was made in the matter of school segregation and increased opportunities for higher education of Chicano students as well as increased opportunities for older adults to learn English.

At our first meeting of the California Federation of Civil Unity, we learned about the Community Service Organization that had been working with Fred in Los Angeles. Two or three young men showed up to ask the support and help of the Federation, and also to join with us to further our objectives. The following year we gave them a special place on the program and financed their representatives to participate. One young man impressed me deeply by his clear thinking, great modesty and sweet gentleness. In talking with him I learned that as a youngster he had lived on the other side of the tracks where the play areas were restricted. A favorite game was freight car hopping. This pastime consisted of scrambling between the cars while they were being shunted in the yards. Hermann Gallegos lost a leg in this game. In spite of this handicap, he worked his way through school and college and into a good position in California state government. His efforts to help other minority youngsters to continue education and training influenced a host of discouraged kids to continue the struggle. His counsel is persuasive but his example exceeds even the words he speaks. He became a member of the Federation executive board and helped our negotiations in towns where smaller groups of Chicanos were struggling with problems identical with those in large centers. Many of them had never heard of the USO or of the Civic Unity partnership.

San Jose had the second largest Mexican-American population of any city in California. They, too, lived in a dismal environment on the edge of town and were continually frustrated in their efforts to improve conditions. Some of us living in Santa Clara County became aware of this situation and undertook to find a remedy. As in Los Angeles, so here too, political power provided the key to open doors of housing, employment and education. Most of the whites with Spanish surnames (as they were listed in the 1950 census) lived southeast of San Jose. Traveling on the Bay Shore Highway one could see the slum area as one whizzed past enroute to Gilroy or Monterey. This area became known as *Sal si puedes* (get out if you can).

In 1952 the district was so severely flooded that the children could not get to school. The PTA dramatized this situation by bringing photographers in to take pictures of the marooned kids standing up to their knees in muddy water. The pictures appeared in the Mercury-Herald and the community was made aware of what existed under their very noses. Not long afterward the cesspools overflowed and 125 cases of amoebic dysentery were reported to the Health Department. This came too close to the dwellers on the West Side and they clamored for removal of "undesirable elements" in the community. But there was another answer to this problem. Just as the Chicanos in Los Angeles had taken matters into their own hands, so here too it could be accomplished with a little outside help to break the ground. The Friends Community Relations Committee working with the Civic Unity people obtained a small grant to employ Fred Ross as field worker for six months. I was chairman of the activating group which gave me the opportunity to learn from Fred as I had from Bard McAllister in the farm labor project, how to stir up impoverished people to help themselves. It is hard to know where to begin. At what point is there an opening? In this case a Mexican-American public health nurse was the nucleus around whom the plan developed. The spear-heading group consisted of the nurse, the Catholic priest, a can maker, a prune picker, a packing house employee and four Chicano students from San Jose State College. A series of home calls introducing Fred was arranged by a Committee member who knew the family. The next night, or soon afterwards, that family invited a few neighbors in to meet Fred. These neighbors had other friends and so like a stone thrown into a lake, the circle expanded. First they discussed their grievances and related their previous efforts. One or another would tell of going to the City Hall asking for a dangerous hole in the pavement to be repaired, another might have had his water turned off without warning. Still another recounted his efforts to collect signatures for a petition which was never even acknowledged. And so each person contributed his personal frustration and his sporadic attempts to improve his condition. "But it never worked," he would say. "We've had clubs before, but no one ever paid any attention to us." Fred would then explain the rights granted by the Constitution to every individual and the value of numbers in obtaining those rights. He pointed out that if 2000-3000 voters were registered in a district, the authorities could not afford to ignore them.

Little by little, person to person, the converts were recruited. While developing this project, Fred lived with us. His working hours started about 4:00 o'clock in the afternoon, continuing until midnight or later when he crept into the house and turned off the lights. He had breakfast about ten or eleven o'clock in the morning. I usually joined him. I was excited to hear about the contacts of the previous evening and I think he liked to summarize what had taken place and point up his strategy for the next move. From his description I learned to know many of the characters and could follow the fascinating evolution of political awareness. After weeks of house meetings, a general mass meeting was called at the neighborhood school. About a hundred and fifty showed up. Most of the discussion was in Spanish. At this gathering 25 individuals offered to act as registrars of new voters.

But here the group encountered opposition. The County Registrar who had held the office for X number of years, was not disposed to cooperate with these upstarts. "Such a thing," he said, "had never been done before." Begrudgingly he agreed to authorize one deputy, but said he would "think" about any more. He "thought" for several weeks. The cut-off line for registration was approaching. It looked as if nothing would come from all this effort. At this point the Los Angeles CSO was solicited for help. They responded by putting pressure on the AF of L Central Labor Council in Santa Clara County. Five additional Spanish speaking deputies were accepted. In the evenings till election day Fred's cohorts went from house to house, pulling out the eligible adults (male and female) edging them down to the corner where the deputy sat at an improvised table and helped make out the requisite forms. When all in the block had been processed, the registrar moved two blocks down and his assistants repeated the round-up of two more blocks. Approximately 400 new voters had qualified when election day came round. Approximately 3000 new voters were listed. But even then obstruction was encountered. At one polling place a well-dressed lady challenged every Mexican who entered and made him read aloud a hundred words out of the California Voter's Handbook. In fact, there were such individuals in every voting center throughout San Jose singling out only dark-skinned people to challenge. When Fred expostulated with one of them, she said, "Republican Headquarters has challengers at all the polls on the Eastside. We're going to challenge right and left." "You folks registered your people but we'll see how many of them are going to get to vote." Fred answered, "O.K., but we are providing Mexican-American watchers to challenge your challengers!" To make sure that no one should forget to vote or could not make it to the polls, a passenger car with a loud speaker toured the Eastside streets. "If you haven't voted, hurry up and do so. Vote as you please. Don't be a slacker. Get out and vote! Hurry up! Vote! Get out! Vote! Vote!" So in spite of the Republican ladies, despite inertia, in spite of their weariness and the beans and chili waiting at the supper table, they "got out the vote." And it worked!

Within the next few months the malodorous ditch was dug out, dikes were built to prevent future flooding, cesspools drained, street lights were installed and roads were paved.

Fred wrote up the experience which was printed by the Federation for Civic Unity in 1953. It was called "Get Out if You Can—The Saga of Sal si Puedes," charmingly illustrated by Kay Watson. Many copies were sold. It is now out of print. Reading it over today, it seems to me it is still pertinent and could be used by Chicano groups in similar situations at the present time.

The Service Committee wished to extend voter registration activities in small towns near San Jose—Alviso, DeCoto, Alvarado, Newark and Niles. The project was launched under the guidance of Fred Ross and a Catholic priest who allowed his church to be used by the Committee as an office and promotional center from which the smaller communities could be reached. Before the project was completed, Fred had to leave for an assignment elsewhere. He offered us a substitute. I remember his saying, "He's pretty young and inexperienced, but he has great potential. I'd like for him to take on the job." The Committee interviewed him. Some members thought he was too shy and unsophisticated and might be lacking in drive. But as there was no one else in sight, they hired him. That was the first time I met Cesar Chavez. I think this may well have been his first employment in the field of race relations. After registering the Mexican voters in southern Contra Costa County, he went on to a larger, more turbulent field of action described in the following chapter on Farm Labor.

I consider myself unusually fortunate in having had the opportunity to know intimately people of varying backgrounds. The average person speaks of "minority groups" as a sort of aggregate constituting a mass of homogeneous particles. The notion that they represent a basic pattern and constitute identical social imbalance misses the point. While they all encounter the prejudices of the dominant group in greater or less degree, the problems of adjustment from their point of view differ widely. I think the Chicano is particularly vulnerable. Originally Indian, he was transfused with the Spanish interpretation of life. The Catholic religion so deeply ingrained in its mediaeval intensity, the very close ties of the family unit under the unquestioned authority of the male, the acceptance of whatever fate brings and the capacity for intense joy as well as for sorrow, are characteristics difficult for the Anglo to understand. In reverse, the American institutions are foreign to the Chicano. It is not easy for him to seek help from the Welfare Department, he has never had to deal with health regulations, in the village at home he never pried into the machinery of government, he worked hard, took care of his family, didn't interfere in other people's business and did not ask advice from anyone except perhaps the priest. He was glad to have his children learn to read and write, but the regimentation of the American school system and the social practices of

American youth are beyond his comprehension. What a long way to travel and what a remarkable development is the creation of the Community Service organization and the tenacity of the United Farm Worker's Union and the persistence of many individuals to acquire educational status in a society so different from their native concepts.

Someone has said that the Mexican is characterized by decorum, gravity, honor and a belief in joy and happiness. I wonder if these precious qualities can be sustained in the midst of our industrial civilization? Perhaps it is not too much to hope that some of it might even rub off on us.

XXVII

Farm Labor and Cesar Chavez

Conditions on the land; migrant labor; the work of Cesar Chavez

Through the years there have been a few books exerting such a popular impression that radical changes in social concepts have resulted from their publication. Dickens' vivid portrayal of children in the London slums, in *Oliver Twist* and other books, Marx's *Das Kapital*, and Harriett Beecher Stowe's *Uncle Tom's Cabin* are books that acted as spring boards for social change. Steinbeck's book, *The Grapes of Wrath*, might be called the *Uncle Tom's Cabin* of the farm workers. This powerful book, which was also adapted for the movies, pulled aside the curtain on rural poverty and shocked the public out of complacency and indifference. Also, somewhat comparable to the influence of Negro spirituals and *The Battle Hymn of the Republic*, songs of the folk singers of the thirties and forties dramatized the plight of the dispossessed farm workers, and their tragic wanderings. The Dust Bowl Ballads were heard everywhere, and through their rhythms the forgotten people were revealed in all their stark poverty and fortitude.

"In 1936 there were nearly 1,700,000 farm families trying to live on an average income of less than $500 a year and that $500 included all the food and other products which they raised for their own use. In other words, more than 8,000,000 people were trying to exist on an average income of $2.00 a week per person (or even less)."

The above statement appeared in the bulletin published by the U.S. Department of Agriculture in 1941. It goes on to analyze the reasons for such a deplorable situation, which I summarize here:

1. Overpopulation and the return of young people previously employed in cities, to the farms where they also found themselves unemployed due to the depression.
2. The absence of free government land for new homesteading.
3. The decline in foreign export of farm goods.
4. The great increase in labor-saving farm machinery.
5. Erosion of the land. It was estimated that the wind blew away enough soil every day to have provided two hundred forty-acre farms.

Due to these conditions the great American exodus began. We saw them on the roads in rickety overloaded cars, heading West, all too often stalled for want of gasoline or a vital engine part. Under-nourished children, exhausted mothers, desperate fathers looking for work, tents pitched along irrigation ditches, by the roadside or in empty lots.

Many municipalities did their best to cope with the new arrivals, but the influx was too great for them to handle. In 1937 the Secretary of Agriculture created the Farm Security Administration whose objective was the rehabilitation of farm people by means of loans, adjustment of debts, better land management, clinics, more advantageous tenure contracts, work grants and the development of cooperatives. This was a nationwide program, part of the New Deal legislation conceived by Franklin Roosevelt. In California, the concern was principally with the part-time workers who were needed in large numbers at only certain seasons on the corporate farms in the San Joaquin Valley. The Farm Security Administration, one of the most imaginative organizations ever created by our government, provided mobile portable units to follow the seasonal itinerary. It also established thirteen more permanent farm labor communities in agricultural centers throughout the Valley. These centers provided two-room metal shelters with electricity and water piped to every home, and central utility buildings with toilet and laundry facilities. Most of them had a community center for recreation and group meetings, a health clinic and provision for child care. Some had shade trees and bits of lawn; others were dusty and hot. Families who worked on the crops were eligible to move in, paying only 50 cents a week to the welfare fund. Our friend Walter Packard served on the Committee responsible for the development of the labor camps. He made frequent trips from the main office in San Francisco to the Valley where he checked on the administration and the local programs. Because I had been working with the Friends Service Committee and with other groups concerned, Walter took Frank and me on several of his inspection tours. The camps offered a variety of opportunities for volunteer assistance. As I came in contact with many young people eager to give their time, money and skills, and as I was familiar with the special needs of the different camps, I could often arrange suitable encounters. At the time of the draft for military service, those taking the pacifist position could sometimes be extricated from the system to serve a term of alternate service in welfare, educational or recreational work at the camps. Supplies of all kinds were needed, such as clothing, cooking utensils, toys and linen. I inspired a number of groups in the Bay area to make or assemble similar things. And in the valley towns adjacent to the camps I succeeded in stirring up enough people to visit, to see for themselves what conditions were like. Having seen this, they in turn became active in persuading others to join a committee of service to the workers. They also were important in overcoming the prejudices of their fellow townsmen and the arbitrary patterns of employment. The owners and managers of the giant farms in the Valley were not as a rule concerned with the problems of their hired help and when it came to political issues, they were solidly against changes of any sort in the status quo. I managed to get acquainted with some wives or children of these land barons. Mixed in with others aware of the real situation, such as teachers, church leaders, social workers, they formed a little nucleus to act as leaven in the community.

At home in the Santa Clara Valley there was also a migrant problem. It was not of the same magnitude as in the San Joaquin area, but it was none the less challenging. The State of California had passed certain laws regulating the use of farm labor on private property. Although there were laws, there was practically no means for enforcement—perhaps not more than three or four officers to cover the whole state. In Santa Clara County alone there were hundreds of small migrant families squatting in orchards or empty lots. They had been coming for years, appearing suddenly at the start of the harvest and then disappearing just as suddenly at the close. The employer was obligated to provide minimum sanitary toilet facilities and shelter from the sun, and to have clean drinking water available at all times. County authorities had difficulty in locating isolated units, and they solicited the help of ordinary citizens to report any violations of the law regarding farm labor that came to their notice. I made a superficial survey by exploring in my car some of the small by-ways and lanes skirting fruit and vegetable gardens. Conditions were indeed deplorable. One place had a single dirty privy for a hundred people; in another, water had to be carried in pails or milk cans a quarter mile distant from the field. Often the open irrigation ditch was the only source of water for all purposes. The children, too young to work, had no place to play other than on the rocky ground skirting the work fields. Their only playthings were pebbles, discarded bottles, empty cans and stray cartons. I talked with ranch owners and foremen and obtained permission for volunteer groups to visit once or twice a week bringing craft materials, games and other stuff—sometimes food and cold drinks—to these desperately deprived children. The Migrant Ministry, financed by the National Council of Churches, maintained teams of this nature and I found that local clubs or neighborhoods were often willing to adopt a certain camp and provide services on a personal basis. When conditions appeared really intolerable, I reported to the County Health Department, but nine times out of ten, no one came to check, and even if they did, compliance was difficult to enforce.

Earlier, I described the Donald Watt Work Camp at the ranch and the outreach of the young people to work at one of the larger migrant camps near Cupertino. The parents of the children asked us, "Why do you do this for us?" They were a little suspicious at first, but the children responded at once and soon cordial entente was established with the older folk. They even invited us to an evening of square dancing. We brought some records, but one of their number played the violin and called the steps, which made the evening much more exciting. It was a picture I shall never forget. The lean, work-weary men in patched overalls, swinging their wives and daughters who were dressed in tattered calico dresses and in the same circle our girls with their flaring skirts and happy faces. Children popped in and out in the circle, dancing with complete abandonment, all adversity forgotten in the ecstasy of rhythm and movement. The only light came from an electric lamp atop a distant high pole, which imparted a pastel texture to the dancers and caused a shadow dance behind them, their shadows mimicking each movement with eerie precision as they danced to the high-pitched violin music and the rasping voice of the caller. We felt privileged to be allowed to take part in such an authentic folk celebration.

After the World War ended in 1945, the shipbuilding boom was over, and the need for unskilled employment of all kinds was greatly reduced. A large number of farm workers were also turned off from the south-to-north, north-to-south migratory treks, and they tended to settle on the outskirts of the Valley towns. In so doing, they became eligible for resident county welfare and health programs. Employment was available sometimes in not too distant places, usually through the medium of the labor contractor who provided transportation and arranged the wage scale with the ranch owner, paying himself a liberal percentage for his pains. The fringe settlements were the rural counterpart of the slums in Eastern cities which were crowded with European immigrants at the turn of the century. Jacob Riis had written, *How the Other Half Lives* in 1919, and Carey McWilliams had written *Factories in the Fields* in 1930, describing similar situations. I felt, with a number of others that the Friends Service Committee—which had been so active in foreign relief during World War II—was overlooking many disorganized, disoriented groups of people here at home. Most of the Friends' projects originated in Philadelphia, where the largest number of Quakers were to be found. So it took considerable persuasion to convince the national office that the needs of farm workers in California warranted a concerted appeal for funds. I wrote a prospectus which was presented to several foundations, and eventually financing was obtained in spite of the controversial character of the appeal.

I was chairman of the Community Relations Committee at the time, and I made several trips through the Central Valley with Steve Thierman, executive secretary of the Northern California office to determine the best approach to the conflicting interests involved. We tried to find the most advantageous location in which to install our worker and out of which he could most conveniently operate. We talked with all kinds of people in several counties: growers, migrants, county officials, educators, employment officers, church people. We discovered that Fresno, Tulare, King and Kern counties then raised 30% of all farm products in California, bringing in some $3,000,000 in annual income to growers. Tulare which raised about 200 different crops was our final choice. As a county it ranked second on the basis of agricultural income in the United States at the time of our search. It had 65 sub-standard communities, housing one-third of its population. The communities we visited comprised a racial mixture of Negro, Caucasian and Mexican-Americans (the largest number). As Steve described it in his book, *Welcome to the World* (1956):

> The inhabitants of these settlements have in common a great suspicion toward any outsider and indeed towards one another. Each man is for himself. If anyone tends to assume leadership, he is quickly discredited by his neighbors. The farm worker's vocational skills are limited by his lack of experience, and his sense of inferiority prevents him from attempting new types of work. He does not save. How can he on his limited income? In many settlements there are no street lights and no plumbing, often not even water. Yet these people are vital to the economy of our state, vital to the production of fruit, vegetables, meat, cotton and wine, all of which contribute to our high standard of living. The Farm Bureau Federation, whose membership represented not only the largest and richest farm owners but also merchants, bankers, grocers and other business men involved with the major enterprise, was irrevocably opposed to any increase in wages. Seventy, eight-five cents an hour for fruit and vegetable picking was the going wage. On some ranches pickers were paid by the box. In 1955 they were paid 11 cents for a 50 pound box of tomatoes. Wineries reduced payments for grapes—originally 9 cents a box, by dumping into drums holding 8-10 boxes and cutting the price to 50 cents per drum. When one admired the beautiful displays of produce in the supermarkets in San Francisco or Berkeley, how many of us could see superimposed on that bounty any picture of the human beings toiling in the scorching heat for long hours to earn a meagre subsistence wage? It was very close to slavery. How dramatize it to stir the public conscience?

The Friends Service Committee recruits its workers with an eye to their professional skill and initiative, but considers equally their motivation, their ability to deal with different species of mankind impartially and their personal humility and warmth in so doing. Sometimes it takes months to discover the suitable individual. In this instance, the choice of Bard McAllister, a Southerner, a Conscientious Objector during the war, a Work Camp Director, and a person who could work equally well with his hands as with his head, was a providential choice. He and Olga, his diminutive, thrifty, supportive helpmate, and their four promising sons, settled in Visalia, a convenient place out of which to operate. Bard spent six months studying the economic and social structure of society in the area. He got to know growers and community leaders, the setup of health and welfare services and most important of all, the forgotten people he had come to serve. After his period of orientation, he felt the need of engaging in a concrete project in order to clarify his purpose in being there. Opportunity came at Teviston, a settlement that had been purchased by Negroes during the war. About 80 families were living there in make-shift shacks when Bard came. In talking with the residents it was obvious to him that the most urgent of their needs was water. Only five families owned wells. The rest had to tote water in cans or drums from a distance of two and a half miles, often having to pay 25 cents to fill each container. Not all of these people had gotten along well with the others. The establishment of a water district would make it imperative for every one to participate in the organization. Bard used this objective to bring them together in an initial meeting at which a resident of another nearby settlement told how they had proceeded in a similar enterprise. It took many long drawn-out meetings before the necessary petition could be agreed upon. I attended one of these meetings in the bare wooden church where the Negro men, weary from a long day's work in the fields, and their patient wives, who were no less weary, sat on wooden benches struggling with the rudiments of democracy. Bard sat there, too, primarily a listener, only occasionally speaking to clarify a technical point or help the group move through an impasse in the discussion. I witnessed an example of what it means to help people help themselves. And it was a true revelation. How easy it would have been for Bard to organize the water district for the group in a fraction of time it took them to do it. Instead, he guided the project into their own hands. The process of finding out *for themselves* how to obtain the services to which they were entitled was much more important than any arrangement engineered by a professional worker would have been. I was deeply moved by these earnest Black people struggling to find words to express their thoughts, listening to each other, accepting the leadership of their minister who was chairman, quoting the Bible to emphasize a point and holding out from seven o'clock till midnight. My own eyes were closing with fatigue. These meetings carried on for twelve exhausting nights, and then there were other hurdles to overcome after the initial step was taken. Finally, around Christmas time in 1959, a big trailer truck lumbered past the great farms, turned into the chuck-holed sandy roads of an alkali flat, and deposited its cargo on an empty lot. Ragged children and rheumy old men and women with babies shuffled over, and some men pushed forward and gently laid their hands on the "New Thing"—the long anticipated *water pump*. The Rev. Daniels took off his hat, bowed his head and said, "Father, thank Thee for this wonderful blessing." At the ceremony of dedication he referred to Moses who struck the rock in the desert of Judea and water gushed forth. He referred to Bard as "Our little Moses."

Similar projects followed in other fringe settlements, and eventually the need for decent housing seemed to outweigh all other efforts. The 1961 National Housing Act, allowing government funds to assist rural construction, made it possible for the Service Committee to finance a self-help housing project. This was a cooperative undertaking in which each family qualified for a low interest long-term loan from the Farmers Home Administration. The loan covered the cost of the lot and all materials for a house 900-1200 square feet containing 2 to 4 bedrooms. Each family was required to give 1500 hours of labor to the cooperative efforts. The houses were built according to uniform plans and the work was directed by a Service Committee staff member. It was a heart-warming sight to see the first house under construction at Goshen. The whole family was working—the father connecting pipes, the mother pounding nails (she told me when she first started she hit her fingers oftener than the nail), the older son bringing in siding and the younger children fetching tools and filling water cans. A neighbor was helping the father. Some months later I visited the site again and was invited into the new two-bedroom house. I was served coffee in a living room furnished neatly with a rug on the floor, a sofa, comfortable chairs, a radio in the corner and curtains at the window. It seemed like a miracle. And out of the window I could glimpse two other houses in process of construction. The glow on the face of my hostess was something I shall always remember as she showed me the details of kitchen and bathroom arrangements, and said, "I painted them walls myself. I always did like pink. It's real cheerful." This pilot project led to a national conference in Washington and to the formation of Self-Help Housing Enterprises, a non-profit corporation, operating actively in counties in California and copied in many other states. Self-Help Housing Associates is an international clearing house for information and for liaison with governments and foundations.

A still more ambitious experiment undertaken by the Service Committee was the creation of a whole new town. After funds were obtained, acreage was purchased half way between Fresno and Madera. I don't remember all the organizational details, but I was present when the final decision was made to purchase that particular tract. The developers were Mexican-Americans and several were with us one chilly winter day when we went to gaze around us at a spot in the wide open treeless expanse of the valley. A few sticks to designate corners, an irrigation ditch and two roads at right angles, each one disappearing on its own course into the distance. It was a grey day threatening rain. What we looked at was earth, just plain barren unadulterated *earth*. That is what we Anglos saw. But David Burciaga, the chairman of the

Mexican-American cooperative planning the project, saw something else. He stooped down and picked up a handful of soil and ran it through his fingers. "It's a good land," he said, "Our group has decided to call it *El Porvenir*—The Future." Ten years later I was privileged to stand on the same spot again and see a village with paved streets and front lawns, with children playing on the sidewalk, and pastel colored houses in orderly rows. Here was David Burciaga's vision of "El Porvenir" in all its tangible reality—100 houses, 100 families!—another proof that where there's a will, there's a way.

Sometimes, even when the will is strong, the way is long and weary and fraught with continuing frustration. The exploitation of the workers in our industrial society has been curbed only by long and often violent battles for a living wage. Legislation prohibiting child labor and regulating hours of work and the condition of working areas, safety devices, fair employment practices, and other advances were made possible only by the power of the unions. The past century has witnessed a long series of strikes by mill hands, railway employees, coal miners, dock workers, street cleaners, bank clerks—what have you—slowly fighting inch by inch to achieve bargaining power and a better life for their families. In the case of agricultural workers, the scattered places of work made concentration of effort immensely difficult, whereas the relatively few big land owners could easily find a place to meet, to decide on wages for that season and consolidate their opposition to "radical legislation." The helplessness of the farm laborer was also complicated by Federal Law 78, passed during the Second World War whereby braceros (Mexican Nationals) could be imported to the United States and returned home after the harvest season ended. When the wartime manpower crisis ended, the law remained in effect. The domestic worker, demanding an increase in wages, found himself at great disadvantage because of the bracero. An American dollar went a long way in Mexico. The bracero was satisfied to earn 50-70 cents a day and put up with cheap food and substandard housing. He could be counted on not to strike. The grower was very pleased with Public Law 78 and did everything in his power to retain it. Industrial workers are protected by Social Security, but the farm worker was not included. Some of these omissions have recently been rectified, but even now he has not received the full benefits available to all other employees. As with every disadvantaged group, the only hope lay in a farm workers' union whose strength and solidarity would compel concessions from management. In the case of the farm workers, however, the lack of trained leadership, the seasonal work period, and the transitory home bases made organization especially difficult.

I don't remember the exact date, but I was asked if I could provide a meeting place for a small group of Mexican-Americans where they would be safe from publicity or surveillance of any kind. Hidden Villa hostel provided a secret retreat and it was there that the preliminary plans were drawn up which resulted in the first major California strike, conducted at the DiGiorgio Ranch near Bakersfield. This strike continued for nearly two years, an amazing achievement, and it had an effect far beyond the local controversy. Unless they were farmers, most people had no idea of what had been going on. The wide-spread and sustained publicity brought the farm workers' situation before the general public. The workers themselves were encouraged by the fact that their group had the tenacity to hang on so long and that other unions and sympathetic community groups would support their efforts. It was also a danger signal to the big growers that eventually the slave would revolt against the master. A series of sporadic strikes followed but were short lived because of ruthless opposition from growers and county sheriffs. As in every revolutionary crusade, the most necessary prerequisite is a dynamic leader—someone with burning conviction and the kind of magnetism that inspires others to follow his banner. Leadership that draws together disjointed elements of protest into a concentrated cooperating unit transforms a rabble into a movement. What Gandhi did for East Indians, and Martin Luther King for Blacks, Cesar Chavez is accomplishing for Chicanos in California. Like his illustrious forerunners, he is also committed to nonviolent methods of action.

Cesar is a modest, soft-spoken, small brown man. He is incredibly gentle and incredibly tenacious. I have known him for many years and his children have been to Hidden Villa Camp. In spite of being one of the most revered leaders of our time, he is a most simple, loving human being, with a subtle sense of humor and a childlike quality of charm. At the first meeting, a stranger can hardly believe that this unobtrusive, genial personality has the indomitable will, the strength of purpose and the sacrificial fervor of a great revolutionary.

When he first won recognition by his fellow workers, he realized that the initial step towards union was to ascertain where the workers lived. Once found—a few here, a few there, on widely dispersed ranches, or in isolated pockets of habitation—before any enrollment could be obtained, an arduous grass roots education was necessary for the people to understand their rights and become convinced of the value of a coordinated effort. Cesar and a few of his lieutenants carried out this itinerant mission and little by little, by means of personal interviews and meetings conducted in Spanish, the movement grew. Strikes, parleys with growers, publicity in newspapers, magazines and fliers increased public awareness of the cause which resulted in the boycott of lettuce and grapes not bearing the trademark of "la huelga." This trademark certified that the product had been harvested under conditions agreed upon by the union and the grower. Picket lines formed outside stores and angered the business interests and the police. Not only the Chicanos, but sympathizing citizens, especially college students, were arrested and beaten, and occasionally even shot. After several years, two

Cesar Chavez   UPI Compix

or three wine merchants capitulated and accepted the strikers' demands, but lettuce growers were more obdurate. After several attempts in the legislature, Public Law 78 was repealed and the menace of the bracero minimized.

Progress seemed to be well on the way, when the Teamsters Union, in conjunction with growers, arranged to offer a substitute arrangement, side-stepping the functions of the Agricultural Workers Union and offering a watered down version of their legitimate demands. I could not understand how the Teamsters Union justified this unbrotherly action. What does "solidarity forever" mean? As a result, the Gallo Wine Company and some others broke their contracts with the Farm Workers and the only place where one could buy 'honorable' head lettuce or table grapes was at the Consumers' Cooperative. I am told the boycott was effective in many cities in the East where representatives were working on wholesale markets to boycott wine and table grapes. Lettuce boycotts were organized by committed individuals in 21 cities from Dorchester, Massachusetts to Seattle, Washington. The demonstrations continued to be non-violent, in accordance with the absolute ethical insistence of Chavez. Unfortunately, in contrast, the growers and sheriff departments retaliated with brutal and outrageous suppression resulting in the death of several of the workers.

Meanwhile, Chavez and the Union have become well known all over the United States. It is a miracle that one little man of humble origin with no money and no previous business training, but with an unquenchable determination for justice and righteousness can accomplish what he has done. He has no regard for personal safety, and he has many bitter enemies, but he has many more devoted friends. Many advances for farm workers have resulted from this long and as yet inconclusive struggle. There is a health center and hospital in Delano built to supplement medical services too often refused by the regular county services. There is a retirement unit for aged Filipino workers; there is a headquarters building and an office for Cesar slightly removed from the centres of conflict. A goodly number of contributors from church, student and club groups maintain financial support. Clothing, food and other supplies flow in and many young volunteers spend hours in construction work, on boycott demonstrations or on office chores. Special bi-lingual classes at the primary level have been established in Fresno and Tulare County School systems, helping Spanish-speaking children to acquire English proficiency before they enter first grade. All this is good, but it is not enough. The recognition of the union and the extension of social security to include farm workers was still not assured. As Cesar said in a speech, "We have made a beginning but it is not enough. We have suffered. We have struggled. We will continue to struggle. We will continue to suffer. We will, we must, and we know in our hearts that we shall overcome. *Viva la causa.*"

XXVIII

Indians

Group counseling; community service;
Bay Area Indian Council.

In one of our cross country trips from the east coast back to California we travelled on the Santa Fe railroad. We got off at Albuquerque to make a side trip to the city of Santa Fe, where we found buses that offered tours to the museums and to the Indian villages. The guides accompanying these tours were attractive young women, most of them anthropolgical students who had made friends with Indians and who were able to interpret something of Indian culture to visitors like us. They dressed in attractive grey-blue uniforms. Most of them wore gorgeous turquoise and silver jewelry and were on good terms with the Indians whom we visited. I was fascinated by this hidden world within the world I knew. Something entirely different from anything I had ever seen or imagined. The beautiful old faces, the irrepressible children, the dwellings with strings of dark red peppers hanging on the outside walls, the drumming and the dancing. The harmony of the pueblo dwellings with the limitless sweep of the desert all around, gave me a new conception of human adaptability. I shall never forget seeing at Taos the tall silent figures wrapped in white blankets, standing on the roofs of the village watching the sun sink in the west. Just before the sun passed from sight, the desert glowed rose color and the shadows all turned lavender or deep purple. I don't know how to describe the kind of spiritual stirring I felt at that time. On later visits and on attendance at dances in the pueblos, the drums and the chants exerted a hypnotic effect on me. It was as if there remained in my blood primordial memory of ancient rites, buried in the unconscious, but apparently present and responsive after ten thousand years of adaptation. Suffice it to say that such was my only Indian experience until then, and it had never occurred to me before that there were Indians in California.

Just as the annual Asilomar Conference on Civic Unity had brought us in touch with Mexican-Americans, so it also provided the opening of the door to the Indian community. Mrs. Ortega, an Indian who lived in Pala, a tiny village near Palomar in Southern California, had read in the newspaper about the meeting and made up her mind to drive up in her car and tell about her people. She drove all night and arrived just as the morning session opened. I gave her ten minutes on the program which stretched into forty as she passionately described her tribal difficulties, her dissatisfaction with the Indian Bureau and distrust of all white people, including those present. Most of us were taken by surprise, never before having heard of these injustices, but one person present had. That was Dr. Chandler, who had formerly been employed at one of the Indian schools. He corroborated Mrs. Ortega's presentation (in somewhat less dramatic terms) and assured us that her accusations were fundamentally accurate.

As a result of this exposition, I felt impelled to investigate further into the lives of this unfamiliar group. I was not able to find anyone who seemed to know anything about them. I really had never heard of the Bureau of Indian Affairs and the word "reservation" held very little meaning. I resolved to try to find out what it was all about through my own personal observation. There is a good precedent among Quakers for doing just this. It is known as "One Friend's Concern."

First I studied the material given to me by the Indian Bureau, I read the Merriam report and other background material on California Indians. I learned that before the Spanish came in 1769 the Indian population was estimated at 150,000. In a hundred years their number was reduced to 17,000. The white man's diseases, measles, syphilis and tuberculosis decimated whole tribes. After the gold rush, treaties were made which the Indians agreed to in good faith but which were never ratified by the U.S. government. Evictions, massacres and arbitrary resettlement by the army relegated the native population onto lands owned by the government and administered from Washington. In moving them, the federal government had agreed to provide water, roads, housing, medical care and education. But there were always difficulties in obtaining sufficient funds from Congress to carry out these promises. About 30,000 Indians moved off the land into towns and villages. In 1950 there were supposed to be approximately 9,000 still on rancherias, about 2500 of whom resided in Hoopa and Tule River reservations. The rest were scattered in pockets all over the state, mostly in Northern California, in the mountains east of Fresno and in San Diego and Riverside Counties in the South.

Frank and I packed our station wagon and drove to Sacramento. Our first visit was to the branch office of the much maligned Bureau of Indian Affairs (Department of the Interior). Here we interviewed Mr. Hill the regional director who briefed us on the problem from his point of view. He was most helpful and friendly, as was everyone else in his office. From Mr. Hill we obtained maps and a list of all 117 reservations indicating the acreage, the number of residents, school and hospital facilities and a list of tribal council members in each unit. We were stunned at the number of rancherias and reservations and the diversity in size, population and potential. We called next on Marie Potts, a leader in Indian rights organizations, who was well-acquainted with Indians all over the state, especially in the northern and central areas. She edited a monthly newsletter entitled the 'Smoke Signal.' From her we received a detailed account of the problems as experienced by Indians, and a list of key people not necessarily on Mr. Hill's list. She explained to us that the Tribal Council was the Bureau's creation. Voting people into representative control was a new concept to Indians. The real leaders were not evident to an outsider but were recognized within the group.

Our first visit to an Indian rancheria took us to Auburn, a short run from Sacramento. This rancheria consisted of about 30 acres just outside of town. Some of the land was arable but there was difficulty regarding water which, somehow or other, had been diverted into other channels so that the Indians had barely enough for household use. James and Violet Ray were the moving spirits here. Both of them had good educations. James held a steady job in the Auburn Lumber Mill and Violet was a nurse. James was able to purchase materials for building a new home to replace the dismal wooden shack furnished by the government. A new stove and a washing machine were already waiting to be moved into the new kitchen. These two young people were as charming a young couple one might chance to meet. I did not know it at the time, but their position in the community was superior to any that we subsequently interviewed. They understood our motives and gave us additional names which eased the approach in other areas. This rancheria was one of the first to disassociate itself from the Indian Bureau and to take title to the land by direct ownership.

Although we had maps, the business of finding the reservations was not an easy matter. There were no guiding signs. Inhabitants living close by did not seem to know where the Indians lived. Even the post office couldn't help. I developed a technique of going to the nearest town and driving slowly down the main street looking for brown faces. When I spotted one I would jump out and accost the person, "Excuse me, but can you tell me how to find the Indian Reservation? I want to see Mr. So-and so." More often than not he would say, "I'm just going there. Follow my jalopy," or he would get into our car and drive there with us. Sometimes we found it ourselves by recognizing the pattern of shoddy redwood houses, the numerous rusting decrepit automobiles and the sprinkling of unkempt ragged children playing in the dirt between the houses.

When we arrived, I went in and inquired for the individual whose name I had. Coming to his (or her) door, I introduced myself and Frank and quickly explained, "We do not come from the Indian Bureau. We are not representing any church and we are not making a survey." (The last assurance was necessary because of anthropological students who were sent out on assignments and who frequently irritated people by their insensitive questioning.)

As a stranger, how does one venture to intrude on the privacy of another individual—especially if there is an economic gap between the visitor and the host? I discovered that if one offers a sincere desire for friendliness with sufficient simplicity, the barriers fade away. An important element also is tempo. Indians are deliberate. They take time to think before they speak and there is a communication without words that they understand. The many Indians I met on my travels around the state gave me a feeling of great humility. They had endured so much stark poverty and insecurity, and had suffered so much; and I represented the arrogant, over-privileged white oppressor. Yet they invited me into their homes, accepted my advances and shared with me some of their confidential struggles to survive. I recall only two instances when I had to overcome suspicion. In Laytonville where the mud was so deep we left our car on the road and waded in, we called on the people designated as the leaders of the Tribal Council. They proved to be a charming elderly couple, apparently glad to see us, who invited us into their kitchen to get acquainted. We talked about the weather, the seasonal rainfall, the mud, the price of food, improvements they had made on the house, about their grandchildren, and the Indian Bureau which did not keep their promises about repairing their road. Mr. Hill came in for considerable abuse. They asked where we came from and I learned that the wife had spent a year or two in a Santa Clara home when she was a child. This brought up the subject of apricots which we discussed at length. It turned out she had been hankering for some, so I promised to send her a bag after I returned to Los Altos.

While we were visiting, several members of the family of varying ages had come and gone. But during the whole time, at the back of the room, there was a middle-aged man who just sat and watched us, never once joining in the conversation. As we got ready to leave, he rose from his seat, came forward and said somewhat menacingly, "What are you people really after? You don't represent the Bureau, you say you aren't writing a paper, you haven't asked us for money. You aren't trying to get us to join the church. What is it you really want?" The old lady spoke up, "I think they just want to make friends, George." I nodded. We shook hands all round, but George watched us through the window as we made our way back to the car. I wish I could have heard the conversation that ensued.

In Southern California as I talked with Indians round the Palomar Observatory, people kept warning me, "Whatever you do, don't go to see Trinita." "Better pass up Trinita's reservation." "Trinita is rabid against white people." It seemed to me that Trinita must be an interesting and authentic personality. I determined to meet her. Frank and Gordon Stafford and I stopped at the entrance of the road leading to her reservation. I thought it more diplomatic to arrive on foot. A pathway led up the hill, and at the top stood a broad stalwart figure dressed in brown slacks and a green shirt, surveying our approach. I started up the trail, but I had to chuckle to myself when the two men hung back and pretended to be examining the car. I knew they were apprehensive about the sentinel they had spotted on the hill. I continued up and finally encountered Trinita who stood waiting at the top with hands on her hips and a bulldog expression on her face. "How do you do," I said in my most placating tones, "I don't represent the Indian Bureau and . . . . ." "If you did," she broke in, "I'd throw you right down the hill."

"I'm not a social worker and I'm not making a survey."

"Damn lousy people," she ejaculated, "always snooping around."

"Well," I said, "I'm just someone interested in Indians. I've heard a lot about you. I'd like to get acquainted. Do you have time to talk to me?"

She grudgingly assented. By this time the two men, not seeing me in baffled retreat, were starting up the trail. I waved to them to come along.

"Who are they?" Trinita asked suspiciously.

"Just my husband and a friend," I said, and introduced them. Trinita was evidently the leader of one of the Indian groups because outside her house there were two rows of wooden arm chairs, facing each other. "This is where we have our meeting," she said, inviting us to sit down. We talked for some time. She explained her difficulties about water and needed house repairs and continued with a bitter denunciation of Leonard Hill, the California representative of BIA and all the employees thereof. When we stood up to leave I noticed a massive oleander bush almost concealing her house. I admired it and said I had never seen so magnificent a specimen. "You know it's poison," she said, "Yes, I know," I replied, and added jokingly, "Next time some one from the Bureau comes to see you, why don't you make a tea of the leaves and offer him a cool drink?" Trinita looked at me quizzically and then she burst out into a spasm of laughter. "Great idea," she said, and continued laughing. The two men and I joined in and she slapped me on the back and shook hands all round. She even accompanied us down the hill to our car, chuckling all the way. "Don't forget," I called to her as we started up, and we left her waving at us and grinning from ear to ear. So that was the redoubtable Trinita! One touch of humor makes the whole world kin.

And so it was everywhere we went. Humility, compassion, humor, openness, sympathy, all the intuitive qualities seemed to do away with barriers and we found ourselves accepted as potential friends. I realized that my experience of silence in Quaker worship fitted in with Indian ways of communication, and I was not made uneasy by lapses in conversation.

Out of this first-hand exploration of scattered, virtually invisible people I tried to figure out some ways to help them connect more with the main stream of American society and enable them to take advantage of their opportunities as citizens, and avail themselves of health, welfare and educational services. It became evident to me that everyone of the widely scattered 117 units had different problems, and that to expect any unity among California Indians was out of the question. Each group needed individual counseling. Their problems covered the whole range of needs—housing, transporation, employment, education, health, citizenship, and help with the problems of old age and alcoholism. I thought that the Friends Service Committee might obtain a grant to put two workers in the field, one in the north, and one in the south, each equipped with camp trailers to enable them to visit isolated groups. Each worker could evaluate the special needs of the group he visited and acquaint them with services available in every county of which they were usually ignorant. Such a worker also could put pressure on the Bureau to alleviate specific needs and to improve rapport between the Indian groups and their neighboring white communities. Just as I had been, all Californians were so ignorant about their native American population! They needed to be made aware of their presence. I wrote up a proposition calling for three year funding. This was accepted by the Columbia Foundation to provide for the worker in Northern California. It was suggested that equal funds be sought to establish the same program to be funded from Southern California, but this never went through.

Frank Quinn, previously employed by the Conference of Christians and Jews, accepted the assignment. We bought him a trailer. A special Committee, of which I was chairman, was set up by the Friends to direct his activities. And off he went. This was in 1954. His work continued for five years and we published a booklet, "Indians of California," in 1955. It was reprinted in 1960, and for many years it was the only short brochure dealing with the history and current status of California tribes. It was in great demand by social workers, teachers and government officials. He also developed a series of tapes recording stories and songs recorded by aging Indians whose descendants were not interested in preserving them. Frank Quinn's wandering odyssey would make a moving document if he could ever find time to write it up. (Perhaps, like me, when he reaches his dotage he will seek to reconstruct that phase of his life.)

It appeared from general observations that there were several larger reservations that needed more intensive work than an occasional visit.

After funds for the itinerant worker ran out, other grants were received for a short period to support a resident worker at Tule Lake near Porterville, and at Round Valley at Covelo, near Ukiah. The emphasis in both areas was on the lives of young people, including how to encourage school attendance and explore sources of special training, how to organize recreation and purposeful activities such as 4H or garden projects, tours to outside communities, library facilities and strengthening of the tribal council. At Tule Lake the water system had disintegrated. There was ample water, but the springs and storage tanks had been neglected. As a result of pollution, dysentery was widespread and many children died. The organization of a water company, getting an agreement to utilize tribal subsidies, and obtaining matching funds from the U.S. Public Health Service, required two years of patient persistent stimulation on the part of the Service Committee representative. Eventually the local group exerted themselves to dig out the springs, replace broken pipes and mend rotten storage tanks. At the same time pressure was needed in Washington to appropriate matching funds for tribal subsidies which had been promised but which had never actually been delivered. What a change when water was finally piped to every house on the reservation! In addition, the old schoolhouse was converted into a community center where meetings could be held and parties for young and old, and even a child day care center and play yard for games were provided. The Service Committee worker was the catalyst that woke the people up to realize that they need not live in such sordid conditions and that through their own efforts their group could remedy not only their physical handicaps, but also the social milieu of the whole community. Today there are several organizations composed entirely of Indians engaged in improving living conditions on the rancherias and encouraging young people to qualify for employment. The contribution of the Service Committee consisted mainly in arousing leadership within the group and in providing them with the knowledge of current social procedures. At a certain point it was important to withdraw what might be considered parental direction in favor of indigenous responsibility.

When the personal service had fulfilled its main purpose, it seemed important to have a state committee to strengthen the overall emergence of Indian initiative. An older organization known as the Indian Rights Committee had been chiefly concerned at the turn of the century with violation of treaties and infringement of Indian lands in the Southwest. The Committee was not active in 1950, but it retained a small bank account. Charles Elkus, its founder, a prominent citizen who lived in San Francisco, was still concerned about Indians. We pursuaded him and Mr. Armsby, the remaining board members, to revive and reinstate the Indian Rights Association into the California League for American Indians. Mr. Elkus was the first president, and I succeeded him and continued to serve for several years. We continued to encourage young people to stay in high school and helped them attain scholarships and jobs. We arranged conferences and stimulated Indians to put pressure on their representative in state and federal offices for needed legislation. We did a lot of propaganda among welfare, health and education departments at county as well as state level because we found the workers had very little understanding of the Indian background and psychology. We arranged exhibits of arts and crafts and sponsored films illustrative of the Indians' skills and their adjustments to the environment. We contributed funds for the revival of tribal dances and festivals. We sent an Indian to Washington to take part in hearings having to do with appropriations. All along the objective was to get the Indians to be more articulate in demanding their rights, to be less concerned with injustices of the past and more mindful of present opportunities. Little by little the white board members withdrew in favor of Indians, and an Indian assumed the presidency. Eventually, because of the rising tide of Indian Power, the League seemed to have fulfilled its function and terminated its existence in favor of other indigenous organizations.

In line with the objectives entertained by the League, I experimented with a little program on the side. The idea originated with the Southern California Friends who arranged for groups of Indian children to journey from other parts of the Southwest to visit homes in California for two weeks. The cost of transportation proved to be prohibitive and the project was laid down, but I decided it would be less expensive if only California Indian children were involved. With the help of Enid Hilton, social worker in Mendocino County, about thirty youngsters from among her Indian clients were selected. Then I found hosts with boys or girls of comparable ages to entertain these Indian visitors for two weeks in San Jose, Los Altos or Palo Alto. It was a lot of work to orient the families and try to match ages and interests at our end, while Enid was trying to reassure Indian parents, provide bathing suits, and more than one pair of underpants, warm sweaters and bus tickets at her end.

We carried this on for several years but then I got too ambitious and decided that we should try to include some of the lovely teenage girls who were school dropouts in Round Valley and Hopland, arranging for them to live with a family, working for their room and board while going to high school in the Bay Area. The plan seemed to be working well for the fall term, but the regular routines to which they were unaccustomed and the strain of adapting themselves to white living styles proved too irksome. Also, the sex motif entered into the picture. One girl asked her hostess for a weekend off to visit an aunt in Marin County. Instead she went junketing to the Gay Way at San Francisco Beach ending up being raped in the dunes by a car load of boys. Another girl disappeared while on a shopping errand for her foster family, arousing much anxiety until a police call from Fresno identified the girl as one in a group of juveniles arrested by the highway patrol. Another of the girls called me at 3:30

Josephine Duveneck (with Raphael Malsin, President of Lane Bryant, Inc. and Helen Gahagan Douglas, former California Congresswoman) recipient of Lane Bryant Annual Award in 1954.

one morning and asked me to come to the Palo Alto jail and rescue her. I decided after all this and more that my efforts were resulting in more harm than good and that I had better leave the adolescent girls to work out their own destinies in their own communities.

Through work with the California Indians we came in touch with another whole set of problems dealing with out-of-state Indians who were being transported from reservations all over the United States to work in the industrial plants on the West Coast. The Bureau paid their costs of resettlement, found them housing (usually miserable) and placed them in jobs in urban areas where workers were in demand. Uprooted from the simple communal life in Oklahoma, New Mexico and Arizona, sudden immersion into the hurly-burly life of cities like Oakland or San Francisco was an incredible contrast. There was no place to which they could go to meet other Indians. The Friends' Indian Committee became deeply impressed with the need for a Center where Indians could find one another and receive counsel and fellowship to assist in their adjustment to city ways. Money was obtained to rent a dwelling house in downtown Oakland in 1955. We named it the Intertribal Friendship House. Four years later, these quarters proving much too small to meet the demands of the many Indian groups, the Committee acquired the Ming Quong Home, a larger building formerly a home for Chinese orphans. Through the efforts of Judge Peters, a citizen of Oakland and a dynamic member of the Committee, the House was adopted into the Community Chest's budget which eased the financial burden. Raising enough money had been a never-ending problem facing the Committee. It is always a headache to have to put time and energy into raising funds when one is involved in a program. Beginning in a small way with clubs, a clothing exchange, evening classes, basketball teams, dances, weekend parties or excursions, attendance increased and a new cohesion developed despite the differences in tribal antecedents. The work of the house: hospitality, responsibility covering the necessary tasks of house cleaning, cooking, dish washing, answering the telephone, child care, etc., was carried on by the Indians themselves. A counseling service became vital. And eventually the Bay Area Indian Council was organized by the Indians themselves with branches in San Francisco and San Jose. All along we had insisted on Indian membership on the Board. At first it was difficult to persuade them to join and to express themselves at monthly meetings, but gradually the older members gained confidence and as younger ones were drawn in, they began to feel that the Intertribal Friendship House did in reality belong to them. The wave of the future, the third world revolution, the example of Black Power, whatever you want to call it, finally dawned for the Indians and they realized they could do it themselves—could organize and plan ahead to liberate their people from the white man's condescension. It happened at Friendship House in such a dramatic way. The Board, composed of Indians and Whites met for the usual monthly business. The Indian spokesman arose and announced that the Indians felt they could now run their own show and would the white members of the Board all go home please. This was a complete surprise, but to their credit, they got up without a word and complied with the request. It was a tough repudiation after months and years of dedicated work. After hurt feelings subsided, they realized that this was essentially what they had been working for from the beginning and here it was coming true at last. I have been fascinated by the declaration of independence that has been manifesting itself in the dark skinned people. It is the same phenomenon that occurs when the child in the home moves out of adolescence into adulthood and is through with parental control. Woe to the parent who resists this newly achieved self-sufficiency. The new relationship of equality can be achieved only by willing acceptance of the changed status. I think the same psychology is at work in our society. We can no longer work *for* the underprivileged, but only *with* them for *mutual* benefit.

I have come to realize more and more that oppressed and desecrated though he has been, the Indian has made a profound contribution to our civilization. I think the current emphasis on ecology and conservation, the reverence for all living things and the increasing sensitivity for preserving our resources, that has finally begun to penetrate our callous and greedy minds, had direct connection with the way the Indian acted towards his environment. It is not the first time in history that a physically subjugated people have so permeated the culture of their conquerors that the transformation is in truth a victory. Not by weapons, but by the strength of the spirit.

XXIX

Quest (Four)

Comparative religion and application to everyday life.

I have sometimes thought about the traditional symbols associated with different religions: the Sword and Crescent of Islam, Shiva dancing through Hindu cosmology, Buddha in meditation on the lotus seat, Moses with the Tablets of the Law, Jesus on the crucifix. How expressive these representations are of the varied approaches man has made to explain the universal mystery of life! Seemingly dissimilar, the basic concepts are really not so far apart. Man's need for God, his adjustment to the world and to the other creatures, who, like himself, inhabit that world. Worship of the Infinite and adherence to a moral law are fundamental to all religions. The emphasis differs. What a paradox that Christianity, the one most dedicated to brotherly love, should find its followers to be the most ruthless agents of violence in the modern world! I often wonder if mankind can survive the present trend towards materialism and competition. Will he resemble those creatures that were unable to adapt to changing conditions and so go down to oblivion like the dinosaurs? "Where there is no vision the people perish." When there is so much beauty on the earth and in the hearts of men—how sad that ugliness should seem to dominate the present picture! Perhaps the younger generation who rebel against war and conformity will save our "perishing republic." May they find the power to redeem us who have so miserably failed the dream!

When I was a little girl one of my favorite books was *The Pilgrim's Progress*. I re-read it about once a year. I remember one of my sisters saying, "I don't understand what you see in that old book. We had to read some of it in English class and I think it's terribly boring." I am sure that at the age of eleven or twelve I did not get all the implications of that remarkable work, which was written while the author was in prison. Since then I have read a great many books by the great initiates describing the journey of the soul through all phases of the mystic way, but none of them equals Bunyan as a dramatic story teller. He writes for the common man, using symbols without self-consciousness and without the extravagant language of St. Augustine or St. John of the Cross. But he makes his points in true puritan restraint which is no less authentic. At any rate, because I read it so many times, it must have meant a great deal to my youthful searching. It is characteristic of all adventures of the spirit, in whatever culture they originate, that progress does not move steadily forward, but entails long periods of aridity and many moods of uncertainty and doubt. Mention is often made of "the dark night of the soul" and of the sudden unanticipated flash of ecstacy — the lowest and the highest points in the journey. In between these two supreme opposites there are many variations of emotional response.

After the enlightenment I received at La Crescenta I enjoyed a sort of easy summertime of certainty in which I could slip into meditation with little or no effort. And I could go about my business with a heightened sensitivity and effectiveness. Of course it didn't last.

There was a Vedanta Center in San Francisco with another Swami in residence. Hither I betook myself in search of further instruction, reading material, and possible association. The building on Vallejo Street dates back to the turn of the century and is characteristic of the flamboyant style of early San Francisco architecture with turrets and carved entrances and mansard roofs. This particular building was crowned with an onion-shaped bulge reminiscent of Russian church edifices. Inside there were offices, living quarters, conference rooms and a large rectangular room which served as the temple. On entering for the first time I was shocked by two enormous, more-than-life-size, framed oil paintings facing the worshippers at the side and in back of the altar. One represened Ramakrishna in meditation, scantily dressed in a dark blue robe, his black hair and profuse beard framing a heavy, dingy face singularly devoid of spiritual radiance. The other depicted Jesus in filmy *pink* drapery encircled by doves, a most effeminate, insipid figure with wispy golden hair, lacking any visible bone structure and certainly not imbued with religious exaltation. These two overpowering paintings offended me deeply. Even when I closed my eyes, I could still see Ramakrishna's glaring masculinity and Jesus' floating formlessness. It was a great contrast to the simplicity of the little chapel at La Crescenta. I never returned more than once or twice. The Swami also was not at all like Swami Paramananda. His approach was far more intellectual. He was well grounded in scriptures and in techniques of worship. He had obviously "arrived" through a long process of training; his discourse was profound and articulate but he lacked the warmth and gaiety that characterized the La Crescenta community. I had come to feel that as one approaches nearer to divine reality one should become less austere and more joyous; one should be less analytical and more tolerant. According to the light one has received, one ought to be able to pass something on to less fortunate people. Meditation should cause one to be more sensitive to all living things and especially to the unspoken thoughts and desires of one's fellow creatures.

"Thou shalt love the Lord thy God with all thy heart and all thy mind and all thy strength and thy neighbor as thyself." A few simple words that sum up the whole duty of man.

I felt I had come to a fork in the road and I needed to study a map before proceeding. I wanted to take a long look at the fundamental implications of Hindu and Buddhist philosophies as I conceived them. I wanted to find where those philosophies related to the Christian ideals and where they differed. I realized that I was a product of Western culture. My roots were in the Western world and that I could not assume a heritage alien to my race without violating something very deep within myself. I gradually withdrew from the Vedanta Society but continued to practice what I had learned while exploring more deeply the ruling principles of Oriental religion.

It seemed to me that there is great similarity between Brahma, the Supreme Being of ancient India, and Jehovah, the Almighty, as described in the Old Testament. Jehovah is a father-rule figure who created the world and who treats man as a wayward child who must be disciplined. Brahma, also the creator, is omnipresent, diffusing all that exists in the myriad forms of the Universe, including the Self (the Atman) within every human being. Even though we find other names that appear as gods to be worshipped—like Krishna, Vishnu and Shiva, they are really only aspects representing different powers of the Absolute, impersonal indescribable Being. The doctrine of Karma emphasizes that man is the creator of his own fate. The conditions of his present life are determined by the dynamics of his previous incarnation. The sole purpose of existence is to overcome all earthly desires and to so purify the ego that it is no longer subject to rebirths, but attains Nirvana, its identity absorbed by the Universal spirit. The methods of attaining this state of perfection are described in the ancient *Vedas* and in the Buddhist scriptures outlining the "Noble Eightfold Path." The Christian mystics, employing a different vocabulary, outline a similar endeavor. They lay great emphasis on sin, on penance and retribution, on the need for purification. But ultimate redemption is available only through the grace of a Saviour, Jesus Christ. This world is looked upon as a preparation for a future state where virtue is rewarded by everlasting bliss and wickedness doomed to suffer retribution for all time.

The idea that a person's condition is due in large measure to his own previous behavior is demonstrated again and again even in one life.

Whatever choices we make and whatever actions we assume will unquestionably determine the subsequent pattern of our lives. The precept of reincarnation seemed to me to offer the only logical explanation for the differences in people. I do not believe that all men are born equal. Even taking the environment into consideration, the inequalities of natural endowment, the innate strength or weakness of character, the inherent disposition cannot be explained as direct inheritance. Now and then, not often, I have met people who impressed me as being very old souls. They have a depth of serenity and wisdom so authentic that I feel their roots must reach far back in time. I have known two quite young children to possess this mysterious quality. And yet, logic aside, the idea of transmigration from death to rebirth seems so preposterous. It is bad enough for a baby to carry on the genes of ancestry, but to imagine the weight of repetitive life cycles jammed into the consiousness of one small creature emerging from the womb, this seems too fantastic for even a credulous person like me to swallow. A transference of this kind would represent such a manipulation of psychic chemicals that even a supreme transcendental Power could hardly perform such a miracle.

Nevertheless, I took to heart the truth that discontent and difficulties are the result of one's own attitudes. "You are your own worst enemy" is a common adage seldom understood. Surely the obligation rests on each individual to discover the why and wherefore of his problems and to endeavor to change the nature of them. This goes for one's self. But to judge other people from this standpoint is something else. Right here comes the point at which I found myself not in accord with Oriental philosophy. If I knew someone sick, suffering, or impoverished, or someone unhappy from economic or emotional causes, I could never dismiss them with the thought that this was their Karma, previously accumulated and it was the law of life which they themselves must seek to remould. Such a belief would encourage indifference to suffering and would make loving kindness irrelevant.

In India where there is so much poverty and so much wealth, so many highly intellectual Brahmins and so many illiterate outcasts, there has been very little concern on the part of the well-to-do until recently to improve the condition of the poor. Even now the initiative for improvement has largely come from England or from America or from English-educated Indians.

If we analyze the great theologies of mankind we find that the great religious teachers have all uttered fundamentally the same message, couched in different terms with unfamiliar vocabulary and alternative rituals. I made a list of some quotations bearing on the basic principles underlying all these creeds. Here are a few dealing with human relationships:

from the Rig Veda (Hindu)
The riches of the liberal never waste away while he who will not give, finds
none to comfort him.
Let the rich satisfy the poor employee and bend his eye upon a longer
pathway.
Riches come now to one, now to another and like the wheels of carts keep
rolling.

from Buddhist Scripture
Hatred does not cease by hatred at any time:
hatred ceases by love. This is an old law.
Do not speak harshly to anyone; those who are
spoken to will answer the same way.
To one in whom love dwells, all in the world are brothers.

from Tibet (the Golden Rule)
That which one desireth not for oneself, do not do to others.

from the Old Testament
If thine enemy be hungry give him bread to eat; and if he be thirsty give
him water to drink; for thou shalt heap coals of fire upon his head and the
Lord shall reward thee. Oppress not the stranger, the fatherless and the
widow and shed not innocent blood.

from the Koran
No one of you is a believer until he loves for his brother what he loves for
himself.

from Confucius
What you do not want done to yourself, do not do to others.

from Taoist sayings
Return love for hatred—otherwise when a great hatred is reconciled some
of the bitterness will remain. To the good I act with goodness. To the bad
I also act with goodness.

Running through the thoughts above, the motivating force seems to
derive from the expectation that charity and kindness given will make you a
better, more moral person. In contrast, it was written in the New
Testament, not because you should be just, not because "right action
makes for enlightenment" but because:

"Whoso has this world's good and seeth his brother have need and
shutteth up his bowels of compassion from him, how dwelleth the love of
God in him? My little children, let us not love in word neither in tongue,
but in deed and in truth. . . . no man hath seen God at any time. If we
love one another, God dwelleth in us and His love is perfected in us."

Our records of the life of Jesus are very scanty but in all episodes the
central emphasis is on love, a spontaneous response to human need,
whether it be physical or spiritual. He was a great mystic, "I and the

Father are one," but he was also a great companion. He liked to play with children and he preferred the company of simple folk like fishermen to the erudite stuffy congregation of priests and governors. More clearly than any of the other great initiates he emphasized that the love of God and the love of man are reciprocal. Peace and goodwill— what has happened to the Christian Church that it obscures this self-evident truth? Where it is possible to strip off the encumbrances of the church as an institution, and dispose of its pomp and idolatry, we find a testimony so simple and so universal that it is like a shining jewel in a bed of gravel.

I labored for years under the conviction of original sin. I think that is a vicious and wicked doctrine that has no relevance to the essential purity of Christ's teaching. I looked around among Christian sects to see if any of them reflected a real image of the Master. To some degree a few seemed to achieve it. Certainly not the most well attended or well organized. Rather unconventional, somewhat bizarre gatherings represent different stages of revolt against tradition.

All my life I had played around the outskirts of organized religious groups. I was attracted to the Catholic Church because of its aesthetic appeal, to the Church of England for the beautiful language of the Book of Prayer, to the Unitarian Church for its unity and social service dedication and to the Vedanta for its depth of mystical communion. But I could never join any of them because there was always something missing. Part of me was satisfied, but only part.

For some years I had been going occasionally to a small meeting held on Sunday mornings at the home of Professor Augustus Murray, head of the Greek Department at Stanford, and a Quaker originally from Philadelphia. We met in his study, a shadowy room lined with books from floor to ceiling. An open fire burned on the hearth in winter time. It was a very small group that gathered in silence. Sometimes it happened that someone spoke but often only the silence was eloquent. I was moved by the sincerity of these people to inquire into the background of their Quaker faith. I read the Life of George Fox its founder and John Woolman its practitioner, Elizabeth Fry, Isaac Pennington and William Penn. What a bunch of individualists! Courageous, upright, humble seekers of the Kingdom of Heaven within themselves and in the world outside! Thomas Kelly's *Testament of Devotion* was echoed word for word in my thoughts. Rufus Jones and Howard Brinton were personalities I met, living examples of the faith they professed and practiced.

The assurance of the Inner Light and the recognition of "that of God in every man" expressed the two deepest convictions that I had come to out of my long searching. The balance of these two ideals often considered antagonistic, seemed to converge into a unity that satisfied my mind and opened my heart. The way of worship, waiting in silence for illumination, represented fellowship at the deepest level. I felt completely free to join in this communion. Since Friends require no doctrinal pledge, the way was open.

At this time, and as a result of trying rigorously to evaluate what I had discovered in relation to my own needs and desires, my sense of direction had become quite clear. To practice the presence of God and to minister to His children in whatever way I could, summarized the way of life that I hoped to fulfill. A very simply formula. Why had it taken me so long to arrive at such an obvious conclusion?

While these perceptions were stabilizing themselves at the deeper level of my consciousness I was outwardly involved, through the American Friends Service Committee, in working with refugees from Europe, Japanese evacuees, Negroes from the south and young people facing emergencies resulting from the war. Trying to assist with these problems often required more insight and more flexibility of judgment than I possessed. But I began to discover how to really listen to people and how to sense intuitively the nature of their burdens. I found that it was not so much advice that they sought, but a chance to talk about their problems to someone else, frequently arriving at solutions through the process of verbalizing. Being aware of "that of God in every man" made every encounter, however trivial, a sort of sacrament. If love is present, rapport between human beings is easily established, brushing aside differences in culture and economic status. I had always had this kind of free communication with children, but with adults I had not been able to establish compatability unless the other person was likeminded in background and intellectual interests. Aspects of me got in the way, critical reactions, desire to dominate and impose my ideas, sophistication, boredom, sometimes embarrassment because of being so much more fortunate than the other person—aspects no doubt of a dissatisfied ego.

As I try to recall this period extending over my middle years it seems to me that it was the beginning of a greater harmony between the conflicting motivations that I had found so difficult to reconcile. I could probably have become a career woman but so much involved in that was distasteful to me. Competition, publicity, endless meetings, pressures of various kinds and subordination of family and my private life—I was not willing to make that sacrifice. I could have withdrawn into study and meditation but the world held too much fascination for me to forego it. My life still operated on two levels but the distance between these levels was narrowing and the separate objectives were tending to merge.

XXX

Hidden Villa Camp

*Camp activities; childrens' problems and
their reactions to camp life.*

The Experiment in International Living and the Friends'
Workshop which I have described in the chapters on European refugees
and Farm Labor had used the Hidden Villa Hostel for living quarters for
the summers of 1940, 1941, and 1942. We had acquired equipment to
meet the basic needs of about fifty people. It was available for
independent groups on a temporary basis. The first camp for blind
children was conducted here by Rose Reznich. The San Francisco Boys'
Chorus organized by Madi Bacon also tried out a week's sojourn. Both
groups have since developed their own properties. The trial experiences
at Hidden Villa focused their objectives and indicated the kind of
financial and organizational resources they would need for the development of independent camps. I decided the time had come for me to
establish an ongoing regular program using the facilities already set up
on the premises.

Beginning in 1945 as an experiment in race relations, Hidden Villa
Camp has existed for thirty years as an independent institution. It came
about in this way. During the time I served as chairman of the
Community Relation Committee (Northern California Friends), I
attended a great many meetings and conferences with other agencies
working for minority groups. Beside the Johnson Survey which I had
participated in, there were other surveys and conferences to determine
the nature of the problem. It seemed there was no end to the lengthy
discussions of housing, education, employment, police and court
discrimination. I got awfully tired of these deliberations which

duplicated what we already knew and seldom resulted in positive action. I wondered what I could do as an individual to make an actual concrete program to combat discrimination and further integration. What did I have at my disposal to use in such a cause?

It had been borne in on me that adults immersed in accepted social patterns were extremely slow to accept change. In the abstract perhaps, yes, but in the making of day to day living adjustments to new relationships considerable time was required. It seemed to me if one could get hold of children *before* prejudice intervened there might be a good chance to prevent its development. A group accustomed to one another from the cradle should be able to work together harmoniously on common interests all through life. Since retiring from Peninsula School, I missed children. A lot of them came to the ranch and seemed to enjoy what it had to offer. It was a ready-made surrounding. Why not organize a summer camp aimed at multicultural understanding? My experience at Peninsula School and with my own kids, my familiarity with camping techniques and outdoor living and the availability of open space and simple accommodations made it seem entirely feasible. I began to sound people out. It was like the Peninsula School all over again. People said, "It's a nice idea but it won't work. The children will never mingle." "The white parents won't send you their children." "The black parents will not trust you to take care of their kids." Same old nonsense! But in any case, I thought I should give it a try. I had a pretty good reputation as an educator and organizer and because of my work in community relations I knew personally quite a few minority group leaders. At first I considered doing it as a Friend's Service project, but when I thought about the lengthy committee meetings that would be involved, I decided to proceed independently. I invited a small mixed group to help me as an advisory committee and I found a Negro girl to be director of the first camp. She had just graduated from Mills College with a degree in playground and recreation work. She was an enthusiastic, bubbling sort of person with great physical vitality, a keen sense of humor and had a natural way with children. She and I planned a spur-of-the-moment program, based on her knowledge of playground skills and games, and my familiarity with kids and with the environment. We mimeographed the plan and the registration forms and purchased athletic supplies. With the help of our advisory committee, we solicited enrollment from a variety of sources. Black or white, rich or poor, any boy or girl between the ages of 7 and 13 was welcome. To our amazement, recruiting was not at all difficult. Within a few weeks we enrolled sixty-one children in three two-week sessions, representing Black, White, Filipino, and Mexican families.

The Hostel was used as camp headquarters where food was prepared and served and group meetings could take place. The Hostel house parent's apartment was turned into the office where there was a telephone and registration and health records could be kept. It was also a place for counselors to relax and enjoy each other when off duty. It was "out of bounds" for campers. I think it important in any camp to plan a place for staff free time. Living twenty four hours a day with kids can be very fatiguing. Counselors need opportunities to escape, to relax, to follow their own concerns and to enjoy each other unmolested by small fry. For young adults the exchange of ideas is an important part of growing up. In camp the responsibility shared by each counselor leads to vital discussion of ideals, methods and attitudes. Indeed the philosophy of life inherent in each individual's thinking becomes manifest to his or her co-workers. If the staff represents a variety of backgrounds, the encounter provides a broad spectrum of human motivation and results in greater tolerance and mutual respect. Over the years the fellowship developed between counselors during the summer months has been remarkable and has often lasted for years. Sometimes there have even been marriages (five in all). Some camps have problems with staff. I think it is usually due to lack of consideration by the director. It is just as important for counselors to experience opportunities for learning and growth as it is for campers to flourish and expand. A satisfied, well-oriented staff is probably the first requisite for a happy camp.

I did the recruiting and screening of campers and staff, visited families, dealt with county regulations, managed the budgets, purchased food and other supplies, set up menus and out-lined schedules. In case of illness, I took care of the child at our house. During the time camp was in session I didn't do much of anything else. Enrollment before camp and evaluation afterwards required a certain amount of clerical work during spring and early fall. It was always an exciting day when the children poured in. Many of them were brought direct to camp by their parents, but we met the largest number at the Southern Pacific depot in Palo Alto. Those who came from San Francisco, Berkeley, Oakland or Marin County met our counselor at the train in San Francisco. It was quite a sight to see them tumble off the cars onto the station platform, followed by a deluge of suitcases, blanket rolls, sleeping bags, guitars and miscellaneous duffel which the conductor tossed off into the luggage van while the engineer leaned out of his cab to see why he had to wait so long before continuing his run. Four station wagons and a truck sufficed to transport the campers and the gear on the ten mile drive to the ranch. The new recruits were quiet and slightly apprehensive about what they were getting into, but the old timers were very verbal asking such questions as "Who will be my counselor?," "Is So-and-So going to be there again?" "Do you have any new horses?" "How is Shortie, or Chief or Manchita?" "Is the donkey still there?" etc., etc., coupled with many explanations to the younger ones. Arriving at camp, meeting the counselor, checking in and allotment of living quarters and the sorting out of equipment and staggering off with it to cabin or outdoor area seemed to take forever, but by six o'clock everybody and everything was sorted out. New companions, supper time, Capture the Flag or Prisoner's Base, darkening world, gathering for campfire, kept everybody too busy to feel homesick. And the thrill of lying under the stars rolled up in the new sleeping bag—what an adventure *that* was!

We divided our children according to age—younger boys and younger girls in cabins, older ones divided into four groups, the *Vale* and the *Tree* for girls, the *Pit* and *Bluff* for boys. We placed two or three minority youngsters in each group. This allocation was made before they came to camp. One time this careful plan was upset. I had three nine-year old boys from Chinatown to accommodate in two cabins with four bunks in each. I divided them up leaving two Chinese and two white boys together and two white, one Negro and one Chinese boy in the other. In the morning I noticed one of the white boys looking very disconsolate. "Jim," I said, "Is there anything the matter?"

"Sure is," he answered. "Those guys!"

"What guys?"

"The guys in my cabin."

"What do they do to you?"

"I don't know what they're talking about. They jabber all the time and I can't understand one word."

Come to find out, it appeared that the counselor had allowed the third Chinese boy to swap bunks so that three celestials occupied the same cabin where the remaining white occupant was unable to share their conversation. When I questioned them, they assured me that their cabin was *"Hidden Villa Chinatown."* We had a good laugh about that, but shifted berths to a *United Nations* habitat.

It was surprising to me and very gratifying that there were practically no conflicts due to ethnic differences. Of course everyone was prepared before coming to expect differences in color and background. I used to call it "The Camp of Many Colors" which applied to natural surroundings as well as to the human beings. I remember only one instance of name calling when some boy started the verse about "Chink, chink, Chinaman Sitting on a fence. . . ." and the term "chink" was bandied about. I brought up the subject at a morning meeting and asked the kids to think up other name tags that were equally uncomplimentary. We collected quite a list: Nigger, of course, Kike, Heinie, Wop, Hunkie, Frosh, Mick, Mug, Hun, Gringo, Jap, Raghead (East Indians wearing turbans), Kook and Wetbacks, etc. All of us except Indians belonged in one of these categories. The staff was also included. We could discuss our own reactions and explain how uncomfortable it made us feel when such derogatory labels were applied to us. A similar approach was used in regard to swearing and "dirty" words, which sometimes constituted a problem with the younger boys. The male counselors and one or two of the most mature older campers handled this discussion. Everyone was encouraged to bring out his favorite samples of profanity or vulgarity to which the leaders evinced no surprise or censure. The discussion emphasized the notion that time and place were important factors in restraint and while the words were not wicked in themselves, they offended some people and it was bad taste to introduce them into polite conversation. The older boys were the most persuasive because they told the younger boys how they had gone through this phase "when we were your age," but now, having grown up (the difference between nine and twelve!) they didn't have to show off anymore. As the story was related to me, they were particularly emphatic about their speech in the presence of females. Chivalry in jeans!

Traditions seem always to develop in any ongoing institution. We had a few at Hidden Villa Camp which were distinctive. One was the morning assembly held immediately after breakfast while campers were still at tables (dishes cleared away). I gave a great deal of thought to these few moments in which the tone and philosophy of the camp could be expressed. I felt it to be the time of invocation, worship if you will, a sharing of the deeper consciousness. I did not seek to proselytize, but only to draw forth from each one his own response to the "communion of saints." A moment of recollection to start the day and rededicate one's energies. I built up a little treasury of poems, stories, prayers, proverbs, legends. Sometimes I brought in a plant or a rock or a picture to explain and to share my wonder. Sometimes a current issue arising out of a camp situation could be aired and discussed and a solution found acceptable to all those involved. A period of silence followed. This was often a surprise to new children. They felt self-conscious and wanted to laugh. As time went on, they understood, for some it became very meaningful. For me, it served to emphasize the underlying purpose of the camp above the pressures of detail planning. And then we sang. I played the piano and one of the counselors led the singing. Songs used in most camps at that time were pretty awful. We used the little books of folk songs published by the National Recreation Association, or, if we had a capable leader, she would teach the words and the tune orally. This is the best way. By the end of their camp session, the children knew a large number of songs. Singing was heard everywhere—on hikes, overnight camping, at the craft cabin and around the camp fires. The last evening of the summer we held a little ceremony at the swimming pool. Each group made some kind of a boat or raft decorated with flowers and a candle for each member of the group. When it got dark we all went down to the pool where candles in paper bags *(luminarias)* had been placed at intervals along the edge. They were reflected in the water. The children with their counselors gathered in small groups along the water's edge. At a given signal, they lighted their candles and set their vessel afloat while the group made a wish for the camp and sang their favorite song. The lights were reflected in the water and the voices rang out in the stillness. Then after a pause the next group launched their craft, made their wish and sang their chorale. The

Hidden Villa Camp days.

final song was one in which everyone joined. We watched the dancing reflections till all the candles burned down and darkness enfolded the silent pool. Then the road back to camp was filled with dim shapes of children scurrying back to their beds

The after-lunch rest period was another habit which I felt was important. During the hottest part of the day if you can get youngsters to relax their bodies and their minds, many tensions due to fatigue can be avoided or resolved. The middle and older children came up to my house. In hot weather it is always cool. I have about 40 cushions; my living room is large. Had you ventured in around one or two o'clock of a summer afternoon you would have been amazed to see the room transformed into a veritable flop house. At this hour I would have been sitting in an arm chair reading aloud such things as *The Jungle Book*, *Kontiki*, *Black Beauty*, *A Tale of Two Cities*, or other delightful books. Many of the disadvantaged children had never been read to before. They were restless at first, but usually settled down to listen when the book began to get exciting. I used to worry sometimes about exploiting a captive audience, but it seemed to me the benefits warranted the imposition. Almost every day a few children went to sleep curled up on the rug with a soft cushion under their heads. So peacefully they slept through the exodus of the others and well into the afternoon. Over some the magic of the great books wove a spell that remained in their memories. I have heard twenty or thirty year old alumni tell me how vividly they still remember ths stories I read or told and how much the quiet periods meant as a respite from outside heat and the intense activity of camp living.

That activity consisted of all the occupations traditionally offered by summer camps. Hiking and overnight camping, cookouts, picnics, sunrise surprise trips, specimen hunting and collecting. Active games such as Capture the Flag (a favorite), volleyball, baseball, tetherball, races and track events, and swimming. The most popular of all the outdoor programs was, of course, riding. This was available to all the campers every other day. It was amazing how quickly they learned. From that first agonizing moment when a child felt himself up on top of what seemed to him a huge unpredictible monster till the last few days of camp when he felt completely at ease in the saddle and could go on a trail ride along the creek and maybe up on the mountain, feeling himself completely secure with his four-footed buddy. They knew all the horses by name, visited them in the pasture, dreamed about them. And remembered their personalities long years afterward. The horses were *so* good and patient, round and round the ring all morning with little heels kicking them and reins held too tight or too loose, with human bundles on their backs going bump bump bump. If anyone fell off, the horse stopped instantly. I hope the love and admiration they received recompensed the animals for the tedious hours spent in the service of these young riders.

As a member of the community, every child helped with necessary chores. Table setting and serving (those on duty known as the hoppers), sweeping the main hall, the washrooms, drying dishes, yard clean up (what hundreds of little scraps appear on the ground just over night), vegetable gathering and preparation, hoeing out the weeds, peeling potatoes, shucking corn, helping feed the animals, making cookies and churning ice cream.

Another category was creative hand work. We tried to use native material such as olive or madrone wood for rings, or pendants or ornamental plaques; we made necklaces from seeds or beads, and belts from strips of leather. Block prints and wrapping paper embellished with original designs, tie dying on torn sheets or white T shirts, the coloring made from native dyes, boats to float on the pool, head bands for riding, toys for younger brothers and sisters—no end to invention and innovations.

We often did folk dancing and dramatics, depending on the genius of that summer's staff. Special events broke through routines. It might be an international dinner or a fiesta, a talent show, hat night, dress-up night, ping pong tournament, water carnival, track meet, song fest, puppet show, hay ride, treasure or scavenger hunts, and of course evening camp fires that brought out all manner of stories, skits and community singing. At the close of evening camp fire we held hands in a big circle and sang a goodnight song. My favorite was:

> Peace I ask of thee, oh river
> Peace, peace, peace
> When I learn to live serenely
> Cares will cease.
> From the hills I gather courage
> Vision of the days to be
> Strength to lead and faith to follow
> All are given unto me.
> Peace I ask of thee, o river
> Peace, peace, peace.

That ring of childish faces lit up by the flickering light of the dying campfire always moved me deeply. I loved these children so much, each one and all together. I was mindful of the frustrations and compromises that lay ahead for many of them. They were the hope of the future. The words in the Episcopal service of Evensong came to mind, "Lighten our darkness we beseech Thee, o Lord, and in Thy great mercy defend us from all the perils and dangers of this night." But instead of 'night' I substituted 'dangers of this *life.*'

So many precious memories! They would fill a huge book and even then I could not put down the reverberations of each brief episode. A few of them come vividly to mind at this moment. One had to do with a dramatized version of Hidden Villa history beginning with Indians and ending with the arrival of the Duveneck family in a covered wagon.

When it came to assigning parts, Freddie, a diminutive Chinese boy insisted that he was going to act Mr. Duveneck. His friends tried to dissuade him. They said he was too small. He was completely determined, "I'm going to be Mr. Duveneck." So they had to give in, provide him with a mustache and an oversized green hat. Mrs. Duveneck was played by the tallest Negro girl in camp. It was a motley offspring that emerged from the covered wagon with these parents, but no one noticed any discrepancies.

Another episode recalls Bertie, a boy from Czechoslovakia, who was a natural with animals. One day he was late for lunch and when he came to the table where his counselor sat, explained that he was late because he had caught a rattlesnake. The counselor asked, "What did you do with it?" He answered, "I tied it to a tree."

"You did *what*?"

"Yes, I tied him to that little tree by the clothesline."

The rest of the gang hooted, but the counselor, knowing the boy, thought he had better go take a look. Sure enough, there *was* a small snake with a noose of light string around his neck, fastened to a sapling. Certainly Bertie had a way with wild creatures!

Barbara came to us by recommendation of a psychiatrist. She refused to eat due to complicated home problems. Every meal at home had been a losing battle. She was tall, thin as a telephone pole and a year or two older than most of our campers. I agreed to take her although I had misgivings. Before her arrival I alerted the staff and explained to the girls in her living group that no one was to make any remarks about eating or not eating, to just ignore her abstention. I also urged that she be included in as many activities as possible. After two days of untouched meals she started to nibble a bit of bread. Nobody noticed. Gradually her plates became empty and Sunday's ice cream and cake called for a second helping. Three of the girls came up to tell me of this remarkable event for which we shared the credit. Groups took a hike that afternoon to what was known as the White House, visible from the valley floor. When they returned, hot and sweaty, I did not see Barbara. I asked one of the counselors who said she was with the other group. The other group leader said she was with the first group. Children said she rushed ahead to out-distance everybody and she was last seen heading down the trail as fast as she could go. It became evident that Barbara was lost. By that time it was nearly dark and we started to organize a search party with flash lights, etc., when the telephone rang. A faint faraway voice said, "This is Barbara."

"Where are you?" I asked excitedly.

"I'm in the White House. I took the wrong trail and missed the group. I didn't know what to do."

"Are the people home?"

"No, I smashed the glass door and got in and found the telephone."

"Stay where you are, Barbara, and I'll be right up to get you as soon as possible."

It's a long drive by road to the White House though a short distance by trail. Meanwhile the owners of the house, driving home from San Francisco on the Bay Shore Highway, could see their house which was prominently located on a hill. They saw it all lighted up and figured that thieves were at work. They speeded up in consternation. After rescuing Barbara, I met the returning owners on the road. I stopped them and explained what had happened and assured them that I would be responsible for the smashed door (I wished Barbara had chosen the window—much less costly). They were not very nice about it and talked about "illegal entry" while Barbara shivered in my car. When I got her back to camp she gobbled down a huge hot meal. The kids all gathered around and wanted to know all about it and how she felt and what she did. She became a heroine. Her status in camp was assured and her appetite phenomenal.

One high experience was contrived by me. I have always been fascinated by the accounts of Midsummer Eve rituals in Britain and in some European countries. Midsummer Eve really comes at the Equinox in June. Since that is at the beginning of the camp season, I decided the July moon was going to represent midsummer for us. We couldn't roll a flaming wheel off a hill because of fire danger, so we had revels around a big fire in the outdoor fire pit and witches and goblins and soothsayers danced about. I had figured the time that the moon would come over the hill by timing it exactly several previous nights, adding an hour each night. There was some sort of Treasure Hunt after supper and I arranged that the two older groups of boys and girls would find their final clue on top of the knoll and that they would arrive just in time for moonrise. It worked perfectly. They met on the hill just as the full moon edged over the rim of the mountain and found themselves suddenly enveloped in the silvery light that deluged the valley. The kids just sat down and were silent for about ten minutes, surprised and awestruck by the magic of moonlight. Great happenings like that are never forgotten.

Robert was a stocky, strong Negro boy whose father had disappeared and whose mother supported herself and her son by house-cleaning by the day. He was a discipline problem in the classroom and was referred to us by the school psychologist. The first three days at camp Robert tried to fight with everyone his size or larger. But he didn't get much of a rise out of anyone. All of a sudden he snapped out of his aggressiveness and became the most enthusiastic participant in everything from horseback riding to singing. He practically took over the dining room routines and ordered the dish washers and dryers to adopt his ideas of speed and efficiency. He took one or two of the younger children under his care. Towards me he behaved like a Sir Walter Raleigh, giving me his arm (which I didn't need) and escorting me into my car or into the Hostel as if he were my gentleman-in-waiting. It happened that one Sunday an outside group asked to use the riding ring for a horseshow. All the children were interested but Robert was particularly involved. He did not hesitate to tell the rather snooty lady how she ought to run things. She brushed him off several times and finally said, "Little boy, I think you better go back to camp now."

"Oh," he said, "Lady, this *is* camp. All round here," waving his arm, "All this *is* camp. And it all belongs to *us*."

I don't remember any statement about the camp that pleased me more, with the possible exception of a remark by a local psychiatrist who told a mother, "Oh, yes. That's the camp where a kid can lie on his back and spit at the sun if he wants to."

My memory teems with incidents like these—funny, tragic, enlightening, nostalgic. I think I am terribly fortunate to have known all these wonderful, unfolding young personalities and to have had a small part in stimulating their search for self-realization and happiness.

I never did any advertising for the camp except to send out brochures to individual families. The time came when I had to cut down on white quotas so that I could save space for other groups who made up their minds more slowly or who were short of money. I made camperships available where necessary. In order to keep the camp finances separate from the family and ranch business, I decided to form a non-profit corporation entitled 'Hidden Villa Camp, Incorporated.' Of course, the land, the buildings, the equipment were not owned or rented from the family, but the income earned by the camp operation and the expenses of staff, food and other operational items were in a separate Camp account. We managed to just about break even. I made an annual report to the Federal and State Income Bureaus as a tax exempt organization. It was a wise move which facilitated subsequent programs of service to schools and youth agencies.

Every year after camp ended I tried to evaluate what had taken place. Two or three weeks is a short time in which to enlarge horizons and increase awareness in young children. Had we provided the important elements to produce growth? Growth in physical, intellectual, social and spiritual stability? Had we met the needs of each individual child in these areas? Had the love that was at the roots of all our efforts really infiltrated? I never felt completely satisfied. Some years were better than others, but always there was room for improvement—new ways to be tried, adjustments to the temper of the times, reconstruction of values, searching for more effective ways of approach. It was hard to judge your measure of success. When most of the kids wanted to come back, you felt it couldn't have been too bad. Sometimes afterwards I received touching letters. Here are a few heart-warming excerpts on little scraps of brown wrapping paper.

> I really don't know how to put my feelings about these four years at Hidden Villa into words, but I'll say this, it's been one of the most wonderful experience. I've loved just about every minute of camp.

Dear Mrs. D——: Even though the poem you wrote about camp tells a lot about it, I don't think any words could describe how I feel. The only way you can know this feeling is to go to your camp and feel it for yourself. I wish I could of gone for many years before and I wish I could come for many years to come.

A mother writes: Thank you for having provided the weeks of utter bliss for my daughter this summer. She talks about it constantly and *slowly* like a mosaic. I'm able to reconstruct what it must've been like.

A Mexican-American girl wrote: "I love you very much. I love you more than an aunt of mine. Thank you."

I will never forget Hidden Villa. And I hope my children (she was 14 years old) get to go just like me.

While I was at camp I got over my fear of water where I couldn't touch the bottom of my feet. I learned to crochet. I just sold a dress I crocheted to a friend of mine. I am thinking about a career in dress design. Not only did I get experience at camp about camping, but about people and a lot about myself.

A camper after several years: "The really remarkable thing about your camp was that everybody loved each other and were happy to contribute to the good times and well-being of their fellows. Perhaps the only exceptions were the mice who made nests in our suitcases. I still have the brown sweater you mended for me after the mice gnawed it.

The following letter seems to hit the highest point:

My son has been telling us about camp. It was the right experience coming at just the right time for him. We were curious to find out about the not so perfect times and in a casual way asked him what he liked *least*. After some hesitation he said, "I think they had oatmeal for breakfast too often."

Former President Eliot of Harvard University said that the most important and unique contribution to education that had ever been made in the United States was the development of the summer camp. I am more than ever convinced after thirty years of operating Hidden Villa Camp that this is a true statement.

The years of childhood just preceeding puberty are of tremendous psychological importance. This is the time when the individual criterion of values begins to develop often determining the subsequent course of life. Impressions, influences, examples present themselves to him and he is confronted by the need to choose between different modes of thought and action. He is still open and receptive. As Whitman says, "he becomes what he observes." This is the great opportunity of the summer camp. There the child, released from the domination of parents, teachers and conventional behavior, can come into contact with realities of life on his own. Also, provided the camp can arrange varied membership, he can experience the brotherhood of man, unencumbered by superficial barriers.

Civilization has endowed us with many gifts but it has often robbed us of our inheritance. Cities get between us and the natural world. At camp a child can get close to the earth, lie on it, roll on it, nestle into it—earth is the ultimate cradle. A child can follow the course of the seasons and the cycles of day and night. What a revelation to sleep under the stars and wake at dawn to the song of birds and watch the light seep over the mountain top into the valley. Hot sun, stormy wind, inky darkness, running water, trees, flowers and the creatures of the wild: all these are fundamental verities. From such things one can learn the secrets of existence.

I have always been opposed to an over-busy camp schedule. Some activities require set periods but I feel there should be a lot of free time in which a child can choose his occupation or choose to do nothing. Time to relax, to reflect a little, to savor himself. To become familiar with and feel comfortable in a certain limited environment is reassuring. It has been called to my attention again and again how important it is to many that the ranch is still the same. It is as they remember it. They look for a certain rock or the barn door to see if the marks on it are the same. One boy, back from Vietnam, seemed enormously relieved that the shoe scraper on the front steps shaped like a Scottie dog, was still there. In our modern society there is so much change. People move from city to city, from house to house, from school to school, from job to job. It appears that the ranch represents a point of stability to many of our ex-campers. They return to reassure themselves. Human beings need roots in the soil just like plants, specific spots where kinship can be established. Even if in later life it exists only in memory. The Indians recognize this sacred bond. It is the secret of their survival.

I mentioned earlier the obligation the summer camp has to ensure the well-being and growth of the young people who serve as counselors. To many of them it is the first experience of responsibility for persons younger than themselves and also the first experience working in a cooperative team with a common purpose—i.e., the welfare of the kids. It cannot be anything but a rigorous learning situation, involving as it does, a twenty-four hour stretch of duty. I tried to give the counselors more than training in the techniques of teaching, more than skill in group leadership. I hoped that the beauty of the environment would kindle their appreciation of the world. I believed that by living so closely with folk from different backgrounds they would be able to develop a loving and creative environment for the children under their care, thus exerting a profound influence on their ideals and objectives despite cultural differences. I envisaged a relationship emerging which might afterwards become a frame of reference. Some years this seemed really to happen. Not always. However, as I found out at Peninsula

School, it is almost impossible to ascertain when growth really takes place, nor how, nor why. You can test knowledge but the response of the spirit is too secret and subtle to evaluate. Occasionally such evidence is vouchsafed. I have been deeply moved by some of the letters I have received from time to time indicating that the growing edge had been served. Because their words so poignantly confirm what I hardly dared hope for, I cannot resist quoting excerpts from a few.

From an ex-camper and several years' counselor:
I've wanted to say to you for so long how important and unique Hidden Villa seems to me. I hope there will be some way that it will continue. As the "outside" world "progresses" a Hidden Villa becomes a pressing need. A place for children to grow sanely. I keep hoping.

From an Indian Counselor:
Many times this summer and last summer I have seen the results of Hidden Villa on the children. I shall always remember the smiles on their faces and the experiences I have come in contact with. I wish I could express how much it has meant to me.

From a Mexican-American Counselor:
I just don't know what to say about Hidden Villa. I loved every minute while I was here and I wish I could come back many years to follow. One enjoyable thing is to see all the kids' smiles and happy expressions on their faces.

From a Negro Counselor:
I find it hard to express the kind of job I've had being part of Hidden Villa this summer. It's almost as intense as the sorrow of leaving. I feel undeserving at times knowing how people are unable to enjoy the kinds of things which *are* Hidden Villa. It almost seems unfair to be paid for enjoying oneself. It is sad that the vibrations may only last for two or three weeks out of the summer because they are so important, so beneficial that I cannot comprehend the wonderful change that would occur in the world were this approach to life universal . . .

From a Chinese girl, ex-camper Counselor:
It's hard to put into words the feelings that I have for Hidden Villa. Even as a camper, the camp held a special place in my heart and I got too old to come, I refused to go elsewhere. After being a counselor here I now see the philosophy behind the camp and I try to build those beliefs into my own life. My experience here has spurred my growth of the last few years: depths of joy, love, depression, anger and frustration have all been felt and learned from. You've helped me to become a full person, with a depth of understanding and love for my fellows that I would not have gotten on my own.

From an Eighteen Year old ex-camper Counselor:
Hidden Villa is one place so full of all these important things: emotion,

thought and compassion. There is no institution, if you'll excuse the expression, of more value and not one that will be of more value in the future. It is difficult to control one's own destiny much less those of others. But to this end as a purely spiritual force, environment serves as a chief compelling force. And that's what is supplied here, beautiful surroundings which do more than anything to bring us all together.

From a College Senior ex-camper Counselor:
Living—what a unique and most wonderful experience. And I treasure its very existence knowing that there will be both joy and sorrow to come. It is the uniqueness of people that gives living such a special quality. How different we each come, how different we each leave, but somewhere in the middle we have reached out and shared one summer at Hidden Villa. I wish I might bear its mark for eternity—for peace in the minds of men.

From a 17 year old girl, ex-camper Counselor:
Hidden Villa spirit will always live in campers and counselors. It will change but there is some indescribable *core* within all of us that never alters. This special spirit must never stop expanding and being shared with all people. I love it!

From a History Research Major diverted to Camp:
Hidden Villa has done two things for me. Both started last year and culminated in this. The first is my growth in confidence. The second is to feel really attuned to nature and to silence. This morning at chapel I suddenly understood what people mean by "world soul" and "acceptance of life," and what the Buddhists mean by being filled with the "sacred breath." At any rate, I love this place, this institution or whatever, with all my being the threads of its life are woven with the threads of mine, like a Turkish carpet.

From a young Jewish girl:
I realized how much I really loved this place while I was walking down from the old cabin in the darkness with Lynn one night. There was no fear of the dark because I knew only beautiful and warm plants, animals and people were hidden in it. A warmth that was to expand in the morning sun—or fog. Sometimes there were tensions and fiery anger but I am left with a deep calm from the whole summer.

From a Farm Worker's daughter:
At all places I have been to, there's nothing to compare with Hidden Villa, the reason being is that there are no such warm and wonderful people to make Hidden Villa what it is. I express my warmest thanks for being given this opportunity to work with such wonderful people as these and also to thank you for giving the understanding of living and learning in a new environment. I shall long remember.

From a Camp Cook and Counselor:

This summer I have been able to find peace in myself. Thanks and love. To have had a small share in the unfolding lives of so many children and young people has been a privilege for which I am deeply thankful. My reverence for the earth and all its creatures, my love of children, my zeal for brotherhood all came together in carrying out Hidden Villa Camp. In its operation my experience in organization opened the way and because I was not responsible to any outside authority, I could use my imagination in devising new and experimental programs. I had so much fun. And so many wonderful contacts and relationships, so much to learn and comprehend about human beings, so many lessons of intuition and perception, such beautiful cooperation from the young workers who were the real creators. Because of them I have come to have faith in the future. To them I could say like the Najavo:

> May you walk in beauty
> In beauty may you walk.
> May you walk in beauty
> Down the path of life.

XXXI

From Wilson's League of Nations to Roosevelt's United Nations

Political climate; first United Nations session, San Francisco, 1945.

Back in 1919 after the close of World War I the crusade of Woodrow Wilson in support of his "14 points" and the League of Nations filled us with hope. We did not fully realize then the nefarious provisions embodied in the Treaty of Versailles. When the debate in Congress revolved around the ratification of the League by the United States, we had high hopes for peace between the nations of the world and we urged our representatives in Washington to give an affirmative vote. However, the bitter opposition of Henry Cabot Lodge, the leader of the Republican party in Congress, succeeded in preventing ratification of the League which our country had been instrumental in originating. This was a tremendous disappointment to peace lovers all over the world. The name of Henry Cabot Lodge took on the connotation of something reactionary, prejudiced and evil. The tragic collapse and death of Wilson was one of the saddest political events of our time. Like so many other martyrs who died disgraced and disillusioned, he is being recognized years later as a leader ahead of his generation and a prophet of a new era.

Succeeding Wilson we had the dismal era of Harding and Coolidge as Chief Executives. Harding died under very strange circumstances. He was returning from a trip to Alaska and after leaving the boat, he went to a hotel in San Francisco when he was taken ill and passed away in less than a week. The strange thing was that he was not removed to any local medical facility, neither to the Army hospital in the Presidio nor to the University of California Hospital staffed by some of the best doctors in the whole United States. None of them were called in for consultation.

It would seem that if a President were ill away from Washington, that the best medical resources of the community would have been at his disposal. Instead, the only care he had was from the naval doctor who had accompanied him on the trip. We thought, as did many others in the vicinity, that he either took his own life or someone wanted to get rid of him. The scandals of Teapot Dome reached into high places, not unlike Watergate in more recent times. Coolidge was re-elected after serving out Harding's expired term because it was thought that he had settled the police strike in Boston which, it was revealed later, was really settled by the chief of police. Coolidge was a thoroughly inarticulate and mediocre politician and the country slid from bad to worse during his regime.

We were not very happy either with Herbert Hoover. When he refused to even talk to the veterans who had marched from all over the country to present their grievances at Christmas time, we were outraged. The name Hooverville was applied in hundreds of communities to the area of shacks and lean-to's located along irrigation ditches and railroad tracks where the unfortunate derelicts of society huddled together around meagre camp fires. Herbert Hoover had done a magnificent job of relief work in Belgium but, although he was a good business administrator, he seemed to lack the quality of loving kindness. He lacked courage or perhaps his imagination could not stretch to understand the plight of impoverished and under-privileged families. His name is indelibly linked with the Depression. His wife, Lou Henry Hoover, was much more approachable. She was a person of great charm and understanding. She was national head of Girl Scouts. I worked with her on forming the Palo Alto chapter and admired her greatly. If she had been able to influence her husband as Eleanor Roosevelt later was able to influence President Roosevelt, Hoover might have been more effective at the time of national crisis.

When Franklin Roosevelt ran for office and was elected our hopes were finally realized. In his first term in office, a tremendous number of social reforms were inaugurated and carried out. Among them were the CCC camps for boys, the Farm Security Administration and the whole gamut of New Deal legislation which changed the climate of American life from despair to hope and resulted in a whole series of readjustments. It was an exciting period and the "Fireside Talks" beginning always with "My Friends" were listened to almost with reverence by some of us. That bell-like voice and the clear and beautiful diction, the choice of words and the content of his speeches have not been equalled since.

Confronting him in his second term of office was the certainty of war and the momentous decision perpetrated by the Japanese attack on Pearl Harbor on December 7, 1941. With incredible speed President Roosevelt set in motion all the potential of the American people to produce weapons of war and provide manpower for army and naval

reinforcements to the Allies. His choice of personnel to carry out
assignments both at home and overseas, was strikingly astute. Before
the termination of the war he was already looking ahead to the peace
that was to follow and for the opportunity to create some sort of lasting
agreement to end forever the danger of international violence. The first
step of cooperation and the final departure of the United States from the
"watershed of isolation" started with the Lend-Lease Agreement to obtain
food and raw materials for Britain in Latin America. Already in 1941 the
London Declaration, adopted by all the countries when at war with the
Axis, suggested that steps be taken "so that, relieved of the menace of
aggression all may enjoy economic and social security." On August 9,
Roosevelt and Churchill met secretly off the coast of Newfoundland,
Roosevelt traveling there on the U.S. cruiser Augusta and Churchill on
the H.M.S. Prince of Wales. As a result of the meeting of these two
great leaders, the Atlantic Charter was issued, and in the following
January twenty-six nations, then fighting the Axis, signed the United
Nations Protocol. One of the weak points in forming the League of
Nations after World War I had been its connection with the Peace
Treaty of Verssailles. By thus planning ahead, the American and English
leaders believed, the two issues could be handled separately. In May,
1942, England and Moscow agreed that both parties would cooperate
after the war and in 1943 when the American war effort was at its
height, a long debate was held by the Committee on Foreign Affairs in
Washington with the result that the United States was committed to
support a post-war cooperative agency against aggression. Conferences
in Quebec and in Moscow drafted a bill for basic discussion. Churchill,
Stalin and Roosevelt met at Teheran and at Dumbarton Oaks in
October, 1944, where a Proposal for the Establishment of a General
International Agency was released. In 1945, Churchill, Stalin and
Roosevelt (then a thoroughly exhausted man) meeting at Yalta, issued an
invitation to a United Nations Conference for International Organization
to be convened on April 25 in San Francisco. Forty-six governments
accepted. The question of who should chair the conference was a thorny
one, but Roosevelt maintained that the United States, as host, was
entitled to select the chairman and Edward R. Stettinius, representing
the Department of State, was chosen for that responsible position. It
seems ironical that the person most responsible for the creation of the
United Nations could not have been present at its opening. His death
was a great sorrow to the whole nation. I cried when, instead of the
well-loved voice of the Fireside Talks, I heard the rasping mid-Western
twang of Harry Truman on the radio.

Preparations for this momentous gathering stimulated a tremendous
degree of planning in San Francisco. The mayor created a whole series
of special committees to deal with the varied aspects of services required
by the great number of delegates and accompanying staffs. The press,
both native and foreign, demanded accommodations. Most of the hotels

in the city were reserved between April and June. Restaurants, places of amusement, museums, theatres were alerted to give preferential treatment to the guests no matter what color nor how oddly dressed they might happen to be. An amusing story in this connection was told me by two black students from the University of California. They tried to dine at one of the fanciest hotels and were turned down by the head waiter. They went back to their house and took towels out of the bathroom to wind around their heads like a turban. Then they returned to the same hotel and were welcomed with warm ceremony by the same head waiter who figured they must be distinguished Africans.

Mrs. Harry Potter Russell headed up the hospitality committees. She arranged for receptions and dinners and teas given by organizations and individuals throughout the Bay Area. The problem of transporting the foreigners to these social affairs and making sure that they would arrive on time at the Opera House where the meetings were held, was a prodigious challenge. It was solved by recruiting a large number of voluntary chauffeurs, mostly young women, and providing a fleet of cars available to the delegates and their staffs throughout the length of the conference. Our daughter Elizabeth who had been working in the Housing Department of the Farm Security Administration, took leave of absence to drive one of these official cars. It was an interesting experience for her as she encountered a great many distinguished people. One of these who developed a liking for his chauffeur, asked her to bring him to her family's country home. This is how we met Henri Rolin, a delegate and head of the Socialist party in the Belgian Senate. He was a most delightful individual. We developed a real friendship with him that continued through the interchange of letters for many years. The diplomats were not on duty over the weekends and this leeway allowed him to spend quite a little time at the ranch which he seemed to enjoy. He liked to ride but he had only seen Western horses and equipment in the cinema. Nevertheless, he went trail riding with us in his business clothes. Then one Friday night he arrived with Elizabeth, resplendent in a wide brimmed hat, gay cowboy shirt and blue jeans. He insisted on a photograph to send home to his family to demonstrate his new style of equestrian outfit.

We also entertained representatives of other countries. The Committee had some difficulty in obtaining home invitations for some of the dark-skinned representatives. I had indicated my desire to meet Arabs and Africans and my attitude on race relations was well known. The Ethiopian representatives and those from Liberia were particularly interesting. I think it was the Minister of Finance from Ethiopia who described his grand-daughter at length in very nostalgic terms as he observed a tiny blonde child who was visiting me. I gave him an American doll to take back to his little one and received a letter after his return home on official stationery thanking me in diplomatic terms for this "gracious entente."

We also had English, French, Dutch, Norwegian, Danish and South American visitors. It was very exciting. I hoped to see a Russian, but as far as I know the only trip made by Molotov and his body guards was a race through Stanford University and a quick lunch at (of all places) the "House of Lords" restaurant on the Bay Shore Highway and back to his special warship anchored in the bay. He would not trust himself to any San Francisco hotel. The pier from which the tender picked him up every night and brought him back early in the morning was heavily guarded by the State police and his own soldiers. I daresay he had a special armored car to drive from the pier to the Opera House.

On April 25, the day the Conference convened, the Russian army lay siege to Berlin. The end of the war in Europe was in sight. But no one knew when it would end in the Pacific. Reports about the meetings at the Opera House were given every evening over the radio to which we listened eagerly. And the newspapers carried additional reports and pictures of all the celebrities. I remember that at one point in the proceedings it was reported that the Conference was in danger of breaking up over voting rights in the Security Council and only the British and American diplomats in Moscow were able to persuade the Soviet Union to agree. This was a most anxious period for the listening public. The tension among the participating members must have been extreme.

Tickets to attend the meetings were not easily obtained. I got to attend two sessions, one early in May and one during the final days. It was indeed a thrilling sight to see the flags of all the countries arrayed around the Opera House and to actually *see* the distinguished statesmen we had been hearing and reading about, and to realize that we were present at an amazing assemblage of world powers. The first global gathering in the history of the world, uniting to solve disagreements without recourse to war.

I heard Eleanor Roosevelt make her impassioned plea for Human Rights, and I was present on one of the days when the five official documents were being signed by the members. Two hundred delegates from 46 nations took over eight hours to complete the signatures. President Truman, who had been unable to attend the opening, closed the Conference on June 26. Six days later the United States Senate confirmed the Charter. By October 24, the necessary number of ratifications had been received from other countries and the United Nations became a reality.

Idealists like me thought that mankind was really going to change. Given an instrument conducive to arbitration, how could we fail to use it? I thought my country would lead the way in arbitration. I could not imagine that we would become one of the worst offenders against peace in the last half of the 20th century. Nor did I foresee the deadly developments of competition in nuclear power that now leaves all humanity in danger of annihilation at any hour of the day and night.

Like so many others, I have become disillusioned little by little, witnessing demonstration after demonstration of man's depravity. In spite of all indications to the contrary, I do believe that we are not stupid and not careless enough to permit a holocaust. And if we do survive, I am sure that a United Nations will endure in some form and that just as it happened in our own United States, a court of law will be established on a world wide basis. Technology has brought us close together; there are scientific and political solutions for almost all our problems. We have the know-how. I wish before we extend ourselves all over outer space, that we could stimulate our *inner* space to concentrate will and vision towards achieving the brotherhood of man on this one little planet. On the occasion of celebrating United Nations Day on October 24, 1960, Dag Hammarskjold said: "Experience has shown how far we are from the end which inspired the Charter. We are, indeed, still in the first movements. But no matter how deep the shadows may be, how sharp the conflicts, how tense the mistrust effected in what is said and done in our world of today, we are not permitted to forget that we have too much in common, too great a sharing of interests, and too much that we might lose together, ever to weaken in our efforts to surmount the difficulties. We must turn the simple human values which are our common heritage, into the firm foundations on which we may unite our strength and live together in peace."

Despite all difficulties, I do believe mankind will find a way to overcome the menace of fratricide. It may take years, with many setbacks, but eventually the only possible solution will result in unity and cooperation among all nations.

XXXII

The Role of Grandparents

Grandchildren growing up in the 1950's and 1960's; adaptation to the new morality.

Each period of life presents a new unfolding. It is like the iris in my garden whose flowers open for a day and shrivel up in the evening only to be succeeded by new blooms on the same stalk, equally beautiful.

After your children are married and leading separate lives, you expect a somewhat monotonous and uncomplicated personal condition. If there are grandchildren, however, a whole new relationship develops, reminiscent of what has gone before, but different: a new intimacy, a new set of values, a new challenge. Being a grandparent is not a simple matter. In many ways it is one of the most delicate of human situations. It involves acceptance of in-law personalities and a household set-up which may not conform to your elderly notions. Gears have to be shifted in the middle of the hill. I was the kind of person who could have easily exemplified the proverbial, horrible mother-in-law. In fact, I am fairly certain that my sons' wives often had that impression, sometimes justified, sometimes not. At any rate, I learned to keep still, to listen, to observe and to wait for the right cue and the right moment. Most of all, when misunderstandings arose, which were inevitable, I tried to bring them into the open, to talk about them and analyze the point of disagreement and so resolve the bitterness. Petty grudges unexpressed can build up into nagging resentments. Unless these hurdles are overcome, it is hard to enjoy a natural, spontaneous relationship with grandchildren.

Once rapport has been established, discretion is still incumbent on you. The old ideas of nutrition, schedules and training may have become obsolete. If you want to share and be useful in the young family's plan of nurture, you have to learn the latest scientific practices. It is odd how notions of baby care seem to go in cycles. In my day pacifiers were considered unhealthy and habit forming. Now they appear out of the mother's coat pocket at a moment's notice and in they go to the baby's mouth without even being washed off under the faucet. One generation is too strict, the next too permissive. And so the pendulum swings back and forth, rarely staying halfway between extremes.

Only one thing does not change. And that is the child's need for love. I remember once when I was in the home of an Indian woman, whose fifteen year old daughter had become pregnant. We had been discussing the possibility of permitting the unwanted baby to be given for adoption at birth. This would make it possible for the girl to continue her education and to grow up normally. Such a course was just about decided when the old grandmother, who had been huddled over the stove in the corner and who had taken no part in the conversation, suddenly spoke up. She said, "This child must be welcomed into the world. *I* will take care of it."

This welcoming is a natural for a grandparent. There are always little chinks of need that busy parents overlook. Without assuming undue responsibility, there are a multiplicity of small services that contribute to a child's wellbeing and security. The varying moods, the fears, the surprising phases of mental and physical growth, the emerging talents and the individual traits are often more easily shared with someone other than a parent—someone who is close and warm and perhaps a bit over-indulgent.

Our first grandchild was born in 1942 to our son Francis and his wife Betty. He had already been working in the Civilian Public Service Camp at San Dimas for several months. Betty lived in Glendora, the nearest town. Her own mother had died years ago and there was no one in her own family to be with her. I was delighted to be of some use and she did not seem to object to my coming. It was a lonely situation for her in a strange community, the wife of a pacifist and able to see her husband only at rare intervals. A week ahead of the estimated date of the baby's arrival, I traveled south to the little house where she lived and found it immaculately scrubbed and clean, windows and curtains washed, floors polished. All the new baby things were arranged in a drawer and on a shelf in the bathroom. Castile soap, baby powder, nose tabs and safety pins were ready at hand. Preparations were really too complete because there was nothing left to do. Just wait expectantly, and then wait some more. For two weeks I racked my brain in the morning to devise some activity to fill the day. We could walk up to the orange grove and pick up a few oranges, or go downtown to the library or the store, we could purchase ice cream cones, a newspaper or a spool of thread—anything to break the monotony of the long spring afternoons. However, two events in life are always sure—birth and death. So the baby finally arrived: bald, beautiful and breast fed. They named her for the heather-like chaparral that grows over the mountains where the camp was located—*Erikamaria*. She was christened thus but as the elaborate name tended to suggest a skin lotion or shampoo advertised on TV, the parents wisely decided to drop the *maria* and allow her to continue as plain Erica.

For me it was a very moving experience to care for a tiny creature again and to share well-remembered skills with a young woman in the initial stages of motherhood. I felt particularly reassured by my son's sensitive response to his tiny daughter. Over the years I have continued to feel a special tenderness for this child. She loved stories and songs at bedtime and was always finding precious little things outdoors—such as colored leaves, sculptured stones, fascinating worms or curious insects. She was a high-strung sensitive little creature and had her childish problems. I used to rub her back and "creep mouse" her forehead till her tensions would relax and she would drop off with a drowsy smile into a sleep-fantasy world. Grown ups are prone to minimize the griefs of children. Because of the child's immaturity, they discount the depth of despair and frustration that he or she may be undergoing. It is only in the last fifty years that we have begun to realize that childhood is not just a preparation for life, but is indeed a period in its own right, a unique authentic transition with its own emergencies and exigencies.

At a funeral service I once attended for one of my pupils, I remember that the preacher spoke of the sad fact that this child had been prematurely removed before he had had a chance to know life. This was not true. This particular boy had lived an exceptionally vivid, exploratory and event-filled life, completely absorbed in a short span of years. In that phase of being, he had come to full fruition.

Our second grandchild was born only two or three days before Bernard, our youngest son, left to serve in the United States army medical corps in France in World War II. The mother and baby spent considerable time here at the ranch with us and also with her own family in Berkeley. "Little Bern", as he was called, was a quite unusual baby. He had a strong, well-coordinated body, and even at an early age a poise and personality usually not noticeable until much later. He seldom cried, but crawled cheerily about, investigating whatever he happened to bump into with whimsical curiosity. There was something very wise and serene about him, and one almost felt that here was an old soul inhabiting an infant body. Perhaps I imagined such things because of the emotional tension I felt at knowing that his father, Bernard, was on the battlefield, and this little boy might turn out to be his only inheritance. At any rate, in my mind's gallery of portraits, I can still see the little fellow sitting at the top of the living room steps, chewing on something and smiling at the group of persons seated across the hall at the dining room table. It was as if he were taking us all in, but making no motion to join us, content just to be near friends, contemplating us and the new surroundings in which he found himself.

As things turned out, his sojourn in this world turned out to be very brief. While staying in Berkeley, he crawled off independently from a group chatting on the lawn and made his way to the swimming pool. No one heard the tiny splash and there was no outcry. When his absence was discovered it was too late. I well remember that I was in bed with the flu when the telephone call came from Bliz, little Bern's mother. With her characteristic directness and realism, she insisted on telling me herself. It was one of the most poignant sorrows in my life.

Little Bern was fifteen months old. After Bernard returned from France, he and Bliz carried the small box of ashes up to the Windmill Pasture and buried it there under a big oak tree. Within a few years, they produced a bevy of other children, and sadness in their first loss was absorbed by joy and delight in their increasing brood. It is strange, but even now after all the years, I do sometimes dream of Little Bern. When I wake, I wonder wistfully about what really happened to that tiny illuminated spirit who drifted in and out of our orbit so many years ago, and who left so little trace of his passage.

Eventually we had eleven grandchildren—five girls and six boys, three of them born in the year of the baby explosion after World War II. They, too, were faced with the draft at age eighteen. One served in the navy, two of them spent two years in alternate service, the others just missed the menace of Viet Nam.

I was very fortunate to be able to see a good deal of most of my grandchildren and to share intimately in the transitions of their growth. Much of it was beautiful, but there were also times of agonizing anxiety and unconsolable heartache when destructive forces seemed to overwhelm the orderly development of personality and there was very little that anyone could do except to stand by and hope.

The young people who grew up in the 50's and 60's appear to me to represent a unique phenomenon. I don't know if it ever happened before that the older generation, seeking to educate the young in accordance with well-accepted precepts, found themselves inadvertently being educated to deal with the changing conditions of civilization of which they were barely aware. The repudiation of the past happened so quickly and penetrated so deeply into ethical and sociological traditions. A hundred years from now historians, if they still exist, will be analyzing the causes of this swift rebellion. We are too close to it now to distinguish the solid reality from the dust of disturbance. Uprisings of peasants against landlords, strikes against low wages and long hours of work in factories are familiar to all of us. But the present day rebellion is aimed at a *decrease* in material advantages, a *disassociation* with affluence. The aim is not success in the competitive market. The object is to be unencumbered by possessions and to find how little a man requires to satisfy his basic human needs. It is really a spiritual revolt against materialism and conformity. Intellectual superiority is under suspicion and intuitive sensitivity is taking its place. How to achieve simplicity in one's individual life in the midst of a highly industrialized society is certainly a challenge for even the cleverest and most courageous experimenter.

In my own case, I am free to say that my well-rooted concepts suffered a series of shocks. Long hair and messy beards, necklaces and headbands for men, abbreviated three-inch skirts and scanty breast covers for girls, false eye lashes and African hairdos were somewhat repulsive to me. I had difficulty recognizing children I had known behind their new, hairy facial jungles. Only the eyes still offered a clue to identity. I didn't like the rock and roll and even less the raucous electric guitars and the exasperating prevalence of ongoing primitive rhythms (a travesty on the drums that emerge from pueblo kivas and reverberate all day and all night for the ceremonial Indian dances). Smelly bodies and dirty feet offended my olfactory nerves, and the new vocabularies kept me guessing. Alternately I laughed at them, or got angry, or felt like crying over their woebegone aspects and their forlorn insistence on deprivation. Their unskilled attempts at organic gardening and subsistence living were usually so pitiful and unrealistic! But how could you say as much to a starry-eyed convert to the new crusade? I tried to keep stressing the praise-worthy motives behind the outrageous manifestations and telling myself to reserve judgment, to let the chaff fly and to keep on believing in the life-renewing quality of the grain being sifted.

All these considerations were somewhat superficial. I came to disregard the obvious absurdities and respect the motives that inspired the aberrations. When it came to accepting the changing concepts of sexual relationships, I experienced a great deal of resistance. According to my code of behaviour the course of true love consisted of mutual attraction, courtship, engagement, marriage. Deviations from this sequence seemed to me to be regrettable misdemeanors and I could not bring myself to offer hospitality in my home to such couples. But as time went on, the young people whom I loved best and in whom I had the greatest confidence became involved in similar arrangements and forced me to think through the basic biological facts and to really observe the outcomes of extra-marital intimacy. In the face of mounting divorce rates, the trial period of co-habitation seemed to produce a more solid basis of union. Of course, the ability to avoid offspring was a major consideration, and this is what finally persuaded me. I had seen so many little children distraught by conflicts between parents, and unhappily aware of their unwanted status in the family picture, that it seemed to me that if two people could wait till they were sure of one another and sure they really wanted a baby, that the little one would have a better chance for love and acceptance. I continue to feel repelled by promiscuity, and I am amazed by those who live together for twenty five years and then go hunting another mate hoping to renew their youth.

Another aspect of the times arouses my greatest sympathy. The

multiplicity of philosophical and religious groups that have appeared during the last ten or fifteen years is truly incredible. All the way from "encounter" to strict Oriental disciplines and fundamental Jesus discipleship. All Christian churches, whether Catholic, Protestant or unorthodox, have felt the impact, and tried, not very successfully, to harness this new enthusiasm to their congregations. But the winds of freedom are blowing and the young are not easily enticed back into the fold. That they are searching for fundamental reality is the most hopeful indication of their sincerity and of their future effectiveness. I wonder sometimes if they may not turn into arch conservatives when *their* children come to adolescence.

In the meantime, I welcome my young visitors warmly by asking, "Do you want a double bed or singles? I have both." "Do you eat meat? If not, we have lots of vegetables." "Do you get up at 5 o'clock to meditate? We don't have a *bo* tree, but there are many bay trees all over the ranch." And so I accommodate them and they tolerate me. The mysterious and elusive quality known as empathy can overcome differences in age and attitude.

XXXIII

Late Travels to Far-Away Places

The Orient and the Near East revisited.

For many years I had longed to revisit the Orient. The trip I made in 1914 just after my marriage had given me a taste—but only a taste—a little like enjoying hors d'oeuvres without continuing on a more substantial repast. In 1959, as the time clock began to tick towards seventy years, it seemed to suggest a now-or-never urgency. Our oldest granddaughter Erica was seventeen. Frank and I decided it would add to our pleasure in the trip to include Erica and her friend, Susan Mellquist, as our travel companions.

Crossing the Pacific in 1914 had taken us three weeks by boat to pass over that huge body of water. This time, approximately 18 hours in the air sufficed. We went first to Tokyo, where we stayed at International House not far from the Friends' Girl School. A typhoon hit the city during the second night. It was a wild night, and great pieces of corrugated iron were ripped off the roof and crashed on the pavement outside the building. But we were not endangered, nor were we really aware of the fury and power of the storm until several days later, when we travelled by train from Tokyo to Osaka and passed the town of Nagoya. At this place there had been a tidal wave accompanying the wind. It swept up the beach and surged into the river already swollen by torrential rains as it came down from the mountains. A lumber mill at the junction of these two colliding mountains of water was smashed into splinters, and the logs and boards were either torn to pieces or carried out to sea. The houses that were left standing had their roofs covered with *futons*—the comforters laid down at night on which the Japanese sleep—drying out in the sun. In the street below, house owners waded in water up to their waists, searching for possessions that had floated away. I saw one man wringing out a child's kimona and a silken *obi*. Still another fished up a teapot and a fragile teacup that had somehow survived the flood. The Emperor declared it a disaster area and sent out a request for funds. International Red Cross set up relief stations in the next town where the survivors were fed and sheltered. It took many weeks for the waters to recede and for the people to bury the dead and restore the shattered dwellings and city streets. Most of the houses were beyond repair—the school, city hall and the mill were totally wrecked.

On our return from Osaka we spent a whole day in a bus encircling Mt. Fujiyama, catching glimpses of it between clouds from every angle. The road was full of potholes and the bus was old and creaky, protesting noisily at every stop. Country people got in carrying little bundles tied up in large squares of colored cloth. As we bounced along, occasionally hitting the ceiling, they laughed at us and with us. This wordless camaraderie of amused discomfort lasted till the next village where they disembarked, bowing as the bus continued on its rollicking way. But although our neck and shoulder muscles ached, we did manage to see the sacred mountain every hour of the day in its serene white ethereal majesty. Our journey ended in opalescent clouds of sunset, and we had been most fortunate in this whole day, for others told us of waiting days for the white lady to unveil herself for their view.

In Hong Kong we had letters to a variety of people differing greatly in social status. We had dinner in one of the fashionable Kowloon restaurants where our two young companions encountered their first cabaret with unfeigned amazement. We also visited a huge school run by a Chinese educator trained at Stanford and Harvard. But the most memorable contact was with the grandmother of a young student, Hamilton Chin, who had been a counselor at our Hidden Villa camp. He owed his coming to the United States to the insistence of this old country woman who walked miles with him from Western China. She had put him on a boat at Hong Kong harbor headed for San Francisco, with a label sewed on his coat indicating that he was to be educated and could lay claim to American citizenship through his grandfather. The latter had produced a son in California after working with the coolie gang constructing the Southern Pacific railway. Hamilton Chin told me about this remarkable old lady living in Hong Kong and asked me to get in touch with her and deliver a gift package. She turned out to be a tiny miniature lady, dressed all in black, whose quick movements made one think of a humming bird. She spoke no English, but when she came to the hotel she brought with her a young Chinese boy who worked in an English bank. She asked many questions about her grandson, seeming especially anxious to know how much money he made. She was much less interested in his educational career. By arrangement we were to meet her the following day to have tea. Someone conducted us through the streets to an apartment house. Here we were told to climb to the top story where we would find Mrs. Chin. On the way up we were observed on every floor by residents peeking through doorways opened just a crack for curious eyes. Tea was brewed on a small charcoal stove. There was no other furniture in the room except the stools we sat on. After tea, the old lady indicated by gestures that I was to go somewhere with her. So down the stairs we hurried and out into the crowded alley. Here she seized my arm in a vise-like grasp and steered me through the crowds in and out to show me different kinds of stores and tradespeople. Frank and the girls were following in the rear, and they had a hard time to keep us in sight because we went so fast. I tried to get loose, but that iron grip on my arm made it impossible. Finally we reached the shop which seemed to be the desired point of call because there was a box tied up Chinese style which the old lady took from the store keeper and pressed into my hands, telling me about it most emphatically. I did not need to understand the words to know that it represented an especially choice gift. I thanked her with gestures and smiles as best I could, wondering of how many meals she must have deprived herself to give me this mysterious token of friendship. On our return to the hotel we opened the package. The contents consisted of small red cherries preserved in some kind of villainous tasting sauce! For about ten years after that visit, I sent her small sums of money, in care of her banker friend, at the time of the Chinese New Year.

Surprisingly enough, there was a tiny Friends Meeting in Hong Kong. Meetings took place in one of the small class rooms in the University and were attended by two English couples, three Americans, an East Indian and three or four Chinese. The Americans were running a child care program and a trade training center for teenagers. I admired their courage in establishing such a minute island of service in the sea of poverty which was visible everywhere—in the enormous apartment houses erected by the British government, in the fishing boat community in Aberdeen, in the caves on the sides of the hills surrounding the leased territory, even in doorways or on strips of matting on the sidewalk, where the total possessions of a family could be just a mat, a tiny coverlet and one little pot set on a half pint size charcoal stove. I never saw such poverty before. It made me hate the tourists that crowded into the bazaars and vaunted their opulence in the restaurants and hotels. Perhaps the most shocking thing of all was the English cricket club—a residue from the Colonial era—which occupied a large acreage in the middle of a city where thousands were crammed into living space no bigger than a horse stall.

The harbor of Hong Kong is certainly one of the most beautiful outposts of the once farflung British Empire. Hong Kong itself is an odd excrescency on the body of mainland China subject to toleration by the Communist government. It is a small island supplemented by the leased territory of thirty miles along the harbor known as Kowloon. From the highest point one looks across the river at the misty, somewhat ominous, expanse of Communist China. This is a way of escape for a trickle of malcontents. Macao Island at the further bend of the harbor (still administered by Portugal, strangely enough) is another stepping stone to freedom. The lease is supposed to expire in this century and no one knows what will happen then. In the meantime the open port and access to world trade has proved beneficial to China.

Singapore, at the tip of the Malay Peninsula, is another city we visited which, like Hong Kong, is also indelibly stamped with English imperialism. Raffles Hotel, the last of the great caravansaries, still stands as a monument to past glory. The spacious dining rooms, the lofty hallways, and the slow-turning huge wooden paddles designed to fan sleepers under mosquito netting, have been adopted for tourist trade by the native government.

From Singapore, fascinating for its history and its situation at the crossroads of the world, we went to Thailand, Cambodia and Bali, places which epitomize the fascination of Oriental culture. In Bangkok we got up about five o'clock to visit the market. (If you want to observe the people of any country you should go to the market.) The river, or *kong*, from the back jungle country flows into the bay. Where the waterways converge, hundreds of sampans laden with produce crowd together in a thick mass bumping and edging each other, the owners manipulating the craft with long poles, shouting to attract purchasers. It reminds one of the traffic congestion at the peak hour on Madison Avenue in New York, only here the street is water and there are no cops. Each fellow is out for himself. The dwellers in the houses built on the banks of the *kong* carry on a lively trade with the vendors, children splashed in the water, women can be seen cooking or washing in apartments wide open to view. At that hour of the morning the heat was intense; later in the day it was intolerable.

We were fortunate to be in Bangkok on the king's birthday. There was a procession and we saw the young king and his enchanting shy little bride—exquisite, petite and dressed in beautiful Thai silk, riding in the royal Rolls Royce. The University *is* amazingly modern, attended by boys and girls in Western attire and behaving much like college students in all parts of the world. They were very friendly and anxious to talk to us, wanting to know about life in the United States. The hottest night I ever spent was in a bedroom in an old English hotel where the wooden blades of the creaky fan in the ceiling barely sent any air through the stifling mosquito nets draped over the beds. After we moved to a more modern hotel, the dining room air conditioning system which had recently been installed, but was not well regulated, kept the temperature at just about freezing. We put on our heavy winter coats when we went down to dinner, and our bodies were subjected to temperatures ranging from about 32 degrees in the dining room to 102 degrees as soon as we left it.

Cambodia provided our first ride on an elephant. We climbed up about a dozen steps to a platform from which the elephant allowed us to seat ourselves sideways on his cushioned saddle. He went very slowly round a track and returned us to the steps, lifting his feet slowly and ponderously, making no sound. Our two days at Angkor Wat were not long enough to give us more than a faint inkling of that vast, unbelievable architectural metropolis, shrouded and throttled by the jungle. The main temple has been redeemed from the rapacious growth, but beyond that for miles the greedy vines and ravening trees have literally swallowed up the temples and court yards. Great slabs of sculpture have been torn off and all this tremendous array of masonry constructed by human effort to placate the unseen powers has been reduced to rubble and dust. So great is the power of living organisms! I was reminded of the Greek statue of Laocoon and his sons being crushed by serpents, only here the strangulation was on so colossal a scale.

How different from this grim scene was the island of Bali—that exquisite tropical island edged with sand and surrounded by a coral reef with its rim of ocean foam a half mile beyond the shallow tide! It would be hard to imagine a fairer paradise. When we were there in 1959 it was still untainted by western sophistication. One could linger all day in the shade of undulating palm branches lulled by the hum of bees and the rustling of palm fronds, watching birds and butterflies busy at the hibiscus flowers. Walking slowly along the beach or on a path worn smooth by generations of bare feet, one came across little shrines half concealed in the jungle and met processions of beautiful slim brown people carrying trays of fruit and vegetables on their heads. These fruits of their toil were offered to the deity or deposited on the grave of a departed relative. The figures moved straight and silent in their brightly colored sarongs—a rhythm of motion and color and primitive dignity. Often after twilight we would hear distant music. Following the sound down the lanes and past native huts and rice fields, we would come on the musicians in a temple garden or in an open space between dwellings. Here the age-old sacred dramas of the *Mahabarata* were enacted to the incessant music of the ganelon orchestra playing sometimes all night long. Our presence did not seem to distract the players or the audience. They made room for us on the benches. Once in a while someone who spoke English would try to explain the story to us. The recurrent theme seemed to be the struggle between Good and Evil, personified by malicious devils and warrior angels.

When we were not traveling enroute from country to country, I had to try to tutor the girls in the high school courses they were missing by absence. Before leaving on the trip, I had arranged with their teachers to follow through so that they would not lose credit for graduation. I tried to persuade the history teacher to let them study Oriental culture, but he said no; that didn't come till they went to college, and first they had to learn about Greek city states and the rise of the Roman Empire. It seemed a bit incongruous to be reading about Caesar's conquest of Gaul and Britain while we were on the other side of the world. The warm breeze lifting the palm branches and the fragrance of ginger blossoms were not conducive to intellectual research, and the teacher was as bored with the assignment as the pupils. However, we somehow managed to cram in enough and produce the necessary papers to satisfy the authorities so the girls were not penalized later for their temporary dropouts.

When we reached the Philippines on our trip, we had come to the chapters in the history book about the Hebrews. Neither of the girls knew anything about the Old Testament. They had heard of Adam and Eve, Noah and the Ark, and Jonah and the Whale. But Abraham and Isaac and the captivity in Egypt and the story of Moses and the Promised Land were totally unknown. As luck would have it, when we were staying at Baguio in the mountains north of Manila, the movie production of "The Ten Commandments" was advertised to be played on Saturday night in the basement of the hotel. There a theatre had been improvised from a storage room fitted with wooden benches. It seemed a golden opportunity to concentrate on the history of the Jews (Hollywood version). This we did for four sweaty, hard-sitting hours and disposed of the assignment on the development of the Hebrew race!

We had been asked by the Filipino houseboy, Felix, who had worked for us in California to contact his brother, whom we found a short way from Manila. His home was a native hut built on stilts to avoid flooding. We climbed a ladder and found tiny bedrooms separated by walls of straw matting where we sat on floors also covered with matting. The kitchen was downstairs on the ground under the house shared with chickens and pigs. Frank was in great need of a haircut and Felix's brother turned out to be a barber by trade. He set up a chair and enveloped Frank in a large sheet and took his shaving tools out of a little bag. Unfortunately, I did not have a camera to take a picture of the operation with the background of native house and jungle and little pigs snuffling round Frank's feet as he sat in the barber chair. Such friendly people and such simplicity of hospitality!

Several years later, we traveled with two other granddaughters in the Near East—Egypt, the Arab countries, Israel, Turkey and Greece. Since our earlier trip before World War II and again in 1963, some thirty years later, the changes were startling. English controls in Egypt had been totally removed, the old Palestine borders were obliterated, Jerusalem was a divided city, Bethlehem was Arab territory, and Constantinople had been transformed into Istanbul. I have always found that even a brief visit to a foreign country enables me to interpret the news with much greater understanding. The muddle of unrest between Israel and its neighbors, disputes about the Suez Canal, Turkey at odds with Greece in Cyprus, the menace of Russia in the Black Sea, all these

In Cambodia, 1959 and Egypt, 1963.

intricate and delicate tensions can be more easily interpreted if one has been on the scene and talked with people actually living on both sides of the struggle.

Small episodes come to mind that stand out from the regular sightseeing schedule. In Egypt the girls wanted desperately to ride across the desert on Arab ponies. I made arrangements to satisfy this craving and they were called for by a dashing dark Egyptian cavalier with whom they disappeared in a cloud of dust in the direction of the Sphinx. I spent an anxious two or three hours wondering if I would ever see them again or if they would have to be rescued from the tents of the Bedouins among the sand dunes.

On the outskirts of Giza I heard about a school for native arts and crafts sponsored by a wealthy citizen of Cairo. Here we found girls ranging from ages seven to fifteen weaving tapestries that depicted the life around them, creating patterns as they wove, without design to guide them—fresh creative fabrics, each one a masterpiece. I especially liked the portrayal of the Nile, deep blue, flowing south to north bordered with vegetation and showing donkeys and camels, temples and pyramids, boats and laborers, all done in the brilliant colors as the girls pushed the shuttle back and forth with sure flying fingers. I talked to the promoter of this project. He said the sad part of it was that at fifteen his girls had to stop working. They were expected to marry and their husbands were never willing to have them employed outside their homes.

My romantic leanings were gratified by a few personal indulgences apart from the general tour. One was on Mt. Nebo, the mountain top from which Moses and his wayward band could look down on the Promised Land. After his long and arduous journey, Moses was not allowed to continue further, only look down at the lush gardens along the River Jordan while his followers descended under the leadership of their new leader, Joshua, dancing as they went, and singing paeans of praise and rejoicing for their deliverance. There was a flat rock at the edge of the precipice. I sat there and thought about the weary old leader having fulfilled his mission, satisfied to let his children enjoy their reward. Total abnegation—"Into Thy hands I commend my spirit." Surely the ultimate sacrifice. The thought of the old man waiting up there for the Angel of Death was made more poignant when I, too, went down the hill and marveled at the lush gardens of Jericho. Excavations were in progress 20 feet underground disclosing the skeleton framework of the ancient fortress where long, long ago "the walls came tumbling down."

The only remaining native grove of the cedars of Lebanon, the wood used to construct the Ark, is high up in the mountains. It consists of five or six ancient windbattered giants huddled together in the snow. The lodge nearby was ridiculously incongruous—a ski hut run by Austrian young people, some of whom were playing and dancing to Tyrolean folk music. Others enjoyed what looked like Munich beer served in heavy pottery steins with black bread. On the way home from this snowy expedition, my eye caught a small roadside sign which said "House of Kahlil Gibran." At my excited exclamation the driver pulled off the main highway into a little village. What a surprise! In a chilly second floor apartment hung the originals of Gibran's drawings for the Prophet and his other books. There was his bedroom, kitchen and workroom—a faint residue of his presence in the empty shell that had once been his home and where the evidence of his genius hung on the walls accumulating dust and cobwebs. Kahlil Gibran's "The Prophet" speaks apparently to the condition of the younger generation more than any other book. It is widely read and represents the modern gospel of spiritual guidance. After I returned home and told my young friends where I had been, they said, "Were you really there? In Kahlil Gibran's home? And you saw the original drawings? How absolutely marvelous!"

I received a similar response from a widely different group to whom I spoke of my pilgrimage to the international headquarters of the Bahai faith at Haifa. Abdul Baha lived here after he was released from prison in 1908 and a beautiful sanctuary has been built on Mount Carmel surrounded by gardens planted with cypresses and all manner of desert plants. The building was built by contributions of individuals from all parts of the world. Its golden dome is visible when approaching the harbor from the Mediterranean. Inside there is one large open space with altars against the wall at the four different points of the compass. These altars are decorated with flowers and lights, but there are no images, only prayer rugs laid on the floor. The doors were all open when we were there, and a few butterflies floated in on the warm breeze. An abode of peace, consecrated to the oneness of all mankind. (So it seemed ten years ago. I cannot imagine what has been happening there since then.)

This journey to the Near East ended with a few days in Istanbul, Greece and Italy. It was a fascinating experience to see these familiar places through the eyes of our young companions to whom everything was new and fresh and exciting.

For many years I had dreamed of going to India because of my interest in Hindu and Buddhist philosophies. In October, 1968, this wish was finally realized, and we joined a Harvard University Alumni tour which took us to Bombay via New York and London. In Bombay I was again impressed by the aftermath of colonialism. Prominent in the harbor approach is the so-called "Gateway to India," the huge archway erected in honor of a British royal visit there. "Gateway to India," what arrogance, I thought. Yet now, after the sun goes down, hundreds of people gather under the arches and along the balustrades to enjoy the cool of the evening. Some bring little braziers and cook their suppers, vendors wander in and out seeking customers for popcorn, peanuts, potato chips, gum, cigarettes and paper toys. If it were not for the

Gateway there would be no cool place for the poor to sit near the water and watch the boats in the harbor. Our hotel was the Raffles type, and the government buildings were typically English architecture. Outside the city we passed acres of corrugated iron huts resembling the most ramshackle of agricultural labor camps in the United States, except that here the squalor was enhanced by stagnant water remaining from flooding monsoons.

The most sacred places in India seem always to be in caves near the top of cliffs and mountains. There you discover in dim recesses the most marvelous carvings, hewn from solid rock—pillars, porticos and high reliefs depicting the life of Buddha, or the dancing of Siva and Krishna's changing forms. A myriad of lesser tributary gods, demons and angels, even animals crowd each other in intricate proximity. The work must represent life-time labor by hundreds of dedicated priests for a thousand yeas. Brahma was presented as having four heads. Siva on the left, Vishnu on the right, Ravana—the Lucifer image was shown being slain, but from his blood more demons arose till Siva got a cup with which to catch the blood and prevent its spreading. (This meant that you must prevent evil *at its source*.) These were the oldest caves. More recent ones, discovered by a British soldier in 1819 near Aurangabad, were decorated between the 2nd century and 7th century A.D. honoring three currents in Indian religion—Brahminism, Buddhism and the Jain sect, a form of Islam. The story of Buddha is painted on the walls and ceilings of twelve of the thirty-four caves. The colors are as fresh and bright as if they had been applied yesterday. The contrasts in India are so omnipresent. You have on the one hand esoteric practices of holy men and the demonstrations of mass superstition on the steps leading to the sacred river Ganges where believers are cured of their physical maladies and their spiritual transgressions by bathing and drinking the terribly polluted waters.

I had been hoping to visit Santinikitan Rabindranath, Tagore's school, but it would have taken more than a day to travel there from Calcutta. So, instead, I went to the headquarters of the Vedanta, the Rama-Krishna Mission at Belur Math on the Gooly River. Here I was escorted to Vivekenanda's room and to the Temple of the Divine Mother and through the large main temple of the order. The old monk who accompanied me was fluent in English and a saintly soul, but I was disappointed by the temple architecture which was ornate and grandiose and did not at all express the simplicity of the Vedanta teachings.

Much more in keeping with my ideals was Mahatma Gandhi's room in Bombay. It has been preserved just as he left it. A small room, the only furniture a pallet on the floor, a pillow, writing materials, two spinning wheels and a telephone in the corner—only the essentials. The anteroom was filled with pictures of Gandhi at various times in his life. The most beautiful was taken while he was talking to Jawaharlal Nehru. Both great men were smiling at one another with deep understanding.

I also retain the memory of another shrine in India where there was an enormous tree in a temple garden whose leaves were heart shaped. Could this be the sacred tree where Guatama was meditating before he became the Buddha—the scene of his enlightenment? I questioned our guide and he said, "No, not the original tree, but a tree grown from one of the seeds of the original." I gathered a few of the leaves and still have them. I recalled that all the temples in Thailand have golden *Bo* leaves fluttering from the eaves.

I was enormously interested in the New India: the influences of the colonial era still strong in social arrangements, the disappearance of the Maharajahs and the dispositions of their palaces and estates, the display everywhere of birth control propaganda and the efforts of the young people to dispose of the caste system. The English paper published in Delhi had several pages of advertising for marital partners. Many of these specifically stated "caste no barrier."

Nepal, a country closed to outsiders till after World War II, showed very little western contamination when we visited there. From the foothills of the Himalayas early in the morning we were able to see Annapurna and Mt. Everest. I had never expected to really see Mt. Everest, but there it was, a distant mystical peak, shining white in the sunrise. It gave me the same feeling as when I first saw the Acropolis in Athens from the harbor of Piraeus. Before we left the viewing hill, the mists from the valley seeped up and drew a curtain around the majestic skyline. Later that same day we visited the shrine where Buddha was supposed to have given his first teaching after he came down from his long period of solitary ascetic retreat. Further up the hill a great golden temple celebrated this event. The group I was with continued up the path to visit the building. I stayed by the stupa which commemorated the spot where he preached. I was left alone for an hour and had a beautiful meditation on this sacred spot.

Another vivid recollection is of the Tibetan Refugee Camp established by the International Red Cross to take care of the Tibetans who left when Communist China invaded their country. About a thousand people living in makeshift dormitories, spending their days in a great workshop where they prepared wool for spinning and weaving, or worked silver and other metals into jewelry and ornaments. They turned out beautiful rugs and coats which could be ordered and sent to addresses in the Americas. The Tibetans were determined to make a new life for themselvs in this colony. I have never seen such hard workers anywhere. It was touching to see the men, women and children of all ages absorbed by the common goal of rehabilitation through their own efforts. A large Tibetan flag floated above the camp. There was a multitude of prayer sticks, and I saw one prayer wheel. The Dalai Lama was at some unknown place of refuge in India.

Our travels ended with brief sojourns in such widely distant countries as Iran, Ireland and the Pacific Islands of Fiji, Tahiti and Samoa. I never felt drawn to Australia or New Zealand. With the exception of Guatemala, the great world of Central and South America remains outside my first-hand experience.

If there is another life time on this earth, perhaps I shall find myself on the banks of the Amazon or on a mountain slope in Peru. Who knows? Suffice it to say that the lands I visited have given me a perspective on the endless richness of nature and on the great diversity of human thought and accomplishment. As I relive in memory the scenes that seemed significant, I get a sense of unity that fundamentally there are not two worlds, nor is there a third world, but only one world despite variations in colors and culture, and that there is some portentous evolution going on, leading either to enlightenment or disaster. When I learn about the disappearance of great empires of the past like the Mayan or the Chinese, I wonder what really happened. Where did all those people who built the colonies in Britain around Stonehenge go? Why did homo sapiens have to begin all over again with stone tools and primitive social practices? In our present-day society there seems to be a race between self-destruction and enlightenment, and I sometimes wonder if we deserve to survive.

XXXIV

Quest (Five)

Personal religious thought.

During the fifteen or twenty years that I was involved with organizing work in the field of community relations I had to attend many committee meetings of one kind and another. I met the leaders of active groups, local as well as national. Among them were government officials, teachers, lawyers, ministers, social workers, business men and individuals who became the moving spirits in grass roots movements for social change. In working with such people, I became aware of varying qualities of leadership. I met the dictator, the conciliator, the compromiser, the intriguer and the obstructionist. It has been said that power corrupts those who possess it. This tendency can be observed in lowly situations as well as in national or international crises. The original motive may have been completely altruistic, but when it meets with a certain measure of success, the ego is flattered and the pure thrust of the original purpose becomes tinged with self-satisfaction. Carlyle called it "the sixth insatiable sense." Some of the ablest people I knew seemed to run off the track somewhere along the way. What started out as unifying procedure resulted in divisiveness. Persuasion turned into coercion. And often very questionable means were utilized to obtain desirable ends. I think I was bothered most by the subtle manipulation of people who were unaware of what was going on. Perhaps this troubled me particularly because I was tempted to use this technique myself when it represented a short cut to a desired end.

Wondering about the causes of conflict that sometimes arose within groups dedicated to the same objective, I came to perceive what a very important part motivation plays in corporate effort. The role of the expert is dangerous, and the organizer must be constantly aware of the why and how of his recommendations. He must guard against the vainglorious urge to dominate and the treacherous trap of infallibility. Truly to retain a moral frame of reference while wholeheartedly espousing a great cause, requires an abnegation of self and an unfailing loyalty to the inner vision that very few people attain. In our time I think that Martin Luther King and Cesar Chavez are the shining examples of this kind of constancy.

It was concern for motivation that made me prefer to work with Quakers on social problems. The concept of "that of God in every man" is a very revolutionary idea. If accepted as a basic belief it involves a new apprehension of deity and an exacting approach to man. I found that Friends were very sensitive to the basis for action and that the requirement for arriving at decisions by agreement from all members of the group reduced the danger of domination by any one person. There was no question of majority or minority vote. The necessity to think through a proposition with those in disagreement was an excellent discipline for me. I used to get pretty impatient with the time it took to arrive at decisions, but in the end I had to admit that the final result was better than what I had hoped for in the first place. The practice of opening every meeting with "a few moments of silence" quieted the mind and focused the sincerity of intention. Closing with a similar period served to establish direction. I found it easier to reconcile my inner awareness with outer performance when I worked through Friends. I took an active part in the Friends Service Committee and also in the Palo Alto Meeting for Worship where I was often moved to speak from urgent inner compulsion. Some of these messages were very surprising to me. I don't know where the words came from. I seemed to be only an agent through whom an idea was articulated.

One of the signs of spiritual growth is the simplification of life. This does not mean that daily routines cease, although inconsequential items do become less insistent. What counts is not so much concerned with outer complexities as with the inner conglomeration of desires, thoughts and aspirations that confuse and irritate the mind. When the center of consciousness becomes well established, this welter of mental distraction diminishes. The wayward themes seem to become harmonized; impulses relate themselves to a total pattern. It was very easy to open the self to meditation at the beginning of the day and at the end (if one could stay awake) but there are many hours between, when recollection needs to be sustained. "That which I will not that I do." It is like learning to drive a car. You have to *remember* to do certain things at first, but gradually your reactions become automatic and you don't need to think about it any more. Just enjoy the scenery. Coinciding with this, when the Inner Light shines brightly nothing can intercept that steady beam. It is not necessary to adjust the vision. It just happens.

But to establish the practice of the presence of God so that it becomes as natural as breathing—that requires a rigorous apprenticeship. When I think about it now it sounds silly, but I resorted to some trivial and seemingly ridiculous ways of keeping myself reminded. For instance, I fastened a large safety pin to the front of my dress and I carried a button in my pocket that I felt every time I reached in to find a pencil or a handkerchief. These objects were preferable to Moslem prayer beads which, although they serve the same purpose, called for questioning, whereas no one suspected a safety pin or a button. I also kept in my purse a small notebook in which I wrote short quotations from many sources. I still have the little blue book although I no longer carry it with me (it is somewhat battered). The sources of sayings range from the *Bhagavad Gita* to the Bible, St. Augustine, The Catholic Missal, Marcus Aurelius, Baha Ullah, and others, and are short little sentences that could be read at a glance. St. Francis' prayer is there:

> Lord, make me an instrument of Thy peace
> Grant that I may not so much seek
> To be consoled, as to console
> To be understood, as to understand
> To be loved as to love, for
> it is in giving that we receive—

One line, "Lord, make me an instrument of Thy peace" came to be a recurrent refrain in my mind. Many religious disciplines recommend this type of expedient. Sometimes it is called a *mantra*, sometimes an individual *secret phrase*. I believe the recent popular movement known as "Transcendental Meditation" has adopted this approach and found it to be psychologically effective. At any rate St. Francis served me well—"Lord, make me an instrument of Thy peace." How does one nourish the subconsious response of love to all human beings so it becomes a positive attitude? It is not enough to feel "I don't like you" and then simply to think "but I have to be tolerant." The mere suppression of a negative attitude is not the same as opening oneself to "That of God in every man." The achievement of a positive attitude requires deeper intuition, not just intellectual or critical judgment.

Before entering anyone's doorway, I made a practice of inaudibly invoking a blessing on the house. This was an old Hebrew custom and interestingly enough, I found it still carried on among the simple folk of Ireland. When joining a group or meeting an individual, I thought "May God accompany me." At the beginning of a Committee meeting and during the course of discussion I tried to imagine God was there among us as an invisible, but somehow participating extra entity, not an embodiment but an essence—an unsubstantiated presence that could ease tensions and flow into decisions, and assure the moral justification of compromises; and above all, hopefully, never weary from the tediousness of irrelevant details. At first this seemed a bothersome, idiotic obligation but gradually the effort subsided into habit. My patience expanded with practice. In all of life, the processes of growth are gradual, unhurried and related. "He who opens the rose, does it so simply," wrote Tagore. In all the natural world this principle is demonstrated. Only human beings get so mixed up because they fail to divest themselves of encumbrances and never discover the simplifying axiom that underlies all existence in this "little gleam of time between two eternities."

It was interesting to me, in making contact with American Indians for the survey for the Service Committee, to observe that the open attitude on my part made communication much easier. In most occasions in white society one feels embarrassed by silence, if it occurs. One has to think quickly to say something to fill the gap. When you confer with an Indian, however, it is not unusual to sit quietly for several minutes after the initial introduction before he will venture a remark. But during that time you are aware that communication is taking place. You feel that mutual understanding is on the way. No pretense avails against such careful inner scrutiny. If you pass this test, confidence is established and a relationship can proceed from there on.

During this period of the Quest my diary was, as usual, written in very intermittently. Reading those entries now, I realize they represent not so much an analysis of my state of mind then as what might be termed letters addressed to the deity, using a variety of terms of address. They indicate the nature of this pilgrim's progress at that point of the journey better than I can remember it now, so I end this phase of the "deeper level" with a few of those letters.

I.

Lord, I thank Thee for the alterations between night and day, for night which gives rest to tired limbs and covers with forgetfulness the foolish and irrelevant anxieties of a burdened mind and for each new day that brings me back to consciousness. One emerges from oblivion and finds Thee waiting like a dear friend from whom we have been separated. Each day is an adventure in companionship ever new, unexpected, full of surprises and challenge. Grant me to walk sensitively this day with faith and steadfastness.

II.

Holy Spirit, purify my mind and heart that I may be able to speak of holy things without contaminating them.

Vouchsafe to grant me the Angel of Thy Presence to protect me from self-seeking and irreverence. Impart to me the sense of things eternal, imperishable and prophetic.

III.

Lord, Thou art very great and my vessel of comprehension is so very small.

IV.

Dear God, How little I know of the true nature of life. All so close around me and yet my eyes do not see, nor my ears hear. Blindly I plunge forward and act without thought, speak hastily without knowledge and so disregard the holy laws of charity that I turn away from the Kingdom of Heaven and lose myself in confusion. Clear away the mist, pierce through the layers of callousness. Blind me, if need be, with the searing light of reality that all lesser manifestations may dwindle and drop from sight. So may I serve only the Inner Light and fill myself utterly from its source.

V.

We cannot know the end of Thy mysteries, Lord. We sense a purpose but our finite minds are not able to comprehend the goal. I can only lay my work with relinquishing hands on the altar of Thy Omnipotence.

But as Thou art present in the infinitely Great, so must Thou also be present in the infinitely Small. In microcosm as in macrocosm.

As the water drop holds within it the secret of the mighty ocean, so does every moment of time articulate the whole mystery of eternity. Not by spreading out wide to the far reaches of the Universe but by drawing in to penetrate more profoundly the depths of consciousness in the fleeting instant, is The Eternal Verity to be found. In the realization of Immanence the purpose is implicit and the essential unity of the spirit is fulfilled.

In the lesser as in the greater.

VI.

Heavenly Father, in the midst of the conflict of the world let me work only for love. Help me to strip off every irrelevant concern and simplify my desires so that my purpose will be one-pointed and undeviating. Against the immensity of the present world chaos one cannot struggle. But within the radius of an individual existence one does have choice whether it shall be greed and fear or goodwill and courage. Oh Lord, I will put my heart in Thy keeping forever and ever.

VII.

O God, I bow before Thee
Light of all knowledge
Support of all worlds
Lead me from darkness into light
From the Unreal to the real
From death to immortality
Reach me through and through myself
And evermore protect me from ignorance and malice
So that I may know the Truth and the Truth will make me free

VIII.

O ineffable Creator, Thou who art the true fountain of wisdom and light, vouchsafe to pour upon the darkness of my understanding the double beam of Thy Radiance removing all ignorance and selfishness. Instruct my tongue and pour into my lips the grace of speech. Give me quickness of understanding, capacity to retain subtlety of interpretation and sweetness of persuasion. Guide Thou my going out and my coming in.

IX.

Dear Lord, Thou hast been with me all the days and all the nights and in Thee do I find my comfort and my strength. I cannot go anywhere beyond Thy love. That is my rest and my peace and my cup of fulfillment running over. Having Thee, I have all.

XXXV

Memorable Happenings

Guests of many nations and faiths.

Over the years Hidden Villa Ranch has been the setting for a number of varied and extraordinary gatherings. Close to a fast-growing urban center, it has offered unusual facilities for small grass-roots groups to hold meetings at little or no expense in a place where they could be assured of non-intereference and privacy. Larger groups have used the picnic area for church outings, inter-racial parties or to raise money for welfare organizations. The riding ring has been available for horse shows, for annual 4H demonstrations or for the starting point for long distance equestrian endurance rides. The autumn Hidden Villa Horseplay, a combination of English and Western equitation, interspersed with games, has provided opportunity for any child, with any old nag, with or without fancy equipment, to participate in horse fun. Originally sponsored to raise funds for Peninsula School, it has become an annual community tradition now in its thirty-sixth year. Once in awhile the remnants of a defunct Hunt Club re-enact bygone days, complete with hounds, stirrup cup and scarlet coats.

It is well-known among minority groups that they are welcome on the premises. It is not always easy for them to find suitable places. One such was a birthday party for the patriarch of a Santa Clara Mexican-American family who started the line with 10 children. Each of them had married, so there were 10 spouses; and each couple had at least four children. The offspring in turn had produced great numbers of great-grandchildren for the widening family. All the picnic tables were filled on that memorable Sunday.

A few weeks before World War II the Hostel offered hospitality to another group. This was the Youth Fellowship from a Japanese-Methodist Church. The Methodist Church had been active in this country and also in Japan for introducing Christianity to a large number of converts. A group of about fifteen or twenty earnest young people with their pastor conducted a Lenten retreat for a weekend in the Spring. Part of their program consisted of writing down on slips of paper a record of all the sins they could remember having committed. They asked to borrow a shovel and went up into the woods where they dug a hole and into it dropped all the little papers to bury their sins. It was very touching to see these gentle young people so sincere in carrying out their religious ceremony. The little girls made me think of early spring flowers, so delicate and graceful they were. I often thought about this episode in the days following Pearl Harbor.

Thinking about religious ceremonies recalls to mind a baptism that a Negro sect arranged in our swimming pool. Originally they wanted to plan the ceremony in the creek, but late in the spring the flow of water was too low to allow total immersion, so the Reverend asked about the swimming pool. Some twenty-five or thirty elders stood around the edge while the appropriate scripture was read. The postulant shivered in her white shroud. Finally she waded gingerly in at the shallow end of the pool led by the barefoot preacher. He gave her a little shove and ducked her under with an invocation of blessedness. She let out a throaty gasp and all those encircling the pool gave a sigh of relief and shouted, "Praise the Lord." The dripping lady, the wet sheet clinging to her ample contours, then emerged from the water sputtering, but ecstatic. While she retired to the bathhouse to remove her chilly raiment, the crowd continued chanting hymns. The ceremony ended with a chicken barbecue at the picnic ground.

Among other uses of the Hostel was a group of Moslems for whom one week in June was set aside. They wanted to conduct a training session for their children to familiarize them with the rituals of their faith. From twenty-five to thirty children were involved, with miscellaneous parents and teachers. Their countries of origin were widespread, including India, Malaysia, Egypt, Lebanon, Syria, Jordan, Saudi-Arabia and Afghanistan. They dressed in their native costumes, including the one or two white American women who had married Arabs and adapted themselves to the manners and dress of their husbands. Prayers began in the morning at daybreak when, in place of a mosque, the call to worship was shouted forth three times from the top of a hill by a young Arab boy: "There is no God but Allah and Mohammed is His prophet." Under the olive trees at the edge of the road, rugs had been spread out, and the company repaired there and prostrated themselves, facing the rising sun and Mecca, to the accompaniment of chanting. This worship took place six times in the course of one day. This seemed to impose a great deal of drudgery on the part of the ladies who could only attend after bathing and putting on freshly laundered saris for each performance. In walking round the ranch some of them came upon the pen where the pigs are kept. This caused a minor panic because the pig is an unclean, tabooed animal for Moslems. The very sight and sound and fragrance of swine disturbed their peace of mind. However, opposite the pigpen the sheep had their abode. And the sheep is the favorite animal throughout the Arab world. The visitors conceived the idea of purchasing one of our lambs to slaughter and cook according to their orthodox traditions. It would make a fitting culmination, they said, to their week's retreat. We were glad to cooperate in the project. Their white cook was neither Arabian or Indian, but an inexperienced neophyte in the doctrine, as well as an amateur in culinary arts. She came to me one afternoon saying she knew I had nothing to do with the group, but she needed some advice. She was about ready to quit her job because different ones kept coming to tell her how she should cook the meals according to their individual preferences, and often they would have heated arguments right in the kitchen in the very limited space where she had to work. She didn't care less whether her methods were Egyptian or Hindustani, but she couldn't work with all the criticisms and contradictory advice. I suggested the simple expedient of locking the doors into the kitchen to keep everyone out, telling the leaders that the food would be prepared her way, otherwise they would have to find someone else to cook for them. Apparently, the ultimatum worked because she stayed on to the end. One rather amusing sidelight developed in connection with this group's stay, which happened at the time when the so-called Black Moslems were causing considerable commotion throughout this country. They had put a sign, "Moslem Camp," on our gate. One of our friends noticed it and called up, saying, "I knew you were pretty tolerant, but I didn't know you'd go as far as encouraging the *Black Moslems.*" To protect our visitors from undesirable repercussions and to protect our own reputation, with the group's permission I changed the sign to read "Islam." Probably only one out of twenty of those who passed by had ever heard that term. At least, it did not arouse any public indignation.

One spring afternoon, about the time when the British Empire withdrew control from India, finally acceding to that country's demand for independence, an English friend of ours, Kenneth Saunders, telephoned to ask if he could bring an East Indian prince to visit us. Kenneth had long been a spokesman for the Indian people, and he was a friend of Gandhi and Nehru. He had written many articles and books about Oriental thought and religion and the necessity for Britain to completely withdraw from the scene. Among the powerful maharajahs who governed large ancestral holdings there were some who were educated in England and who were deeply concerned for the well-being of their people. One such was the Gaekwar of Baroda, who had come to the United States under the guidance of Kenneth to study American institutions and scientific developments. He had brought a sizeable staff with him. When Kenneth brought him to the ranch, he was accompanied by his doctor who also acted as his secretary. The Gaekwar was a small compact little man who moved quickly with birdlike gestures and asked questions about everything he saw. He went around the garden with Frank who had to identify every tree and flower. The doctor-secretary carried a little black notebook and fountain pen and walked three steps behind the Gaekwar wherever he went. As Frank gave the name of the plant, the Gaekwar would turn his head halfway round and say, "Write that down." And so it was recorded. When he looked through the big window in our living room, he said, "It reminds me of Kashmir, the most beautiful place in all of India."

Our introduction to the Gaekwar led to a later encounter in Rome. Kenneth was traveling with him there, and by chance, we met them at St. Peter's. Kenneth invited us to come up that afternoon for tea and birthday cake. "You'll cheer up the old man," he said. It was the Gaekwar's birthday and according to custom, the poet who traveled in his suite had written a birthday poem for his master. The trouble was that the Gaekwar didn't like the poem and was in a bad humor. (In olden days the poet would have been beheaded.) So, somewhere on a high terrace overlooking the whole city of Rome, we drank tea and munched cake and tried to enliven the day for the disappointed Gaekwar. We must have succeeded because on parting he invited us to come to his palace in India. "I will send five elephants to meet you at the station," he promised. Unfortunately, we did not get to India till many years after he had died. His nephew, and successor, was not as hospitable as his uncle.

Over the years we often allowed Native-Americans to use our picnic grounds for dancing and feasts. One time there was to be a giant pow-wow with hundreds of Indians congregating from all over the United States. They required open space in which to set up teepees and toilet facilities, and above all, a large flat area for dancing. After inquiring at many places such as ball parks and state campgrounds, they decided Hidden Villa was best for their purposes—and least expensive. We reserved two large fields for their use. They were to stay from Thursday till Sunday noon. I waited for them all Thursday afternoon and evening, but there were no arrivals and no word. About Friday noon I telephoned to San Francisco. Oh yes, I was told, they were still planning to come, but not quite so many—and they would not be arriving until Saturday noon, and they were counting on dancing all day Sunday in our big field. Saturday came—and still there was not a redskin in sight, nor any message. Early on Sunday morning a bus and a large number of dilapidated automobiles arrived, out of which emerged a hundred or more expectant young white people planning to join the dance. But there was nary an Indian until later—when two Indians arrived from San Jose expecting to find their brothers and the tomtom drums! Word had apparently gotten around among the so-called "hippy" population in San Francisco that the Indians were going to dance at Hidden Villa, so they had come to join the pow-wow. Much to the dismay of the conservative employees of the ranch, these bearded, straggly-haired, barefooted, amazingly clad couples spread out all over the ranch, poking into barns and corrals, shed and picnic tables, and wandered up the trails along the creeks and into the garden. Eventually they settled down with their paper bag lunches and guitars for a jazz festival, and then a circle dance was organized which lasted almost till midnight. By then I had received a telephone message saying that the Indians had decided to stay in San Francisco and would not be coming after all, but "Thank you for the offer!"

Several small groups of students had used locations on the ranch at different times for the setting of amateur movies. So I did not think much about it when Peter Corbetta, a drama major from Foothill College, asked if a friend of his could use a secluded place one Sunday to make a film based on the painting of the Garden of Delight by Hieronymus Bosch. I designated the canyon, which seemed satisfactory to Peter. On Sunday morning I went off to Friends Meeting in Palo Alto. When I returned, I found crowds of people in the lower field gathered around a helicopter, and another crowd of people dancing around a huge sort of pillar erected on the knoll above the canyon. These dancers appeard to be nude. Presently the helicopter zoomed up over them and let down a cloud of pink smoke which drifted in rosy swirls around the actors and the huge phallic symbol. Someone in the neighborhood was alarmed by the glow and summoned the fire department. Neighbors appeared on adjacent hilltops, busy with binoculars, and the sheriff received a number of calls from outraged parents demanding "some type of preventive action," to which he could only reply, "I can do nothing since it is on private land." A nearby resident happened to be a Harvard alumnus who was celebrating his 25th anniversary with some other members of his graduating class. When the pink smoke blew down their way, he and his guests became curious and migrated to the scene. The "entertainment" attracted more and more spectators, who appeared from every direction and included gentlemen of the press. Monday morning headlines read "Hills jump as 200 cavort in nude for art's sake." I found out afterward that the film was a product of Sinca Films, Ltd., which was connected with the San Francisco Art Center. Hobbs, the director, had hired two busloads of volunteers recruited from the city streets of San Francisco at five dollars a head (or perhaps one should say, a body). I never did see the film, entitled "Roseland." It was shown in Pacifica and South San Francisco, but never locally.

Over the years, we entertained large numbers of musicians at the ranch—quartettes and choral groups and individual musicians. The Stanford Music Guild was formed in our living room. I remember that Joan Baez, when she was still in high school, sang at a Friends'

Christmas party for children. Her parents attended Palo Alto Meeting. But the most memorable occasion took place on March 21, 1976, on the anniversary of John Sebastian Bach's bithday. Margaret Fabrizio, a harpsichordist of note, always celebrates this anniversary. Her housing space is limited, so she suggested using our house. On this occasion, harpsichords were set up end to end to accommodate the Bach concerto for *three* harpsichords. Most of the furniture was moved out onto the porch or hall to make room for other instruments and performers. From two in the afternoon until ten o'clock at night, trios, quartettes, cantatas, chorales followed one another in quick succession as musicians arrived with suitable instruments. Every available space in dining room, kitchen, hall and outdoor porches was crowded with music lovers paying tribute to the great master. All kinds of bread and cheese, cold meats and hors d'oeuvres, coffee and beer were spread out on tables. At six o'clock Margaret served sauerkraut soup which had been simmering all day on the kitchen stove. (Bach's favorite? Not mine!) Margaret had invited a hundred guests. I am sure each one brought two or three friends. I was afraid the walls might get pushed out, but they—and we—survived the pressure.

The most beautiful and the most mysterious gathering I ever witnessed at the ranch took place one June morning. Driving out from Palo Alto I noticed a great many butterflies flying along the road as if they were escorting my car. I stopped to get a better look. It was true. A steady stream of Monarch butterflies came floating by—flurries of them coming on and on, all heading in the same direction. As the car approached the Hidden Villa gate, their numbers seemed to increase. It was like traveling through an orange mist. When I walked over the bridge towards the house, a marvelous sight met my eyes. The lawn was completely covered with butterflies. There were thousands and thousands of them. More and more kept dropping from the skies and crowding into the glowing mass, covering the lawn so thickly that there was not even one tiny spot of green grass visible. It looked as if a giant had laid a huge embroidered coverlet over the whole expanse. They stayed there all afternoon. The dogs came by and sniffed at the edges of the path but turned away, unimpressed. A few birds flew low to inspect the phenomenon but decided they were not interested in such a gathering. But all the Ranch people came to observe and to marvel at this unusual sight. Towards evening it seemed as if all the butterflies in Northern California must have arrived. The air was clear except for an occasional tardy drifter. When we went to bed, they were still there. But in the morning just after sunrise, they all vanished in a sudden silent irridescent cloud, swirling over the tops of the bay trees, trailing a few stragglers and disappearing the way they had come. The lawn was green again. I never knew where they went. They never came again. And no one has ever been able to tell me why we had that unique visitation. Man has not yet penetrated all the secrets of nature. There is still so much to learn.

XXXVI

Conservation and Environmental Education

Friends of Hidden Villa; a farm—wilderness approach to ecological concepts.

A tremendous change has taken place in the general attitude of the public toward open space. Years ago, when I was a child living in Massachusetts, there was a land beyond the setting sun which we referred to as "the West." Out there, all manner of potentialities seemed to exist for the stouthearted. Fortunes could be built up in the mines, in salmon fisheries, in orchards, or in the cattle markets. Bridge building, construction work or furnishing hitherto undeveloped services in rapidly growing towns and cross roads provided other opportunities. It seemed there was no limit to the possibilities. Those who departed for this vast unsettled area were often considered venturesome, or even somewhat foolhardy. I remember the astonishment aroused by one of the Lyman girls who chose to attend the University of California in Berkeley instead of sticking to Radcliffe, Bryn Mawr or Vassar. Most Bostonians could hardly conceive of the existence of cultural or educational advantages on the West Coast. But it certainly was taken for granted that the western lands were limitless and, when all else failed, that almost anyone could come by land for a modest outlay of cash, provided he were willing to start from scratch and work strenuously to develop it. In my early days I never heard anyone mention the need to preserve open space. True, there had been parks and playgrounds established adjacent to the eastern cities. But still the emigrants from Europe kept on coming to New York and continuing across country to settle homesteads in states with romantic names like Colorado, Oklahoma or Wyoming, without having to be concerned with possible future amenities such as "undeveloped open space."

After the assassination of McKinley it was fortunate for the United States that Theodore Roosevelt succeeded to the presidency. He had always been a great lover of the out-of-doors; he explored wilderness areas and was familiar with the resources and beauty of wild country. He was greatly influenced by his friend John Muir who introduced him to the Yosemite, the Yellowstone and the High Sierra. The story is told of an episode when officials waited at a certain railroad station to welcome the Chief Executive. But instead of allowing himself to be officially received, he slipped off the train and hurried unseen to the back of the depot where John Muir was waiting with two saddle horses to spirit the President away to the wilderness. The crestfallen members of a welcoming delegation had to put their speeches back into their briefcases and furl the flags and silence the band. This disregard of protocol lost Roosevelt some votes and dismayed the leaders of his party, but it certainly benefitted posterity. It was he who established the national program for forests and parks and elevated the Department of the Interior to a place in the Cabinet. It happened just in time to save some of the great scenic wonders in our country. Not everyone appreciated these efforts for conservation. However, the conflict of interests aroused by the expenditure of large government subsidies to purchase monuments helped to publicize the issues and ultimately led to greater awareness on the part of the general public. At least a score of citizen organizations dedicated to the preservation of natural resources were soon formed.

After Frank and I moved to California in 1918, we became aware of this conservation movement and gave it our enthusiastic support. We always attended the conferences of the Pacific Camping Association (which was later absorbed by the American Camping Association), and we joined the Save-the-Redwoods League, the Wild Life Federation, and the Audubon Society. We participated in the campaigns to protect priceless parcels of mountain and seashore visits against private ownership and commercial development. One of the most important local accomplishments was the salvation of the Butano Forest near Santa Cruz. Lumber interests were on the verge of cutting down the magnificent virgin redwoods and madrone that grew in that canyon. If they had not been checked, the lovely little stream with its waterfalls and banks of shoulder-high ferns and wild azaleas would have been lost forever.

The Sierra Club, organized originally by John Muir and supported largely by a small group of mountaineers and outdoor enthusiasts, became the leader in the fight to conserve our natural resources. Membership increased enormously, and it spread from state to national importance, providing the strength needed to arouse public opinion and to influence legislation. The Sierra Club is a good example of the power of citizens to influence government procedures constructively if they are sufficiently motivated, well-organized and articulate. With the increased size of the Club, however, there was increasing danger of losing the personal contacts that had inspired much of its activity. To counteract this trend, it became expedient to form local chapters based on the geographical concentrations of members. Some who lived south of San Francisco became interested in forming such a unit on the mid-peninsula, and planned a hike to discuss it. A group of about twenty-five of the most active Sierra Club adherents joined the hike up Adobe Creek to an area we had set aside as a Boy Scout Camping Ground. At this place the hikers took out their lunches and discussed the matter of establishing a smaller unit. The decision was made to incorporate the group into a new chapter, which took the name of Loma Prieta, the highest peak in the Santa Cruz Mountain chain. That was in 1933. Since that time the Loma Prieta Chapter has become the second largest in the country. In 1974 the Sierra Club installed a metal tablet on the Camping Ground commemorating the spot where its inception took place. For the first year or two of its existence, we used to host the Loma Prieta Christmas party. But when the number of members increased, and I found myself involved in cooking for a hundred and sixty guests, who were squeezed into every nook and cranny of our house, I decided they would have to go elsewhere another year. Numbers are important for political action, but size certainly does destroy intimate personal contacts.

When we bought Hidden Villa Ranch in 1924 and later added adjacent property to insure the control of the watershed, we had no idea that its financial value would increase so enormously in our lifetime as a result of the great influx of population and the proliferation of subdivisions. We looked upon the ranch simply as our home and an environment in which to nurture plants, animals and children. Its location combined the advantages of a rural setting with proximity to a big city and to a college community. It seemed to provide the surroundings to carry out the way of life we had chosen to follow. Luckily for us, the great changes in the population and the local development did not occur until after our children were grown. How free and pleasant those years were which can never again be repeated!

With the metamorphosis of the Garden Valley into the urban sprawl, land took on a different significance. From being a source of lifegiving natural fertility, it became only the underpinning for a series of man-made buildings calculated to produce unearned profit to its owner. In China, time is reckoned by specifying the Year of the Bull or the Year of the Cock or the Pig, or the Horse. But in Santa Clara and San Mateo Counties, the period between 1950 and 1970 might well be designated as the Era of the Realtor. The development demon was on the rampage. All available open space was viewed with avaricious eyes, and—none too soon—park and recreation departments received belated public support. Spontaneous conservation associations sprang up in many of the small towns and threatened areas.

Hidden Villa Ranch represented one of the largest easily accessible intact holdings left in this area, comprising 2500 acres, the greater part of which consisted of virgin wilderness. Naturally, the real estate interests cast longing eyes towards the flat land and jingled money bags in our direction. Adjacent towns held out allurements of annexation, and recreation departments reflected on the possible use of eminent domain. We began to realize that we had inadvertently become the custodians of a most precious heritage and that we were responsible for its ultimate destiny.

Over the preceding years, in addition to the summer camp for children and the use of the Hostel and picnic ground for groups, we had welcomed an increasing number of individual hikers, campers and riders to share the trails and campsites that gave us so much pleasure. Occasionally a school in Los Altos or Mountain View would ask permission for a class to visit our animals. With the reduction in farm and orchard activities and restrictions on the use of city lots, what earlier had been a trickle of visitors developed gradually into a steady stream. We were glad that so many people were "getting back to nature" and that children could be exposed to what Whitman called "the primal sanities," but the increase in numbers necessitated scheduling and setting up a few restrictions in order to safeguard the fragile environment.

Our family came to the agreement that a large part of the wilderness area, including the creek and its pristine watershed, should be dedicated at our death to public use as a permanent wild life sanctuary. We let it be known that such was our intention. The wise choice of the appropriate body most likely to fulfill our wishes in the future was not so easy to determine. State? County? Audubon Society? Nature Conservancy? Sierra Club? Which of these agencies would best insure continuance? Much would depend on the administrative policies at the time of transferring custody, and it is not always easy to foresee future developments.

In the meantime, our facilities became widely known and their use increased from season to season. The schools, especially pre-school, kindergarten and primary grades, discovered that the children could see more than one kind of domestic animal at the ranch. Hitherto animals had been visible to them only in picture books or on the TV screen. Horses, cows, sheep, pigs, goats, ducks, geese, chickens, rabbits, peacocks now could be seen, all in one excursion. Thus, during the autumn months and from March to June, yellow school buses may be seen trundling up Moody Road, where they pass the iron gate and park by the big tin hay barn where excited young occupants and their teachers scramble out to meet "Mr. Brown" who is their guide on the "Ranch Tour." In addition to Mr. Brown, the group is chaperoned by Shannon, the Irish setter who leads the way, and by Tammie, the Scottie who brings up the rear. Last year we entertained about seven thousand visitors from schools within a radius of fifty miles of the Ranch.

When the toddlers get back to the classroom, they draw pictures of what they have seen, and the older ones write thank you letters. Our mail box if often filled with large manila envelopes which contain the varied records of these student impressions.

Trips such as these serve as an introduction for very young children to the world outside their homes, a world which furnishes them with food and other necessities of life. But such sightseeing trips are not enough for them as they grow older. Most outdoor education programs are totally inadequate; they skim the surface in the text books and in silly little experiments featured in the classroom, but they seldom, if ever, come into actual contact with living forces. I first came to realize the great importance of this learning experience when I observed the effects on children in my summer camp that resulted from their first-hand contacts with nature. There is something in it deeper than knowledge, although knowledge may well be included. The emotion of wonder can so easily be evoked in a child, who, in one sense, becomes what he sees. He is still open to discover "intimations of immortality." Those who dwell only in city streets rarely acquire such perspective, and their scale of values is limited by the artificial environment in which they live. Becoming aware of the relationships of all living things to other living things is the key to knowing ourselves. It is the basis for understanding the intricate web of life. By what means can such experience be brought about? The challenge for the teacher is to set the stage so that this kind of learning can take place.

I often saw this deeper learning experience during the few weeks that children were living at camp in summer, especially with some who returned year after year. But always it has seemed as if we should be able to reach a larger number. There were so many to whom camp was not available. During the past few years, with the help of three young teachers, we have experimented with a program geared for school children between grades four and eight. We made contact with public school principals, offering to provide a series of 4-6 all day sessions at the ranch, if the school would provide transportation and insurance and would pay for some specially trained teachers. In return, we arranged for the orientation of classroom teachers at the Ranch. We held a planning session at the school with the children. On visitation days, the dividing up of the class into groups of six to ten under the direction of a special teacher-guide insured participation. Plans were carefully made ahead of time involving content, time, the age of the students and the availability of interesting phenomena. For instance, if piglets had recently been born, if a field were being ploughed, if a storm had caused the creek to overflow, or if someone had found a woodrat's nest, a whole series of questions arose which led into many avenues of ecological research. Or it might be that the order of the day would be to emphasize the process of preparing raw wool from the sheep into usable yarn, or the conversion of acorns into mush such as Indians used to make, or finding what plants are suitable for vegetable dyes, or trying to prevent erosion along the banks of the creek and a hundred other projects which stimulate curiosity, observation, skills and knowhow. Because the groups were small everyone had a chance to participate actively. Just before the bus came to take them home, the individual groups gathered together to share what they had seen and done. Sometimes, before leaving the ranch, they asked how and when we bought it, what was it before it was a ranch, how old the house was, had we always lived in California, and so on. When they returned to school the interest aroused could be used by the teacher to motivate a great variety of learning.

Up to this time the opportunity for the schools' excursions described above has been available only to those schools having extra-curricular funds. Some of the less opulent are unable to meet the fees for the special teachers, yet they are the very ones most in need of curriculum enrichment. Twenty years ago I organized Hidden Villa Camp as a non-profit corporation. By means of camp and hostel fees, scholarship donations from foundations and from individual supporters, I have been able to run the operation on a self-sustaining basis. Of course, the taxes, utilities, much of the maintenance and capital improvements are taken care of by Frank and me, but the actual activities of Hidden Villa Camp, Incorporated, have been carried out independently, and each fiscal year has ended with a small balance. However, with the increase in the use of the land and the development of the educational contribution that we are able to make, we have come to feel the need of additional funds. Some of our neighbors and friends and members of the community who have benefitted from trails, picnic or camping areas have conceived the idea of "Friends of Hidden Villa." This organization, based on different types of membership, will support the ongoing structure of Hidden Villa and make it possible to include underprivileged groups.

The farm-wilderness combination constitutes a unique approach to ecological concepts. There is something here for all ages from pre-schoolers through college graduates, including the individual researcher, child or adult. In carrying out such a program there are a few major considerations. First is the selection of data to be presented and the need for skill and understanding in its interpretation. Equally important is the protection of the land and other resources so that too constant use may not result in the destruction of the very quality that constitutes its appeal. I have been fortunate to have been able to enlist the interest and enthusiasm of half a dozen young teachers and a score of volunteers who are developing the concept and practice of environmental education. They exude enthusiasm for the cause and demonstrate a beautiful and creative approach to the subject. They also revere the setting and are almost fanatical guardians of all the wild and tame life that makes up the total environment. It is very exciting to me to listen and watch what they are doing. Being limited in mobility and staying power, I can only share vicariously in the fulfillment of an idea, and I suppose I should call myself retired. But, although I may feel a little tired at times, I do not feel withdrawn. There seems to be a center of energy from which many filaments spread out. I feel very close to the whole operation and deeply involved with every detail of its progress. The younger leaders who are carrying on are very kind to me, and they permit me to share their objectives, failures, successes and their resulting conclusions. Best of all I like to share the children's comments. A fifth-grader wrote, "You have to learn about Nature in person. You have to taste it, feel it, see it and hear it. I felt like sitting there all afternoon listening to the trees and leaves." And a fourth-grader commented, "At Hidden Villa we made animals our brothers. Sometimes I think about people who don't care about beautiful forests and pollution, but if they went to Hidden Villa they would just go to work to clean it up."

I have always felt that no one can *own* land and that custodianship is a sacred trust that involves great responsibility along with the enjoyment. But to share with children and to be able to contribute vital educational experiences to their growth is a great reward in itself.

XXXVII

Gathering Up Loose Threads

Fiftieth Wedding Anniversary; writing; books published; biography of F. Duveneck.

The decade from 1960-1970 was certainly a stormy period in the United States. The unrest among young adults played havoc with educational systems. Minority leaders refused to be satisfied with token integration. Labor unions voiced their discontent and engaged in prolonged strikes, disruptive of business and public services. Antagonisms that had been seething below the surface for many years erupted into violent and bitter public demonstrations. The assassinations of John F. Kennedy and Martin Luther King seemed to epitomize the turbulent and tragic temper of the times. Above all, the war in Vietnam tended to stimulate aggressiveness and to support the philosophy of power. The American public came to accept scenes and stories of atrocities perpetrated by our armies. Newspaper stories and TV presentations gradually dulled our reactions. When our own government endorsed ruthless methods of control in foreign lands, it was inevitable that people at home should substitute violence for arbitration, and coercion for persuasiveness. The democratic idea and the American "way of life" appeared to have been laid aside, and an era of tolerance for the gratification of the rich and powerful and of indifference to the poor seemed to possess our whole society. A new type of imperialism was established by business expanding its foreign markets, thus inevitably leading to the insidious control of internal politics.

Right in our own neighborhood the real estate interests plotted against our beautiful lands in order to establish vast areas of subdivisions, enormous freeways and endless shopping complexes. It was a matter of political pride that our state of California had, by 1962, surpassed all the other states in population. Everything was getting bigger. Bigger meant better, and better meant bigger. The only use for land was to make money.

Perhaps only when a situation becomes intolerable will change occur. Revolt then becomes mandatory. Out of havoc new solutions emerge. The episode of Watergate and the related revelations really broke through our national complacency. People began to realize what had been going on and what they themselves had been responsible for. I am convinced that the downfall of Richard Nixon and his amoral confederates saved the United States from becoming a dictatorship. I thought it a pity that the impact was weakened by the pardon, but still the lesson was clear and the results far-reaching. We stopped taking a lot of things for granted and began to analyze our institutions. Our codes of morals and behavior were dusted off and scrutinized for relevance.

Gradually it became evident that the seemingly anti-social doings of the younger generation had a deeper significance than just making a disruptive, impatient gestures. To avoid taking part in a war in which they did not believe, they were willing to go to jail or to emigrate to another country. Refusing to conform to out-moded life styles, they experimented with other means of survival, earth utilization, manual skills, music making, new art forms, cooperative living, rudimentary relationships, self-sufficiency. Simple, basic occupations provided workable alternatives for college degrees and professional achievement. Some of it seemed pretty crazy to old fogeys like me, but there was a sincerity and an earnestness in their efforts that one had to respect. Such a revolution against affluence and materialism represented hope for the future. Unfortunately, disillusion with government tends to result in a negative attitude towards civic responsibility: "Why bother to vote when both parties are equally bad?" "I don't want anything to do with politics. It's nothing but a big mess."

A positive aspect of the time, however, was the significant increase of public awareness in regard to natural resources. Whereas the Sierra Club had battled virtually alone for years, all at once it found itself supported by a multiplicity of small agencies and dedicated individuals. Friends of the Earth, Nature Conservancy, Audubon Society, National Wildlife, Regional Parks, Open Space, Green Foothills, Save the Redwoods, Save the Bay, Save the River, Save the Coast line. Save everything! Stop pollution and waste of all kinds, develop recycling techniques, abolish strip mining, explore solar energy. At times it seemed there was almost a frenzy for conservation.

These developments were of course most acceptable to me, and I took part in a number of campaigns, either opposing bad practices or endorsing salutary measures. Also, I became disturbed by the growing indifference regarding the United Nations. Too many people failed to realize that despite its limitations its existence was still an essential factor for peace in the world, and the work carried on by the international committees and special commissions were constantly laying foundations for cooperation between nations. I wrote letters to a number of people prominent hereabouts, suggesting the need to actively support the United Nations. Starting with a small group, we gathered enough to create the Mid-Peninsula Chapter of the U.N. Committee. I was president for a few years, but gradually passed the leadership into more capable hands. The group has since developed a center in downtown Palo Alto with a successful gift shop, library and information service.

Consistent with my concern for integration and my experiences at Hidden Villa Camp, I tried to get other summer camp directors to realize the importance of including minority group campers. About a dozen camps showed interest, and I arranged confrontations between White leaders and Negro parents. We had some amazing meetings. They really talked to each other, barriers down, the Blacks revealing all their resentments and the Whites on the defensive in regard to living up to their democratic ideals. With the help of campership funds, we were able to introduce several non-white children to hitherto restricted camps, and we prevailed on Black parents to trust their children to the new situation. It entailed a lot of work for a relatively small number, but it worked for them. Hence, it was an important entering wedge. A number of camps removed their restrictive clauses, and a few were sufficiently converted to actively solicit and underwrite racial participation.

It became evident, as we were able to get the non-white children into camp, that the staff counselors were practically a hundred per cent white, and that if camps were really going to serve children of various backgrounds, it was important for them to have leaders to whom they could comfortably relate. This consideration led to efforts to enlist older teenagers and college students to apply for positions. If and when we found suitable candidates, it was absolutely mandatory to do some extra training to acquaint them with the objectives and methods they would be encountering. To find the proper candidate and to persuade him or her to undertake a summer promising a lot of hard work and relatively little remuneration, took a lot of persuasion. And then the camp director also needed to develop understanding and patience, and be willing to prepare other members of his staff to accept the newcomer.

This project was really difficult due to the fact that most of the Black and Oriental and Chicano applicants counted on earning enough money in the summer period to carry them through the following school year. But here again, the very few who got a toe, even if not a foot in the door, served to demonstrate a new pattern. This toehold applied to both camp directors and young Black counselors.

In 1963, our children and nephews and nieces put their heads together and decided that on June 7th our 50th wedding anniversary should be celebrated. Whoever heard of such a party? It lasted three days—a long weekend. Beginning on Friday night with a supper party to include all kin on the West Coast and my dear friend Agnes deLima imported from New York, it extended to Saturday when a host of friends and associates spread over the lawn. At least five hundred people, all ages, all colors, drawn from a wide sphere of activities in which we had at one or another time been engaged. Not only for Frank and me, but for those who came, it was like old home week where they also renewed old associations. Not content with this magnificent gathering, our impressarios staged a barbecue at the picnic ground on Sunday to which the "larger family"—those who had lived with us for a season, all the ranch inhabitants and those who had been most closely connected with us at some period of their lives, were included. At the end of the afternoon I felt as if, to climax all this excitement and adulation, we should somehow be gathered up in a golden chariot and disappear over the horizon in a luminous cloud. However, such an apotheosis did not take place, and we resumed our regular lives still aglow with the love and friendship we had been showered with. It was indeed a golden occasion.

This anniversary party impressed me with the passage of time. From my earliest years I had wanted to write. When I was in college, I wasn't sure whether my ambition centered on short stories, travel pictures, plays or poetry, so I tried my pen at all kinds of writing except novels. I

had not lived long enough nor had enough human contacts to follow through on character development, and my first-hand emotional experiences were too meager to enable me to construct a convincing plot. I wrote a few stories in a moralistic tone, very dull, some descriptive outdoor scenes, a play and a great many poems. Few were ever published and I did not persevere. I had too many possibilities. I was curious about the world, I wanted to have children, I had to live in the country. I always had to be teaching something to somebody, so I just let writing slip between the boards.

As a matter of fact, though, all through my life I really did a lot of writing on the side. Teaching plans and programs, addresses to parents and teachers, committee reports, surveys of one kind or another, proposals for financial grants. Every Christmas I composed a Christmas Chronicle of some length, often illustrated with snapshots, describing the highlights of our past year in considerable detail. A hundred mimeographed copies served to keep up relationships with family and friends living in many distant places. During the year replies came drifting in, the network was not broken.

It had been my intention, starting way back in 1915 to write the story of my father-in-law's life. His one-man exhibit at the Panama Pacific Exposition in San Francisco in 1915, where he was awarded a special gold Medal of Honor, had brought him out of oblivion and reinstated him as one of the important figures in American painting. For the previous twenty years he had succeeded in avoiding publicity somewhat to the detriment of his career. He was recognized by other painters, but little known by the general public. Written material was negligible. Unless you lived in Cincinnati, it was hard to find out anything about him except through a slender book written by one of his pupils or in articles in magazines and newspapers. From a human point of view, as well as from the standpoint of his artistic accomplishment, the story of his life fascinated me. During the first few years following my marriage to his son I saw him often, and he told me a great deal about his childhood on the frontier, his student days in Germany and his spectacular success as a teacher and as a portrait painter. I made detailed notes as he talked. During the winter that I spent in Cincinnati, I verified dates from old church records, and collected data concerning pioneer days in Cincinnati. I even visited Piqua in northern Ohio where Duveneck's mother grew up on the land homesteaded by her German father. Later, I made contact, either in person or by correspondence, with many of his former students and with contemporary artists who had known him at different periods of his life. Having been in Munich and Florence, I could more easily comprehend the background of his European experiences. And since I was familiar with Boston, it was not difficult for me to reconstruct the story of his wife, Lizzie Boott.

From time to time I wrote up certain sections of this biography, but work on it was sandwiched in between other activities. Along about 1960

I had decided that if ever I was going to carry out my intention and my promise to Frank Duveneck, I had better go about it soon. I overhauled the fragments I had written, organized my materials, translated letters written between 1870 and 1876 in German, discovered old photographs and constructed a bibliography and a list of paintings indicating in which museums they were to be found. I thought I had a book. I sent it to quite a few publishers, some of whom kept the manuscript for months only to return it with a pleasant but unconvincing compliment and a definite refusal. I got tired of wrapping packages and using up postage, and one day pushed the manuscript into a drawer, where it rested for several years. But it still kept bothering me as an unfinished enterprise, and finally I pulled the manuscript out once more, listened to some good advice from professional people, found editorial help from a knowledgeable young friend and a printer, a painstaking craftsman who created a handsome format for my book, *Frank Duveneck, Painter, Teacher* which was published in 1970. It had some good reviews and it sold moderately well. It was not sufficiently publicized, however, and I was a little disappointed that it did not receive wider distribution.

Having partly fulfilled my deferred lifelong ambition of creative writing, I thought, "Why not write up some of the stories I tell the children at campfire time?" I had often been asked to write them down, but I had always been too lazy to do so, but at long last the time seemed to have come, so I did. I sent the finished manuscript around. But once again I experienced negative results: "It won't do. It's not a book." So, I pulled the manuscript to pieces again and separated the stories. The ones that related to olden times could (by a little stretching of the imagination) be called historical. These were published by the California History Department of DeAnza College as a small paperback selling for $2.50. This little book had a picture of our entrance gate on its cover, and it was called *Hidden Villa Tales*. It was followed by "Hidden Villa Animal Tales"—also a paperback—which had a different colored cover. Children seem to enjoy both of these books, and teachers like to use them for supplementary reading. Having had fun writing several books, I decided to embark on my latest literary endeavor, an autobiography— and it, too, has been fun for me.

XXXVIII

Finale

A summing up of personal beliefs.

> ". . . Last scene of all,
> That ends this strange eventful history,
> Is second childishness and mere oblivion,
> Sans teeth, sans eyes, sans taste, sans everything."
> —*As You Like It*

Shakespeare presents a dismal picture of man's last appearance on the stage of life. To be sure, we have all witnessed sad examples of similar deterioration, but in our time, life expectancy has increased and advances in medical knowledge have alleviated many problems of old age. During the past decade I have observed an increasing interest in death and dying. Books have been written on the subject; courses are offered in the colleges. It has become almost a "conversation piece." Strangely enough, in my generation—or perhaps I should say in Victorian society—the subject was rarely mentioned. It was not considered good taste to talk about money, religion, sex or death. You could gossip comfortably about birth, childhood, maturity, illness and diet, but not about dying. This is another example of how far removed we were from fundamental realities. All primitive civilizations associated death with their most sacred rituals. Indeed, it was death that gave life its significance and provided the goal for all endeavors. A sort of proving ground for Nirvana.

I was well along in years before I ever witnessed an actual death, but I have two childhood memories related to the subject. The first was when my grandmother died and I was considered too young to be allowed to go to the funeral. My mother and sisters had been busy fitting themselves out in new black dresses and hats. And gloves—I vividly remember these sombre black gloves. I watched from an upper window when they all squeezed into the funeral carriage. I was angry at being left out. So I went into the large dress closet oustide my nursery and sat myself down in the dark on a pile of hat boxes under the hanging dresses and coats and tried to produce a few tears of sorrow. I succeeded, but they were undoubtedly tears of frustration, rather then bereavement.

The other episode was the destruction of my favorite doll, Esther. I was sitting on the porch in Cohasset with my brother Jim. I had placed the doll in the crown of my broad brimmed hat which was lying between us. Jim picked up the hat by the elastic and swung it around over his head. It was inconsequential action, but Esther crashed to the ground in a thousand pieces. I wept bitterly. Jim kept saying, "I'm sorry. I didn't mean to do it." I felt no resentment towards him, but I was inconsolable. I picked up the shattered fragments and watered them with my tears. There was no possibility of reconstruction. The offers of another doll provided no comfort. It was an irreparable, final, complete loss. I cried myself to sleep that night and appeared red-eyed at breakfast the next morning. My governess worried and, with extraordinary insight, she suggested that we might have a funeral. This idea appealed to me and Jim cooperated by offering one of his most treasured possessions—a small black Civil War knapsack—as a casket suitable for the occasion. We made a procession to the croquet court and Jim dug a hole. For several days I returned to the spot and wept. About a week later my governess saw me getting a shovel from the tool house.

"What are you going to do with that?" she asked me.

"I want to see what Esther looks like now." I answered.

She was relieved. I had apparently accepted the idea of finality. Scientific investigation prevailed over grief. Of course, Esther was not a human being, but she was real to me and the concept of mortality came to me just as forcibly through her dissolution as if she had been a living being.

All my life I have been blessed with an abundance of physical energy. Although I was born with a defective foot which caused arthritis in later days, I never paid much attention to it. When my children were young I had no difficulty in keeping up with them, and when I was at school or involved in other activities, I did not have time to worry about discomfort. I could work long and hard, and when I got tired I could always count on a kind of reserve tank of energy which would keep me going a little longer, like the second wind of a long distance runner. The first indication that the reserve tank was running pretty low happened one day when I was preparing for a dinner party of ten or twelve people. All of a sudden my engine stalled. My legs refused to move, my backbone seemed to crumble, my neck and shoulder muscles atrophied—it was even hard to breathe. There was nothing to do but flop on the nearest bed, to lie flat and motionless and utterly relaxed. This inertia lasted about fifteen minutes before I was ready to resume activity. After several similar instances, I learned to anticipate the symptoms of collapse and to do my flopping before the crucial moment.

After my eightieth birthday, other limitations developed. As the sage in the Forest of Arden prophesied, my faculties declined. My hearing decreased, my eyes developed cataracts (this handicap has been transformed by an operation and special glasses), my sense of balance became uncertain and I found it expedient to carry a sturdy cane that someone had left hanging in one of my closets. It was discovered that I had leukemia, and after two attacks of pneumonia which landed me in the hospital, I realized that my pace would have to be altered. The faithful machine—my body—that served me so well through the years, was now deserving of a little more consideration.

I found it somewhat difficult to reorient my daily life into a more sedentary regime. Above all, I found it difficult to accept help graciously. Instead of being the giver, I found myself in the position of recipient and this was a new discipline for my proud and independent personality. Whereas I had always tended to say "Yes," now I felt obliged to say "No" to active participation in new forms of social evolution. Surprisingly enough, however, I do not feel pushed into a corner because my young friends are keeping me informed and in touch with their progress. I have books and TV programs to enjoy without stirring from my easy chair, and I correspond with a number of people in many parts of the world. I even have an electrically powered golf cart to take me around the ranch to see the animals and growing things and on into the woods, even up to a high point where I can sit in the sun and look at my beloved hills and watch the birds. When I go on such excursions I am accompanied by my dogs. While I meditate they explore the underbrush and deer trails, returning frequently to make sure I am still parked in my lookout. I am a very pampered old lady, surrounded by love and kindliness.

Looking back to the last phase of my quest, the practice of the Presence did become a habitual accompaniment of my days and nights. I am not sure at what point and how it came about, but I gradually drifted from an identifiable personified companionship to a more abstract but all-pervading sense of Immanence—a deep persuasion of the unity of all life. The earth itself, all living things—plants, animals, humans and the limitless Universe that flows around us—all this immensity entered into my comprehension, absorbing doubt, fear, guilt, and self-analysis.

As I look back and seek to define the influences that contributed to this new awareness, I discover clues through seemingly highly divergent sources. During the years in which I had become acquainted with simple, less intellectually-oriented people, I encountered a whole scale of values differing from those to which I was accustomed. The "Third

World" seemed to have an important message for me. Especially the Native American. His affinity to the earth and to the forces of Nature revived my early childhood impressions when I sought refuge in the out-of-doors. All through life the woods and mountains have offered me solace and inspiration. For many years it was my custom when weary to lie down *on the ground.* People used to laugh to see me curled up asleep on the lawn. But I knew the earth under me was recreative. I could feel the stored up sunshine seeping into my body. This feeling seemed to echo the Indian way of life. As I became more familiar with Southwest Indian religion, I began to understand the significance of the dances, the chants, rituals and other observances. All their art and their actions were related to other-world consciousness, familiarity with the Great Spirit—As illustrated by the following prayer from the Tewa Pueblo.

> O our Mother the Earth, O our Father the sky.
> Your children are we
> And with tired backs we bring you the gifts that you love.
> Then weave for us a garment of brightness—
> May the warp be the white light of morning,
> May the weft be the red light of evening,
> May the fringes be the falling rain,
> May the border be the standing rainbow—
> Thus weave for us a garment of brightness
> That we may walk fittingly where birds sing,
> That we may walk fittingly where grass is green
> O our Mother the Earth, O our Father the sky.

I found the same motifs in the books written about the Bush People by Laurens van der Post, who was born in South Africa and was nurtured by a native nurse. His descriptions of the Bushman's sensitivity to the ever-changing moods of the veldt and its animal life seemed to echo the Indian's wisdom. He speaks of the "intimate conversation of nature—the voice of the lion, the passionate intense cough of the leopard. . . . the croaking of frogs by some precious starfilled water hole. . . . and overall the smell of the incense of the devout earth evoked by the first fall of dew."

Although he was the offspring of European parents, the instinctive primitive feeling that Van der Post derived from his native nurse carried him through great emergencies in his life. When he was captured by the Japanese in World War II, he sustained himself and his men with stories of African lore. They endured incredibly harsh treatment, in spite of which he comprehended the compulsions and motivations of his captors and held no rancor. "Forgive them, for they know what they do." His profound faith in the relatedness of all life enabled him to detect the common humanity he shared with his tormentors.

Another source of inspiration came to me from the words of Dag Hammarskjold, general secretary of the United Nations during the critical years from 1953 to 1961. I had admired his brilliant mind and his comprehension of different world cultures; I knew how completely dedicated he was to the attainment of peace through negotiation. What I did not know was his profound religious motivation, which resulted in the creation of the Meditation Room located just off the public lobby in the General Assembly Hall. He wrote the introductory pamphlet which is given to everyone entering the room. It says in part, "We all have within us a centre of stillness surrounded by silence. This house, dedicated to work and debate in the service of peace, should have one room dedicated to silence in the outward sense and stillness in the inner sense." How beautifully expressed! There is no altar, no symbol of any kind, only in the middle of the room a shaft of light from a high window strikes the side of a great slender tapering obelisk of iron ore. This is a symbol of how "light of the spirit gives life to matter." People of many faiths can respond to this universal symbol.

On September 10, 1961, Dag's life ended in a plane crash. It happened in Africa where he was negotiating for peace in the Congo. He was not unprepared because he knew he had many enemies and had often been warned of their hostility. In 1964 his notebook, called *Markings*, was published in English translation. It revealed his secret, interior life which no one knew about. Dag had left this slender little record to a friend with a request to edit and publish it if the entries were considered worthy. He designated the document as "a sort of white book concerning negotiations with myself—and with God."

Markings is a beautiful book, a worthy counterpart to the *Confessions* of St. Augustine or the writings of Pascal and Saint Teresa. This slender volume laid bare the source of Dag's incredible strength and energy. Most of the famous European mystics led cloistered lives, but he carried on in the thick of hot disputes and tangled controversy. W. H. Auden stressed this in his Foreword to *Markings*. "It is an historical document of the first importance as an account of the attempt by a professional man of action to unite in one life the *via activa* and the *via contemplativa*."

I was greatly moved by *Markings*. It confirmed my growing conviction that an individual could be seemingly engrossed in worldly affairs, but could at the same time be operating from the basis of moral integrity and in obedience to inner vision. "In our era the road to holiness necessarily passes through the world of action." How sad it is that the apostles of love like Lincoln, Gandhi, Martin Luther King, and Dag Hammarskjold must become martyrs before men can accept the truths to which they bear witness. In spite of peace, we continue to instigate discord; instead of brotherhood we accentuate devisiveness. And yet it has been demonstrated over and over that unless we can give, we never will receive. This law applies to nations as well as to individuals. It is so obvious. There is no other alternative to chaos.

I have watched with interest how, during the last twenty-five years, there has arisen a great burgeoning of concern for metaphysics and simplicity of living. As the younger generation revolted against war and bureaucracy, their protest gradually simmered down from violence to uneasy discontent. The search for panaceas resulted in a great variety of life styles, odd groupings, cults and practices. Older people were dismayed at many of the demonstrations and condemned the participants without considering the causes of their unrest. I have no tolerance for those who try to obtain their ends by evil means, involving destruction of life or property, but I look on the nature followers, the communes, the compost devotees, the vegetarians, even the nudists with a great deal of sympathy.

Meditation has become an end in itself. One can almost say that it has developed into Big Business. I am told that the organization known as Transcendental Meditation promoted by Maharishi, for instance, has hundreds of followers with national headquarters and a network of branches in many cities and colleges. The organization seems to have unlimited funds for promotional purposes. When I was growing up, social rebels became socialists or agnostics and the next generation took refuge in communism and atheism. It seems to me that the present addiction to self-communion may well represent a shift from the pursuit of power to the cultivation of deeper satisfactions. If it is not merely a passing fad, nor an escape from reality, one may hope for a drastic change in social behavior. This possibility fits in with the convictions of Father Teilhard de Chardin, the Jesuit scientist priest who prophesies a new phase in evolution. He traces man's increasing control over the forces of nature from the cave man through Greek and Roman, Medieval and Modern times and insists that civilization has reached a point in esoteric development equal to the tremendous progress in scientific knowledge that has characterized the last hundred years. In his book, *The Phenomenon of Man*, he says mankind is entering on a new sphere of consciousness. Perhaps the modern preoccupation with the psychic aspects of life may indicate the beginnings of such a new search. As men apprehend the dual nature of physical power—creative but also supremely destructive—they come to realize the need for control. There must be adequate checks and balances. The only answer is a moral law more binding than physical deterrents. Perhaps God is not as obsolete as some people believe. At many points science and religion seem to converge; the physicist talks the same language as the theologian.

As I studied history I observed that new movements originate simultaneously in different individuals often far apart in location and engaged in unrelated fields of study or action. A new idea seems to stir up a sort of contagious ferment in the world, perhaps because its time has come.

Such seems to have been the case during the first half of this century when Freud and his associates opened the door of the subconscious to a shocked and incredulous audience. Their discoveries about the latent undercurrents of human emotion revolutionized all previous theories of conduct. A whole new dimension of life had been revealed. Just as the voyages of Columbus and Magellan altered all maps of the world and more recently, the pioneers in flying have recharted the universe, so the explorations of psychology have transformed all our conceptions of human development.

I was first introduced to these new ideas through my teaching in Peninsula School. The Progressive School movement was responsive to psychoanalysis and to allied techniques; indeed some schools based their whole program on the child's psychological adjustment. Our educational vocabulary was enlarged by terms like introvert and extrovert, the father-figure, complexes, schizoid, neurosis, libido, etc. It is hard to realize how recent these words and these concepts are. New tests were introduced into our school; teacher meetings were enlivened by arguments between the converts to the new philosophy and the conservatives who considered all such emphasis mere nonsense. Certainly Peninsula School was greatly influenced by the revelations concerning personality characteristics, and I came to a much deeper understanding of children's problems and adult peculiarities.

During later years when I worked with minority groups, much that I had learned from working with disturbed children helped me to analyze social situations and to comprehend the roots of prejudice. Many people I knew were greatly helped by psychiatric or psychological treatments. On the other hand, I observed others who became more confused than they had been before consultation and still others who continued to be dependent on the doctor for months and even for years. The guidance of another person's soul is a dangerous and exacting profession. It is not enough to be brilliant and highly trained. Unless the guide has attained wholeness within himself, he should not be entrusted with so delicate and sacred a responsibility.

As I became more familiar with the writings and ideas of the leaders in the pyscho-therapeutic movement, Carl Jung stood out as the one who seemed most significant to me. Freud, the great innovator ploughed up the field but Jung sowed the seed that led to the harvest. It was not until I read *Memories, Dreams and Reflections* that I really grasped the stature of the man and realized how far beyond the mere professional activities of the psychologist Jung's vision extended. He has the quality of the ancient Hebrew prophet. I am convinced that as the years go by he will be venerated as the great evangelist of the 20th Century.

It might appear irrational to fuse such widely separated teachings as Indians, Van der Post, Chardin, Hammarskjold and Jung into a synthesis of affirmation, but I think it was William James who pointed out in *Varieties of Religious Experience* that a person seeking truth is led to find his answer in unanticipated ways and not always in the terms of his own culture. The source is less important than the synthesis.

In telling the story of his life, Jung omits any mention of achievement or honor. As a matter of fact, he says in the prologue, "The only events in my life worth telling are those when the imperishable world errupted into the tangible one. That is why I speak chiefly of inner experience. . . . all other memories of travels, people and surroundings have paled beside these interior happenings." Similarly, in Dag's *Markings* there is no mention of his heavy responsibilities for world government. To follow his career you have to read another book. Jung alludes to the course of his life as one "singularly poor in outward happenings." Another instance of similarity between these two men was their reverential feeling for *stone*. When Jung was building his house in Bollingen, he obtained a massive stone on which to carve Greek and Latin inscriptions. This he set up in the center of his enclosed garden. For him it was a symbol of the Unknown and the Occult. Dag's obelisk at the United Nations expressed the illumination of all life by the light of eternity.

As I came to understand Jung's theories and beliefs I found the solution to some of the problems of relationships that had eluded me. His analysis of the collective unconscious explained the primitive pagan allegiance I felt for the earth and the excitement aroused by folk rituals and ceremonials. All my life I have been puzzled by the ubiquity of evil that in spite of my optimistic tendencies, I have never been able to deny nor to shove out of sight. It always lurked in the background of my mind. Jung's symbol of the *Shadow* gave a clue to the origin and persistence of wickedness which has to be acknowledged in the world and also *in one's self*. "The Shadow is the invisible saurian tail that man still drags behind him," he said, and again, "the immaturity of man is a fact with which we have to reckon."

Jung explores the whole category of myth and legend and points out the theories that occur over and over again in divergent cultures which express the fundamental drama of human existence. The symbols may be different and the language unfamiliar, but the meaning is the same. In every generation, what is important to remember are not the wars and triumphs, not the changes in national boundaries, not political successions, but the vitality of the spiritual concepts relevant to that period. Jung, more emphatically even than either Hammarskjold or Chardin, emphasizes the importance for present day man to rediscover the life of the spirit. "God himself cannot thrive in a humanity that is psychically undernourished." Unless a higher consciousness gains precedence and control, the irresponsible drive for wealth and power can only lead to disaster.

It is almost impossible to assess the trends of one's own time. There is no way to evaluate the relative strength of current ideas, because our judgments are formed by the milieu in which we live. We do not often come in contact with basic assumptions differing from our own, and we tend to ignore the majority groups that cling to the status quo or those that would take us further down the road to materialism. I cannot

Photo by Betty Estersohn

believe that the powers of darkness will eventually prevail over the children of light. The revolt of the young, manifest in all sorts of groups, sane and insane, earnest, idealistic, aspiring, worshipful—all these are signs that the old order is changing. The day of deliverance may be at hand. I shall not see it happen, but I believe it will come and is even now on its way.

Meanwhile, in the short span of life that remains for me, I know I must leave the world to its own course and concern myself with the subjective reflections of old age. It is time to gather the picture puzzle pieces of life together and find out how they fit into the framework of time and place for myself—a microscopic facet in the cosmic pattern.

A few pages back I used the word *Immanence* to describe a state of mind—I cannot account for the sharpened awareness which has come to clarify my perceptions. The episodes of every day life have a sacred quality. Sleep, dreams, waking in the morning, the breaking of bread, sunlight and shadow, meeting with friends or strangers, children, dogs, music and fragrances, my beloved hills and the sky, mid-day weariness, even petty annoyances, bring dual impressions—a tangible reality and an intangible aura—which is still more real. Once in a public meeting Jung was asked, "Do you believe in God?" He answered, "I do not believe—" He paused and then he added, "I know."

I, too, know.

There are no words to express this inner certainty. But it is based on the evidence of unity within all things, on the creative power of love and the pervasive energy of the Spirit flowing through and transcending human endeavors.

This is what I mean by Immanence—a merging of the outer and the inner. No longer two levels of life, but a reconciliation of opposites—a conclusion of my quest.

Index